Praise for *American Caliph*

"[*American Caliph*] adeptly weaves together narratives of the hostage negotiations, of feuding American Islamic groups, and of Khaalis's life, which was shaped by race, theology, and the faulty 'machinery of American justice.'"
—*The New Yorker*

"Fascinating and meticulously researched . . . *American Caliph* provides a nuanced portrait of Khaalis . . . A haunting book."
—Jonathan Darman, *Air Mail*

"Mufti immerse[s] himself in the story . . . [His] efforts add up to the most complete picture yet of what happened—and why it mattered."
—Andrew Beaujon, *Washingtonian*

"[*American Caliph*] richly recounts an event that was years in the making, unearthing new information and masterfully tying together multiple storylines stretching from D.C. to the Middle East and involving everyone from local police to a Libyan dictator . . . Mufti meticulously builds the story of the 1977 siege through the different threads that led to it."
—Martin Austermuhle, *DCist*

"[A] gripping, meticulously researched history . . . Expertly drawn from FBI files, wiretap transcripts, and interviews, this captivating history fascinates."
—*Publishers Weekly* (starred review)

"In crackling prose, journalist Mufti delves into Khaalis' connections to Elijah Muhammad's Nation of Islam . . . Mufti deftly weaves America's cynical Middle East policy, the star quality of Muhammad Ali and Kareem Abdul-Jabbar, and the tortured production of a biopic about the prophet Muhammad into this real-life thriller."
—Lesley Williams, *Booklist*

"Mining thousands of documents from FBI files and Department of Justice records, trial transcripts, and interviews . . . , journalist Mufti fashions a tense, often grisly account of the events leading up to the two-day standoff and the arrests, trial, and aftermath . . . [An] engrossing work of investigative journalism."

—*Kirkus Reviews*

"Mufti skillfully explains what led to the 1977 attack and three-building hostage situation that shut down Washington, DC, for days . . . The hostage siege is narrated in nail-biting detail."

—Laurie Unger Skinner, *Library Journal*

"*American Caliph* is a kaleidoscopic and utterly enthralling tale of an audacious crime that forever transformed our national conversations about race, terrorism, and Islam. Shahan Mufti elegantly weaves together the stories of a slew of fascinating characters to create a stranger-than-fiction saga that will make you gasp and marvel. This is one of the mightiest feats of journalism I've ever had the good fortune to savor."

—Brendan I. Koerner, author of *The Skies Belong to Us*

"A fast-paced thriller that reads like the best John Le Carré novels, except this story isn't fiction. *American Caliph* is a wild whirlwind of a book with a crazy cast of characters—some of them familiar, all of them unforgettable—and a plot that would be hard to believe if it weren't all true. Shahan Mufti is a terrific writer."

—Reza Aslan, author of *Zealot* and *An American Martyr in Persia*

"*American Caliph* is a fascinatingly detailed retelling of one of the most mystifying American dramas of the 1970s. With a cast of characters that includes Malcolm X, Muhammad Ali, and Kareem Abdul-Jabbar, *American Caliph* reveals how the struggle for Black civil rights also nourished the rise of an American Islamic movement, and how, to an uncanny degree, its early ructions offered a foreshadowing of things to come, in America and beyond. A necessary, immensely readable book for troubled times."

—Jon Lee Anderson, staff writer for *The New Yorker* and author of *Che* and *The Fall of Baghdad*

"*American Caliph* is a meticulously reported and gripping account of one of the more bizarre chapters of U.S. history. In this unforgettable tale, Shahan Mufti brilliantly brings to life a part of our country's past that has been largely forgotten, but whose reverberations are felt to this day."

—Rozina Ali, contributing writer at *The New York Times Magazine*

Dmitry Gudkov

SHAHAN MUFTI

AMERICAN CALIPH

Shahan Mufti is the chair of the Department of Journalism at the University of Richmond and a former daily news reporter for *The Christian Science Monitor*. He is the author of *The Faithful Scribe: A Story of Islam, Pakistan, Family, and War*, and his writing has appeared in *Harper's Magazine*, *The New York Times Magazine*, *The Atlantic*, and *The Nation*, among other publications.

AMERICAN
CALIPH

PICADOR

FARRAR, STRAUS AND GIROUX

New York

AMERICAN
CALIPH

✴

THE TRUE STORY
OF A
MUSLIM MYSTIC, A HOLLYWOOD EPIC,
AND THE
1977 SIEGE OF WASHINGTON, DC

✴

SHAHAN MUFTI

Picador
120 Broadway, New York 10271

Library of Congress Control Number: 2022022946
Paperback ISBN: 978-1-250-87263-0

Our books may be purchased in bulk for promotional, educational,
or business use. Please contact your local bookseller or the Macmillan
Corporate and Premium Sales Department at 1-800-221-7945, extension 5442,
or by email at MacmillanSpecialMarkets@macmillan.com.

For book club information, please email marketing@picadorusa.com.

picadorusa.com • instagram.com/picador
twitter.com/picadorusa • facebook.com/picadorusa

1   3   5   7   9   10   8   6   4   2

CONTENTS

AMERICAN
CALIPH

PROLOGUE

Late in the morning on March 9, 1977, seven men stormed the Washington, DC, headquarters of B'nai B'rith International, the largest and oldest Jewish service organization in America. Armed with a staggering assortment of weapons and ammunition, firing guns and flashing knives, the attackers quickly took control of the building and held more than one hundred people, mostly employees, hostage inside.

The men were members of a group who called themselves the Hanafi Muslims. They were nearly all African American, converts to Sunni Islam, headquartered at an imposing house on a charming stretch of Sixteenth Street in Northwest Washington, six miles up the road from the White House. The building had been purchased six years earlier by the most famous member of the group, the NBA superstar Kareem Abdul-Jabbar.

The group's leader and spiritual master was a fifty-four-year-old man named Hamaas Abdul Khaalis. A U.S. Army veteran and former professional jazz drummer, Khaalis had become acquainted with Malcolm X, one of the best-known Muslims in America, in New York in the 1950s, when both men were young members of the Nation of Islam, the powerful Black nationalist organization. Like Malcolm, Khaalis went on to become one of the organization's leading officials at its Chicago headquarters, answering directly to Elijah Muhammad, a man his followers considered a prophet of God.

In the late 1950s, after a bitter split with the Nation, Khaalis embraced a more traditional creed of Islam in Harlem. His new teacher was an immigrant Muslim mystic who claimed to have extraordinary spiritual powers and taught Khaalis that the Hanafi school of Sunni Islam was the "Prophet's side" of Islam, the true path to salvation. Under the tutelage of his new master, Khaalis claimed to develop remarkable mystical powers of his own. In the early 1960s, Khaalis and a few others registered the Hanafis as a nonprofit organization in New York. In the early 1970s, after his spiritual master died, Khaalis moved the organization to Washington, DC, with the support of his star disciple, Kareem, and adopted the title of "khalifa," or caliph.

The caliphate is an Islamic institution born at the deathbed of the Prophet Muhammad in the seventh century. Muhammad named no successor, leaving his followers to decide not only who would inherit his authority and mission but also how it would continue to pass on so that the faith might survive. Some argued for the leadership to pass down through the bloodline, while others insisted that the most knowledgeable and pious of men, regardless of relation to Muhammad, should become the caliph of Muslims. The issue of succession would eventually turn bloody and fracture Islamic civilization into Sunni and Shia. Over centuries, countless people would claim the title of caliph, all over the world wherever Muslims lived. For the Hanafi Muslims of Washington, that man was Khaalis. "Islam," one of the hostage takers explained to a caller on the phone, "will rise in the West and there will be one to lead it." That one was "our leader Hamaas Abdul Khaalis," he said, "the khalifa, the man of the West."

A little over an hour after the assault on B'nai B'rith, three other Hanafi disciples of Khaalis's entered the Islamic Center of Washington, located on the city's storied Embassy Row. The Islamic Center was the largest and one of the most important mosques in America, situated in one of the glitziest neighborhoods of the capital. The three men were brothers with clean records, but they had spent nearly their entire lives in Anacostia, one of the poorest and most crime-ridden neighborhoods in the city. Armed with handguns, rifles, and machetes, they took over the mosque's office complex, where they held more than a dozen men and women hostage.

The hostages at the Islamic Center were nearly all Muslim. They hailed from half a dozen different countries. Among them was one of the Hanafis' prime targets, Muhammad Abdul Rauf, the Egyptian-born director of the center and one of the most prominent Muslim religious leaders in the United States. Soon after 1:00 p.m., the gunmen at the Islamic Center put Rauf on the phone with Khaalis, who delivered an ultimatum.

A movie about the life of the Prophet Muhammad was to play in New York City that afternoon. Rauf's job was to convince his diplomatic and religious contacts to use their influence to shut down the film's premiere. If Rauf failed, Khaalis explained, the Hanafis would begin beheading hostages and drop their heads out of windows.

The producer of the film was Moustapha Akkad, a debonair Muslim immigrant from Syria who had arrived in the United States more than two decades earlier with dreams of Hollywood glory. He had studied film at UCLA and the University of Southern California. The biopic of the Islamic Prophet Muhammad was Akkad's debut film and had taken him almost a decade to complete at a cost of $17 million, making it one of the most expensive movies in film history. The project had invited controversy throughout the previous decade. Many influential Muslim groups and powerful religious and political leaders in Asia, Africa, and Europe had been campaigning against its production and release because in Muslim societies, depicting the Islamic Prophet has been a widely accepted taboo for a thousand years.

The film had already sparked riots in several countries and opened up fissures between nations and world leaders. Akkad was able to complete the project only after Muammar Gaddhafi, the renegade military ruler of Libya, offered Akkad sanctuary and bankrolled his project with money from state coffers.

As the film began playing at the Rivoli Theatre in Manhattan at 2:00 p.m. that day, and as police in Washington and New York scrambled to halt the screening, two other Hanafi Muslims entered the District Building in downtown Washington, a few hundred yards from the White House. With weapons concealed under their clothing, they marched up to the fifth floor of the building, where the mayor of Washington and all of the District's legislators had their offices. A firefight broke out between the Hanafis and security. One guard was shot in the head and rushed to the hospital. A news reporter lay dead on the cold, cracked, marble floor. Marion Barry, an ambitious council member with dreams of becoming the mayor of the capital, sat on the floor moaning, clutching the left side of his chest as it oozed blood.

By three o'clock, almost four hours after the Hanafis began their assault, downtown Washington, DC, had ground to a halt. Courts and city offices were evacuated, all the monuments were closed to visitors, and congressional and city officials moved around the city under heavy guard. Some synagogues and Jewish schools in the District closed for the day. Snipers from the police department and the FBI took positions on rooftops all over downtown Washington, while ambulances and squad cars raced down the streets blaring their sirens. The American capital looked and felt like it was under attack.

President Jimmy Carter had been in office for fewer than fifty days. That day, he was busy hosting the prime minister of Israel, Yitzhak Rabin, who was on an official visit to Washington to discuss the new American president's proposal for a grand peace bargain between Israel and its Arab neighbors. Carter directed the FBI to assist with the hostage situation. The FBI code-named the crisis DISTAK: District Takeover. Carter's top White House aides, meanwhile, huddled in the West Wing to chalk out a strategy. America's anti-terrorism apparatus was nascent, launched only a few years earlier under President Richard Nixon after Palestinian gunmen shocked the world by attacking Israeli team members at the 1972 Munich Olympics. It was virtually untested.

Hamaas Abdul Khaalis was hardly unknown to law enforcement. The FBI had started monitoring him more than two decades earlier when he became involved with Malcolm X and the Nation of Islam. In the 1950s, the FBI placed him on its infamous Security Index—a list of people thought to pose a threat to American national security and who could be immediately arrested by order of the president. The FBI continued its surveillance of Khaalis as he shot up through the ranks of the Nation, then broke away and formed his own Hanafi group and eventually settled in Washington. During this time, the Secret Service had met with and questioned Khaalis on two different occasions, once after he had seemingly foretold the assassination of John F. Kennedy in a series of communications addressed to the president. Federal prosecutors had pursued criminal charges against Khaalis twice but dropped them both times.

The Metropolitan Police Department of Washington also knew Khaalis intimately. They first learned about the Hanafis in the early 1970s, soon after the group moved to Washington and requested a charter from the National Rifle Association for a Hanafi Rifle and Pistol Club. They claimed to be a gun hobbyists' club, but the police were alarmed by the number and variety of weapons they were purchasing from local stores. The police informed the FBI, who in turn alerted the Secret Service, and law enforcement began surveilling the Hanafis closely. Then, one day in January of 1973, the Hanafi headquarters was invaded by members of Elijah Muhammad's Nation of Islam, on a mission to annihilate Khaalis's Hanafi organization. They left seven dead bodies inside the Hanafi Madh-Hab Center. It was the deadliest mass murder in the history of Washington, DC. The Washington police and the FBI, both of whom had been secretly surveilling the Hanafis from a distance for months, were suddenly inside their headquarters, cooperating closely with Khaalis and his followers to investigate and prosecute the murderers.

The 1973 murders at the Hanafi Center made Khaalis a public figure. In the four years between the murders and the hostage taking, *The Washington Star* and *The Washington Post*, the two largest newspapers in the capital, ran more than one hundred news stories about him and the Hanafis. They reported on the horrific massacre at the Hanafi headquarters and then followed Khaalis's very public campaign against the Nation of Islam and the series of dramatic criminal trials that followed. Rarely did a month pass in those four years without a story about Khaalis or his community appearing in the news somewhere in the country. Khaalis was a guest on the *Today* show on NBC, the most watched morning show in the country, and the Hanafis were featured on the major networks' evening news programs, watched by tens of millions of Americans every night.

By the time the two Hanafi men in the District Building were holding nearly a dozen hostages in a fifth-floor office, Khaalis had articulated a second demand: he wanted the murderers from the Nation of Islam who had attacked the Hanafi Center four years earlier to be delivered to B'nai B'rith. There, it was expected, Khaalis would have them executed. In addition, Khaalis demanded that two other preeminent American Muslims be handed over to the Hanafis: Wallace Muhammad, who had inherited control of the Nation of Islam from his father, Elijah, and Wallace's most famous disciple, the heavyweight boxing champion Muhammad Ali. They too, presumably, would be executed by the Hanafis.

The saga of the Hanafis and their bloody feud with the Nation of Islam had played out prominently in the media throughout the 1970s, as the press simultaneously covered the geopolitical drama around Akkad's major film production based on the life story of the Islamic Prophet. Most Americans, meanwhile, were paying much closer attention to the news of Muslims in faraway lands, such as Africa and Asia, including the violent conflicts in the Middle East, especially between Israel and its Arab neighbors. In truth, all these apparently detatched stories were slowly crashing into each other. The strains in the Middle East, which America was seeking to manage from afar, were tearing open fissures at home between Muslims and non-Muslims and within American Muslim communities. The three-part synchronized attack that finally erupted in the heart of Washington, DC, on the morning of March 9, 1977, had been bubbling just under the surface for years.

The Hanafi takeover of Washington remains, to this day, the largest hostage taking in American history and the first such attack by Muslims on American soil. The attack, which had been planned and executed by Americans right under the noses of American law enforcement, found the nation's capital stumped. To pacify the situation, the hostage negotiators in Washington, who represented all levels of law enforcement and nearly every federal security and spy agency, needed to act quickly but carefully. The lives of nearly 150 hostages depended on it. To save them, the negotiators needed to understand how a biopic of the Islamic Prophet directed by a Syrian American immigrant in Hollywood was tied to the massacre at the Hanafi Madh-Hab Center by a rival African American Muslim group, and how all of this was bound by America's intricate and aggressive Cold War maneuvering in the Middle East.

Ultimately, investigators would have to trace the path of Khaalis's entire life. They would need to understand how and why this Black man—descended from slaves, born two years before the global Islamic Caliphate fell in the aftermath of the First World War—came to acquire the title of caliph for himself. They would need to understand how Khaalis, who had lived through landmark moments in American history—the civil rights movement, the Hart-Celler Immigration Act of 1965 that fundamentally altered America's demographics, and America's Cold War with the Soviet Union—was fundamentally shaped by them. In short, the task of understanding Khaalis was the task of understanding America and its place in the world in the mid-twentieth century.

Outside of a brief European jazz tour in his twenties, Khaalis had never set foot outside his country. He had scarcely left Washington since he had moved there six years earlier. The only people with whom he had spent much time in the city, other than his family and other Hanafi associates, were American law-enforcement officials, attorneys, and judges.

Khaalis had conceived of and executed his attack while caught deep within the machinery of American justice. Hamaas Abdul Khaalis may have been acting under the Islamic title "khalifa," but he, and his actions, were, above all, American.

Khaalis had said as much. In a book titled *Look and See: The Key to Knowing and Understanding—Self-Identity, Self-Culture and Self-Heritage*, which he published only months before the massacre in 1973, Khaalis was unequivocal about his feelings for America. "Islam is not following political ideologies of unbelievers, nor is it working against your country, nor spying against your country," he wrote at the book's beginning. "A Faithful Believer in Islam," he wrote, "is a sincere patriot." Toward the end of the book, he wrote a short poem that contained this stanza:

> America,—my country, you are me,
> I am you,
> For all the tragic events and blessings too—,
> Old and young—people of every hue,
> Work, study and strive
> Make our ideals come true.

"You are me, I am you." At some point between publishing those words in 1972 and launching his historic attack on Washington, Khaalis lost faith in America. On the morning of March 9, 1977, as he set out, ostensibly, to defend the honor of his beloved prophet, Khaalis also hoped to win something for himself: the justice promised to him by his country and by Allah. And there was one more thing he was after: to be recognized the world over as the one and only, undisputed American caliph.

PART I

1.

PSYCHOLOGICAL WARFARE

On June 22, 1944, two weeks after Allied forces stormed the beaches of Normandy to liberate France from the Nazis, Hamaas Abdul Khaalis reported to the psychiatric ward of the Station Hospital at Fort Huachuca in Arizona for an evaluation. The twenty-one-year-old, known at the time by his birth name, Ernest Timothy McGhee, was almost six feet tall and broadly built, weighing close to 170 pounds. His brown face had striking features, including a strong angular jaw that was frequently clenched. He was a good-looking man, but he bore a stern expression. Within weeks of his August 1943 arrival at the base, people were talking about his strange behavior. He always seemed bothered around others. He chewed his nails and muttered under his breath. Other soldiers heard strange noises at all times of the day and night. Sometimes he would weep; other times he cackled loudly.

Khaalis was a Buffalo soldier, a private training to become a reconnaissance scout by learning to read maps and study terrain, in a field artillery battalion with the 92nd Infantry Division, one of two all-Black American infantry units in the Second World War. It was a decisive moment in the war, and the 92nd was months away from deployment in Europe. The only other all-Black American division in the war, the 93rd, also trained at Huachuca and had been deployed months earlier to battle the Japanese for control of remote island outposts in the Pacific.

The dry, oppressive Arizona heat was sapping the morale of many soldiers in Khaalis's 92nd. Close to one thousand men from the division, dismissively termed "the Casuals," were being camped separately at the time, watched over by superior officers while being treated for ailments that frequently proved to be completely imaginary. The army doctors might have suspected that Khaalis, like many others in his division, was looking for an easy way out of a war he did not want to fight.

The incentive to leave the army was greater that morning than ever before. More than two thousand miles away at the White House, President Franklin D. Roosevelt had signed the Servicemen's Readjustment Act of 1944 into law. Commonly known as the GI Bill, it offered veterans unprecedented benefits like tuition and living expenses for college or vocational training, low-cost mortgages, low-interest business loans, and unemployment compensation. All that was required to qualify was active-duty status, which Khaalis held, and a discharge that was anything but dishonorable. If Khaalis was deemed unfit for service and ejected from the military on medical grounds, he would be toward the front of the line to receive the new benefits instituted that morning.

Khaalis's path into the army was an unusual one, especially for a young Black man. America formally entered the war after the Japanese attack on the Pearl Harbor naval base in December 1941. As tens of thousands of Black men enlisted in the military over that Christmas, Khaalis was preparing to go off to college at Purdue University. Khaalis grew up not far from Purdue, in Gary, Indiana, on the southern tip of Lake Michigan. Khaalis's father, Sylvester, was born in Alabama, and his mother, Cecile, in Mississippi. They had both journeyed north before the earliest wave of the Great Migration and were married in Gary in 1913. Khaalis, the couple's seventh child, was born on August 30, 1922.

Gary was named for the chairman of the board of the United States Steel Corporation and built to serve the giant steel plant that opened its gates in the city in 1908. It was the largest steel plant in the world at the time, employing almost seven thousand people, who produced hundreds of thousands of tons of steel each year. Khaalis's father was one of those factory workers. Gary was a planned city, built on a grid and advertised to developers and laborers as the "City of the Century." At first, it attracted mainly immigrants from Greece, Poland, Russia, the Balkans, and other parts of southern and Eastern Europe. African Americans fleeing Jim Crow and Ku Klux Klan terror in the South soon followed.

Gary, like many northern cities where African Americans settled, was starkly segregated. It was fraught with tension between people of European ancestry, both native-born and immigrant, and new Black residents. At the steel mill, they all worked together. Among them were also some of the earliest Muslims to arrive in America from the Balkan provinces of the Ottoman Empire. They were fair skinned, so they lived in white neighborhoods, but many buried their dead in a cemetery less than a mile from the McGhees' residence. The family might even have seen the traditional Muslim funeral processions go by. The Muslims also established a "Benevolent Society" mutual aid group with an attached coffeehouse and mosque not far from the McGhees' house.

Khaalis spent his early childhood in a house a mile from the plant, in a part of the city that would be labeled "hazardous" on the earliest redlined municipal maps. He was still a young boy when the family moved to a new house on the much broader 25th Avenue, right across the street from the newly built all-Black Theodore Roosevelt High School, which Khaalis began attending as a teenager, along with a few of his siblings who were in grades above him.

The McGhees were not a friendly bunch. They kept mostly to themselves. Sylvester, a thin man of medium build, was an authoritarian with a deep religious streak. He appeared to hold the large family in his tight grip. They were Seventh-day Adventists who attended the nearby Mizpah SDA Church and observed a strict Sabbath on Saturdays. Neighbors who lived alongside them for years felt like they hardly knew the family.

At school, Khaalis was a quiet, serious, and introverted loner. He did not swear, he did not drink, he did not smoke, and he drew little attention to himself. He rarely smiled. The only time anyone recalled him getting animated or angry was when things were not done precisely according to the rules, and especially his rules. He also had little tolerance for filth or messiness. What most people remembered him for, however, was his natural gift as a musician. Khaalis would mesmerize on the vibraphone. He and his brother Julius, who was a year ahead of him, also played the drums in the school band.

Khaalis graduated in 1940, ranked 27th in his class of 135. Thanks to a global hunger for steel during the Second World War, Gary was being swiftly pulled out of the Great Depression. Khaalis began working at the steel mill alongside his father while taking music courses at Gary Junior College and playing in a sixteen-piece brass band with kids from his former high school. Later in life, Khaalis would tell a psychiatrist that he was admitted with music scholarships to both Tuskegee University, in his father's native Alabama, and to Wilberforce University in Ohio. Where he did end up was Purdue, fewer than one hundred miles away from home. Before he left for university, in what must have been the strongest rebuke to his father, Khaalis walked into St. Monica's Catholic Church, right by the newly constructed rail tracks, and was baptized as a Catholic.

Khaalis enrolled mostly in science and math courses at college and studied German, English, and government in his first year. Purdue was not a welcoming place in the 1940s for a serious young Black man like Khaalis. He was one of only a handful of African Americans among the six thousand students. Even finding a place to live was a challenge. Decades after Purdue had admitted its first Black student, the university still did not allow African Americans to live anywhere on its West Lafayette campus with the white students. The only place that would house Khaalis was the International House, which was home to students from places like Korea, China, Czechoslovakia, and Peru. He could live among the foreigners in his own land. At the end of his first semester, Khaalis began boarding in a house across the tracks in the town of Lafayette. There, ten months before he would have been eligible for the draft, Khaalis decided to volunteer for the military, registering with the U.S. Army's Enlisted Reserve Corps in October 1942.

In November 1942, American troops began fighting in the first major Allied operation of the Second World War. Operation Torch, a joint effort with the British, was an amphibious assault on the coast of North Africa meant to seize control of the mostly Arabic-speaking and Muslim region from Vichy France. It was a fitting place for American soldiers to enter the western theater of the war. In many ways, colonial America's history had begun in these waters. In the fifteenth century, European expeditions encountered the New World while seeking routes to India that bypassed the coasts of Africa and the Middle East, which were dominated by Muslim empires and kingdoms. Then, centuries later, under the presidents Thomas Jefferson and James Madison, a newly independent United States of America fought its first overseas war in these same waters to protect American merchant ships from Muslim Barbary pirates.

America returned in World War II posing as a liberator. Under the leadership of Dwight Eisenhower, the commander of Allied forces in the region, thousands of American and British soldiers landed at several spots along the North African coast. In advance of these landings, aircraft had dropped five million French and Arabic leaflets created by the Psychological Warfare Branch of the Allied forces. The leaflets, bearing the image of President Roosevelt and the scrawled signature of General Eisenhower, made America, rather than Britain, the friendly face of the invasion. "We come to you to liberate you from your conquerors, whose only desire is to deprive you of your sovereign right to worship freely and your right to live your way of life in peace," the message read. The leaflet ended with a promise that America would never be able to and never meant to keep: "We will leave as soon as the threat from Germany and Italy will have been dispelled."

Khaalis was called up a few months after Torch ended. He left Purdue for processing at nearby Fort Benjamin Harrison in August 1943 and was shipped off to Fort Huachuca in Arizona, near the Mexican border. Life at the base followed the same basic patterns of segregation and humiliation that Khaalis had come to expect everywhere. Huachuca had an especially bad reputation in the military for its strained race relations. Black and white soldiers were housed separately, and the base even had two separate hospitals, one exclusively for Blacks, which was staffed almost entirely by Black nurses and Black doctors, when available. With 946 beds, Station Hospital was the largest African American hospital in the United States at the time.

At his evaluation, Khaalis described psychiatric symptoms to the doctor. He reported having visions of white horses on the walls. He said he heard voices that told him to harm himself or, sometimes, others. When he was muttering, apparently to himself, he was actually in conversation with Fred, Jerusha, and Gary Richardson, Khaalis explained, the three stocky white dwarves who visited him in his mind. The doctor noted in the records that Khaalis had no recorded history of psychiatric illness. Khaalis insisted that he had started feeling this way years before, when he was still a high school student in Gary.

The doctor was unconvinced and decided to administer sodium amytal to induce narcosynthesis, a hypnotic state that doctors believed encouraged truth telling. Khaalis held steady under the influence of the "truth serum." He expressed no extreme emotions and repeated the details of the visual and auditory hallucinations he had been experiencing. This time he said that these visions had been there for as long as he could remember. Other than that, he deviated from his original story very little. Khaalis was ordered hospitalized while a panel of doctors decided to meet at a later date to discuss his fate. He underwent a battery of tests. They checked his urine and blood. They tested him for syphilis. They X-rayed his lungs. The physical examinations found no symptoms of any organic disease, nor did they detect dementia. Khaalis appeared to be completely fine. His fits, meanwhile, became more severe and violent.

Finally, on July 7, 1944, a few months before his battalion would be deployed to Italy, a sanity board ruled that Khaalis suffered from "psychosis dementia praecox paranoid type." It was a mental disorder that had been recognized relatively recently, commonly known as schizophrenia. It did not allow him to serve his function in the army. The board recommended a Section 2 discharge—a "separation because of personality disorder." The panel directed that he be placed in a psychiatric facility immediately, where he would presumably be lobotomized. Less than a month later, however, Khaalis was released into the custody of his mother. She told the army that she wanted Khaalis cared for in a facility of her own choice in Gary.

Khaalis never went to a hospital. He filed for unemployment compensation and disability that he was now entitled to under the GI Bill. He waited. Had he successfully manipulated the system, fooling the military medical bureaucracy into cutting him loose and paying him benefits? Or was he truly a mentally disturbed man who simply slipped through the cracks in a country that cared little for him beyond his ability to serve as cannon fodder? Many people would wonder about this in the years to come. During the long, tense hours when Khaalis held hostages in Washington, the negotiators would study Khaalis's military record and wonder if they really were dealing with a psychotic man. A check for $127.25 finally arrived at his home address in August. That summer, with the money in his pocket, Khaalis left his hometown, hoping never to return. He had dreams of greatness—or maybe they were delusions of grandeur.

2.

BLACK IS GREEN

Khaalis arrived in teeming Harlem, New York City, in the summer of 1946. In the two years since leaving the army, he had trained as a drummer at a music conservatory in Chicago and played at jazz venues around that city. He joined Chicago's Local 208, a segregated Black musicians' union whose membership read like a who's who of Chicago blues and jazz at the time. The Midwest—Chicago in particular—had dominated the jazz scene in America for decades, but the Harlem Renaissance had paved the way to a dynamic new stage in New York. There, in small clubs, younger artists were experimenting with an exciting new sound called bebop. Harlem, the new mecca of jazz, called out to a whole generation of musicians like Khaalis.

He quickly found success, playing with big bands on 52nd Street as well as with some smaller West Indian and Spanish ensembles. He had formal training, so he could read music, and he had polished his skills on the timpani, all of which made him a desirable commodity. His monthly disability checks, 70 percent of his army pay, were enough to keep him afloat. There was money to be made in jazz, too. Black is green—that was the word among the promoters, managers, and booking agents in New York City at the time. Black artists were cheap for them, and they had the potential to make them a lot of money.

While playing a musical engagement at Harlem's Salvation Army one day a few months after arriving, Khaalis spotted a young woman serving coffee and refreshments to the guests. Slender and five foot seven and a half inches tall, she was a regal-looking Black woman. Her name was Ruby Copeland, and she was a couple of years younger than Khaalis. She, too, had converted to Catholicism a few years earlier. Her family had moved to New York City at the end of the first wave of the Great Migration when she was a toddler. Ruby's father, the sole breadwinner for the family of eight, worked at a chemical and dye factory right across the Hudson in New Jersey while they lived in the squalid tenements on Old Broadway, a forgotten alley east of Broadway close to 125th Street. Khaalis and Ruby fell in love, and on New Year's Eve, 1946, they walked into the Church of the Annunciation on 135th Street in Harlem and got married.

Khaalis got his big break soon after, while playing gigs with the scorching Texan trumpet soloist Oran "Hot Lips" Page. The Music Attractions Agency, a small New York City promoter, approached him with an opportunity to travel. Europeans had not seen American jazz performed live since Duke Ellington toured parts of the Continent in the 1930s. With the war over, Europe had once again opened its doors to American talent. The agency's plan was to assemble a band of lesser-known artists who had played with famous big bands whose names could be used to draw large audiences in Europe. They had booked several members. Austin Cole, the leader of the band, had played with Duke Ellington; a singer named Maxine Johnson had performed with Count Basie, Franz Johnson, and Cootie Williams; Shad Collins, the trumpeter, had backed Cab Calloway; the bassist Jimmie Wood and guitarist Willie Houston were from Sy Oliver's big band. Khaalis fit the bill perfectly as a drummer and signed on for the tour.

The Harlem Madcaps, as they called themselves, took off from the New York airport in April 1947. They landed in London and began blazing a trail through Europe that Count Bassie, Charlie Parker, Duke Ellington, and many other more famous artists would travel in the months and years that followed. The Madcaps had dates scheduled in London, Antwerp, and Stockholm when they started, but they kept adding more as the buzz around them grew. Soon, they were being billed as "America's most popular negro orchestra." They hopped from one European city to the next, playing for almost entirely white audiences. Khaalis appeared comfortable and assured sitting atop a platform at the back of the stage with his name, "Ernie McGhee," printed in big, neat, bold letters on the kick drum facing the audience.

A couple of months into the tour, Khaalis received news from Ruby announcing that she was pregnant. The Madcaps were on a hot streak, and some of his bandmates were already landing gigs—or European girlfriends and wives—that would keep them on the Continent for much longer. The letter forced Khaalis to consider the option of returning. He had left his own family behind for good in Gary. Ruby, and any children he might bring into this world with her, were his real family now. In August of 1947, he made his way back, first to London, and from there to New York. In November, Ruby gave birth to their first child, a boy they named Ernest McGhee Jr. Khaalis, now twenty-five years old, would begin shaping the child in his own mold, something that would cost the boy his life when he reached that age himself.

Khaalis had become a father in revolutionary times. He had traveled through Europe just as its empires were contracting, giving birth to new nation-states all over Asia and Africa. The trip across the Continent had made Khaalis curious about the world in a way that he had never been before. Soon after he returned, he enrolled at the City College of New York to complete his bachelor's degree. He was no longer interested in science. Instead, he took courses in history, philosophy, and sociology.

Khaalis graduated with his bachelor's in social science in the spring of 1951. He ranked 96th out of his class of 113, but more important, almost a decade after he first enrolled in college, he had completed what he started. That same spring, Ruby gave birth to their second child, a daughter they named Eva Cecile after Khaalis's mother, who still lived in Gary. Khaalis and Ruby moved to a new, larger apartment in Central Harlem near the Harlem River. The baby was not even a year old when Khaalis's mother died suddenly at the age of fifty-two after suffering a stroke. Khaalis traveled back to Gary, where his name was entered on her death certificate as the one who reported her death.

In the fall, using the educational credit left on his GI benefits, Khaalis enrolled in courses at the Graduate School of Arts and Sciences at Columbia University. One of the courses he attended in the fall of 1951 was titled "Diplomatic History of the Near East," taught by a young professor named J. C. Hurewitz. Middle Eastern Studies did not yet formally exist as an academic field in America but if it had, Hurewitz would have probably been its unofficial dean. He was not much older than Khaalis and had served on the battlefield in the Second World War as an intelligence officer in the Near East Section of the Office of Strategic Services, the precursor to the CIA. Israel and Palestine were the central subject of Hurewitz's research, and his newly published debut book, *The Struggle for*

Palestine, described the conflict that Hurewitz argued was at the heart of growing unrest in the region. In Hurewitz's course, Khaalis learned about the creation of the Jewish state and was introduced to the complex and sprawling history of Islamic civilizations stretching from Europe to South and Central Asia.

Five years in New York City would have given Khaalis an intrinsic familiarity with the traditions of Islam. It was impossible to be part of the jazz scene in Harlem at that time and not be exposed to the religion. Many of jazz's most famous names were associated with the religion, and many had taken on Muslim names. The saxophonist Charlie Parker, one of the pioneers of bebop, took the name Saluda Hakim. Sahib Shihab, the alto-saxophonist who played through the 1940s with Thelonious Monk, was another one of the early converts. Art Blakey, the drummer and band-leader, took on the Muslim name Abdullah Ibn Buhaina and followed the Ahmadiyya sect of Islam. Along with the drummer Talib Dawud, he housed the Muslim Mission religious organization in his own home. While Dizzy Gillespie devoted himself to the Bahá'í faith, his band was frequently made up almost entirely of African American Muslims.

A long feature article in *Ebony* magazine detailed this Muslim jazz subculture. The article, titled "Moslem Musicians: Mohammedan Religion Has Great Appeal for Many Talented Progressive Jazz Men," centered on a lesser-known tenor saxophonist named Lynn Hope. Over seven pages of the magazine, he was featured in ten photographs in various poses, studying Arabic script and reading the Koran, for example. There were also several photos of him wearing a white turban while playing his saxophone standing atop a bar at a club, flanked by other Black musicians wearing fez hats and surrounded by a mostly white audience. According to the article, nearly two hundred jazz musicians claimed to be Muslims. It was almost fashionable. Langston Hughes had captured the trend in a pithy poem, "Be-Bop Boys": "Imploring Mecca / to achieve / six discs / with Decca."

For many in Harlem who embraced the faith, Islam was also truly the religion of Black empowerment. Most of the earliest slaves who arrived in North America were from North and West Africa, regions that were heavily Muslim, and historians estimate that there were tens of thousands of Muslims from these regions living in colonial and antebellum America. Islam, as such, helped some African Americans connect with their pasts before the slave ships had come for them. Christianity, with its white Jesus, was the religion of the slave master, of lynching and death. No one had seen images of Muhammad, on the other hand, and so, by contrast, in the imagination of many in Harlem and around America, the Islamic Prophet became a Black man. In the eyes of Allah, many African Americans came to believe, all races were equal. Khaalis had been feeling the pull, too. Around the time that he enrolled in the Near Eastern studies course at Columbia, he had started calling himself a Muslim.

3

NO. 7

The Black Muslims who gathered in a designated space at the Harlem YMCA on 135th Street every Sunday spoke of Allah as their god like all Muslims around the world do. For these Black Muslims, however, that name did not refer to the great, unseen divinity of unlimited power and vision, as it does for most other Muslims. For them, Allah was a flesh-and-blood man. In fact, Khaalis would have even seen a photograph of him when he first began attending these sessions at the Y. He was light skinned, ethnically ambiguous, his combed dark hair neatly parted on one side. In the most commonly used photo of him, he stands, intently studying a book held in his hands. Some of the older "brothers" and "sisters" in the group had even met him in person.

This mysterious individual was known variously as Wali Dad, Wallace Dodd Fard, Wally Ford, Professor Ford, and many other names, but the people in his organization, the Nation of Islam, called him Master Fard Muhammad. The earliest recorded appearance of Fard is in the town of Paradise Valley near Detroit, Michigan, in the early 1930s. He had seemingly come out of nowhere, as a door-to-door salesman, hawking fabrics in the most depressed Black neighborhoods at the beginning of the Great Depression. He was a charming and convincing salesman who told his clients that both he and his fabrics came from the East. He introduced himself as an "Asiatic" man from Arabia, and he spoke with a distinct foreign accent that some understood to be "Hindoo." Wherever he was from, he was undoubtedly an immigrant, and he spoke English well enough to ingratiate himself with clients.

He often ended up joining families for meals inside their homes. One of Fard's favorite topics of conversation was health and nutrition. The poor African Americans living in crowded slums ate poorly and frequently suffered from seasonal ailments, especially in the harsh winter months. Fard offered cures as well as advice on a proper diet—giving up pork, for example, or eating only one meal a day. As word spread among people that Fard's sage advice resulted in better health, more and more people began to seek him out. Soon, he began to host large gatherings of his own. He told his followers that the source of all his wisdom was the teachings of his faith, Islam.

Islam was not new to the city. A sizable Arab Muslim immigrant community had developed in nearby Detroit by this time. A mosque in the Highland Park neighborhood of the city had existed since the early 1920s. Just as the steel plant at Gary had attracted thousands of Muslims from the Balkans at the turn of the twentieth century, after the First World War the Ford Motor Company, with its $5 a day wage promise, pulled in thousands of Arab immigrants to its major plant in Dearborn. Detroit was a brutally segregated city at the time, and the police were frequently vicious, especially when dealing with the Black residents, who were effectively barred from living in Dearborn, where the Arabs settled. The Black families that Fard nestled with would have had little or no exposure to the Islamic or Muslim traditions practiced by the lighter-skinned Arab immigrants.

Instead, Fard's teaching struck notes reminiscent of the Universal Negro Improvement Association led by Marcus Garvey, as well as the quasi-Islamic Moorish Science Temple, which was led by a Black man from North Carolina named Noble Drew Ali who claimed to have traveled through the Middle East and Africa. These movements had been hugely influential among African Americans earlier in the twentieth century. Both movements, especially the Moors, borrowed heavily from Islamic tradition in preaching a dogma of Black empowerment and freedom. Fard's ban on pork, for example, may have sounded familiar to those with any exposure to the older African American movements. By the time Fard arrived on the scene, though, these movements were starting to wane, and he saw an opportunity to fill the vacuum.

As Fard transformed himself from sage to prophet, he built his own original, fantastical dogma on the foundation laid by Garvey and the Moors, adding in a hodgepodge of Islamic ideas as well as elements of astrology, millennialism, and what is best described as science fiction.

Islam, Fard told his followers, was the original faith of Africans before they were kidnapped and enslaved. They belonged to the ancient tribe of Shabazz rooted in Central Africa that had built the pyramids of Ancient Egypt. The Black race, he said, was a divine race, and their spiritual home was Mecca. The white race, on the other hand, was the product of an ancient eugenics experiment gone awry. A scientist named Yakoob, he explained, had slowly drained the pigment from humans, but in the process also drained them of all humanity. What resulted were pale-skinned beings—a devil in human form. These white devils were the ones who had kidnapped Africans and brought them to the wilderness of North America. Fard explained his presence in Detroit as a divine mission to find the lost tribe of Shabazz and restore its members to their lost glory.

As his congregation began growing into the hundreds, Fard set up a "Muslim Temple of Islam" in Detroit, where he would host weekly meetings. He also opened a "University of Islam," a school for the young children of his many followers. Local authorities started looking into the "Muslim cult" when they noticed a large number of African American families pulling their children out of the public school system and opting for Fard's University of Islam. In 1932, when a mentally disturbed Black man claimed he had murdered his roommate by driving a knife through his heart on orders of the "Gods of Islam," the authorities saw an opportunity. The suspect was found to have links with Fard. The police raided Fard's temple, arrested him, and uncovered a great deal of literature and correspondence that gave authorities the first deep look into the group. Fard was released only after agreeing to a deal with the cops: he would leave town and never return. Fard moved to Chicago, where he continued to receive visitors for a while. A couple of years later, though, just as he had appeared seemingly out of nowhere, he disappeared forever.

Fard had left a Nation of Islam with between four and eight thousand adherents. After a brief but vicious succession battle, Elijah Muhammad, one of Fard's closest disciples, inherited the organization. Born Elijah Poole, the son of slaves from Georgia, he had nearly wrecked himself drinking before meeting Fard and becoming his trusted disciple. He was light skinned enough that the FBI once mistook him for an Asian man. Sobered up and under the tutelage of Fard, Elijah had emerged as a skilled and sharp operator. After Fard's disappearance, he began running the organization from the headquarters in Chicago with national ambitions. He was imprisoned for several years in the 1940s, along with several of his followers, after refusing to register for military service, but he continued his mission upon his release.

The Nation of Islam had three temples when Elijah took over as its leader—the original one in Detroit, a second one in Chicago, and a third in Milwaukee. Over nearly two decades Elijah had added several more in the Midwest and on the East Coast. The temple in Harlem, where Khaalis encountered the message, was No. 7. It was a significant number in traditional Islam and a powerful number in Fard's complex numerological universe, and many members of the Nation believed that, someday, some "wise man" would rise from within its ranks.

Khaalis, the seventh child of his parents, might have wondered if he was the chosen one. He threw himself into the Nation with the zeal of a convert. Like everyone who entered the Nation, Khaalis took on a new name: Ernest X, the X replacing the false "slave" surname given to him by the white slave master. Khaalis began dressing, like the other Muslim brothers, in sharp black suits and bow ties. Ruby took on the X surname, too, and began dressing in all white, with her hair concealed under a pinned scarf. "Assalamu alaikum, brother," the women were taught to greet the men, with their chins gracefully pointed up. "Walaykum Salam, sister," the men would reply respectfully. In poor Black communities, members of the Nation stood out starkly because of their regimented and healthy lives. The men, in particular, underwent complete transformations, inevitably finding employment, appearing healthy and successful, and eliciting curiosity and sometimes reluctant admiration from others.

Just as Khaalis was feeling the embrace of the Nation of Islam, he was being pushed away by the nation of his birth, America. His GI Bill educational credit ran out after only one semester at Columbia, and Khaalis was still without a job. "Since my graduation from City College of New York," Khaalis wrote in a letter to the Department of Veterans Affairs in the summer of 1953, "I have tried vainly to get jobs in private industry, in government relations, and it has been impossible." The mental illness discharge was haunting him in the job market, he explained. "They seem to fear me," he said of would-be employers. "I am now being rejected by society as an outcast." He concluded his long letter with a request: "It is my desire that you grant to me—if you wish to extend to me justice— more GI extension under Public Law 16, whereby I might be able to study an independent career in medicine." He said he wanted to attend Columbia School of Medicine. "It is my desire to be an asset to society and not a detriment." He ended by emphasizing his earlier point: "I ask for Justice, not mercy." He signed the letter "Ernest X."

Khaalis demanded justice, but the truth of the GI Bill was that it was written by mostly white lawmakers with white soldiers in mind. It was never really meant to benefit Black soldiers like Khaalis—and it was certainly not intended to help them become doctors. Vocational training was one thing, but a young Black man applying for medical school, and at Columbia instead of a historically Black university, was beyond what the bureaucracy would allow. In the best-case scenario, the fact that Khaalis signed his name "Ernest X" would have confused the bureaucrat reading his request. Khaalis received his formal letter of denial in the mail that fall.

In order to keep his benefits, Khaalis presented himself for another psychiatric evaluation at the VA a few months later. He was judged to have improved, and so his monthly pay was reduced from 70 percent to 30 percent of his army salary. For the first time since leaving home a decade earlier, Khaalis started to fall behind on bills. In October 1953, he faced his first debt-collection lawsuit for $596.75. He began working as a mail carrier for the U.S. Postal Service while dedicating his spare time in service of Temple No. 7, even holding a fundraiser at his home with Ruby.

In 1954, as Khaalis was sinking to one of the most desperate lows in his life, a new arrival in the Harlem temple promised to buoy him. Elijah Muhammad had assigned No. 7 a new minister. He was a young man, a few years younger than Khaalis, named Malcolm Little. In the Nation, he was known as Malcolm X. He, too, was the seventh child of parents who had moved north during the Great Migration. He had found the Nation while serving a prison sentence in Massachusetts and, following his release in 1952, had quickly become a close and trusted aide of the Nation's leader, Elijah Muhammad.

With his sharp intellect, a lyrical oratory style, and bottomless charisma, Malcolm was injecting the Nation with a vigor and energy that no one in the organization remembered seeing before. He wore spectacles and spoke assuredly, like a scholar, but with the raw passion of a preacher. The wry smile he would sometimes flash left his adversaries shaken and his followers empowered. Spotting Malcolm's talent, especially his knack for inspiring the young, Elijah Muhammad had made him a roving minister. He hopped from one city to another, galvanizing congregations along the way. Before arriving in Harlem, he had erected a brand-new temple for the Nation in Boston, Temple No. 11.

Harlem was Malcolm's most exciting assignment to date. He knew the city well—in his earlier years he had peddled drugs in the streets and in jazz clubs. Elijah Muhammad and many others believed that the Harlem temple was full of potential, but it had somehow always lagged. Within months, Malcolm pulled hundreds of new congregants into the fold. It grew so fast that soon they moved to a new, larger space on West 116th Street to hold their weekly meetings. As he always had, Malcolm X delivered in Harlem.

One of Malcolm's unofficial assignments was to find and recruit promising young Black men and women into the ranks of the Black Muslims and funnel the best of them to the messenger Elijah for important posts. Khaalis, a graduate of City College who had attended courses at Columbia University, would have stood out instantly as an exciting prospect. His serious demeanor and attention to detail must have caught Malcolm's eye. So, in 1954, as Malcolm prepared for his next assignment of erecting Temple No. 12 in Philadelphia, he recommended Khaalis to Elijah Muhammad and suggested that the young man might be a great asset to the Nation working directly under the messenger in Chicago.

The messenger liked what he heard about this young man named Ernest X. Only a small fraction of Nation members had college educations at that time, so Khaalis's credentials made him an obvious choice to lead the University of Islam in Chicago, the largest of the Nation's schools, which dictated the curriculum taught to children around the country. A few months later, Khaalis, Ruby, and their two children, Ernest Jr. and Eva, moved to Chicago, where Khaalis reported to his new boss, the messenger Elijah Muhammad.

4.

THE SHEIK

In August 1954, Moustapha Akkad, a Syrian man in his early twenties, arrived at Idlewild Airport in New York City aboard a Scandinavian Airways flight from Copenhagen. The trip had started days earlier when Akkad, wearing a stifling woolen suit, boarded his first-ever flight at the airport in Damascus. There, his father had presented him with a pocket-sized copy of the Koran and $200 in traveler's checks. Akkad carried the money and the holy book in his pockets all the way to America.

From New York, his journey continued as Akkad climbed aboard a cross-country bus headed to his final destination: Los Angeles. He was starting a bachelor's degree at the University of California—or, as Akkad told himself: he was headed to Hollywood. He certainly had the looks for Hollywood. He had a sharp, finely chiseled nose and the large, sparkling brown eyes of his mother, framed by eyebrows that looked like the strokes of a calligrapher's pen. The dimple in the middle of his chin gave him a boyish charm even in his twenties—he was not exactly sure of his age because there was no formal record of his birth. Akkad was not remotely interested in being in front of the camera, though. He wanted to become a filmmaker, like Alfred Hitchcock, whose movies he had fallen in love with as a child at the theater in his hometown, Aleppo.

Akkad was the eldest of seven children. His parents gave him the name Moustapha, one of the Islamic Prophet's most famous monikers, meaning "the chosen one," in Arabic. Aleppo, his birthplace, is one of the oldest cities in the world, and the Akkads had deep roots there. The family name itself hearkened back to the ancient Mesopotamian past of the city. The region was conquered by Muhammad's Muslim armies in the early seventh century and became an important cultural and economic hub of the early

Islamic world. Akkad's father, Bakri, was born a subject of the Ottoman Empire, which was also the seat of the Islamic Caliphate. By the time Akkad was born in the early 1930s, the Ottoman Empire was gone, dismembered by the Allied powers in the aftermath of the First World War, and the caliphate it housed had fallen. Akkad grew up in a Syria that was a protectorate of France.

As a young child, he attended Arabic schools, but Bakri eventually sprung for a bilingual French education for his firstborn. Akkad's father held a good job as a low-grade bureaucrat in the revenue department of the Syrian government while his mother raised the children and ran the home. There was not always enough money for luxuries, but the house had furniture and carpets on the floors—it was comfortable. In the aftermath of the Second World War, when the European powers finally began giving up their colonial holdings in the region, Syria freed itself from the clutches of France and declared independence. Not long after that, Akkad switched to Aleppo American College, an English-language school supported by the Presbyterian mission from the United States.

It was there that Akkad began thinking seriously about becoming a filmmaker. The cinema had captured his imagination as a young boy. Aleppo had a handful of movie theaters, and as he sat in those darkened halls with his friends, the flickering images on the big screen worked their magic on his mind. He was entranced by whatever films Hollywood saw fit to export to the Middle East, whether they starred Flash Gordon or Laurel and Hardy. Still, making movies for a living felt like a fantasy even wilder than the things Akkad saw on the big screen.

At American College, Akkad met a teacher named Douglas Hill. The freshly ordained Presbyterian minister with dark horn-rimmed glasses was a recent graduate of Macalester College in Minnesota. For his artistically inclined students, Hill built a theater production workshop in the basement of one of the school buildings. Akkad practically moved in. Soon after graduating, Akkad told his parents that he was saving the money he made from his bank-teller job to go study film in Los Angeles. The acceptance letter from UCLA arrived in the mail in the spring of 1954. He was the first in the family to leave the country.

By the time Akkad landed, Syrians had been arriving on American shores for more than a century. It is estimated that between 1860 and 1914, nearly 180,000 arrived in America and nearly a fifth of them were

Muslims. They came aboard ships at first, becoming peddlers or open-ing restaurants and other small businesses. Others were homesteaders and moved to places like North Dakota or took up farming in the heart of the corn belt. Akkad's arrival marked the era of a new kind of Syrian travel to the United States. He came on an airplane, and his passport, in French and Arabic and adorned with the newly independent country's hawk crest, contained a student visa, which only became possible in 1952, when the United States overhauled its immigration system for the first time in decades. While the new immigration act maintained quotas on the numbers of immigrants from specific countries, it finally did away with the prohibition of immigration from most of the Asian continent that had been in place since 1917. It was the start of the Cold War, and America needed as many friends as possible around the world to counter the Soviet threat. The student visas were a way of targeting upwardly mobile, middle-class youth from Asia and Africa and pulling them into an American orbit.

Islam was still an enigma to most Americans when Akkad arrived. If the word "Muslim" meant anything, it applied to the sharply dressed Black followers of Elijah Muhammad who sold bean pies on street cor-ners in a few big cities in the Northeast and the Midwest and on the West Coast. As their numbers grew, though, things were changing. Muslims were making their presence felt in America like never before.

The summer that Akkad landed in New York, the Arabian Islamic Prophet Muhammad himself was making surprise headlines in the city's newspapers.

An eight-foot-tall Vermont marble statue of Muhammad, weighing almost half a ton, was one of ten statues of famous lawgivers that had lined the roof of the Madison Square Courthouse in Manhattan since 1900. That summer, the statues were lowered for routine repair. The Is-lamic Prophet, his lanky frame covered in a flowing robe with a beard to match, was delicately cradling a long scimitar in his sinewy hands. He wore a turban on his head, which was turned to the right. The city's Muslims recognized him immediately.

It was not an unflattering depiction, especially not by Western stan-dards. After all, Europe's history, especially during and after the Cru-sades, was in some ways defined by its battle against Muslim empires. For a millennium, whether in Dante's *Divine Comedy*, Voltaire's *Mahomet*, Salvador Dalí's paintings, or the earliest European motion pictures,

Muhammad was almost always cast as a villain. In European depictions, whatever the medium, Muhammad was lecherous, treacherous, and violent. America absorbed some of this European cultural context—Voltaire's play, for example, was performed in the American colonies—but the statue atop the courthouse exemplified America's relatively more ambivalent attitude toward Islam and its Prophet.

In Islamic civilization, the depiction of Muhammad in any medium has never been popular or broadly accepted. Muhammad had delivered the message of one unheard, unseen God, Allah, and his life's mission was to triumph over the many divinities of pagan Arabia, who were worshipped in idol form. Muhammad had, with his own hands, toppled the statues of these pagan gods when conquering the city of Mecca in the seventh century. Depictions of Allah, the divine, were strictly forbidden. This taboo extended to Allah's prophets, especially Muhammad, and had hardened over time, especially with the development of the printing press, which allowed for mass distribution of media. In some places the taboo transformed into a full-blown ban on depictions of Muhammad. Many Muslims considered creating an image of the Prophet to be blasphemous, a crime punishable by death. The Muslims in New York wanted, at the very least, for the statue of Muhammad to be gone for good.

In the absence of any leading central Muslim organization in the city, foreign Muslims took up the cause. The Pakistani, Indonesian, and Egyptian ambassadors to the United Nations, which had opened its headquarters in the city a few years earlier, relayed their concerns to the State Department, which put two junior diplomats from the newly formed Bureau of Near Eastern Affairs on the job. The decision was not the State Department's to make, of course. Final authority rested with the New York City commissioner of buildings in the Department of Public Works, to whom it might have sounded like a lot of hassle for nothing. When the renovations were complete, only nine statues were returned to the roof. Muhammad was gone forever. Muslims in New York had made their mark, however small, on the Manhattan landscape.

ACROSS THE COUNTRY, in Los Angeles, Akkad settled right in. In his second year at UCLA, he joined the Delta Sigma Phi fraternity—their emblem was the ancient Egyptian Sphinx—and moved into the house with his new brothers, who became his close friends. There were few Arab students whom Akkad could have befriended even if he had wanted to and certainly none in his theater arts courses. The Arabs he did find in film class were on the screen, and they were a deeply unsavory bunch, in the mold of the evil Muhammad of medieval Europe. The 1921 movie *The Sheik*, starring Rudolph Valentino, perhaps best captured the negative stereotype of Arab men that had endured in Hollywood since the silent era. It also did great business, making $1 million at the box office, and it solidified Valentino's status as Hollywood's most sought-after leading man. It also spawned two sequels in the subsequent decade and spurred a trend of Arab-themed Hollywood films with titles like *A Café in Cairo*, *The Desert Bride*, *A Son of the Sahara*, and *The Thief of Baghdad*.

Akkad had completed his second year in college when, in the summer of 1956, America's relationship with the Middle East was forever transformed. When Gamal Abdel Nasser, a former Egyptian military officer and the president of his country, suddenly nationalized and seized control of the Suez Canal, the stakes were high. The waterway, which had been built almost a century earlier when Egypt was a territory of the Ottoman Empire, cut through Egyptian territory and connected the Red Sea with the Mediterranean. It was one of the most important shipping lanes in the world. Not long after the canal opened to traffic in the late nineteenth century, Britain began its colonial occupation of Egypt, and it maintained control of the canal even after Egypt negotiated its independence in the twentieth century. Nasser's decree made the canal the property of Arabs for the first time ever.

In late October, Israel, Britain, and France launched a military attack on Egypt. The war was fought on land, in the air, and at sea. Dwight Eisenhower, who had led Operation Torch in North Africa during World War II, was now president of the United States. He knew the complexities of the region as well as anyone in his administration, and he watched gravely from the sidelines. The United States had been dabbling in Middle Eastern affairs ever since the Cold War started. Eisenhower's predecessor Franklin D. Roosevelt had forged close ties with Saudi Arabia, for example, and negotiated a sweetheart oil deal for America even before the country had dropped the atomic bomb on Hiroshima. Under Eisenhower, the CIA had toppled a popularly elected government in Iran and had unsuccessfully tried to back a coup in Syria.

The war in Suez was no business deal, however, and there was nothing clandestine about it. Getting involved in Suez would mean upstaging Britain and France in their own colonial backyard and setting a new precedent of policing conflicts within the Middle East. The conflict in Suez was also a Cold War entanglement. Nasser had been accepting large amounts of military aid from the Soviets, and by November 1956 the Kremlin was making not-so-subtle threats of intervening in Suez on behalf of Nasser. With little space to maneuver, and uneasy about a military confrontation with the Soviets, Eisenhower decided to lean on his allies instead. By December, Britain, France, and Israel had all but withdrawn from Egyptian territory. It was a victory of sorts for America, but more important, in the aftermath, it was clear to the world that America now held the reins of war and peace in the Middle East.

While Akkad was watching these historic events unfold in and around his home country through the summer and fall of 1956, he also watched another historic battle between Egyptians and Jews play out much closer to home in Los Angeles. *The Ten Commandments*, the epic biopic of the Prophet Moses, the great lawgiver of the Abrahamic religions, was released in the midst of the Suez Crisis, in November 1956. The film, directed by Cecil B. DeMille, was shot on location on the Sinai Peninsula, and when it premiered at the Criterion Theatre in New York City, French, British, and Israeli jets were still pounding the Sinai with bombs. The reviewer for *The New York Times*, who attended the premiere, noted how this "coincidence was profound," and wrote that the "conflict between Egypt and Israel" actually "has its preamble in the Book of Exodus." In its time, it was the most expensive film ever made—and also the most financially successful in Hollywood history. It was nominated for seven Oscars and won one.

A few months later, in Washington, President Eisenhower cut the ribbon at the Islamic Center of Washington, DC, on the capital's famed Embassy Row on Massachusetts Avenue. Constructed on a prime, thirty-thousand-square-foot piece of real estate, the Islamic Center was born of the joint desire of many newly formed post-colonial Muslim governments in Asia and Africa to establish a pan-Islamic presence in the heart of the American capital. It was a beautiful, unique complex that had taken nearly eleven years and $1.25 million to complete. Designed by an architect from Italy, the complex contained a mosque with a magnificent chandelier imported from Egypt; the handwoven rugs were from Iran; the marble of the pillars was cut in Turkey—all encased in an Alabama limestone facade. It was a melting pot of Islamic civilization—a truly American project. There were no images inside, only intricate Arabic calligraphic designs of Islamic holy text decorated the walls.

Eisenhower's visit was the first by an American president to an Islamic house of worship. In his remarks, he walked a thin line between religion and Cold War politics. "My Islamic friends," he began, "under the American Constitution, under American tradition, and in American hearts, this Center, this place of worship, is just as welcome as could be a similar edifice of any other religion." Freedom of religion, he explained, "is indeed a part of America, and without that concept we would be something else than what we are." He celebrated America's "strong bond of friendship with the Islamic nations," and reminded his audience of Muslim worshippers, ambassadors, and diplomats that "like all healthy relationships, this relationship must be mutually beneficial." He concluded with this: "As I stand beneath these graceful arches surrounded on every side by friends from far and near, I am convinced that our common goals are both right and promising."

His mostly immigrant audience could read between the lines, as they already knew how America viewed the region after Suez. Eisenhower had unveiled his new Middle Eastern policy months before in the form of a presidential decree. The Eisenhower Doctrine, as it came to be known, allowed any Middle Eastern country to request American military intervention if it felt threatened by the Soviet Union. One of the first tests for the doctrine came a few months after Eisenhower's speech at the Islamic Center, when Turkey asked the United States to send its military forces to Syria, which Turkey said was threatening its security by leaning on the Soviets. What followed was a disastrous engagement, "a period of the greatest peril for us since the Korean War," secretary of state John Foster Dulles told Eisenhower. The task of policing the Middle East would not be an easy one. Syria was so badly spooked by the episode that it decided to place itself formally under the protection of Nasser's Egypt, creating a new country called the United Arab Republic. Nasser, the hero of Suez, became its president.

A few months after his country had ostensibly disappeared from the map, gobbled up by Cold War Middle Eastern power plays, Akkad still chose to list it in the program for his UCLA graduation ceremony. Sandwiched between Abbey from Pasadena and Albert from Los Angeles, Akkad from Aleppo, Syria, received his degree in theater arts in May 1958. In the time that it had taken for Akkad to complete his degree, the Middle East had gone from a fringe American concern to a central focus of both American policymakers and filmmakers. David Lean, one of the most admired film directors in the world, had signed up for his next project: a biopic of T. E. Lawrence, a British diplomat and spy who, during the First World War, helped organize the Arab revolt against the Ottoman Empire that led to the fall of the Islamic Caliphate. "How excited I am by the Lawrence of Arabia idea," Lean wrote to Harry Cohn, the president of Columbia Pictures. "I can't think of a better subject for my first film in America."

Akkad was more determined than ever to leave his mark on Hollywood. He enrolled in the film school at the University of Southern California for a master's degree in cinematic arts. America no longer had use for recycled colonial tales about Muhammad, Arabs, and Muslims—America was starting to write its own Arabian adventure. Akkad, a lonesome Arab on the periphery of Hollywood, was starting to see himself as a messenger of sorts. In a studio system developed by Jewish immigrants from Europe at the turn of the century, Akkad was positioning himself as the Arab who would tell the Muslim story.

5.

HOMEGROWN

In January 1958, Elijah Muhammad sent a cablegram to Gamal Abdel Nasser, the president of the United Arab Republic, on the occasion of the Afro-Asian Peoples' Solidarity Conference hosted by the Egyptian government in Cairo. Elijah, who had been taught by Master Fard that Blacks in America were an "Asiatic" race, had already formally endorsed Nasser's seizure of the Suez Canal in public statements and his newspaper columns. In Nasser's stand against the British, French, and Israelis, the Nation saw a reflection of its own fight against white supremacy in America. In his letter, Elijah wanted Nasser to recognize these parallels too.

"As-Salaam-Alikum." He began the letter with the traditional Islamic greeting. "Freedom, justice, and equality for all Africans and Asians is of far-reaching importance," he wrote, "not only to you of the East, but also to over 17,000,000 of your long-lost brothers of African-Asian descent here in the West." He ended the letter with a prayer for "the unity and brotherhood among all our people which we all so eagerly desire."

Nasser, fueled by the ideologies of Pan-Arabism and socialism, was no fan of religiously motivated Muslim activists. At home, he had already imprisoned leaders of the Egyptian Muslim Brotherhood whose vision of a modern Islamic state in post-colonial Egypt ran contrary to his own. In contrast to Elijah, who would appear in public wearing his trademark kufi African hat embroidered with a crescent moon and star, Nasser favored finely tailored suits and ties. Still, over the years, since the arrival of Malcolm on the scene, the Nation of Islam had gone from a fringe cult organization to one of the most influential—and fastest growing—African American organizations in the country, and it demanded to be taken seriously at home and abroad.

With its central message of economic self-reliance, the Nation had developed a vast network of business enterprises. In the mid-1950s, the Chicago temple had an associated grocery store, a restaurant, and a bakery, which employed a combined forty-five Muslims who served the large and fast-growing community. The Nation was constantly encouraging its members to start private businesses of their own, too. Elijah's own wealth had ballooned to an estimated $1 million, not including his home and other real estate owned by the temple. His annual income, largely from donations from the dozen or so temples, as well as from profits from the Nation's businesses, was approximately a quarter of a million dollars. For Black Muslims, the group's numerous business enterprises and the wealth of their holy apostle were a point of pride. They signified both God's favor for the movement and the Muslims' ability to work together to improve the lives of Black Americans.

This newfound wealth and influence attracted the unwelcome attention of J. Edgar Hoover's FBI. Hoover had built the FBI from the ground up and had been the chief of the bureau since 1924. In the decade since the end of World War II, the FBI had doubled in size to nearly seven thousand agents. The zealous new recruits, encouraged by their rabid boss, saw enemies everywhere. Any individuals or organizations that exhibited potential to subvert the American government quickly fell into the FBI's crosshairs. The Nation of Islam, with its strong emphasis on community, separatism, and Black supremacy, was an obvious target for surveillance.

The FBI circulated its first major internal report on the Nation in 1955, soon after Khaalis arrived in Chicago to begin his work at the headquarters. The report, nearly one hundred pages long, described the Nation of Islam as a "fanatic negro organization," an "especially anti-American and violent cult." The monograph, distributed to all the bureau's major field offices, was mandatory reading for all field agents in cities where the Nation of Islam had a significant presence. The report explored the murky history of Wallace D. Fard, known as Master Fard Muhammad by adherents, noting that he had once told the Detroit police that he was "the Supreme Ruler of the Universe." It also dedicated several pages to Elijah Muhammad and the story of his ascension from humble disciple to absolute ruler and holy apostle of the Black Muslims.

Most of the report detailed the sprawling and complex structure of the Nation. The Nation's temples were concentrated in the Midwest and

Northeast at the time, with one in San Diego. Each temple had a minister, who oversaw religious matters. A secretary under each minister took care of day-to-day operations of the temple. The Fruit of Islam, modeled after the muftis of the progenitor Moorish Science Temple organization, was a paramilitary force of men who trained in martial arts and combat at most of the Nation's temples under the supervision of a captain. The captains of each unit of the Fruit reported directly to a supreme captain in Chicago who answered directly to the messenger Elijah. The women, meanwhile, trained in homemaking, cooking, and sewing, and in doctrines and theories of the Nation's theology. The children of the members were encouraged to attend the University of Islam for schooling wherever one was available.

By the time Elijah sent his letter to Nasser in early 1958, Khaalis had already shot up through the ranks of the Nation to become the secretary of Temple No. 2, the de facto national secretary of the Nation of Islam, in charge of operations across the country. Khaalis, now in his mid-thirties, fit more snugly into his suits, and he lived with Ruby and the two children, Ernest Jr. and Eva, in an apartment inside the Nation's Chicago compound in the Hyde Park neighborhood.

The FBI had started tracking Khaalis when he was still at Temple No. 7 in Harlem. Months before he left for Chicago, two special agents of the bureau found a pretext to interview him about his role in the organization. Khaalis did not make a good first impression. In a memo to Hoover, the special agents reported that Khaalis "manifested a belligerent and hostile attitude" and "an open and great hatred towards all members of the white race." Khaalis told the agent that he had been Muslim his whole life and "his leader is Allah and the Prophet Elijah Muhammad." Khaalis complained that the United States had "denied him and members of his race their rights of citizenship, their freedom, justice and equality." Months after that encounter, the FBI added Khaalis to the notorious Security Index.

As secretary of Temple No. 2, Khaalis became one of Elijah's closest and most trusted aides, answering directly to the messenger. Elijah trusted Khaalis to make his personal travel arrangements to visit temples around the country. Some in the Nation also believed that Khaalis was the person actually writing Elijah Muhammad's weekly column,

"Mr. Muhammad Speaks," in the *Pittsburgh Courier*, the leading African American newspaper in the United States. At the weekly Sunday congregation at Temple No. 2, Khaalis would often rise after the messenger had finished addressing the faithful to make his own announcements about the affairs of the university, fundraising efforts, and other mundane organizational matters. As he became more deeply embedded in the organization, though, he began touching on more sensitive topics. An FBI mole reported that in a meeting on May 22, 1957, for example, Khaalis stood up and began railing against the FBI, which, he told the gathered members of the Nation, was infiltrating the ranks of the organization. He might have struck some as overly paranoid.

Soon, the messenger began inviting Khaalis for dinner at the family home, a privilege reserved for only the most elite and trusted members of the Nation. At the dinner table, in the company of Elijah's immediate family, Khaalis dwelled on potential threats lurking in and around the organization. On one occasion, he suggested that the entire headquarters required new security measures. He suggested introducing background checks for new members. At another dinner table conversation, also reported to the FBI, he began rattling off names of people he thought should be turned away from the Nation of Islam because he suspected them of being informants.

His obsessive focus on potential threats put Khaalis on a collision course with Raymond Sharrieff, the supreme captain of the Fruit of Islam, responsible for the entire organization's security. Sharrieff was a few years older than Khaalis, broadly built, with eyes that always appeared to be scanning. Unfortunately for Khaalis, Sharrieff was married to Ethel, Elijah's eldest daughter. He was one of the most influential people in Elijah's close orbit. Many in the messenger's family were already wary of Khaalis, just as they were of any outsider who got too close to Elijah, even Malcolm. When Khaalis began butting heads with Sharrieff, the entire family quickly turned on him.

The spats stemmed mostly from the overlapping responsibilities. Once, for example, Khaalis spotted one of the Fruit of Islam soldiers vacating his post during a public meeting, leaving a stash of weapons unguarded. Khaalis demanded an apology, but Sharrieff refused to let the soldier give him one. The tensions would occasionally spill out at the dinner table when both men were present. Elijah was forced to mediate, and it began to wear on him. Elijah complained to others that Khaalis did not know his place.

It all ended spectacularly, one evening in September 1958. Khaalis had been invited to sit in on a trial administered by the Fruit at the Nation's headquarters. A sister named Thelma who worked for Khaalis at the University of Islam had been accused of writing letters in which she had criticized one of Elijah Muhammad's daughters, Lottie, for interfering with the workings of the university. Criticizing one of the members of the messenger's family was a grave offense and not something Elijah allowed. Elijah had decided to adjudicate the trial himself.

The proceeding went on as anyone might have predicted. Elijah appeared intent on defending his daughter no matter the facts presented by the other woman. As Khaalis watched, he understood that the sister from the school never had a chance at getting justice. Khaalis had always had a hard time biting his tongue when he saw something being done incorrectly. Elijah was about to announce a punishment when Khaalis suddenly stood up and began shouting in defense of the convicted woman. Muhammad's daughter, Khaalis yelled, was clearly interfering. The accused woman had done nothing wrong.

Khaalis and Sharrieff had already had a run-in earlier in the day in Elijah's presence, and the messenger had little patience for Khaalis. He exploded from the bench, telling Khaalis that he had crossed a line, and commanded him to apologize to his daughter on the spot. Khaalis stood silently. Raymond Sharrieff suddenly lunged at Khaalis, and the two men tumbled to the ground, grappling, throwing punches, and yelling obscenities. Members of the Fruit jumped into the scuffle, finally separating the two men and removing them from the courtroom.

A few days later, Khaalis submitted his resignation to Elijah Muhammad. He knew that excommunication awaited him anyhow. As Khaalis and Ruby packed up the apartment and prepared to leave the compound, he warned other members that the Nation had become a self-serving family oligarchy. He had been at the family dinner table, and he had come to believe that it was corrupt to the core. Elijah Muhammad, meanwhile, regaled his new dinner guests with stories about the time that Khaalis had spent in the "nut house."

Khaalis and the family checked into a hotel in Chicago. Khaalis could not shake the feeling, though, that they were being followed. Wherever he went, he saw men that he recognized from the ranks of the Fruit. Finally, in December 1958, four years after he had arrived to serve one of the most important and powerful African American leaders in the country, Khaalis returned to New York City. The family had nothing, so they moved in with Ruby's parents at their new home in the borough of Queens.

In the summer of 1959, the Nation finally broke into the national consciousness of America through a five-part public television documentary series titled *The Hate That Hate Produced*. The series, hosted by journalist Mike Wallace, and reported by a young Black journalist named Louis Lomax, raised the alarm about the threat posed to America by the Nation of Islam. "These homegrown negro American Muslims are the most powerful of the Black Supremacist groups," Wallace said in his introduction. The Nation, he explained, "now claimed a membership of a quarter of a million Negros." Millions of Americans watched and were shocked by the images of young Black men from the Fruit of Islam training in martial arts overlaid with the audio of Elijah Muhammad's speeches denouncing the "devil" white race as the ultimate enemy. Elijah Muhammad was introduced a little more than four minutes into the first episode when a black-and-white photograph appeared on the screen. "Here you see Manhattan Borough President Hulan Jack shaking hands with Elijah Muhammad the leader of the Muslims," Wallace said. In the photo, two other men stood by Elijah's side as he greeted the politician. On his immediate left was Malcolm X, and next to Malcolm stood Khaalis, Minister Ernest X.

The two men could not have ended up further apart. Khaalis was once again delivering mail for the USPS, and the FBI had removed his name from the Security Index soon after he left Chicago. Malcolm, meanwhile, was the undoubted breakout star of the documentary. In the months that followed, he regularly appeared on television to debate prominent figures, and he began touring the country on a speaking circuit. The Nation reaped the rewards. Membership doubled to sixty thousand people in the weeks after the series aired. It became the largest organized Muslim group to have existed in America, and, in the midst of the civil rights movement, one of the largest and most important groups of African Americans in the country. When the first episode aired, Malcolm was traveling through Africa and the Middle East as Elijah's emissary meeting many important world leaders, including Gamal Nasser's deputy and future Egyptian president, Anwar Sadat.

At the 1959 annual Saviours' Day convention, when the Nation celebrated the birth of Master Fard, Elijah finally received the message that he had been anticipating for almost two years. A leader of a Pan-African organization took the stage and read a letter addressed to the "brother peoples" in the Nation of Islam from the President of Egypt, Gamal Abdul Nasser.

"Unity and solidarity are the two indispensable factors for realizing our liberty," Nasser wrote in his message to the Black Muslims. "This lesson must be seriously taken to heart and maintained against imperialist forces seeking to undermine our integrity and convert us into disintegrated groups which can easily be victimized and made to serve their selfish interests." Islam, "our great religion and traditions and ways of living," Nasser concluded, "will serve as the cornerstone in building the new society based on right, justice and equality."

6.

SAILOR'S CLUB

At some point, soon after his return to New York, Khaalis came under the tutelage of a man named Tasibur Uddein Rahman, a Muslim immigrant from the Bengal region of South Asia. Rahman was a slight and small man, only five foot six inches tall with skin a shade lighter than that of Khaalis. Khaalis called him Dr. Rahman, but he was not a doctor in any formal sense. He was a faith healer, a mystic who claimed to possess knowledge that gave him supernatural abilities, including glimpsing into the future and other hidden realms. His disciples believed that he could convene with spirits and with *jinn*—infernal semi-human beings—and that he obtained some of his knowledge from them. He even had the power to control the physical world around him, and he boasted of being a Houdini-like escape artist. Once, he said, he was arrested by the New York City police for performing unlicensed medical procedures in his apartment, but when they took him to jail, the door to his cell would not remain closed, no matter how many times the officers tried. Eventually, he said, they gave up and let Rahman return to sleep in his own bed.

Rahman followed a branch of Sunni Islam called *Ahle-Sunnat wal Jamaat*. The Arabic translates to the "Keepers of the Prophetic Tradition and Community." In Rahman's native South Asia, the tradition was commonly known as Barelvi Islam, named after the town of Bareilly in the north of colonial British India where the branch's original seminary was established in 1904. Barelvis flourished in colonial South Asia, where the British had overthrown the Muslim Mughal Empire that ruled over much of the region. It was a time marked by religious revival of all sorts, as Muslims, Hindus, and other religious traditions searched for explanations of the catastrophic failures that led to the European takeover. Barelvi Islam tethered itself to the theories and practices of the Hanafi school of juris-prudence, one of the four major schools of Sunni legal scholarship, but it also borrowed heavily from mystical Sufi traditions that had been popu-lar in South Asia for almost a millennium, as well as symbology, astrol-ogy, and numerology.

If there was a defining feature of Barelvism, it was extreme—some called it fanatical—reverence for the figure of the Prophet Muhammad. Barelvis elevated Muhammad from the status of a mere mortal, as he is be-lieved to be in most Sunni traditions, to that of a superhuman figure. The Barelvis believed, for example, that Muhammad had knowledge of what existed in the heavens, otherwise known only to Allah. One of their more controversial beliefs was that Muhammad was not a flesh-and-blood hu-man but was instead composed of pure light that presented in the form of a human being. Muhammad, they said, cast no shadow. Because of these beliefs, Barelvis, more than any other branch of Islam in colonial times, and perhaps any other in history, were committed to violently defending the honor of the Prophet. Within a few decades of its establishment, it had become the largest branch of Sunni Islam in the subcontinent.

It is possible that rather than any specific interpretation of the divine will or sharia law prescribed by the Hanafi school, Khaalis was drawn to the meaning of the actual word "Hanafi." In Islamic tradition, the *hanif* were the monotheistic people who lived in the Arabian Peninsula before Muhammad ever brought the message of Islam to them. In a desert of idolaters, polytheists, and heathens, Muhammad encountered these people like an oasis of truth who had somehow always known to follow Allah's will. They were the rightly guided ones, like Abraham, the orig-inal *hanif*. When these men and women encountered Allah's message as revealed by Muhammad, they accepted it readily—the truth had always lived in them, after all. As Khaalis began learning about Hanafi Islam from Rahman in Harlem, he felt as though he was like the *hanif* of seventh-century Arabia—he had always known this to be the truth.

Khaalis's new immigrant mentor was born at the turn of the twentieth century near the city of Calcutta, the largest city in the Bengal region. He first arrived in America around the time that Khaalis was born. Like Khaalis, Rahman had once served in the white man's army. In his immi-gration papers, Rahman reported that he was part of a British Royal Field Artillery regiment during World War I. He would have been no more than fifteen years old at the time, one of the thousands of child soldiers from the Bengal region to serve in the British army in far-flung theaters of the war.

The British Indian soldiers, especially those fighting in the Middle East, were in a painful bind. They were fighting for the Allies and against the Ottoman Empire, the seat of the global Islamic Caliphate. The caliph, Sultan Mehmed V, issued a decree directing all Muslim soldiers to declare jihad against the Allied forces. Some British Indian soldiers refused the orders of their British officers, some deserted or laid down their arms, and a few even rebelled.

At the end of the war, the Ottoman Empire defeated and disintegrating, the British Indian soldiers returned to find a massive social movement led by a handful of prominent Muslim professionals and intellectuals sweeping British India. The Khilafat movement was rallying Muslims across South Asia in street demonstrations to pressure the Allies to preserve the Islamic Caliphate. The movement adopted the crescent and star of the Ottomans as their symbol, and its representatives traveled around the world with it, lobbying world leaders, statesmen, and even the Pope, to ensure that the Islamic Caliphate did not become the final casualty of the European War.

The caliphate, after surviving uninterrupted for more than fourteen hundred years, was finally extinguished in 1924, when the new secular Turkish government formally deposed the caliph. The legacy of the caliphate, however, lived on in Muslim minds and hearts, and also politically. The crescent and star of the Ottoman caliph ended up on the flags of dozens of Asian and African Muslim countries that gained independence after the end of European colonialism. It was the same crescent and star that Master Fard had introduced to his African American followers in Michigan in the early 1930s, and that had landed on Elijah Muhammad's signature kufi hat.

By the time the caliphate fell, Rahman had already left British India. As thousands of former British Indian soldiers did during that time, Rahman would line up for work at Calcutta's busy port and hop on and off British merchant vessels that traversed the globe. As many South Asian men, especially Bengalis, had done in those days, Rahman jumped ship one day at the port of New York and melted into the crowds to start a new life. America was an inhospitable place for people like him. The 1917

Immigration Act, passed by the U.S. Congress and overriding President Woodrow Wilson's veto, had introduced, among other restrictions, an Asiatic barred zone, which covered almost all of China as well as most of South, Central, and Southeast Asia. While barring most Chinese from legally entering the United States, the law also effectively barred most of the world's Muslim population from immigrating, stemming what many feared was a "tide of the turbans" arriving on American shores. The act also introduced a literacy test and several other excludable classes of people, including alcoholics, idiots, people with contagious diseases, and polygamists, a term that could theoretically be applied to any Muslim anywhere in the world as Islam allows men to have multiple wives.

Many of the undocumented Bengali immigrants living in New York illegally settled along the west side waterfront or on Manhattan's Lower East side, but Rahman ventured farther uptown toward a burgeoning community in Harlem. He would have soon found what some have since called Bengali Harlem, a large community of Bengali seamen who formed a thriving subculture in upper Manhattan. The British Merchant Sailor's Club of Indian Seamen opened its doors in 1943, occupying the two upper floors of a four-story building on West 138th Street, and became the beating heart of the community. The club had a recreation room with a film projector, a radio, a gramophone, and a piano, as well as Indian stringed instruments. A mess hall could seat eighty people. A small library contained newspapers, pamphlets, and other reading material from India. The club's members were mostly Muslim, and the prayer room had twenty-five copies of the Koran.

In January 1944, *Life* magazine ran a three-page spread on the club with a large photograph of the prayer room accompanying the write-up. As the members of the club prepared to pray, the article said, "they take down the portraits of the British King and Queen, because Islam considers that any picture of a living thing might tempt Moslems to worship that image rather than the invisible God." The photograph showed, however, a large American flag hanging vertically by the doorway, remaining up as the men prayed.

Many of the South Asian men in this community married Black and Puerto Rican women and raised multiracial children in multicultural and multireligious families. Their families frequently entered the restaurant business, creating a local variant of South Asian cuisine favored by many jazz musicians. (Miles Davis was known to frequent Bombay Indian Restaurant on 125th Street.) The restaurants also became a political node in Harlem where the anti-colonial sentiment of the Indian migrants found common cause with African American groups fighting for civil rights in America.

In July 1946, when President Harry S. Truman signed the Luce-Celler Act into law, allowing people of Indian origin to finally legally immigrate to the United States, Rahman applied for his papers and became a legal resident. By the time Khaalis met him in the late 1950s, Rahman was an American citizen. He had married an African American widow named Mary Ann Smith, and, together, they had a young boy named Jalal. Rahman worked as a cook at Michael's Restaurant on West 114th Street and practiced spiritual healing on the side for extra cash.

Khaalis was entranced by the life story of his new spiritual master. Though the diminutive mystic was from a faraway place that Khaalis knew little to nothing about, the older man's life story strangely reflected Khaalis's own. Rahman explained to Khaalis that the supernatural powers he possessed were made possible by the knowledge that had been transmitted to him by his own teacher. His teacher, in turn, had received them from his own spiritual master, all part of a cryptic line of saints leading back to the Prophet Muhammad of Arabia himself. Rahman, claiming to be a modern saint, presented himself to his mainly African American followers as their direct link to the Islamic Prophet.

Rahman told Khaalis that he had been wandering in America, north and south along the Eastern Seaboard, for more than a quarter of a century searching for a worthy student whom he could train to become his khalifa, or caliph. Rahman claimed his mission was to bring his special knowledge to America, where no one yet possessed it. When Rahman met Khaalis, the seventh child of his father, he said he saw the clear light of knowledge burning inside of him. Rahman had found his khalifa. Khaalis instantly took an oath to follow his new master's teachings. He had finally found the religion he would die for.

Khaalis told Rahman about his experience in the Nation of Islam and his conflicts with Elijah Muhammad and about the corruption and nepotism he had seen in the top ranks of the organization. The Bengali mystic, in response, told Khaalis that the Nation of Islam was a sinister plot masterminded by Zionists. Elijah Muhammad was a mere pawn of

Jews, tasked with misleading African Americans in order to keep them away from the true Islam of the Prophet Muhammad. Master Fard, he told Khaalis during his tutorials, was a drunkard named John Walker, a petty criminal who was coopted by the Zionists to derail the growth of Islam in America.

Rahman and Khaalis hatched a scheme to infiltrate the Nation of Islam and attempt to steer it from the inside toward Sunni Islam. Rahman, excited by having a top-level defector from inside the Nation under his guidance, might have seen an opportunity to gain control of the enterprise for himself. In December 1960, Khaalis resurfaced at the Nation of Islam headquarters in Chicago and begged Elijah for forgiveness. After a formal trial at the Nation's headquarters on December 14, 1960, which was attended by the organization's top brass, Khaalis was readmitted. With fresh access to headquarters, Khaalis went to work immediately. He began whispering to anyone who would listen that he had learned from an "unimpeachable Indian source" that Master Fard was a drunken fool and Elijah Muhammad was part of a sinister Zionist plot.

Within a week, he was openly advertising his reasons for rejoining the Nation. "If the Messenger does not start teaching real Islam," one of the FBI's moles inside the Nation reported Khaalis as saying, "it is my intention to see his whole kingdom is destroyed and his family wiped out." Before Christmas, Khaalis confronted Elijah Muhammad himself and made his blunt pitch. Khaalis wanted to start teaching the children at the University of Islam the *shahada*, the traditional Islamic proclamation of faith that he had learned from Rahman: "There is no god but Allah, and Muhammad is the Messenger of Allah." Elijah understood what Khaalis was saying—Master Fard was not Allah; Elijah was not the Prophet Muhammad. Elijah erupted and turned Khaalis away for the last time.

Days later, Khaalis was back in New York City to reconvene with Rahman. Elijah, Khaalis reported, was a lost cause. The Hanafis would need to find some other way to spread the true message of Sunni Islam. On January 16, 1961, Khaalis; Ruby; Rahman's wife, Mary Ann, who now went by Maryam; and another married couple who followed Rahman walked into a courthouse in Manhattan to fill out paperwork to register a new organization. They listed the name as the American Social Federation for Mutual Improvement, Inc. They registered the following as the organization's charter:

1. To provide for the voluntary mutual benefit and improvement of the members.
2. Social and moral improvement of the membership.
3. Propagation of the faith/religion of Islam through mutual cooperation.
4. This is a non-profit corporation.
5. The benefits are voluntary.
6. The above purposes are to be carried out by discussions, meetings at various times, research in the religion of Islam to improve the social and moral improvement of the membership, by providing adequate facilities for that purpose.

At the bottom of the form, Khaalis's wife signed her new name, which had been given to her by Rahman: Khadija, after the Islamic Prophet Muhammad's first wife. Khaalis signed the document with the name that he had been given by Rahman: Hamaas Abdul Khaalis, meaning the "zealot in service of purity."

A few months later, Khaalis's name appeared on a series of letters intercepted by the FBI that were addressed to the Nation of Islam and written on the stationery of "Sunni Islam Madhab." The letters threatened holy war or jihad against the Nation of Islam. The bureau's New York office traced the source of the letters and found a sign for the American Social Federation for Mutual Improvement hanging from a third-floor apartment window in a building on West 125th Street, two blocks east of the Apollo Theater.

At the same time, the FBI was eavesdropping on Elijah Muhammad and heard him discuss the letters on the phone with a subordinate. "I could have them beat up and killed too, if I wanted," Elijah Muhammad said on the phone, "but I don't want to do anything like that unless, you know, they actually on the scene tried to do something like that. Then we'll go after them with fingers and toes." He instructed his deputy to stand back, for now. "As long as they are just talking, well, then pay no attention. Just watch them."

7.

WORLD LEAGUE

At around the time that Khaalis and Rahman attempted to steer the Nation of Islam toward Sunnism, Wallace Muhammad, the seventh child of Elijah Muhammad, was also trying to turn his father toward the more orthodox forms of Islam that many immigrant Muslims in America practiced. Wallace had developed doubts about his father's dogma early in life, particularly when it came to one of the fundamental tenets of the Nation's doctrine: the divinity of Master Fard, and Elijah's own claim to prophethood. He shared these doubts with his mother when he was young. She listened but counseled Wallace to avoid a confrontation with his father.

Wallace was a quiet, soft-spoken man who never courted controversy. *Playboy* magazine once described him as having "the charisma of a post office clerk." His bushy mustache, nasal voice, and bulbous eyes gave him a friendly appearance, but he hardly looked the part of the rising star in the Nation of Islam—especially not one who was poised to take over the Nation's leadership from his father, as many believed. He was born in 1933, right before Master Fard disappeared forever, the only child Elijah had with his wife, Clara, during their brief spell with the mysterious immigrant. Elijah claimed that Master Fard had named Elijah's seventh-born himself, bestowing on him the "W" of his own name. The messenger had never made any secret about his own desire for Wallace to be his successor. Wallace was barely out of his teens when Elijah made him the minister of Temple No. 12 in Philadelphia, which Malcolm had established years earlier.

Wallace's drift toward traditional Islam strained his relationship with his father. Like Khaalis, Wallace had fallen under the tutelage of a South Asian Sunni Muslim immigrant—in Wallace's case, he was named

Muhammad Abdullah. His new teacher taught Wallace the Koranic scriptures and gave him training in languages, including Arabic and Urdu. Wallace arranged meetings between his new teacher and Elijah with the hope of injecting some Sunni orthodoxy into his father's sermons and teachings. A growing number of Sunni Muslims in America, especially immigrants from Asia, Africa, and the Middle East, were becoming publicly critical of the Nation and casting it as a heretical faith. Elijah had made token gestures to appease his fellow American Muslim critics. The Nation began referring to their houses of worship as mosques instead of temples, for example. In his sermons, Elijah began quoting the Koran more and more and the Bible less and less. Still, when it came to the fundamentals—his own claim to prophethood, and the divinity of Master Fard—Elijah did not budge, not even for his son.

Wallace chose not to press his father. Elijah Muhammad's health was fragile. His bronchitis was terrible, and he hacked through speeches and conversations. He had always been thin, but now he appeared frail. On a doctor's advice, he had moved to an estate in Phoenix, where he slept under an oxygen tent, while the Chicago headquarters was effectively being run by his family members. It was only a matter of time, Wallace might have thought, before the organization fell into his lap. In any case, Wallace had more urgent problems—he was facing prison time. At the instruction of his father, Wallace had refused to register for the military draft and was convicted of the federal crime of draft evasion. In the fall of 1961, after Wallace's final appeal was denied, he surrendered himself to begin serving a three-year sentence at Sandstone prison in Minnesota.

Elijah might have hoped that prison time would temper Wallace's activism. Instead, upon his parole in January 1963, Wallace emerged more convinced than ever that the religion of his father was a heresy. Wallace had spent his time in prison studying the Koran and other traditional Islamic texts with Sunni Muslim inmates, and he no longer kept his views secret. "If Fard was standing in front of me right now," he confided to one of his cousins after his release, "I'd grab that dude in his collar and I'd snatch him out of his shoes, God as my witness."

In September 1963, Wallace got word that Malcolm X was interested in meeting privately. Wallace had heard rumors that in his absence, Elijah had started grooming Malcolm as his successor. He was surprised, therefore, when Malcolm shared his own doubts about Elijah. A decade after joining the Nation of Islam as a young, fiery parolee, eager to inspire and please Elijah, Malcolm had grown into a sober-minded leader with national recognition and influence. He and his wife, Betty, whom he met through the Nation, were now parents to three young daughters. Like many others, Malcolm had heard rumors about Elijah's extramarital affairs and the children born out of wedlock to many secretaries, but he had always rejected them as smears engineered by the FBI and other enemies of the Nation. As the details grew more convincing, however, Malcolm became more concerned. He had come to Wallace for his opinion, and Elijah's son did not hesitate to confirm what he knew: Elijah had fathered at least half a dozen children with his secretaries over many years. More troubling for Malcolm was the fact that some of them were women he himself had steered toward the Chicago headquarters. For Malcolm, the news was devastating—he would never again view Elijah with the same reverence.

Sensing a rebellion brewing, Elijah went on the offensive. First, he moved on his son Wallace, suspending him from the minister position at the Philadelphia temple. Wallace went into hiding, convinced that the Fruit of Islam had been secretly ordered to assassinate him. A couple of months later, Elijah found a pretext to cut down Malcolm. In the days following the assassination of President Kennedy, as most Americans mourned in shock, Malcolm had made blunt remarks to the press about America's "chickens coming home to roost." The assassination, Malcolm said, was the result of the violence that America was unleashing in Vietnam and other parts of the world. "Being an old farm boy myself, chickens coming home to roost never did make me sad," Malcolm quipped in his signature style, "they always made me glad." Elijah summoned Malcolm and reprimanded him, suspending him from the Nation and barring him from speaking to members and to the public for ninety days.

The FBI spotted its best opportunity in decades to disrupt the Nation, or even destroy it. The bureau's illegal Counter Intelligence Program, or COINTELPRO, had been using misinformation and subterfuge to target all kinds of organizations, including various civil rights groups, for a decade by this time. Using the playbook, the FBI began spreading rumors through the ranks of the organization about how Elijah was embezzling the Nation's funds to enrich himself and the "royal family." They also planted stories in the press. An article in the *Los Angeles Herald Exam-*

iner, for example, with the headline "Black Muslim Founder Exposed as White," claimed that Master Fard was a white man from New Zealand with a Polynesian mother and detailed his rap sheet and prison time at San Quentin prison near San Francisco.

Notwithstanding the failure of their earlier conspiratorial venture to convince Elijah to embrace Sunni Islam, Khaalis and Rahman spotted a fresh opportunity. This time they targeted Elijah's children, hoping to find someone who would defect. Knowing that Elijah now lived mostly in Phoenix, Khaalis periodically called the Nation's headquarters. He vacillated, sometimes within a single call, from being persuasive to proselytizing to pressuring. Ethel, Elijah's oldest daughter and wife of Raymond Sharrieff, the man responsible for Khaalis's ouster from the Nation, confided in her mother after receiving one of these calls. Khaalis, Ethel told her mother, wanted to meet her and her brother Herbert in person. She felt that it was a bad idea. "He is crazy," she said, adding, "It might be another trick." In 1964, Khaalis and Rahman traveled to Chicago to meet with Wallace in person. They made their best pitch for Wallace to join the Hanafis, but Wallace demurred. It was the last time Khaalis would look for a meeting with Wallace until he finally demanded his presence as a condition for releasing the hostages that he held in 1977.

Malcolm, meanwhile, was nowhere to be seen. His ninety-day suspension had come and gone, with no sign of him at headquarters in Chicago. He had retreated to the home that the Nation had bought for him in Queens, New York, only a mile or so from where Khaalis had lived after being ejected from the Nation several years earlier. Finally, in March 1964, Malcolm resurfaced on the front page of *The New York Times*. "Malcolm X Splits with Muhammad," read the headline. The report said that Malcolm had plans to create a new "black nationalist party," as well as another religious organization, Muslim Mosque Incorporated, which followed orthodox Sunni Islam. It was already drawing recruits from the ranks of the Nation. A month later, as a way to mark the new beginning, Malcolm booked a plane ticket under a new, Arabicized name, Malik el-Shabazz, and flew to Mecca to perform the hajj, the Islamic pilgrimage.

When Malcolm returned to New York that summer, he was a changed man. He began speaking publicly about his transformation and attributed his new worldview to his experiences during the Islamic pilgrimage. Standing alongside millions of other people of all races in Mecca, praying to the same Allah, had fundamentally altered his views on race relations, he said. He had experienced a spiritual reawakening. He was now an "orthodox Muslim" and he opposed no one based on their skin color. Malcolm's appearance had changed as well. He had dropped the clean-cut look preferred by the Nation and now sported a full goatee—though he still flashed that same wry smile for the cameras lined up to document his return.

The country had also changed radically in his absence. President Johnson had signed the Civil Rights Act into law in July 1964. It was a great victory for the civil rights movement and for its most charismatic leader, Martin Luther King Jr., and his Southern Christian Leadership Conference. Members of the Nation, Malcolm in particular, had long ridiculed and derided King for his more conciliatory stance in demanding civil rights for African Americans, but now Malcolm struck a more civil tone with him and echoed King's concerns about African American human rights.

In the fall of 1964, after two months of nonstop campaigning around the country for his new political and religious organizations, Malcolm embarked on another, more elaborate multistate international tour. Over the course of three months, Malcolm traveled through more than a dozen Arab and African countries, meeting with heads of state and political and religious leaders along the way. He received attention and admiration that no American Muslim leader had ever come close to receiving. He made stops in several historic cities of Islamic civilization and even made a politically charged visit to a Palestinian encampment in the Gaza Strip. One of the most important stops on his itinerary was the Al-Azhar Institute in Cairo, Egypt. Al-Azhar, Arabic for "the Luminous," was more than one thousand years old and the most prestigious and respected Islamic seminary in the world. After the fall of the caliphate, it was left as the single most respected religious authority in Sunni Islam. Malcolm received a hero's welcome there as he was lavished with attention and praise. He was also offered financial grants, including scholarships for dozens of African Americans of Malcolm's choice to be trained at the institute in Sunni Islamic jurisprudence—an offer to train a new generation of religious elite in America.

Next, Malcolm traveled to Saudi Arabia, where he met with officials from a relatively new but important organization called the Muslim World League. The league was a Saudi challenge to Al-Azhar's religious monopoly, and it was buying unprecedented influence around the world by funneling petrodollars to poorer Muslim countries, as well as eyeing Muslim minority communities, especially in Western countries. At the World League, Malcolm received a warm welcome. They assigned one of their top religious scholars, a Sudanese imam with a bushy white beard by the name of Ahmed Hassoun, to accompany Malcolm back to the United States and act as his religious guide and teacher.

In October 1964, toward the end of Malcolm's foreign trip, *The New York Times* published excerpts from a letter Malcolm had written from Mecca. "For 12 long years I lived within the narrow–minded confines of the 'strait-jacket world' created by my strong belief that Elijah Muhammad was a messenger direct from God Himself," Malcolm wrote. He lamented representing and defending him "even beyond the level of intellect and reason." Malcolm promised, "I shall never rest until I have undone the harm I did to so many." Finally, he made his conversion official. "I am a Muslim in the most orthodox sense; my religion is Islam as it is believed in and practiced by the Muslims here in the Holy City of Mecca."

The rector of Al-Azhar in Cairo issued a formal letter certifying Malcolm's bona fides. Malcolm, the letter proclaimed, was "of true and correct faith." It was "his duty to propagate Islam and offer every available assistance and facilities to those who wish conversion to Islam." To anyone watching, it was becoming apparent: Malcolm was Al-Azhar's man in America. He was the Saudis' man in America. He was the closest anyone had ever come to being the caliph of American Muslims.

Betty Shabazz, Malcolm's wife, met with Wallace and asked him to join forces with Malcolm, presenting him with the note from Al-Azhar. Just as he had declined to join Khaalis, though, Wallace declined the overture from Malcolm. Wallace had his own designs and, more important, he probably knew what was coming. When Malcolm returned to New York the following month, it was clear that he was a marked man. A little more than a week after his arrival, Raymond Sharrieff, the supreme captain of the Fruit of Islam, who had once wrestled Khaalis to the ground in Chicago, sent a brief and blunt telegram to Malcolm X:

"Mr. Malcolm: We hereby officially warn you that the Nation of Islam shall no longer tolerate your scandalizing the name of our leader and teacher the Honorable Elijah Muhammad regardless of where such scandalizing has been." Signed: "Captain Raymond Sharrieff."

Malcolm's home in New York was firebombed on February 14, 1965. On February 21, in the middle of the day, while speaking to a crowd of four hundred people in the Audubon Ballroom in West Harlem, Malcolm X was gunned down by members of the Nation of Islam. Malcolm had bullets lodged in his chest and face when he arrived at New York Presbyterian Hospital, where he was declared dead on arrival. His final rites were performed by the Sudanese imam that the Muslim World League had assigned to him, and he received a traditional Islamic burial. A few days later, Temple No. 7, where Khaalis had met Malcolm X at the beginning of their spiritual journeys, was burned to the ground and destroyed by Malcolm's furious followers.

The assassination had eliminated a man who posed a threat to the Nation of Islam and to America's security establishment, both well prepared to crush any potential threats. It also sent a warning to all those who still dared to consider challenging the messenger Elijah. Wallace heard the warning loud and clear. A few days after Malcolm's murder, at the annual Saviours' Day celebration in Chicago, Wallace appeared onstage in front of tens of thousands of Elijah Muhammad's followers to announce his return to his father's organization.

He began with a confession of guilt: He had publicly judged his father, "a man who has a title and a history that makes it permissible for God Almighty to judge him and not me." He regretted the mistake and prayed that Allah and his father would forgive him and, "if it's necessary," he told the crowd, "that you also accept me and permit me back in your midst as a brother." He ended with a metaphor from masonry, the trade that he had earned a living with since his exile from the Nation. He had used a hammer to knock, however, "I wasn't knocking to destroy," he explained, "I was knocking to repair." It was "a great mistake," he conceded. "I'm sorry for it."

His words were chosen carefully. At no point did Wallace renounce his own Sunni Islamic faith. He never embraced his father's controversial beliefs either. He simply apologized for judging him. As far as Khaalis was concerned, Wallace had just sold out. He knew that Wallace and Malcolm had followed in his footsteps, breaking away from the Nation on religious principle. To see Wallace stand by his father's side days after Malcolm had been gunned down left no doubt in Khaalis's mind: Wallace was a hypocrite—the word used in the Islamic holy book to describe the absolute worst enemies of Islam.

Later that year, Malcolm's posthumous autobiography—composed with the author Alex Haley—would be published and begin inspiring thousands of people to follow his path into activism and into Islam. Still, his assassination left a powerful vacuum in the leadership of American Islam. For the final few months of his life, Malcolm was perhaps the first and only American caliph, effectively anointed and recognized by the most powerful and revered centers of Islamic power in the world as the spokesman for Muslim interests in the world's most powerful country. While he was now gone, Malcolm had left behind the blueprint for ascending to the top. Wallace strategically repositioned himself close to the levers of power in the Nation of Islam. Khaalis, on the other hand, convinced of his own righteousness and grandeur, began charting his own path to the top. He was, after all, the "zealot in service of purity."

8.

JIHAD PRODUCTIONS

In January 1966, as jury selection was beginning in New York for the criminal trial of the three Nation of Islam hitmen accused of murdering Malcolm, Khaalis encountered a charming and ambitious young man on the streets of Harlem. The young man had watched from a distance as Khaalis preached to a youth group on a street corner. When Khaalis finished, the young man approached him, saying that he had heard enough—he was ready to become a Muslim right on the spot. Khaalis took stock of the man—slender and handsome, wearing spectacles—and decided to introduce him to his teacher, Tasibur Rahman. On January 20, 1966, the man recited the *shahada*, the declaration of faith, and became a Muslim. Rahman gave him a new name: Abdul Aziz—the "servant of the powerful one."

Khaalis had been on a recruiting spree in New York, even calling public meetings to spread the word about the Hanafis and against the Nation of Islam. Aziz was a special find and would quickly become Khaalis's right-hand man, something like what Malcolm had been to Elijah. He would also play a key role in Khaalis's takeover of the American capital a decade later. Aziz had passed through the thick of the civil rights movement earlier in the decade. As a nineteen-year-old student at Howard University, he was one of the founders of the Nonviolent Action Group along with a few friends, including his once-roommate, Stokely Carmichael. After a year of agitating for civil rights in the Washington, DC, area, Aziz and Carmichael, along with a dozen others, rode the Illinois Central Railroad from New Orleans to Jackson, Mississippi, in the summer of 1961 as part of the Freedom Rides, a campaign to desegregate public transportation in the American South. Aziz, Carmichael, and several others were arrested and jailed in Jackson, where they briefly shared a cell with a young man named John Lewis, who was an activist with Martin Luther King's group.

After Malcolm's murder, Carmichael went on to become one of the pioneering leaders of the Black Power movement, which grew in reaction to the slow progress in the fight for equality that followed the landmark civil rights legislation of the mid-1960s. The new movement, forged in dozens of fiery riots across the country following Malcolm's assassination, adopted a more aggressive rhetoric that sometimes faintly echoed the Nation of Islam. The Black Panther Party, an armed militant group of mostly young African Americans inspired by the Black Power movement, was established in 1966 in Oakland, California.

Aziz was a poet, however—more of an artist at heart than a militant. He left Howard just fifteen credit hours short of an undergraduate degree and, in Harlem, found a group of Black revolutionaries who were using their art for Black empowerment. The Black Arts movement, as it was known, had its home at the Black Arts Repertory Theatre and School (BARTS) on West 130th Street. It was established by the famous Beat poet LeRoi Jones, who had burst onto the scene in 1964 with his one-act play *Dutchman* and was instantly radicalized by the murder of Malcolm. "For Great Malcolm a prince of the earth, let nothing in us rest until we avenge ourselves for his death," he wrote in "A Poem for Black Hearts," right after the assassination. He embraced the Islamic faith, changed his name to Amiri Baraka, left behind his wife and two children in Greenwich Village, and made a symbolic pilgrimage to Harlem to open BARTS. He also started an associated record label and named it Jihad Productions.

When Khaalis met Aziz, he was employed as a production manager at BARTS, working with Black artists and musicians who reveled in the rough-and-tumble revolutionary spirit of the place. Through Aziz, Khaalis's Islamic message began spreading at BARTS, and several people in Baraka's close circle converted to Sunni Islam. By the spring of 1966, the wheels were starting to come off as the artists and militants who passed through the space began feuding. When these conflicts turned violent, Baraka suddenly left Harlem and moved to Newark, leaving a vacuum at the top of the organization. Aziz saw an opportunity. The elegant-looking four-story brownstone that housed BARTS, Aziz proposed to Khaalis, would make a perfect headquarters for the Hanafis, who had been conducting their business out of Khaalis's apartment. Aziz recruited an old

classmate from New Rochelle, who took on the name Abdul Latif; the classmate would help out along with two other Hanafis. Their plan was simple:
they would move in with guns, clear the place out, and settle in.

The takeover happened on March 9, 1966, the same day that a jury
convicted three men of murdering Malcolm X and exactly eleven years
before the Hanafis would take over downtown Washington. It was swift
and successful. The *New York Herald Tribune* reported news the following morning about a new "Hanafi Mussulman School of Islam" that had
set up at the former headquarters of BARTS. The article quoted Khaalis,
identifying him as a "brother" in the community, saying that the purpose
of the organization was to teach the basic principles of Islam to whoever
wanted to learn. "Islam means respect for all people and for everyone,"
Khaalis was quoted as saying, an attempt to draw a distinction between
the Hanafis and Elijah's Black Muslims. "We are not teaching hate." The
Hanafi community, the article said, numbered in the hundreds.

Only days later, the building was back in the news. A raid by nearly
fifty police officers had led to the arrest of half a dozen armed men camped
inside, including Abdul Aziz and his friend Abdul Latif. The police recovered an eighteen-inch pipe bomb, a loaded .22-caliber rifle, and an M-1
carbine rifle, along with bandoliers full of shells, slingshots, crossbows,
knives, and clubs. They also found marijuana and smoking pipes. In the
basement, cops discovered a shooting range with bizarre signage: "Weapons are to be cleaned and sharpened each day at 6 P.M. All weapons are
subject to inspection by the Khan. All officers will be obeyed. The penalty
for disbelievers are [*sic*] death. This law was given to our fathers. It has not
been enforced in 1400 years. It will be enforced now."

The newspapers reported this as the discovery of a "new and super
militant Black nationalist group which calls itself the Hanafi Musselmen."
The police told reporters they were looking into a "secretive organization
of extreme black nationalists" known as the "Pakistani Muslims," which
"appears to be far more fiercely militant than the Black Muslims." Abdul
Aziz and a few of Khaalis's other disciples were charged with felonious assault and violation of public health laws. Less than a week later, however,
all the charges were dropped. There was insufficient evidence, a New York
judge opined, to prove the charges beyond a reasonable doubt.

The release only emboldened the Hanafis. Khaalis explained to Aziz,
Latif, and the others under his command that they were the vanguard of

a new, empowered Sunni American Muslim community. To fulfill their destiny, they needed to wage jihad, or a struggle for Islam, and for that, they needed cash, and lots of it. It was time, Khaalis instructed, to rob a bank. On April 1, 1966, Aziz, Latif, and another Hanafi hijacked a taxicab and drove it to a Chase Bank location at 135th Street and Fifth Avenue in Manhattan. Once inside, the Hanafis wrestled the lone guard on duty to the ground. The safe, the guard told them, had $200,000 in it—it was more than enough to kick-start a national Hanafi movement. The Hanafis could not get it to open in time, though, and had to flee in a getaway car when they heard the police sirens. By the evening, all three men had been arrested. This time a grand jury indicted the Hanafis, and a trial was scheduled for the summer.

Khaalis, who had helped plan the heist, was furious but also nervous. He walked into the New York office of the U.S. State Department a few days later and inquired about the process of renouncing his American citizenship. An FBI report described the exchange he had with the official. What was his plan after giving up his passport? Khaalis explained that he would seek asylum in "Red China." He did not know anyone residing there, nor could he speak Chinese, but he would teach the Hanafis' interpretation of Islam to the people living there. The agent asked Khaalis if he planned to be critical of the United States when he was abroad. Khaalis, the report said, "would be as critical of America as it had been critical of him."

Ultimately, China was too far away. Khadija and Khaalis now had three children. The third child, a daughter named Maryam, was born in 1962. Moving to a foreign country with a baby and two teenagers was no easy proposition. In the end, Khaalis left Khadija and the children behind in New York and went as far as Washington, DC. There, he found work with the Pakistani embassy, where he ran errands and did odd jobs for the embassy staff. He got another part-time job in the kitchen of the International Club. The job paid $300 a month, half of which Khaalis used to pay his rent.

He had been there only a few months when, on March 11, 1967, exactly a decade before Khaalis would launch his assault on Washington, his spiritual master Tasibur Rahman died. As Rahman's chosen khalifa, Khaalis knew it was now his time. The responsibility to spread the true faith of Islam to all of America rested on his shoulders. First, he needed to arrange a proper burial for Rahman. The Islamic Cultural Center of New York was a popular spot for Sunni Muslims in the city, and Khaalis met with the Egyptian imam to discuss arrangements. Rahman's casket was transported to a Muslim cemetery that the cultural center maintained across the river in New Jersey. The Egyptian led the funeral prayer as Khaalis and other followers of the deceased mystic stood in straight rows behind him, hands folded respectfully. At the conclusion of the ceremony, Khaalis would have thanked the imam for leading the communal funeral prayer. Neither man could have imagined that ten years later, almost to the date, Khaalis would be holding the Egyptian hostage, one of his Hanafi lieutenants pressing a machete to the imam's neck, threatening to behead him and toss his head out of a window.

9

DAY OF DOOM

Muhammad Abdul Rauf, the Egyptian imam, had arrived in New York City aboard a steamship the previous year, around the same time that Khaalis had met Aziz on a street corner. Together with his wife and three children, the forty-nine-year-old with heavy eyebrows and a broad, gentle face, had watched the Statue of Liberty slowly come into view over the horizon on Christmas Eve. Rauf was an Islamic scholar and missionary, trained at Al-Azhar and sent to America by the Egyptian government to become the director and imam of the Islamic Cultural Center of New York.

The city must have felt like a different planet compared to the small village along the eastern bank of the upper Nile where Rauf was born in 1917. The houses there were built with unbaked mud bricks, and few people ever left the village, let alone the country. Rauf's father, an imam of a local mosque and the chief religious authority in his village, claimed direct descent from the Prophet Muhammad. Rauf, his firstborn, arrived in the world on the birthday of the Islamic Prophet. Rauf showed early promise for religious scholarship and had memorized the entire text of the Koran by age eight. In his teens, he began his studies at Al-Azhar.

The United States was Rauf's fourth international assignment as a missionary. After completing his theological training at Al-Azhar in the late 1940s, Rauf traveled to the tiny Arab emirate of Kuwait. Then he lived in the United Kingdom for several years, where he also earned a doctorate from the University of Cambridge in anthropology. He then spent almost eight years in Malaysia, where he helped establish the country's first major Islamic University. Right before he arrived in the United States, he had published a biography of the Islamic Prophet with a British publishing house.

America was always, at best, a peripheral concern of the world's Islamic missions. After the Suez Crisis, and the speech by Eisenhower at the unveiling of the Islamic Center in Washington, Al-Azhar and other Islamic institutions began taking a deeper interest in the great Western power that promised religious freedom in its constitution and began sending missions to America. Rauf encountered a Muslim society of the kind that he had never seen or studied before. There were between half a million and a million Muslims spread across the vast expanse of the country at the time, and they came from every conceivable background. African Americans were still the single largest group, but the demographics were quickly shifting. The Hart-Celler Act, a new immigration law in 1965, passed alongside historic civil rights legislation, had lifted the limits on immigration based on national origins. Previous immigration regimes had suppressed, and often barred, immigration from Asia and Africa. The new law opened the door, for the first time ever, to most of the Muslims of the world to enter America.

The Islamic Cultural Center, which occupied a five-story building on the southern bend of Riverside Park overlooking the Hudson River on 72nd Street in Manhattan, was the closest thing to a central institution for Muslims, both Sunni and Shia, in the city. The center was established by a group of Muslim diplomats serving at the United Nations headquarters, which had opened its doors across town in 1952, five years before the Islamic Center in DC. Unlike the ornate center in the capital, though, the New York center was never meant to serve any diplomatic function. It received meager support and functioned mostly as a convenient space for the diplomats to pray and worship.

Still, because of its location close to Harlem, the mecca of American Islam, the cultural center always played an outsize role in American Muslim life. Rauf's predecessor, another Al-Azhar–trained Egyptian named Mahmoud Youssef Shawarbi, was most often credited with welcoming Malcolm into Sunni Islam. After his break with the Nation, Malcolm had started attending Friday prayers at the mosque on Riverside. He also met with Shawarbi for more detailed lessons on Sunni Islam, taking careful notes like a student. When Malcolm made his first trip to Saudi Arabia to perform the hajj pilgrimage, he required certification that he was a true believing Muslim, and it was Shawarbi who testified to this fact in a written document. Shawarbi also arranged many of Malcolm's important meetings during his second trip to Egypt, including those at Al-Azhar. Malcolm worked so closely with the cultural center that the FBI listed it as an "affiliate organization" of Malcolm's Muslim Mosque Incorporated.

When Rauf's family moved into their apartment on the top floor of the building on Riverside, New York City was still reeling from Malcolm's murder. It did not take long for Rauf to learn the militant ways of New York's Muslim community. One cold winter morning, less than a year into his new job, as he was collecting the mail, Rauf was held up at the entrance of the building by three African American men carrying barely concealed weapons. They all wore sunglasses, and a few were dressed in what might have passed for Arab garb in Manhattan, complete with the traditional *kaffiyeh* headdress. Their leader, a towering light-skinned African American with a mustache who was wielding a scimitar, greeted Rauf with the Islamic salutation "Assalamu alaikum," or peace be on you, and followed it up with the more alarming "today is the day of doom." The man, who claimed to be representing the Honorable Elijah Muhammad, told Rauf that he and his men were there to claim the building and all its resources for the Nation of Islam. He asked Rauf to turn over the property records and deed and surrender the key.

"I welcome anything that promotes the cause of Islam," Rauf replied diplomatically. He explained that the keys to the building were with the secretary, who would return only later that evening. The leader of the group agreed to return, and the men left after touring the entire building, examining the space, and taking an inventory of the furniture and equipment. By the time the men returned that evening, a panicked Rauf had already placed calls to the Egyptian embassy, the UN mission, and the State Department. NYPD officers were waiting inside when the armed men entered, and they were all arrested and jailed. The new secretary of Harlem's Temple No. 7 read the news in the papers the following morning and paid Rauf a personal visit. No true follower of Elijah Muhammad, the secretary claimed, would ever dare threaten Rauf like that. It was all a big misunderstanding, he told a bemused Rauf, who accepted the explanation without question.

Rauf was only beginning to piece together the complex puzzle of American Islam when events back home in the Middle East captured his, and all of America's, attention. The Six-Day War broke out in June 1967 when Israel suddenly launched airstrikes on Egypt, after Nasser had been posturing aggressively on the Sinai Peninsula along Israel's border. Israel's attack decimated the Egyptian air force, which was caught flat-footed on the ground. Israel moved its ground forces into the Sinai via the adjoining Gaza Strip, as well as into the West Bank territory, to Israel's east, administered by the Kingdom of Jordan. Israeli forces also occupied the Golan Heights across the northeastern border with Syria. Israel's Arab neighbors never recovered from the shock of the initial attack, and within a week they surrendered the territory to Israel. Almost 1 million more Arabs came under Israeli occupation. These new borders would set new terms for the conflict for decades to come and would become a central foreign-policy issue for America in its role as broker of peace in the Middle East.

The Middle East conflict came home to America in a way that even the Suez Crisis never did. The Six-Day War occurred as America was fighting its own long war in Vietnam and, more important in the midst of the long, hot summer of 1967, as race riots raged in cities across the country. Detroit, Newark, and other major cities resembled war zones at times, as police unleashed immense firepower against African Americans who took to the street to riot and protest unemployment, poor housing, and police violence. When the smoke cleared, close to one hundred people, most of them Black, were dead. Thousands of people had been injured, and entire neighborhoods were reduced to rubble and ash.

Many African American activists, especially more militant ones, began drawing parallels between the violence Blacks had endured at home and the suffering of Arabs, particularly Palestinians, who came under Israeli occupation that same summer. The Black Panther Party, the Malcolm X–allied Revolutionary Action Movement, the Nation of Islam, and many smaller Sunni Black Muslim groups like the Hanafis made public statements in support of the Palestinians and against Israel. Increasingly, radical civil rights organizations like the Student Nonviolent Coordinating Committee, which was now led by Abdul Aziz's old Howard University friends and fellow Freedom Riders, Stokely Carmichael and H. Rap Brown, joined in the chorus. In a press release published in August, the group assailed "the Jewish refugees and survivors" of the

Holocaust for using "this tragedy as an excuse to imitate their Nazi oppressors—to take over Palestine, to commit some of the same atrocities against Arab inhabitants, and to completely dispossess the Arabs of their homes, land and livelihood."

The general counsel for the Anti-Defamation League, an organization that challenged anti-Semitism in America, fired off a scathing response to this: "It is a tragedy that the civil rights movement is being degraded by the injection of hatred and racisms in reverse," he wrote, adding, "Anti-Semitism is anti-Semitism whether it comes from the Ku Klux Klan or extremist Negro groups." The alignment of some African American activists with the Palestinians came at the same time that American Jews were rallying to the Israeli cause like never before. American Jews traveled to Israel in large numbers that summer to work the civilian jobs left vacant by Israelis serving in the war. American Jewish organizations fundraised nearly $300 million for Israel that year, and Americans held close to $200 million in Israeli bonds by the time the war ended. B'nai B'rith, the largest of the American Jewish organizations, purchased a record $13 million in Israeli bonds. The war, wrote Rabbi Arthur Hertzberg, a prominent American Jewish scholar, "evoked commitments in many Jews who previously seemed untouched by them."

Tensions between American Jews and African Americans were not new, but the 1967 war was the first time that the two groups battled over a foreign-policy issue with such ferocity. Stokely Carmichael traveled through the Middle East that year, speaking out against Israel at every opportunity along the way. Even the most measured leaders, like Martin Luther King, who had visited the Palestinian West Bank and the East Jerusalem neighborhood during his 1959 trip to the Holy Land, was pointing to the plight of the Palestinians days before his assassination.

Immigrant Arabs, caught in the middle of this, became visible in America for the first time thanks to television coverage of the war. Americans still mostly associated the word "Muslim" with the Nation of Islam, but now, Arab interlocutors began appearing in the media and talking about issues that had less to do with the history of the transatlantic slave trade and more to do with prevailing American foreign and immigration policies aimed at Asia and Africa. As the leader of one of the most important Muslim institutions in the country, Rauf became a frequent guest on TV and radio shows and at public events as a representative of Arabs and Muslims in America, where he was often pitted against leaders of American Jewish organizations.

For Rauf, the war had serious personal consequences, too. Nasser, who believed that the Americans had secretly supported Israel in the war, severed Egypt's diplomatic ties with the United States, leaving Rauf, who was only halfway through his four-year quasi-diplomatic appointment, in unexpected legal limbo. He could return to Egypt, but if he wished to stay in the United States, he would have to apply for a new visa that would allow him to continue living and working as an imam in the country. Rauf found that the 1965 immigration act had created a new visa category called Third Preference. If foreigners could prove that they were serving a professional function that an American could not fulfill, they could apply to become naturalized as American citizens. Rauf was confident that he was one of only a handful of people in the country who was credentialed by Al-Azhar to be an imam. If he were to become an American, he might even become the first American citizen to hold such credentials. After consulting with a few lawyers and diplomats, Rauf submitted his immigration application and paid a $25 fee. As he waited, he heard of a potential opening to lead the Islamic Center of Washington, DC, the grand, custom-made structure on the capital's Embassy Row, the real center of Islamic religious power on the North American continent.

10.

SPORTS RESCUE

"Should Black athletes be on the Olympic team, the American team?"

Lewis Alcindor, the seven-foot-two college basketball star from UCLA, was not ready for this conversation. At twenty-one years of age, he was already a national phenomenon. He had scored fifty-six points in his first varsity game and was now leading the best college team in the country and considered by some to be the best college center in history. So overwhelming were his skills that the NCAA had banned dunking in college basketball after his arrival, a move that people started calling the "Alcindor rule."

He had agreed to this live television interview on the *Today* show in July 1968 to talk about his work over the summer in his native New York City with Operation Sports Rescue, encouraging young Black men in the city to consider college while coaching them in basketball. He did not wish to be ensnared in a heated debate about race relations in America. Martin Luther King had been killed by an assassin's bullet months earlier, on April 4. During the summer of 1968, the year after the long, hot summer of 1967 had set America on fire, a new wave of protests and violent riots erupted in more than one hundred cities. The worst of the riots was in Washington, DC. In a fiery speech in the capital, Stokely Carmichael had told crowds that "white America has declared war on black America." Protestors and rioters began closing in on the Capitol, and President Lyndon Johnson called in the National Guard to protect the city. Weeks later, at the U.S. Olympic basketball team tryouts, Alcindor was a no-show. He, along with a few UCLA teammates, had decided to boycott the games. Now, for the first time, he was asked to explain his decision on live TV.

"Well, I know I'm not going because there's just too many things that point against it. I have to go to school and plus, you know, the atmosphere is that it's wrong to represent this country and then have to come back and, you know, face the music all over again."

"But you live here."

"Yeah, I live here but it's not really my country, you know."

"Well then there's only one solution then: maybe you should move."

"Well, you see, that would be fine with me, you know, but it all depends on where are we going to move?"

Born and raised in New York City, Alcindor had come of age in the civil rights movement and was quietly radicalized by it over the years. He was six years younger than Emmett Till and was old enough to remember the news of his gruesome murder and the even more gruesome photos of his lynched body in an open casket. In his teens, he listened to speeches by Malcolm X and read the poetry of Amiri Baraka. During the Harlem riots in July 1964, he faced off against cops firing gas canisters and bullets at protestors. When he left New York for UCLA and grew an Afro, he considered himself part of the Black Power movement. He had also become deeply interested in Islam after reading *The Autobiography of Malcolm X*. In 1967, he was the only college athlete at the Cleveland summit where Muhammad Ali, along with a team of professional athletes, gathered in support of his decision to avoid the military draft during the Vietnam War. The decision to boycott the Olympics was Alcindor's own public political stand.

In an apartment on Manhattan's West 132nd Street, Khaalis was mesmerized by what he saw on TV. The young man was articulating the frustrations with America that Khaalis had been grappling with himself. What really caught Khaalis's attention, though, was what Alcindor wore around his neck: a small pendant in the shape of a crescent and star. Was the young college basketball star dabbling in Islam? Was he under the influence of Elijah Muhammad? Khaalis knew Alcindor's father, a fellow jazz musician who played on the Harlem circuit in the 1940s and '50s. Both families had briefly lived in the Dyckman housing project in Inwood, at the northern tip of Manhattan, in the 1950s. Both men had their firstborn sons a few months apart in 1947. Khaalis passed on a message to Alcindor's father about wanting to meet his son.

Khaalis was still recovering from the death of Rahman a year earlier. In the time that had passed since then, Khaalis had plunged further into the depths of desperation and madness. During the turbulent summer of 1967, living in Washington, DC, and with $16 left in his bank account, Khaalis had attempted to singlehandedly rob a bank in suburban Maryland and was arrested by FBI agents. While he was on parole, Khadija committed him to a psychiatric hospital talking incoherently about things "my teacher taught me that have to be done." He was put on the antidepressant Tofranil, while he smoked incessantly and lost ten pounds within a few weeks. He was discharged later in the summer, after being judged "competent to handle his own affairs."

Khaalis was slowly starting to turn things around for himself. He had found a good job mentoring young high school students through the Street Academy program that had been started by the Urban League in New York in 1966. A college graduate, he was a natural at the job. He also found it to be the perfect place to find promising young recruits for his Hanafi group. Abdul Aziz, meanwhile, had been released from prison after serving a two-year sentence for the attempted bank robbery in Manhattan. He began teaching at PS 113 in Harlem, and he introduced his students to Khaalis on occasion. The ranks of the Hanafis were growing, with promising young people heeding the call.

Still, if competing with Elijah Muhammad and the Nation of Islam was the aim, Khaalis was lagging far behind. After Malcolm's assassination, Elijah had found a new poster boy for his organization, the world heavyweight-boxing champion Cassius Clay, now known the world over as Muhammad Ali. He was as charismatic outside the ring as he was lethal inside it, and he was raising the profile of the Nation beyond what even Malcolm could have achieved. Ali was drawn into the Nation through Malcolm, but when Malcolm and Elijah began feuding, Ali had remained uncompromisingly loyal to Elijah, calling Malcolm a "hypocrite," and once even publicly threatening Malcolm on the messenger's behalf. Elijah Muhammad "will destroy him through Allah," Ali had told reporters. "You just don't buck Mr. Muhammad and get away with it." Ali was now Elijah's exuberant ambassador, roving across the country and around the world. In 1964, Ali took a trip to Africa, which included a stop in Egypt, where he met Gamal Abdel Nasser and posed for the camera shirtless on a camel framed by the pyramids of Giza with his fist in the air, exclaiming "Allahu Akbar," "Allah is the greatest." He was a global Muslim icon.

Alcindor was nothing like Ali. He was quiet and awkward, especially in front of the camera, and reticent with the media. At times he appeared angry and standoffish. Still, he was a phenomenal athlete. There was feverish excitement around his upcoming professional career—he was as high profile as a college athlete could get. Ali's star, on the other hand, had been falling since he was stripped of his boxing titles in 1967 for refusing to serve in the Vietnam War. This stance against the war had also made him a polarizing figure, and even Elijah Muhammad had distanced himself from the controversy and from Ali. For Khaalis, the prospect of Alcindor acting as a superstar ambassador, traveling the country carrying the banner of Hanafi Muslims, was a dream: Alcindor might finally catapult Khaalis to a national level he had yearned for.

A few days after his television appearance, Alcindor came knocking on the door of the cramped apartment where Khaalis lived with Khadija and their three children. Khaalis welcomed the lanky ball player and launched into his pitch. "The first thing I want to tell you is, don't ever say that this isn't your country," Khaalis instructed Alcindor, sounding the notes that his immigrant teacher, Tasibur Rahman, had struck with Khaalis when he found him on the rebound from the Nation of Islam. "Your ancestors lived and died in this country and this is your country. You have to get all your rights as a citizen—don't reject it, affirm it." Khaalis quizzed Alcindor, as he did all his potential recruits, about what he already knew about Islam. Alcindor explained how he had been attending Muslim prayers at a Sunni Muslim mosque in Harlem and had already taken the *shahada*. Khaalis was not impressed. He offered to become Alcindor's mentor, but on the condition that they would start from scratch.

During the summer of 1968, while the U.S. men's basketball team worked its way to the gold medal at the Mexico City Olympics, and Tommie Smith and John Carlos raised their defiant fists in the air on the medal stand, Alcindor immersed himself in Khaalis's teachings. For weeks, he spent every day with his new guru, rising at dawn and spending the day studying the ways of Hanafi Islam. Khaalis explained to Alcindor that he had special knowledge through an "inner line" of mysticism that he had inherited from his teacher. Khaalis had an opinion on everything. He showed Alcindor the proper way to clean behind his ears and between his toes during the ritual cleaning before prayer. He taught him his interpretation of certain cryptic verses of the Koran during their long study sessions. Khaalis frequently quoted his own master, Tasibur Rahman, and shared with the new inductee the details of the supernatural miracles he performed, like how he caused the great Northeast blackout of 1965 that plunged all of New York into darkness for a full day. Khaalis told him that he still occasionally convened with the spirit of Rahman and received guidance from him. He was the chosen caliph, after all.

Khaalis also gave his new student lessons in Middle Eastern politics. He explained the difference between Jews and Zionists. The former, Khaalis said, were brothers who had helped the Prophet Muhammad in his times of trouble. The Zionists, on the other hand, were an evil cabal, the root of all that was ill in the world. The Zionists, Khaalis believed, had even aided in the kidnapping of Africans for enslavement on the American continent. His venom for Zionists and the state of Israel aside, Khaalis struck Alcindor as more balanced than the Black Panthers and other militant African American groups that some of his peers had turned to. Khaalis was more generous, even loving. The color of the skin was of no importance, Khaalis said; the only thing that mattered was the purity of heart. Alcindor was in complete awe of his new spiritual master. For his ritual oath taking, Khaalis instructed Alcindor to shave his head and all his pubic hair. After his new *shahada*, Khaalis granted the young man his new name: Kareem Abdul-Jabbar, "the docile servant of the enforcer."

In April 1969, Kareem was the first overall pick in the NBA draft. He signed a million-dollar contract with the Milwaukee Bucks and moved to Wisconsin, where he occasionally shared his new place with Khaalis's old disciple from New York, Abdul Latif, and other Hanafis when they visited. Even before he had made his first shot as a professional, he was already one of the most exciting sports figures in the country. The Bucks posted a winning record in the league that was second only to the New York Knicks that year, and Kareem was named rookie of the year. The following year, the Bucks had a record-breaking twenty-game winning streak in the regular season. Even though the Bucks failed to win the title, Kareem took the MVP honor.

Khaalis's roster of disciples began to swell with other NBA stars. Walt Hazzard, another UCLA player who had gone to the Lakers, joined the Hanafis. Wallie Jones and Don Smith, two of Kareem's teammates, also professed the Islamic faith. Warren Armstrong, who went to the

New York Knicks in the 1968 draft, converted to Islam and changed his name to Warren Jabali. More important for Khaalis, Kareem became the star roving ambassador that he had hoped for. Anytime anyone approached Kareem after a game to express curiosity about his new name or Islam, Kareem would direct them to Khaalis. His teacher, he would say to them, had all the answers.

In the meantime, just as he had done at the Nation of Islam, Khaalis shot up through the ranks in the Urban League. By 1970, he was the Street Academy's director of the community outreach, in charge of an expansive network that allowed him access to young Black men and women across the city of New York. During this time, he met a twenty-two-year-old Macalester College graduate named Pauletta Hawkins. She was bold and fiercely ambitious. She wore her hair in an Afro and was strikingly beautiful. Khaalis was more than twice her age, but he fell for her, and she, in turn, was enamored with the attention he showered on her. Khaalis asked her if she would become his second wife, and she agreed.

Her parents were shocked. Her father, Reginald Hawkins, a dentist in North Carolina, was a minister and firebrand civil rights activist. In April 1968, Martin Luther King Jr. was scheduled to stay at the Hawkinses' residence in North Carolina when a last-minute change led him to Memphis, where he was assassinated. When Khaalis met Pauletta, who was just starting her graduate studies at New York University, her father was competing in the Democratic primary to become governor of North Carolina. She took her *shahada* with Khaalis, and he gave her the name Bibi Hasna, after his teacher Rahman's mother. Khadija welcomed the young bride into the home with open arms and treated her like a younger sister. Less than a year later, Bibi gave birth to a baby boy, and they gave him the name Abdullah.

The Urban League abruptly shuttered the Street Academy in December 1970, and Khaalis, as he had been so many times before, was suddenly out of a job. That same month, however, the indictment for his attempted bank robbery from three years ago was dismissed after the court decided that he was not mentally fit to stand trial. A few months later, the Bucks finally won their first-ever NBA title. Kareem posted twenty-seven points in the final game. The day after the win, he went public about his Islamic faith. He announced that his birth name, Alcindor, would no longer decorate his jersey. He would now wear the name given to him by Khaalis: Abdul-Jabbar.

Because of Kareem's generous financial support, Khaalis did not feel the financial strains he had in previous times of unemployment. Instead, with his star pupil's encouragement, Khaalis began to think big. If Khaalis was serious about spreading the word of Islam to all Americans, as Rahman had wanted, then Khaalis would need to dedicate himself to the mission full time. While Kareem pledged to continue his financial support for the Hanafis, the two men began scouting properties in Washington, DC. They settled on a beautiful and imposing Tudor-style structure on Sixteenth Street in the Shepherd Park neighborhood in the Northwest quadrant of Washington. It was steps away from Rock Creek Park, a few miles north of the White House, and south of Walter Reed Medical Complex. The racially mixed neighborhood was home to some of the wealthiest and most influential African Americans in the capital, if not the entire country.

The Hanafis moved into their new headquarters in July 1971. The house had over a dozen rooms, almost all with windows that looked over the well-maintained, leafy yard on all sides. Sunlight streamed through from sunrise to sunset. The first floor had a large living area facing Sixteenth Street that the Hanafis used for communal prayer and worship. On the second and third floors, Khaalis and his growing family occupied most of the rooms, with a couple of rooms available for visiting guests. The basement had several spaces—a garage that opened in the back, a laundry room, and several rooms that served as a hostel for young boarders who were training to join the Hanafis. The house was sandwiched between two large Jewish temples. Next door was the Ohev Shalom, the oldest orthodox synagogue in the capital, and across the street was a conservative synagogue. The Hanafis considered their house sacred ground, too. No shoes were allowed anywhere inside.

The Hanafis mostly kept to themselves, and the neighbors, mostly well-to-do professionals, did not seem to mind. The Hanafi women, all of whom pulled their veils over their faces when leaving the house, preferred colorful, flowing, South Asian–inspired dresses. The men appeared busy with their jobs. Most of them started driving cabs, an occupation that afforded them the freedom to set their schedules and pause, when needed, to say their prayers. They were an orderly and polite group. Outside, a plaque read: "Hanafi Madh-Hab Center, Islam Faith, United States of America." Khaalis chose the Arabic term *madhab* to denote the specific school of thought within a vast Sunni Islamic tradition to which the group adhered. Above the front entrance, they raised the American flag. Khaalis was finally headed to where he had long wanted to be—at the heart of American power.

11.

SUBJECTIVE CAMERA

Buried on page twenty-seven of the July 14, 1971, issue of the Hollywood industry publication *Variety* was a story about the Syrian American film director Moustapha Akkad's first film project. "'Mohammed' 3-Nation Coproduction Rolls in Fall to Show Islam Religion," the headline announced. The biopic of the Islamic Prophet Muhammad, a "large scale spectacle," was an "American-Lebanese-Egyptian coproduction," the magazine reported. The story quoted Harry Craig, an Irish screenwriter who, a few months after collecting a couple of BAFTA awards for his work on the sprawling epic *Waterloo*, was working on the screenplay for Akkad. "The film will show the religion of Islam for the first time outside the Middle East," Craig was quoted as saying. "My purpose in writing the screenplay is to lift the veil of ignorance and darkness that prevails outside the Middle East on the birth and religion of Islam." The movie, *Variety* reported, would be simultaneously shot with two completely separate casts, one speaking Arabic and the other English.

Akkad had started thinking about this movie in the summer of 1967, as the Six-Day War raged in the Middle East, at the end of which Syria lost a chunk of territory to Israel. He was married by this time to Patricia, a white American woman from Kansas. They had met at a college beauty pageant in Los Angeles where she was a contestant and Akkad had been a judge. They married in the fall of 1963, and months later, Akkad petitioned the United States to become a naturalized citizen. They had a baby boy, and the small family lived in a two-bedroom apartment in the Brentwood neighborhood of Los Angeles.

What frustrated Akkad most about the coverage of the war were the "spokespeople" for Arabs and Muslims who appeared in American media to give the Arab side of the story, especially on TV. Most who got face time were religious Islamic leaders like Muhammad Abdul Rauf, who had little political savvy and, frequently, a weak command of the English language. The Arabs and Muslims, Akkad felt, could barely get their basic message across to the American mainstream—they did not have a chance of winning the war for American public perception. Akkad had enjoyed moderate success as a producer in the television world working on a syndicated travel show distributed by United Artists. In September, three months after the 1967 Arab–Israeli war ended, Akkad started his own shop. He registered a company under the name Akkad International Productions and began devising a pitch for a film about the Islamic Prophet Muhammad.

Months later, Akkad was sworn in as an American citizen at a ceremony in Los Angeles and began shopping around his idea to Hollywood studio executives. Almost forty years old, Akkad had thick muttonchop sideburns with hints of gray. He frequently had a briar pipe stuck in the side of his mouth. He looked more like a professor than a filmmaker, and it was a tough sell. Akkad might have had TV experience, but he had no real experience in filmmaking—certainly nothing like directing a vast historical epic like *The Ten Commandments* or *Lawrence of Arabia* that he was pitching. More important, there was also an obvious challenge facing any production about the life of the Prophet Muhammad: who would play the title character? There was only one right answer—no one.

Akkad had a workaround. He called it the "subjective camera." Hitchcock had used it in some of his films, most famously in the shower scene from *Psycho*. In Akkad's mind, the camera's point of view would represent Muhammad. No part of him would ever be seen, and his voice would never be heard, but his presence would be confirmed as the audience watched the scene through his eyes. At best, the device was adventurous, at worst, it sounded absurd. How could the protagonist of a film never be seen or heard? One after the other, the studios passed. Akkad suspected the studios also had a bigger concern that was never expressed in his presence: Moses and Jesus were one thing, but who in America wants to watch a movie about the Prophet of Islam?

After a year of trying and failing in Hollywood, Akkad did a most American thing: he packed up, left his home in Los Angeles, and traveled halfway across the globe to turn his dream into a reality. Akkad, Patricia, and their two children—the younger boy was only a few months old—arrived in Beirut, Lebanon, in the summer of 1969. The sprawling ancient city on the eastern Mediterranean coast was, along with Cairo, a modern cultural hub for Arabic-language media. Akkad had received a small investment from an Arab immigrant friend in Los Angeles, and he used it to get an apartment for his family and to set up a lavish office in downtown Beirut near the port. He had been spurned by Hollywood, and from his new base, he began his hunt for Arab investors.

His first stop was the kingdom of Kuwait, a small city-state that British colonial administrators had carved out between Iraq and Saudi Arabia decades earlier. Kuwait was awash in petrodollars and, like several other countries in the region, was getting ready to launch a state-run television station. In the months that followed, Akkad shuttled from one Arab capital to the next, meeting ministers and heads of state and bureaucrats in drab official complexes and in ornate palaces, looking to finance his epic. None of the people he met with had ever remotely considered pouring money into a Hollywood project, but Akkad was pleased with how many appeared intrigued by the prospect.

Within a year of arriving in Beirut, Akkad had handshakes from the governments of Kuwait, Libya, and Morocco and from several Arab sheiks who were considering investing privately. Akkad was especially excited about the interest shown by Adnan Khashoggi, a rotund Saudi businessman notorious for his over-the-top decadent lifestyle. America had tailored a cozy relationship with the kingdom since President Franklin D. Roosevelt met with Abdul Aziz Ibn Saud, the founder of Saudi Arabia, on an American cruiser in the Suez Canal on Valentine's Day 1945. A sweetheart profit-sharing deal on oil production in 1950 was followed by a military pact that allowed Saudi Arabia to become one of the top purchasers of U.S. military hardware. Khashoggi was one of the main beneficiaries of this relationship, becoming a middleman between Saudi arms buyers and American military equipment manufacturers. When Akkad met him, Khashoggi was being paid tens of millions of dollars in commissions—in reality, they were bribes—by American corporations like Lockheed and Northrop. Khashoggi loved to flaunt this wealth. He flew around the world on his private DC-9 aircraft, shuttling among his homes and offices in California, New York, Paris, London, Riyadh, Beirut, and other places. He was particularly excited by the prospect of seeing his name splashed across the big screen.

Still, no one was ready to sign on the dotted line or hand over a dime to Akkad until he had the blessings of Islamic religious authorities. If Akkad's "subjective camera" was a legitimate workaround, he needed to prove it. Like Malcolm, another Muslim American looking to have his genius recognized, Akkad went to meet the Islamic authorities. Like Malcolm, his first stop was Al-Azhar in Cairo. The muftis at the institution, which the *Variety* article had described as "the 'papacy' of Islam," were receptive to the idea. They agreed to read the screenplay. Harry Craig, the Irish screenwriter, had been locked up in an apartment in Cairo for months, studying Islamic religious scriptures and historical texts. When the screenplay was ready, Akkad rented out an entire floor of Hotel Palestine in Alexandria, a tourist resort town on Egypt's northern coast along the Mediterranean, for a multiday reading session with Craig and a panel of scholars and experts from Al-Azhar. For days, they pored over the text, page by page, sometimes wrestling over the smallest details. The meetings went on for almost an entire week and felt conclusively done only when one of the scholars from Al-Azhar embraced the Irishman. Days later, with final scripts in English and Arabic in hand, Akkad marched to the Al-Azhar campus in Cairo and watched as each page received a stamp of final approval. Al-Azhar left him with only one last demand: they would not formally endorse the film until they saw the final cut before release.

Next stop was Saudi Arabia to meet with the Muslim World League. In the years since Malcolm had visited the country, the league had established itself as the most influential religious authority in the Islamic world, eclipsing Al-Azhar at least in the political arena. At the league headquarters in the port city of Jeddah, Akkad sat across from a dozen stern men in a half circle around a conference table. None of them appeared eager to reach for the scripts that Akkad had laid out on the table in front of them. Akkad gave his pitch. He explained the basic contours of the film. It focused on the adult life of Muhammad, beginning with when he receives a visit from the archangel Gabriel in the city of Mecca to inform the Prophet of his mission, to his death more than two decades later. He described, for the Saudi clerics, the proposed subjective camera technique. Finally, he offered to change or remove anything from the script that the council objected to. Still, no one moved.

"Films," one of the clerics finally began, "are *haram*," using the Islamic term for taboo and forbidden. Akkad had come prepared to defend portions of the script, and perhaps his technical choices, but he had not expected to defend the cinematic medium itself. Akkad pointed to the picture of the king on the front page of a Saudi newspaper that lay on a table. How was a photograph of a king any different from a moving image? A still photo, one of the muftis offered, cannot be mistaken for real life. A film, on the other hand, mimics life in motion and sound. The Saudis had recently launched a state television network, Akkad countered. He had watched it with his own eyes in the hotel room. Television broadcasts via the airwaves are ephemeral, a scholar explained. While certainly not admirable, television, the league had opined, was permissible in the kingdom. Films, on the other hand, can move and proliferate endlessly; they are dangerous—and *haram*. It was apparent that it was not necessarily Akkad's script or his techniques that the Muslim World League was concerned about—it was the slippery slope of allowing Islamic history on film that made them nervous. If they endorsed Akkad's project, in other words, how could they stop others in the future?

The chasm between the league officials and Akkad grew wider and wider with every passing minute. By the end of the hour, Akkad was exasperated and furious. The clerics had enjoyed it no better. The Americans have landed a person on the moon, Akkad scolded the league officials as he packed up to leave. Yet here they were, a group of Muslim men, discussing whether Allah has an opinion on filmmaking. "Who has landed on the moon?" one of the robed men asked with a smirk. Shadows and mirrors can trick anyone into believing anything, he taunted Akkad. Akkad picked up his script, thanked the men for their time, and left. The biggest enemies of his Muhammad project, he realized, were the ones living in the Prophet's own land.

12

LOOK AND SEE

The Hanafi community in Washington continued to grow. Friends and fans of Kareem's moved to DC, as did friends and acquaintances of Khaalis's second wife, Bibi, from North Carolina. This included her brother, who took the name Saleem and became a top deputy of Khaalis's. Others made the journey to Washington from New York and from several spots in the Midwest. Many of these new adherents were college educated. The Hanafis began running ads for the group in *The Hilltop*, the student publication of Howard University, and attracted several curious young students from there, too. Soon, the Hanafis occupied a cluster of a half dozen homes, either rented, or owned by Kareem, around the northern tip of the District and in the adjacent Maryland suburbs.

Khaalis's family continued to grow, too. Bibi, who was working toward a master's in early education at Howard University, gave birth to her second child, a daughter, in 1971. They named her, Khaalis's sixth child, Bibi as well. Aziz had married Khaalis's eldest daughter, Eva, at Khaalis's urging. The young woman in her early twenties, who now went by Amina, was tall like her mother and strong-willed like her father. Less than a year after Bibi had given birth to Khaalis's sixth child, Amina and Aziz had their first baby, a girl they named Khadija. Not yet fifty, Khaalis and his first wife became grandparents.

Khaalis also took a third wife, a widow with two grown sons who became Hanafi Muslims themselves. Khaalis gave her the name Hafsa, after a wife of the Prophet who was a widow when Muhammad married her. While Khadija and Bibi were both officially married to Khaalis, one in New York and the other in Washington, DC, Khaalis's marriage to

Hafsa was purely an Islamic marriage, simply requiring an oral contract between man and woman. Although according to most interpretations of sharia law a Muslim man is allowed to have four wives concurrently, Khadija and Bibi gave the third wife a cool reception. Instead of moving to the center, Hafsa lived with her sons in an apartment in a nearby Maryland suburb, Silver Spring. It was an arrangement that would have deadly consequences one day.

Khaalis's firstborn, who now went by the name Daud, was emerging as the spiritual leader of the community. He was in his mid-twenties, and Khaalis had clearly groomed him to be his successor. His knowledge of Islamic religious scripture was impressive, and the Hanafis believed that Allah had gifted him with extraordinary powers of perception, like those that Dr. Rahman possessed.

In 1971, Kareem married a woman from California named Janice Brown; Khaalis named her Habiba after she took her *shahada*. It was a dramatic dawn ceremony at the Hanafi Madh-Hab Center, from which Khaalis barred Kareem's parents—who had come in from New York—because they were not Muslim. The traumatic event tore open a rift between master and pupil that would never fully heal. A week after the wedding, Kareem and his bride set off on a honeymoon that took them through many Muslim countries in Asia and Africa. She gave birth to their first child in 1972, a baby girl they named Habiba, like her mother. It was a large house, and Kareem's small family would share it with several other young families who had joined the Hanafis.

Aziz opened a jewelry store at the mall in the upscale neighborhood of Georgetown in the summer of 1971. The Aram store sold jewelry and antiques that Aziz acquired from dealers in New York, but he eventually started traveling abroad to cut his own deals. He curated the collection of African and Asian pieces that often evoked an Islamic aesthetic. The listing in the yellow pages described it as a place to acquire "hand fashioned Original Designs—Gold and Silver Exotic Jewelry." It was perhaps the only Black-owned business in that mall. When Kareem was in town, he would sometimes spend the day there signing autographs for fans. Despite this star power, the store did not make nearly enough to support the Hanafi community or even the center. It was up to Kareem to sustain the enterprise, which he did happily with money from his NBA earnings and lavish endorsements.

After losing his job with the Urban League, Khaalis had been spending his spare time writing. He had been playing with the idea of a book for nearly a decade, and in May 1972 he finally self-published it with the title *Look and See: The Key to Knowing and Understanding—Self-Identity, Self-Culture and Self-Heritage*. It was part manifesto, part spiritual self-help manual. In this sprawling, sometimes disjointed tract, Khaalis argued against the very notion of race in America, which was so central to the Nation of Islam's creed. "The so-called negro, so-called colored man, so-called black man and so-called white man," Khaalis wrote, "cannot be found anywhere on the planet earth. They do not exist—they are myths." Instead, Khaalis saw the people of the world divided into two camps: captors and captive. The powerful, cunning captors mercilessly exploited the captive. For the captive, there was one path to freedom and salvation: the path of true Islam. Khaalis left little doubt in the text that he was the only American in possession of that truth. The pocket-size book that the Hanafis called the "green book" was soon available in local bookstores for the cover price of $1, and it announced the arrival of the Hanafis on the Muslim scene in Washington.

The capital's Muslim population was small compared to New York's, but the proximity to power gave the few Islamic organizations in the city special importance. The Nation of Islam's Temple No. 4, established by Elijah Muhammad himself in the mid-1930s, was now housed at a permanent structure on New Jersey Avenue, a little over a mile north of the U.S. Capitol. The most prominent place was still the Islamic Center of Washington, however. That institution had recently hired a new imam: Muhammad Abdul Rauf, who visited the new Hanafi Madh-Hab Center in the spring of 1972. His profile had skyrocketed since Khaalis had last seen him five years earlier. He was on a national speaking circuit and in July 1971, the same month that the Hanafis moved to Washington, Rauf had testified for the House Foreign Affairs Committee about competing regional claims to the city of Jerusalem.

America had changed during this time as well. Seven years after the passing of the Hart-Celler Immigration Act of 1965, as immigrants from Asia steadily arrived in the country in unprecedented numbers, the demographics of the United States had shifted remarkably. The face of Muslim America in particular was dramatically changing. Until 1965, African American Muslims had always constituted a majority of the Muslim population of America, but Muslim immigrants from Asia and Africa were fast catching up. Unlike many African American descendants of slaves, these Muslim immigrants were often upwardly mobile and solidly middle class. They built their communities in the suburbs and frequently assimilated into white society, sometimes even absorbing its racial prejudices against African Americans, Muslim or otherwise.

Rauf visited Khaalis at a time when he was caught in the middle of the tense racial divide between Black and immigrant Muslims in Washington. The growing immigrant Muslim population in the Washington area had made the Islamic Center of Washington their domain. Between playing host to foreign dignitaries and catering to the Muslim elites in the diplomatic service, the center had drifted far away from the African American Muslim population in Washington, one of the poorest in the country. Feeling isolated, a group of African American Sunnis had broken away and established a new mosque in the capital that spring, a few blocks from the Nation's Temple No. 4. They called themselves the Islamic Party of North America, and they were led by a man named Yusuf Muzaffaruddin Hamid who, like Khaalis, was a former jazz musician and was drawing inspiration from Islamic political revivalist movements like the Muslim Brotherhood in Egypt and the Jamaat-e-Islami in Pakistan.

In February 1972, the Islamic Party had declared war on Rauf, personally. In only the second issue of its newsletter *Al-Islam*, the party published an editorial titled "Oust Rauf," which demanded that Rauf resign from his post immediately. The party, the editorial said, "expresses shock" that Rauf had appeared at a Nation of Islam rally in New York, "speaking in support of the organization and activities of the heretical 'Black Muslim.'" Weeks earlier, the news of a shootout with police at Harlem's Temple No. 7 that had left one NYPD officer dead had shaken Muslim communities all over America. Rauf's appearance at the Nation's rally was a show of solidarity with them. The editorial quoted from Rauf's remarks there in which he expressed "admiration" for "the beloved leader, the Honorable Elijah Muhammad." The Islamic Party, like the Hanafis and most other Sunni groups, viewed the Nation as a heretical group. The editorial called Rauf's statements "shocking" and demanded that he "either retract his statement publicly or voluntarily remove himself from Directorship of the Islamic Center."

Rauf may have thought that Khaalis, an African American newcomer to the city, would be well positioned to mend fences between the Islamic Center and the party. At the very least, a visit to the Hanafi Center would demonstrate Rauf's eagerness to collaborate with Black Sunni Muslims—and distance him from the Nation. The meeting between Rauf and Khaalis was pleasant and uneventful. At the end of the meeting, Rauf made the customary gesture of inviting Khaalis to the Islamic Center, and Khaalis made a courtesy visit with some of his Hanafi followers a few weeks later.

The Nation of Islam, meanwhile, was breaking new barriers. The front page of the May 19, 1972, issue of *Muhammad Speaks*, the Nation of Islam's official newspaper, came with a full-page banner headline: "The Great Gift of Our Libyan Brothers." A dollar amount was listed below the headline: "$2,978,406.00." In an Arab Middle East defined by the political and religious rivalry between Egypt and Saudi Arabia, Libya stood apart. Its flamboyant and charismatic military leader, Colonel Muammar Gaddhafi, had charted his own course since coming to power in a military coup a few years earlier. He had led a political and cultural revolution, eliminating the opposition and restructuring the state. Thanks to the seemingly limitless oil reserves discovered in the country more than a decade earlier, Gaddhafi embarked on a project to transform the North African state by building highways and entire new cities in the desert.

While he went to work developing infrastructure at home, Gaddhafi had a passion for supporting troublemakers abroad. Any anti-Western, anti-colonial militant movements anywhere in the world could attract his attention and largesse. He was funding militants in South Africa and Uruguay, as well as the IRA and the Red Army Faction in West Germany. The Nation of Islam had reached out to Gaddhafi out of desperation. The organization was searching for a credit line to purchase a new headquarters in Chicago—Elijah had his eyes specifically on an abandoned Greek Orthodox church that had gone up for sale on Chicago's South Side. After being declined by bank after bank in America, Elijah dispatched Muhammad Ali, who was accompanied by his manager, Elijah Muhammad's son Herbert, to Libya as his emissary. Ali and Gaddhafi hit it off, and Ali returned to Chicago having secured a $3 million loan. The Libyan loan made national news and raised alarms at the FBI. It also incensed many Muslims in America, including Khaalis. Why, given all the options in America, had the leader of a powerful and wealthy Sunni African country chosen to throw its weight behind the Nation?

A few months after the announcement in *Muhammad Speaks*, a Washington Metropolitan Police Department detective noticed a sudden cluster of gun permit applications to the department; there were nine in the second week of August alone. The purchases included thirty-five machetes, a Remington 1100 semiautomatic shotgun, three handguns, and plenty of ammunition. All the applications led to three addresses in DC and Maryland. The permits referenced the existence of a Hanafi Mussulman Rifle and Pistol Club at an address on Sixteenth Street, so the detective made a visit to the headquarters of the National Rifle Association. Khaalis's brother-in-law, Salim, had submitted an application for a charter from the gun club, but the NRA was hesitant to grant one. The NRA readily shared the details from the Hanafis' application with the detective. In August, the police tipped off the FBI field office in Washington, which began running the dozens of names on the membership list through their central information system.

At first, the FBI headquarters treated the lead from the Washington field office coolly. That changed on the night of September 5, 1972, when eleven Palestinian men stunned the world by taking members of the Israeli Olympic team hostage at the summer games in Munich. The Palestinians, it emerged, were members of an armed guerrilla group called Black September, which was demanding the release of Palestinian prisoners in Israel. They had trained in Libya and were supported, in part, by Gaddhafi. The operation ended disastrously, with a shootout and grenade explosions leaving all the Israelis and most of the Palestinian hostage takers dead.

A week after the attacks, the new director of the FBI, L. Patrick Gray, who had taken over after J. Edgar Hoover died in May of 1972, fired off a memo to the bureau's Washington field office, specially marked "PERSONAL ATTENTION." The investigation into the Hanafis, he directed, "must be conducted in a most discreet manner to avert publicity." Considering the "relatively large number of individuals associated with this group, it would appear that informant penetration of this organization should receive priority attention." The director wanted spies in the Hanafi Center. The note concluded with an order: "Insure all aspects of this investigation are pursued vigorously and make every attempt to determine the true nature and purpose." He had previously noted "the foreign influence in extremist movements" as a reason to be concerned about the Hanafis.

After the Munich incident, the FBI and the Washington police began a schedule of close surveillance of the Hanafis. Plainclothes cops set up posts inside one of the synagogues near the Hanafi Center. Federal agents made phone calls to the Hanafis under false pretexts to gather information—one even knocked on the front door of Salim's house posing as an interested buyer for a car parked outside. A police chopper took flight over the main Hanafi compound and snapped several photos of the property. In November, they successfully planted an informant among the Hanafis, who began reporting the activities at all formal meetings held at the Hanafi Center each Sunday.

The deadly gunfight at Temple No. 7 earlier that year had unleashed a low-grade civil war among Muslims in America. On October 22, a little more than a month after Munich, Raymond Sharrieff, the supreme captain of the Fruit of Islam, the man who had thrown punches at Khaalis and threatened Malcolm in his final days, was shot and wounded in the neck in an assassination attempt. A bomb went off at the Nation's temple in Rochester on Thanksgiving. In December, several major gunfights between Sunnis and the Nation rocked Atlanta, leaving several of the Nation's men in the hospital and one Sunni Muslim dead. A "wild riot" in Rikers Island prison between members of the Nation and Sunni Muslims left nineteen people, including a guard, injured. One newspaper counted at least eighteen murders, nineteen shootings, and three abductions related to Muslims around the country that fall.

The informant inside the Hanafi Center, in contrast, relayed surprising calm. Khaalis was at odds with everyone, it appeared, Muslim or not. The Black Muslims following Elijah Muhammad were enemies of Islam, he said. "Martin Luther Coon" and "Ralph Abernasty" had been misguided fools. "The Bushy haired" Pan-Africanists were unpatriotic. He even warned his followers about the "false" Stokely Carmichael who, Khaalis said, had been secretly working for the government since 1968. The FBI agents appeared almost pleased with what they were hearing. The group, an agent reported being told by the informant, "is a truly religious type organization and a patriotic one. During this class, no violence or revolutionary ideology was advocated." Again and again, the field office sent reports to headquarters of remarkably little going on in and around the house.

What all the surveillance failed to report, in hundreds of pages, however, was a delivery vehicle that arrived at the Hanafi Center in the first week of December carrying a Xerox machine. The copier was hauled into the house along with reams of paper and ink. Amid all the fighting and bloodshed in American Islam, Khaalis was readying himself to fight a battle of ideas. He had decided to exert his power with a letter-writing campaign—or weekly "lessons," as Khaalis termed them—to the ministers of all fifty-seven Nation of Islam temples in the country. For this reason, Khaalis had decided to invest almost $1,300 to lease a Xerox machine for fifteen months. The Hanafis now had their very own makeshift mass-media operation.

To craft the lessons, Khaalis teamed up with a man named Aly Hashim. He was an old acquaintance of Khaalis's from Temple No. 7 and a fellow breakaway from the Nation of Islam. When the two men first met in the 1950s, Khaalis was making a living as a jazz musician, and Hashim was a prizefighter with at least a couple of major bouts in Madison Square Garden. Soon after Khaalis was dispatched to Chicago to work directly under Elijah, Hashim had a falling-out with the minister Malcolm X and was ejected from the Nation of Islam. He had spent the subsequent two decades studying and mastering various languages—he claimed to speak thirty-five—including Arabic and Hebrew. In Washington, he worked at the Pakistani embassy for years while also claiming to study math and physics at Howard University. When the Hanafis arrived in town, Khaalis put Hashim on a salary to teach Arabic and other languages to the Hanafis.

The first letter by Khaalis on formal Hanafi Madh-Hab Center stationery went out on December 29, 1972. The letter was unsigned but had the Sixteenth Street Northwest address listed. The letter took direct aim at Elijah, the man who claimed to be the prophet of Allah, and was peppered with Arabic and Koranic terms. Khaalis used the title *Al-Gharoor* for Elijah, Arabic for "the deceiver." The letter began with an excerpt from "What Islam Is Not," the introduction of Khaalis's book, *Look and See*. In the two-page letter, Khaalis insulted Elijah in various ways and ended with an ultimatum: "Remember, you cannot use the Holy Quran, revealed to the Holy Prophet Mustapha Muhammad. Your leader must come forward with his own book, as he brought his own Islam."

The second "lesson," which arrived the following week, was more aggressive: typed in all-caps, it carried the signatures of both Khaalis and

Aly Hashim. This time, Elijah's surname was spelled "Mukammad," and a footnote explained that in Arabic, "Mukammad means: sad, grieved and blackened. To be laden with sin. Sorrow bowed because of evil committed through ignorance (error)." This letter turned its attention to W. D. Fard as well, the man whom the Nation believed to be Allah incarnate. Khaalis wrote in the letter that Fard's real name was John Walker, and he described him as "the slightly cock-eyed man," who had served seven and a half years in jail for "stealing a truck load of junk, in Gary, Indiana," and raped a seventeen-year-old white girl. He referred to him as "Baal," a false god mentioned in the Koran. "Your captain Raymond Sharrieff knows this," Khaalis, wrote. "Do you?"

All three pages of this letter were festooned with Arabic text and notes in the margins. While these were likely contributed by Hashim, they gave an impression that Khaalis had some command of the language of the major Islamic holy texts. He knew Elijah Muhammad and his ministers struggled to read it. "It is a pity that none of you ever took time to learn how to read the Arabic language." The letter dripped with condescension. "Then you could have easily seen that Elijah Mukammad was a lying deceiver." In the end, Khaalis repeated the central demand he had made in his first letter: he wanted Elijah and the ministers to stop using the Islamic holy book and the recorded traditions of the Islamic Prophet Muhammad, who "lived fourteen hundred years ago." If they agreed to stop using these texts, Khaalis claimed that they would not hear from him anymore. "But as long as you are deaf, dumb and blind," he warned, "you will hear from us."

Perhaps more than anything else, it was the end of the letter that might have alarmed the ministers of the Nation of Islam and Elijah Muhammad. The letter was signed "Khalifah Hamaas Abdul Khaalis," and underneath was an Arabic phrase that identified him as the representative of the "Global Islamic Civilization." Khaalis, in other words, was delivering this warning on behalf of the nearly one billion Sunni Muslims of the world.

The Nation of Islam did not roll over for just anyone. One of the ministers from Texas responded to Khaalis's letter days later. "Not only do I say that you are a hippocrite [*sic*] and jealous," he wrote, "you are less than a Muslim." The writer caustically noted that the bottom of the Hanafi stationery carried a note about how to make tax-deductible contributions to the center. "If I were you, I would try to clean my own house before I tried to clean that of someone else." James Shabazz, the minister of the temple in New Jersey, whom many believed to have orchestrated Malcolm's assassination, was more pointed in his letter to Khaalis: "Sir," he warned, "I believe this is risky business."

13.

SEED OF THE HYPOCRITE

When the phone rang at the Hanafi Center around eight in the morning on January 18, 1973, it was unusually busy at the house. Bibi, Khaalis's second wife, had just arrived home after giving birth to her third child. The baby boy, Khaalis's seventh child, was named Tasibur, after Dr. Rahman, and was only nine days old. Meanwhile, two other young children were sick at home, and Khadija and Amina were getting ready to shuttle them to the doctor. Khaalis had left home a half hour earlier to take his third wife, Hafsa, to Jefferson Junior High School, where she was a teacher. When Amina answered the phone, the man on the line introduced himself as Tommy Jones and expressed interest in visiting the house to buy a copy of Khaalis's little green book. Hurried and distracted, she handed the phone off to her brother, Daud, who was formally the imam of the center. He told the man to call back later in the afternoon to schedule a time to pick it up.

Soon after, Amina, Khadija, and the two sick children left the center, driven by Abdul Nur, a young and loyal Hanafi adherent. When they returned a little before noon, Khadija departed the house for a grocery run at the nearby Giant Supermarket with her teenage daughter, Maryam, chaperoned once again by Nur. When the phone rang again at around two o'clock, the only adults at home were Khaalis's oldest children, Amina and Daud, and Khaalis's second wife, Bibi. The four children at home were all between the ages of nine days and eleven years. Amina answered again, and the same man on the line said that he was interested in collecting some Islamic literature from the center. The Hanafis were always happy to sell copies of Khaalis's book, and Amina invited him to come by and pick up a copy. The man said he would be over soon and hung up.

The caller's real name was not Tommy Jones, and he was not interested in Khaalis's book—not for the reasons he had suggested anyway. He was John Clark, or John 38X, a member of the Nation of Islam's Temple No. 12 in Philadelphia, and an enforcer in the notorious criminal organization known as the Black Mafia. He had arrived in Washington, DC, the night before with seven other members of the Nation of Islam on a mission to murder Hamaas Abdul Khaalis and end his insurgency against the messenger Elijah Muhammad.

They had heard about Khaalis at the regional gathering of the Nation of Islam temples of the Delaware Valley, hosted in Newark, New Jersey, earlier that month. Everyone seemed to be talking about the pair of letters Khaalis had dispatched to all ministers of the Nation of Islam across the country, accusing Elijah of being a liar and Master Fard of being a fraud. By this time, the Nation of Islam was the wealthiest and most resourceful Black organization in the country, with an estimated net worth of $70 million. Not all the money, however, was clean. Over the previous decade, as the Nation of Islam's message continued to spread like wildfire, particularly through prison populations, the movement had become enmeshed with criminals and organized crime networks in several regions. From coast to coast, armed gangs affiliated with Nation of Islam temples were involved in extortion, money laundering, drug dealing, and plenty of violent crime. The temples in the Delaware Valley were especially notorious, and none more so than Temple No. 12 in Philadelphia. Malcolm X had named it "top of the clock" when he founded it in 1954, bestowing the members with a sense of pride in being the twelfth. Beginning in the late 1960s, however, the temple in Philadelphia had slowly started to merge with a violent criminal drug network in the city.

The Black Mafia's main hustle was heroin. They got their supply from the infamous New York trafficker Frank Matthews and pushed it in the depressed African American neighborhoods throughout Philadelphia. Drugs went against the clean-living ethos of the Nation, but the Nation's message of Black ownership and Black enterprise serving Blacks ironically reinforced the Black Mafia's mission to peddle drugs in Philadelphia's most depressed neighborhoods. If there were going to be drugs pushed on Black people, why should anyone but other Blacks profit from it, the logic went.

The merger between the Nation of Islam and the Black Mafia happened in slow motion. It started in 1967 after a man named Samuel Christian, one of the founders and bosses of the Black Mafia, became a Black Muslim and a captain of the local Fruit of Islam unit. Other members of the Black Mafia soon followed, slowly occupying ranks in the temple hierarchy. Eventually, both organizations saw the clear benefit to joining forces. For the organized crime ring, the Nation was the perfect money-laundering machine, with the added benefit of providing cover from tax agencies and law enforcement and a national network of safe houses found in the Nation's temples. The Nation of Islam, meanwhile, received a substantial stream of money, most of which it funneled to Chicago. By the early 1970s, the Black Mafia and the Philadelphia temple had grown so close that people referred to them by a single name: the Muslim Mob.

Unlike most other criminal enterprises operating under the umbrella of the Nation, the Black Mafia appeared to crave attention. There was a twisted, violent strain in their operation that was fodder for the press. When the Black Mafia hit a furniture store in South Philadelphia in January 1971, for example, they killed several employees and customers during the course of the holdup. Then, for no apparent reason, they doused a few with gasoline, set them on fire, and stomped on and trampled the bodies while fleeing the scene. The city's police commissioner called it "the most vicious crime I have ever come across." One of the attackers in the case would later be found in Chicago, serving as a personal bodyguard for Elijah Muhammad.

At the regional conference, James Shabazz, the same minister from Newark who had warned Khaalis about his "risky business," publicly denounced the letters in a speech. He stopped short of ordering a hit on Khaalis, but Shabazz made it clear that he believed Khaalis was acting as an agent of someone other than God—a reference to the FBI. To members of the Black Mafia in attendance, including one of its founders, Ronald Harvey, Khaalis and his Hanafi headquarters presented a perfect target. The implication that Khaalis was backed by powerful enemies in Washington, as well as a basketball superstar, made him a high-value target. Moreover, nothing would please the messenger Elijah more than the elimination of a "hypocrite" who had dared to leave the fold of the Nation.

When the Black Mafia hit squad arrived in Washington, DC, on the evening of January 18, the city was buzzing with anticipation of the inauguration of Richard Nixon, who had won a second term in a historic landslide victory while waging an aggressive anti-crime, "law and order" campaign. The hitmen had driven all around the city looking for vacant rooms and finally found a couple available at the Downtown Motel on New York Avenue in the Northeast quadrant of the city, two miles from the White House. Ronald Harvey and his associate John Clark, two of the leaders of the group, had booked two rooms under their names and stayed up late into the night finalizing their plans.

Amina was playing with one of Bibi's children in the kitchen on the first floor when there was a knock at the front door shortly after 2:00 p.m. She peered out the window by the front door and saw two men with cigarettes tucked behind their ears. Women at the center typically never answered the door, and the men's appearance did not inspire confidence. And the Hanafis had been on guard ever since Khaalis had sent those letters. So, the six-foot six-inch, 220-pound Daud, the only man in the house, came down the stairs and opened the door a crack. One of the visitors presented him with a $10 bill as payment for the literature. Daud closed the door before turning to grab change. When he returned to the door, there was a third man there. It took a few moments and all three men to overpower the hulking Daud as they forced their way inside the house.

Amina, Daud, and their toddler half-brother, Bibi's oldest son, Abdullah, were the only people on the first floor. The intruders had drawn their weapons and herded them into the living room, where they were forced to lie facedown on the floor with their hands tied behind their backs. The intruders bound their feet and flung loose clothing over their heads. Five other men rushed into the house and captured Bibi and four other children, including the nine-day-old infant, from various rooms on the two floors above. Amina and Daud along with their eleven-year-old brother, Abdul Rahman, Amina's twenty-month-old daughter with Aziz, as well as Bibi and her two other young children, were herded into the basement together.

The intruders seemed unsatisfied and agitated—unsure of what to do next. Some examined the brand-new color TV set. One of them pulled open Amina's diaper bag and pocketed the $10 bill he found inside. Others were searching through drawers for anything they could find. What they were really after was Khaalis, and he was clearly not at home. Khaalis had returned to the center briefly that morning after dropping his third wife off at work, but he had soon left again to meet with Aziz at the Aram jewelry store. Around the time that the center was invaded, he was on his way to collect his wife Hafsa at the end of the school day and drop her off at her apartment in Silver Spring.

The intruders huddled and chalked out their plans in hushed tones while the Hanafis cowered in the basement laundry room. Then, in a burst of action, they began executing their plan. Daud was taken up the stairs first. In the small prayer room on the third floor, he was made to kneel and was shot in the head three times. Next, it was Amina's turn. One of the intruders yelled at her as he shoved her up the stairs: "Why did he write those letters? Why didn't you try to stop him?" Even in the grip of terror, she fought back: "My father knows best. That's his job." The gunmen shoved her to the floor in another third-floor room. "Well, this is best for you," he said as he shot three bullets into her head.

In a different room, another gunman had forced the eleven-year-old Abdullah onto a bed. The little boy pleaded for his life. "I'll do anything you say—just don't hurt me," he cried. "All right," the gunman replied, before pulling the trigger and landing a bullet into his skull. One of the gunmen noticed that Amina, lying still in a pool of blood, was panting. "Damn," he said, "she's still breathing." He then fired a couple more rounds into her head. Her body went limp. Three of Khaalis's four children with Khadija were now lying still in three separate rooms, bleeding from bullet wounds to the head—the fourth was with Khadija at the Giant Supermarket.

Khadija was standing in the checkout line with a shopping cart full of groceries when she realized that she had forgotten her purse at home. Abdul Nur, who had been driving her around the city all day, volunteered to make the short drive back to the center to collect it. When he entered the house several minutes later, three Black Mafia members jumped him. They struggled with the 180-pound Nur and dragged him up the stairs before tying him up on the floor. Just as the bullets entered his right temple, Nur threw up the eggs he had eaten that morning. The gunmen joked about his breakfast menu as they walked back downstairs. In the basement, Bibi, bound and gagged, was surrounded by four children— her three babies, as well as Amina's two-year-old daughter. They were all screaming in hysterics.

Bibi might have heard the water running in a bathtub upstairs. She might or might not have also overheard the intense argument that had erupted between two Black Mafia members, one insisting he had signed on for a robbery, not this. Adults are one thing, but children? I have three children of my own at home. What did they ever do? They're too young to make an identification, so what's the problem? They haven't committed any heresy. The other man was in no mood for arguing. If you don't do what you're told, you end up like the Hanafis. The seed of the hypocrite is in these children, you understand?

Three of the older children were torn away from Bibi as they clutched at her clothes. She screamed and spit pointlessly into the cloth gag in her mouth. One of the Black Mafia men, left in charge of guarding her, examined her squirming helplessly on the floor. Later, he began filling up the deep washing basin in the laundry room. Once it was full, he lifted the nine-day-old baby and slowly lowered him in. Bibi, the mother, could only watch and scream into her gag as the man held his hand in the basin for a long time. Once he was done, the gunman leveled his gun barrel at Bibi's head and pulled the trigger eight times. It was done. All eight Black Mafia members regrouped in the first-floor prayer room, their shoes staining the pink rug red. In the quiet house, they sat and waited for "the head dude." He would return home eventually.

Khadija was starting to worry. Her escort, Nur, never returned. She tried calling the house from a pay phone outside the store, but both lines were busy. She decided to walk to the apartment of Khaalis's third wife, Hafsa. It was a place that she typically avoided, but this felt urgent, and she was desperate. A little after four o'clock, Khaalis and Khadija rushed home in the 1972 Pontiac Firebird registered in Hafsa's name. As they approached the center, they noticed Nur's car parked outside. Neither Khaalis nor Khadija had keys with them, so they rang the doorbell. There was no sound. They knocked. Still, no answer. They began peering through the windows. Through one, Khadija saw the face of a man she did not recognize inside her home staring back at her. It was the face of the ringleader, Ronald Harvey, and it terrified Khadija. She began screaming and ran to a neighbor's house to call the police. Just then, the front door burst open, and someone tried to yank Khaalis inside.

When Khaalis wrangled himself free, the hitmen fled out the back door into the alley and scattered. Khaalis hopped back into the car and started following a gold Volkswagen down the alley behind the house. The car chase did not last long. Khaalis had gone only a few hundred yards around the block when his car collided with another as he tried to turn back onto Sixteenth Street. Khaalis abandoned the car and ran back toward the Hanafi Center. He arrived just as the first officer from the Washington police department, Steven Levow, was responding to the scene. Khaalis stormed inside yelling the names of his children, and the cop followed him closely inside, gun drawn, unsure of what to expect. The first floor was barren. On the second floor, Khaalis found the body of Nur, his brains splattered on the wall. Then, as he was racing up to the third floor, he saw someone standing in the hallway, leaning on the banister, drenched in blood from head to toe. It was Amina. She could barely stand straight, and she looked dazed as she turned over objects looking for something or someone. Khaalis looked her up and down, horrified, and ran off to another room. He found the bodies of his two sons, Daud and Abdul Rahman, in separate rooms. He then entered the bathroom on the second floor and saw three children, blue in the face, lying dead in a bathtub full of water. The police officer kept tailing him. Whoever had done this had set it up like a house of horrors, leaving a new gruesome surprise behind every door. Finally, they burst into the basement, where Khaalis found his nine-day-old child, Tasibur, floating facedown in a large basin in the laundry room. Bibi, his wife, was laid out on the floor, bleeding from her head. Khaalis reached for her. She was still breathing.

The police, along with the FBI, had been surveilling this address from a distance, nonstop, for almost five months. Now, suddenly, for the first time, the center was swarming with cops. Bibi and Amina were put on gurneys and taken to waiting ambulances. Amina was still conscious as she was being loaded up. A flattened bullet fell out of her hair as she turned her head to face her father, who was standing by her side. She was able to get out two words: "Elijah's people." By that evening, soon after sunset, seven Hanafis had been pronounced dead.

14.

ASYLUM

Hanafi Islamic jurisprudence requires that the dead be buried within one day, but the Hanafi Muslims in Washington were not able to bury their dead in time. The bodies were tied up in autopsies. Khaalis had argued against the procedures—he did not want the bodies more brutalized than they already had been—but he was told that it was necessary if there was any chance of bringing the murderers to justice. Weighing his hopes of seeing justice served in this world against the family's ability to enter heaven in the next one, Khaalis allowed it.

When the seven dead bodies were returned, they were ritually washed and cleansed for burial, and each of the seven, even the babies, was wrapped in a single length of unstitched white cloth, as is Islamic custom. On January 20, two days after the massacre, the bodies were placed in caskets and loaded onto four hearses parked in front of the center. Fifty people attended the funerals. Kareem had flown in from Milwaukee the evening of the massacre. At the funeral, cameras flashed from a distance. Kareem carried one of the dead babies' caskets all by himself. It would have appeared miniature in his giant hands. After a service at the Johnson and Jenkins Funeral Home a few minutes' drive from the Hanafi headquarters, the procession began making its way to the Lincoln Memorial Cemetery in Maryland.

The Nation of Islam was making no attempt to keep a low profile. Washington's local Temple No. 4 had arranged for a twisted, callous victory parade to ride alongside the Hanafis' funeral procession. Driving along, the Black Muslims jeered and heckled while waving copies of the newspaper *Muhammad Speaks*. One of their cars was fitted with a bull-horn, and the man speaking through it declared Elijah Muhammad the true savior and the only hope for the Black man. While TV crews filmed the ruckus, uniformed police units assigned to the funeral looked on nervously. The Hanafis did not respond. At the cemetery, they quietly unloaded the dead and lowered them into their graves. Kareem returned to Milwaukee and immediately purchased a Model 8111 .12-gauge shotgun for himself.

Khaalis wasted no time in going on the counteroffensive. On January 22, he held a press conference at the Hanafi Center and declared Elijah Muhammad responsible for the massacre. "America is in trouble," he told the dozens of reporters gathered in the prayer room of the Hanafi Center, a row of microphones in front of him, "when you can't express your personal feelings without the threat of violence and murder." A week later, Khaalis was invited on the *Today* show on NBC, one of the most-watched morning shows in the country. In the ten-minute segment, the host, Frank McGee, peppered Khaalis with questions about his theory. Who, specifically, McGee asked, did Khaalis believe was responsible for the murders? "I will say I know who is responsible," Khaalis replied calmly. He first named Elijah Muhammad (referring to him as Elijah Poole, his birth name); then his son-in-law Raymond Sharrieff; Herbert, Elijah's son who managed Muhammad Ali; as well as the two other sons, Wallace and Elijah Jr. It was the entire top brass of the Nation of Islam. Khaalis described the scene that he had encountered when he entered the center on the afternoon of the murders and relayed the words that Amina had reported exchanging with the gunmen. He recounted how the Nation's followers were caught by TV cameras celebrating and rejoicing at the funerals.

Frank McGee asked Khaalis if he knew anything about the deadly standoff that had recently taken place at a Brooklyn sporting goods store. Right after the attack on Khaalis's home, several African American Sunni Muslim gunmen had taken hostages for two days. The hostage takers, who surrendered on the third day, told police that they attempted the robbery to arm themselves for what they believed would turn into a violent civil war between different sects of American Islam. The American Muslim civil war that had been simmering before the massacre appeared to be kicking into high gear. The Muslims in Brooklyn were not the only ones worried. *The Atlanta Journal-Constitution* ran a story on the front page with the headline "Weary Muslims Arming," describing similar feelings among the Black Sunni Muslims in that city. Khaalis said he knew nothing about the men in Brooklyn. Finally, the host asked if the police had been effective so far: "We cooperate one hundred percent with the police department and I want to give my country a chance. I have two offers to seek asylum in another country. Number one, I feel this is my country; I should get the proper protection here. Even if I went, I would still go as an American and when I return, I would be an American."

The Nation kept firing back but now mostly directed its message to the faithful within the Nation's fold through the newspaper *Muhammad Speaks*. A cartoon strip published in early February showed a Black man wearing a traditional taqiya Muslim cap and a short goatee, unmistakably Khaalis, receiving wads of cash from a TV producer, his "boss," who was wearing a black suit and smoking a cigar. "How was my act?" the Black man asked while counting his money. Later in the month, in a column titled "An American Flag Muslim," a member of the Nation of Islam directly addressed Khaalis and questioned his motivations. "Mr. Khaalis, I noticed on television that you were flying the American flag outside of your home and even wearing it on your body," the columnist, Melvin 12X, wrote. "You are no better than the Arch Deceiver," he wrote, "who has used you, a Black man, to defile the name of Allah's Messenger," referring to Elijah Muhammad.

Amina returned home from the hospital a little more than a week after being shot. The doctors had successfully removed six bullets from her skull and, to the amazement of everyone, she appeared fine, at least on the outside, and at least at first. Setting foot in the Hanafi Center for the first time after the murders was traumatic. She was heavily sedated as she suffered from crippling headaches and was unable to concentrate for very long. She would often break down crying uncontrollably. Khaalis's second wife, Bibi, stayed in the hospital for much longer, and her prognosis was much poorer. She had brain surgery, and the doctors told Khaalis that the twenty-seven-year-old would live the rest of her life in a vegetative state, unable to move, speak, or care for herself. She would be released from the hospital in March, more than two months after being shot. Khadija and Khaalis decided to set up her bed on the first floor, but her moans and howls kept all the others up through the night. Bibi's brother, Salim, who had founded the Hanafi's NRA club, walked into the house one day to see Khaalis tossing a draft of Bibi's master's thesis, page by page, into the crackling fireplace. It was the closest thing to mourning anyone ever saw Khaalis do.

The grounds outside the Hanafi Center were systematically cleared by the Hanafi men. The gorgeous azaleas that surrounded the house were all chopped down. The basement windows were bricked over, while the first-floor windows were boarded up with masonite board. The center transformed from idyllic spiritual home to hardened fortress. Khaalis began sending out pleas for support to immigrant Muslim groups. The foreign Muslims "who don't come to our assistance at this time and declare" Elijah Muhammad "an impostor," he told a news reporter, "by their silence are in agreement with and condone murder. The Sunnis and Hanafis should come together," he said. In a series of personal phone calls to Rauf after his press conference, Khaalis urged the director of the Islamic Center to convince Muslim ambassadors in Washington to end their sponsorship of the Nation of Islam and Elijah Muhammad. He asked Rauf to hold his own press conference with these ambassadors and diplomats inside the palatial Islamic Center and rebuke the Nation.

Rauf did nothing of the sort. Inserting himself in the middle of a dangerous and bloody feud and ending up on the wrong side of the Nation was not a risk he was willing to take. In any case, some of the Muslim governments Khaalis was talking about had been using the Nation as a strategic toehold in American politics for more than a decade, ever since Nasser's outreach to Elijah after the Suez Crisis. An FBI internal memo from the time, however, did note that Libya, which had lent Elijah Muhammad millions of dollars less than a year earlier, was running a back channel through a Libyan man named Muhammad Subhy to urge Elijah Muhammad to address the criminals in his ranks and end the bloodshed. The February issue of the Islamic Center bulletin carried an announcement, with a prayer "that the Almighty may sustain Brother Hamaas in this most unfortunate adversity." Rauf, for his part, simply led a prayer for the dead Hanafis at the congregational Friday service at the Islamic Center.

Khaalis did not attend. By that time, he had written off Rauf for good. A front-page story about the massacre in *The Washington Post* had quoted Rauf giving his impression of Khaalis: "I think his religious knowledge was a little superficial," Rauf was quoted, adding that he appeared "more concerned with the interests of black people" than of Muslims in general. Even though Rauf later disclaimed the remarks in a letter to the newspaper, Khaalis concluded that Rauf was no friend of the Hanafis or of Islam. As far as Khaalis was concerned, he was an enemy of both.

THE MURDER INVESTIGATION was led by Joe O'Brien, the chief homicide detective in the Washington Metropolitan Police Department. He was one of the first cops on the murder scene at the Hanafi Center. The even-keeled, straight-talking, forty-four-year-old former marine from Boston had joined the capital's police force in 1952 upon his return from the Korean War, an experience he had memorialized in a bicep tattoo. He had a neat appearance, a respectful manner, and a nice head of hair. He was seen at the station headquarters frequently with a Lucky Strike in one hand and a coffee in the other. O'Brien was assigned to the homicide unit shortly after joining the force and served on it through the 1960s, the most murderous period in the capital's history. His colleagues believed that he had a photographic memory, which might explain why he excelled in homicide investigations. He had investigated hundreds of murders. The images from the massacre at the Hanafi Center were unlike anything he had ever seen, and they seared themselves into his mind.

O'Brien became the face of American law enforcement for the Hanafis. O'Brien first met Khaalis at around 7:00 p.m. on the day of the massacre, to record his witness statement. The two men had sat together for more than an hour. At first, Khaalis was suspicious of O'Brien and all law enforcement, questioning the pace of the investigation. After the FBI followed up with an in-person interview of their own in February, his suspicions only grew. In the weeks that followed, though, O'Brien managed to break through the haze of paranoia that clouded Khaalis's mind. He would show up at the center at all times of the day and night whenever there was an important development in the case. If Khaalis and Khadija ever called and sounded upset, he would come meet with them in person. He would always remove his shoes, and sometimes while he spoke to them, he would choke up, too. Soon, Khaalis, Khadija, and the Hanafis began trusting O'Brien in a way that they trusted few others outside the community.

The investigation began with a handful of objects found in the bushes surrounding the house, in the alley behind it, and in the neighbors' yards, through which the assailants had made their escape. There was an issue of *Time* magazine and a credit card that pointed to the city of Philadelphia, and that is where the investigation quickly turned. When the Philadelphia police were given the details, they saw the fingerprints of the Black Mafia all over it. A literal full palm print found in the bathroom of the Downtown Motel in Washington matched that of Ronald Harvey, the ringleader. O'Brien dispatched a daring deputy, an African American detective named Ronald Washington, to Philadelphia to poke around at the Nation of Islam's Temple No. 12. The detective shaved his head, put on a suit, and began attending services and public meetings undercover. Several days later, he returned to Washington with a list of names of Temple No. 12 members who, he believed, had traveled to Washington from Philadelphia that inauguration week.

As the evidence accumulated, O'Brien began working with the U.S. attorney's office that was responsible for prosecuting serious crimes in the District of Columbia courts. The office in Washington had 140 lawyers at the time and was being led by Earl Silbert who, like O'Brien, was a Boston native, though he came from a different world. Silbert was Jewish and a bookish lawyer in his late thirties with thinning hair. He had joined the U.S. attorney's office a decade earlier straight out of Harvard Law School. When the massacre at the Hanafi Center occurred, Silbert was just getting started with prosecuting the biggest case of his career. On January 10, 1973, he had delivered the opening statement on behalf of the government in the prosecution of the men who had broken into the Watergate Hotel in Washington. Many believed that Silbert's epic two-hour-long opening statement was the reason that five of the defendants quickly folded and turned in guilty pleas.

The evidence-gathering operation ultimately took up almost four hundred man-hours of Washington police time. Combined with evidence that the FBI had collected through its many field offices across the country, Silbert's team had plenty to work with. Thanks to the extensive law-enforcement surveillance of the Hanafi Center, and infiltration by the FBI that had preceded the crime, they also had an unusual amount of context. For its part, the police in Philadelphia had been on the trail of the Black Mafia for years and had files compiled on almost all the suspects. Silbert could easily place the Nation's hitmen in Washington on the day of the murder and even have them inside the house during the massacre.

The mechanics of the murders, however, were another story. Who pulled the trigger on whom? Where? When? These were questions that would be extremely difficult to pin down in front of a jury. Amina Khaalis was a key witness to the crime—she had been conscious through the entire ordeal. Even she had been in only a few of the rooms of the house during the murders, though—and she'd had several bullets in her head, and her vision had been obscured by a piece of cloth for most of the time. There would be grave questions raised about the reliability of her testimony. Despite all the evidence, Silbert did not feel confident about getting convictions for all the men involved. The government desperately needed a confession.

The investigators and attorneys quickly zeroed in on one of the hitmen, named James Price. Silbert's office already had a solid case against him. They had phone records that placed him in Washington, and Amina had singled him out in a lineup as one of the men she had seen in her living room. He was also the one, it appeared, who had argued against murdering the children with Ronald Harvey, the ringleader. His wife was expecting their fourth child when the massacre occurred. He was one of the youngest in the group, and the most exposed. Silbert's team baited him with protective custody for his wife and children and offered possible leniency for the many other charges he faced in multiple jurisdictions. On June 28, 1973, Price folded and gave the prosecutors a formal written statement describing all the harrowing details of the crime with names of the individuals involved. On July 5, he testified before the grand jury and detailed everything that happened on the afternoon of January 18 at the Hanafi house.

On August 16, 1973, the grand jury in Washington handed down federal indictments for seven men who had broken into the house. All seven were members of the Nation of Islam's Temple No. 12 and known members of the Black Mafia. There was an eighth suspect as well, but he had died the day after being served a subpoena in a hospital bed in Philadelphia. Four of the seven men, including one of the ringleaders, John Clark, were already in custody in Philadelphia on separate state charges. In October the FBI picked up two others who'd been hiding out in Jacksonville, Florida. The only one left was Ronald Harvey, one of the Black Mafia chiefs. He had a long rap sheet—twenty arrests and dozens of criminal charges. He had no convictions, though, because key witnesses would usually fail to testify against him for some reason or another. He had been arrested earlier in the summer for his involvement in another mass murder at the Camden, New Jersey, home of a high-profile Black drug kingpin turned politician, but he had quickly posted his $175,000 bail and absconded. The FBI placed him on its most-wanted list and issued a poster with his face on it. A trial date was set for the remaining six for early 1974. James Price's case, the government had secretly promised his lawyers, would be separated from those of the others right at the beginning of the trial. The stage was set. Khaalis, his family, and his community pinned their hopes on a thing called American justice.

15.

TOP RANK

War broke out in the Middle East again in October 1973. This time it was Egypt and its Arab neighbors and allies that launched a surprise attack on Israel. Syria and Egypt in particular hoped to recapture the territory they had lost to Israel in the 1967 war. On the Jewish holiday of Yom Kippur, Egyptian forces crossed into the Sinai Peninsula, and the Syrians moved into the Golan Heights. The war lasted for nearly three weeks. It was a bloody conflict. Thousands of Israeli, Egyptian, and Syrian soldiers were killed, and tens of thousands were wounded and maimed. When the United Nations finally secured a ceasefire agreement between Egypt and Israel in late October, the Sinai Peninsula and Golan Heights remained under Israeli occupation. The map of the region remained unchanged, but Israel was much less certain of its position in it.

For the United States, what followed the war was far more consequential than the fighting itself. Israel had been able to repel the attack in large part because of the help of the Nixon administration, which had mobilized $2.2 billion in emergency aid and launched Operation Nickel Grass, an American airlift operation that delivered thousands of tons of military equipment to Israel during and after the war. What the Americans did not know was that the leaders of Arab states, including historic rivals Egypt and Saudi Arabia, had met in advance of the war and decided that if the United States entered the conflict on Israel's side, it would pay a heavy price.

Before the ceasefire was signed, the Organization of the Petroleum Exporting Countries, a cartel of oil-producing nations, announced a drastic cut in oil production and embargoed oil exports to the United States. The price of oil on the global market skyrocketed, increasing transport costs and, therefore, the prices of nearly everything. The United States was already struggling because of a weak dollar, and the oil shock of 1973 further hobbled the country's economy, threatening a global recession. The military conflict may have ended with an ambiguous result in favor of Israel, but the oil shock that followed demonstrated to the world, for the first time ever, the awesome power of the Arab oil-producing countries.

For Moustapha Akkad, who was about to embark on one of the most expensive movie projects in the history of cinema, the oil shock did not necessarily spell disaster. The embargo translated to a historic transfer of wealth from North America, Europe, and Japan to the Middle East. The financial reserves of many of the governments and individuals backing Akkad were bloating, not shrinking. Khashoggi, the Saudi playboy millionaire, had pulled out of the deal under pressure from his Saudi religious authorities, but the governments of Morocco, Kuwait, and Libya had all decided that the approval of Al-Azhar was good enough for them to split the proposed $6 million budget among them.

More than five years after conceiving of the project, Akkad was finally ready to begin shooting his film. Filming on location in Saudi Arabia was no longer an option, so Akkad picked a site in the small village of Ait Bouchent, fifteen miles outside Marrakesh in Morocco, whose government was one of the three main sponsors of the film. Akkad had secured permission from King Hassan, the ruler of the country, in a personal meeting. With his consent, Akkad began building a gargantuan set on the northwestern edge of the Sahara, re-creating the entire town of Mecca as it would have appeared nearly fourteen hundred years earlier, when Muhammad received his revelations from the archangel Gabriel. At the center of the life-size set, Akkad erected a replica of the Kaaba, the holiest site for all Muslims in the world, nearly fifty feet tall and draped in a handwoven tapestry from Tangiers. The cost of the entire elaborate set, which Akkad boasted was the most expensive since the film *Cleopatra*, was nearly $1 million.

While his Mecca was being constructed in the desert, Akkad went on a hiring spree for the best talent. Akkad cast Academy Award–winner Anthony Quinn, the hulking and dashing Mexican-American actor, in the lead role of Hamza, the Islamic Prophet's paternal uncle, who was one of the earliest converts to Islam. Irene Papas, Quinn's Greek costar from the Academy Award–winning 1964 movie *Zorba the Greek*, would play the female lead role of Hind, the wife of Muhammad's archenemy in Mecca. One of the central characters of the film was Bilal, a Black Abyssinian enslaved by Meccan traders, who was freed by Muhammad and became one of his most trusted companions. Bilal is believed to have been the first man to sing the Islamic call to prayer that, fourteen centuries later, is a motif of Islamic cultures all around the world. The story of Islam, Akkad had decided, had to be seen through the eyes of the African diaspora that had experienced slavery for millennia. It was a bold narrative choice but also a bet on selling movie tickets in America.

Akkad was in Beirut when he received a phone call from Herbert Muhammad, Elijah Muhammad's third son, who had heard the news of Akkad's project. He was Muhammad Ali's manager and offered the champion to Akkad for the role of Bilal. Herbert, who had recently founded the Top Rank boxing promotion company, would have explained that Ali had some acting experience under his belt. During the time in which he was stripped of his boxing license while fighting a draft-dodging conviction, Ali had appeared in small roles in movies and even performed in a short-lived Broadway show. Akkad's film could be a breakthrough opportunity for Ali to display his Muslim faith and polish his lucrative side-hustle in Hollywood at the same time.

Akkad was tempted. Despite his affiliation with Elijah Muhammad's Nation, Ali had been embraced by the Muslim world at large. He had traveled through dozens of Muslim countries to a hero's welcome. He had completed the hajj pilgrimage in 1972. He had declared the United States the "stronghold" of Zionism. Moreover, casting a star like Ali would guarantee publicity and a global audience. Still, after some thinking, Akkad declined. Ali, he decided, was almost too big a star for the role. The audience, he feared, would never accept him as Bilal. Instead, Akkad offered Ali a minor role of a slave who is hired to assassinate Hamza, the lead character. Later, Akkad received a call from Ali himself while the boxer was in Beirut on a goodwill tour of the Middle East, during which he visited several countries, including Egypt, Libya, and Qatar as well as Palestinian refugee camps. The two men spoke about the possibility of the role but decided to go separate ways. In the end, Akkad hired an obscure Senegalese-born actor named Johnny Sekka, who had enjoyed modest success in British theater and film, for the role of Bilal.

On April 14, 1974, *The New York Times* ran a feature on Akkad's project with the headline "Film Turns Small Town Into Mecca." It was the first mainstream press coverage of the film. The article highlighted Akkad's limited experience and contrasted it with the budget, which it put at $8 million. The article mostly dwelled on the precarious situation involving competing views of Islamic religious authorities on Akkad's project. Akkad had "official approval from Morocco, Libya, Kuwait, Algeria, Syria and Egypt," the article said, but added that he "is approaching his task with some hesitation." The article noted how "few scripts in motion-picture history have been so carefully prepared and checked for accuracy and orthodoxy." While Akkad hoped "for better understanding of Islam at a time of international concern over the struggle between Israel and the Arab states," he also sounded his concerns. "It is a sensitive subject," he told the reporter. "We may still have riots."

16.

STOOL PIGEON

The largest and most elaborate murder trial in the history of Washington, DC, began in February 1974, a little more than a year after the massacre at the Hanafi Madh-Hab Center. It was a turbulent and violent decade, and many American Muslim groups were still steeped in lawless militancy. Over the summer and fall of 1973, a few members of the Nation of Islam had gone on a six-month-long killing spree in San Francisco that left fifteen people dead in what became known as the Zebra murders. Days before the Black Mafia trial started in Washington, there was a brutal shootout at a Sunni mosque in Brooklyn in which four Sunni Muslim men were murdered. That same day, Patty Hearst, a teenage media heiress, was kidnapped from her apartment by a group known as the Symbionese Liberation Army, which had its own strong ties not only to the Nation of Islam but also to Sunni Muslim groups in Cleveland.

The superior court in Washington, DC, was a new court created by an act of Congress in 1970. The local justice system had a hybrid setup, in which the District had its own criminal court, but major crimes were still prosecuted by federal prosecutors from the Justice Department. With more than one hundred witnesses expected to testify, Leonard Braman, the DC judge assigned to the trial, was bracing for a long and challenging few months. Washington police signed an elaborate memorandum of understanding with the U.S. Marshals Service to make security arrangements. A courtroom was remodeled specifically for the proceedings. The windows were covered with steel plates. The jury room had plywood installed over its windows. A metal detector scanned all people entering the courthouse. Special battery-powered lights were on hand at all times in case the power was cut off. Twenty-four U.S. Marshals were assigned to guard the proceedings. Braman ruled that the defense and prosecution witnesses would not be allowed to be in each other's company, and extra security guards would be stationed all around. With a 659-person jury pool, jury selection alone cost $13,000. The trial would cost a fortune, close to $100,000, which had to be financed by a special appropriation from Congress.

Earl Silbert chose to be the lead prosecutor for the case. After an outstanding start in the Watergate break-in trial, Silbert had started receiving criticism for playing it too safe. He was prosecuting the crime well enough, people said, but he was failing to connect the dots to the White House. He stepped back from the Watergate trial in June 1973 and, for a change of pace, began working on the largest mass murder case in the history of the American capital.

One of the first witnesses the prosecution called was Hamaas Abdul Khaalis. He was not particularly useful for identifying any of the intruders; he had had only a brief scuffle with one of them at the door and did not even get a good enough look at him to identify him. Still, with his testimony, the prosecution hoped to establish the motive for the murders: a struggle over the direction of Islam in America. When he took the stand, Khaalis came face-to-face with the murderers of his family for the first time. If any of his wounds had healed in the past year, they burst open the moment he laid eyes on them.

He was asked to introduce himself. He stated his name and described his occupation as "*Masheer*—the guide, spiritual adviser. The man who defends the faith. The man who knows tricksters and murderers and gangsters that deviate on Islam." He had been on the stand only a few moments when he thought he saw one of the defendants smirk at him and blow a kiss. "You don't have to smile, Mister," Khaalis said, rising to his feet in the witness box and pointing at the row of the accused seated in front. The defense attorneys jumped to their feet and asked the judge to stop the trial, but Khaalis was spiraling. "It's over. It's over," he shouted, his booming voice filling the courtroom. "You killed my babies. You killed my babies and shot my women." A swarm of security guards surrounded Khaalis and dragged him out of the courtroom as he continued to shout. Before Braman adjourned the proceedings, several of the defense attorneys moved for a mistrial.

Braman was in no mood to start over again. After Khaalis had cooled down outside the courtroom with Joe O'Brien, he returned more composed. Braman announced that he would hold a special hearing in which Khaalis would be required to present a defense against being held in contempt of court. Khaalis hired a lawyer, and a few days later he offered a contrite explanation in a special court session. "I am very sorry for what I did spontaneously," he said. "I realize that it was wrong." Khaalis guaranteed that the judge would have nothing to worry about moving forward. "I give my word, regardless of what happens in this courtroom, even if someone hits me, I won't do it again." Braman was satisfied. He excused Khaalis but told him that he was not to speak for the remainder of the trial. The judge then dismissed the defense motions for a mistrial. Days later, Khaalis received the invoice from the attorney he had hired for the hearing in the amount of $750. Khaalis would never forget that dollar amount.

Over the months that followed, the Nation of Islam mobilized in a big way. The Nation, and the Black Mafia in particular, were accustomed to dealing with police and local prosecutors, but they had never dealt directly with federal prosecutors. Elijah Muhammad was nervous that the feds would use the murder investigation to start digging deeper into his organization. He had good reason to be worried. Silbert had learned his lesson from the Watergate trial. After trying the people who had pulled the triggers, he fully intended to trace the chain of command to find out who had ordered the hit.

The Nation's immediate aim was to derail the trial. Attorneys had to be assigned armed guards because of anonymous threats they received. Judge Braman and his wife were provided round-the-clock protection by U.S. Marshals, while an explosives unit of the police screened all mail for the judge. Even the judge's son, who was attending college in the South, had a security detail assigned to him after he was mysteriously forced off the road by a speeding car. A reporter covering the trial for *Philadelphia* magazine received photographs of his own toddler son in the mail with his name scribbled at the bottom without any explanation. Some even wondered if the Nation was tampering with the witnesses after bizarre courtroom scenes: when asked to identify the men he had seen running on the street around the time of the murder, one of the prosecution witnesses, a maintenance worker at the synagogue across the street from the Hanafi Center, pointed to the three uniformed marshals present in the courtroom.

When it came to witnesses, the prosecution was most nervous about the stool pigeon, James Price. The government's case rested heavily on his cooperation. As planned, Price's attorneys had moved to sever his case from the other defendants' at the beginning of the trial, and he was now awaiting his own trial date. The other defendants had immediately become suspicious. A few weeks into the trial, a man named David Pasha, a minister at one of the Nation's temples and a licensed attorney, appeared at the courthouse, unannounced, with two towering female bodyguards in blue uniforms by his side. He had Price's wife and two children accompanying him. He demanded immediate legal access to Price. By all reasonable standards, it appeared to be a brazen shakedown from Chicago. Still, Price expressed a desire to meet with the lawyer and his wife and children, so Braman allowed it. "If this tactic is permitted to proceed," Silbert argued in a memo to the judge, "the entire system of fair and equitable proceedings which have been the hallmark of the administration of criminal justice in this nation's capital will be threatened." As Silbert feared, soon after the meeting with the Nation's attorney, Price stopped talking to the government.

Louis Farrakhan, the slick minister at Temple No. 7 in Harlem, and the man who had come to replace Malcolm X as Elijah's main spokesperson, fired warning shots right from the top. On April 1, during a regularly scheduled Nation of Islam–sponsored broadcast on the Washington station WOOK, Farrakhan gave a twenty-eight-minute interview in which he directly addressed the Hanafi trial. The attempt to link the murders to the Nation of Islam, he said, was a government plot to strip "Elijah Muhammad of acceptability and respectability." Farrakhan then described what would happen to anyone who cooperated with the government:

> Let this be a warning to those of you who would be used as an instrument of a wicked government against our rise. Be careful, because when the government is tired of using you they're going to dump you back in the laps of your people. And though Elijah Muhammad is a merciful man and will say, "Come in," and forgive you, yet in the ranks of the black people today there

are younger men and women rising up who have no forgiveness
in them for traitors and stool pigeons. And they will execute
you, as soon as your identity is known.

Days after that broadcast, Price formally backed out as a witness for
the government. He denied knowledge of any crimes that he and his fellow Black Muslims had been accused of. He claimed the written confession was under duress. He also informed the judge that from this point
onward, he would be represented by the Nation's attorney, David Pasha.
The prosecution had gone for forty-nine days and presented 510 exhibits
and 135 witnesses, but the Nation had wrenched the government's star
witness out of their hands in the final phase of the trial, and the case
began to wobble. In May, Judge Braman acquitted the youngest of the
accused, twenty-two-year-old Jerome Sinclair. Price's confession had
identified him as the man who had drowned the three children in the upstairs bathroom with his hands. No one had seen him do it, however, and
Amina had not identified him, nor had any of the other witnesses.

A twenty-four-person jury finally began deliberating over the fate
of the four remaining defendants. Three days later, they found all four
men guilty of first-degree murder. They all faced life sentences. "I want to
give my country a chance," Khaalis had told the host of the *Today* show
days after his family was massacred. More than a year later, his country
appeared to have delivered at least partial justice. The Hanafis made no
public statements. There were still at least two more trials to go. James
Price, the man who never testified, had forfeited his deal with the government and would soon face trial. Ronald Harvey, the criminal mastermind
who was at large at the beginning of the trial, had been apprehended in
Chicago and was, once again, in custody, but this time without bail. He,
too, would face trial soon.

Silbert, the prosecutor, made it clear that the federal government was
also far from done with the investigation. He planned to convene a new
grand jury, he told reporters, to find out "who, if anyone else, was also
responsible for this crime." In September 1974, the DEA carried out a series of raids in Philadelphia that essentially broke the back of the Black
Mafia in Philadelphia. The Nation of Islam's criminal network, however,
stretched beyond the Delaware Valley, and federal prosecutors were eager to trace it all the way to Chicago. One of the assistant U.S. attorneys

described the Department of Justice's strategy in more straightforward terms to a news reporter: "You have to get the little fish first."

The war in the street between Muslim Americans continued unabated. One of the big fish in the Nation, James Shabazz, the minister of the Nation's temple in Newark and widely considered the man who had overseen the assassination of Malcolm X, was assassinated a few months after the Black Mafia trial ended. He was shot in the face several times outside his home. A few months after that, in early 1975, before Judge Braman sentenced the four Black Muslims, a man associated with the Nation of Islam's Washington temple walked into a courthouse in the town of Louisa, Virginia, less than one hundred miles south of the District line, and shot dead a judge presiding in a courtroom. His sawed-off shotgun had the word "Allah" chiseled into its stock. The news made it to the front page of *The Washington Post*, which might very well have been the point.

17.

PILGRIMAGE

Akkad was forced to stop shooting his film for the first time in May 1974. The cameras had been rolling for only about two weeks. The heat on the sprawling, bustling outdoor set was so intense that Akkad would shoot for only a few hours after dawn and before sunset. With the widest-angle lens, Akkad could capture a set with space for five thousand extras in it. One day, as Akkad was directing a sequence in which the slave Bilal is tortured by his Meccan masters for following the new religion of Muhammad, his assistant handed him a telegram from a government official in Rabat, the Moroccan capital:

> ON THE INSTRUCTIONS OF THE MINISTER OF STATE IN CHARGE OF INFORMATION I HAVE THE HONOUR TO INFORM YOU THAT THE SHOOTING OF THE FILM MOHAMMAD THE MESSENGER OF GOD IS SUSPENDED STOP

Akkad did not say a word to anyone. Later that evening, he climbed into a car and drove four hours to Rabat, where the minister of information provided more details. The word of a counterfeit Kaaba, he told Akkad, had reached Saudi Arabia, and the Saudis were furious. It might have been the article in *The New York Times* or maybe just word of mouth. Regardless, over the airwaves in Riyadh, the Saudi capital, a radio broadcast had announced that the crown prince, Fahd Ibn Abdul Aziz, had objected to "the idea of any film on the Prophet Mohammed." The Saudis, the minister told Akkad, had given King Hassan of Morocco an ultimatum: if Morocco allowed Akkad to continue shooting his film, there would be serious diplomatic consequences.

Saudi Arabia had emerged from the 1973 oil crisis stronger and more influential than ever. By leading the oil embargo that brought the world economy to its knees, the country had not only displayed its economic might but also burnished its credentials as the leading voice for the Palestinian cause and the linchpin of Muslim regional interests. Morocco, a country on the periphery of the Arabic-speaking world, on the northwestern Atlantic coast of Africa, had no oil of its own and was entirely dependent on its Arab allies to meet its energy needs. The Saudis knew that they had great leverage over it. Morocco was scheduled to play host, later that fall, to the seventh summit of the Arab League, when the Saudis were expected to formally back Morocco's territorial claims to the Spanish province of Sahara and urge the United Nations to look into the dispute. If Akkad's film was not stopped, the Moroccan king could no longer count on Saudi support.

After fourteen days of frantic lobbying by Akkad, the king relented. He sent instructions to Akkad through his subordinates to continue filming. He was told to be discreet, though, and finish up quickly. The fourteen-day stoppage cost half a million dollars, and the mood on the set was desperate. Akkad knew that it was only a matter of time before the Saudis would return. In July, a bombshell from Cairo landed. Al-Azhar, still the most respected religious authority in Sunni Islam, whose scholars had stamped each page of Akkad's screenplay with their seal, was rescinding its endorsement. The institute issued a formal religious opinion, a fatwa, signed by the top sheik of Al-Azhar himself. It read:

> In my personal name, in the name of Al-Azhar and in the name of the Islamic Research Council which studied the issue of the film called "Mohammad the Messenger of God," in several meetings especially convened for this purpose, I herewith declare our disagreement to the production of the film called "Mohammad the Messenger of God" or any other similar film which present a dramatization of any kind of the personality of the Holy Prophet Muhammad (pbuh) or the personality of any one of his companions.
>
> The reason for this banning is that the projection of this dramatization on the screen in any explicit or implicit form

will decrease the value of this holy personality, in the feelings of Muslims even if the actor is on a sublime standard of character, piety which make him very near to the personality he acts. Since this is not the case at all, the abuse of highest Muslim personality of the Prophet and those of his companions becomes very grave.

The fatwa ended with this directive: "it is totally forbidden in Islamic point of view to produce the movie called 'Mohammad—The Messenger of God' or to show it in cinema houses. We would therefore call the Muslim people and their governments to stop any showing of this film."

It was ominous news, but not unexpected. Al-Azhar was parroting the Muslim World League's argument because the Saudis were calling the shots, political and religious. More worryingly, Akkad thought, if Egypt, the great Arab powerhouse, was caving, how much longer could Morocco resist? Not long, it turned out. The very next month, in August 1974, when Akkad had only about half the film in the can, another telegram came from Rabat ordering the filming to stop once again. This time, Akkad was summoned to Rabat. He pleaded with the king's intermediaries but was told that the leader had made up his mind. In addition to everything else, the Saudis were now threatening to bar all Moroccans for the annual hajj pilgrimage that winter as long as the counterfeit Kaaba stood in the village of Ait Bouchent. Akkad understood. No king, no matter how powerful, could afford to stand in the way of his people's duty to make the pilgrimage. Akkad returned to Ait Bouchent, assembled his cast and crew—it consisted of almost three hundred people from twenty-eight countries—and broke the news. He did not know where they would go from here, he told them, but he made them a promise: "We will finish."

Like the Nation of Islam had in its time of need, Akkad turned to the single Arab leader who stood seemingly apart from all others, immune to pressures of the region and the world—a man who only ever danced to his own tune. The Libyan ruler Muammar Gaddhafi, who had eagerly joined the oil embargo effort in 1973, was the only one still holding the line as all other Arab countries were increasing oil production. Gaddhafi reveled in making the Europeans and Americans—the colonists and neocolonists as he saw them—squirm. Libya was already supporting Akkad's film financially through its Ministry of Culture, and Akkad requested a personal audience with Gaddhafi. This was not about cash anymore—Akkad needed a lifeline.

Akkad's editing team began assembling show reels of both the Arabic and English versions of the film using the footage they had. A few weeks later, leaving behind his cast and crew on the outskirts of Marrakesh, Akkad arrived in Tripoli with the reels and a 35 mm projector. He was received at the airport by a couple of ministers and did his first screening that same day for an audience consisting of Gaddhafi's cabinet and advisors on the top floor of a drab government building that housed the Ministry of Information. The next morning, Akkad was informed by an advisor to the president that Gaddhafi was interested in watching the reels for himself. Akkad was instructed to have everything ready at 8:00 p.m. at the army headquarters.

Akkad had the film loaded and the chairs arranged in a half circle for the president and his entourage when, at five minutes past the hour, Gaddhafi, who famously drove himself around in his austere gray-green camouflage Volkswagen, arrived at the army headquarters. He shook Akkad's hand as he entered and quipped about the admission price. He invited Akkad to take a seat next to him and asked him to explain how he had ended up in this predicament. Akkad briefed him on the Saudi pressure on King Hassan of Morocco, and when he was finished, Gaddhafi asked to see what he had.

At several moments during the hour-and-a-half screening, Akkad heard Gaddhafi whisper "Allahu-Akbar," "Allah is the Greatest." In the glimmering light of the projector, Akkad kept glancing at Gaddhafi, trying to gauge his expression. During the elaborate, David Lean–inspired battle sequences shot with thousands of extras—Akkad was deeply proud of them—it looked like Gaddhafi wiped a tear from his eye. When the reel whirred to a stop, Gaddhafi ordered that the lights stay off. He asked Akkad to start at the beginning once again. This time, Gaddhafi provided commentary as the film played, telling his advisors and Akkad what he thought, elaborating on key moments and sequences, almost like a film critic.

After the second showing, Gaddhafi asked Akkad what he needed to complete the film. Akkad explained that it would be impossible to move the colossal set that he had constructed in the Moroccan desert. He would have to build something new at a new location. He would, however, need to move a lot more. One hundred horses, specially trained for the film's battle sequences, were waiting in Ait Bouchent. There were costumes for the cast and for the five thousand extras. There was the expensive and heavy equipment that went with any film crew—lighting, cranes, and cameras. There were tons of props. There were hundreds on the crew from dozens of countries who would all need visas to enter a new country. He would need extras, thousands of them. He would need a location in the desert where he could house everyone for the months of shooting that remained. He also needed money to cover this unprecedented change of venue and to cover and extend the contracts of the cast and crew of both the Arabic and English versions. In short, Akkad was asking Gaddhafi to bankroll what could become the most expensive film project in history. Close to midnight, Gaddhafi turned to his army chief and his deputy and instructed them to get it all done. The film, he declared, was too important—it must be completed. Gaddhafi rose, stepped outside, climbed behind the wheel of his VW Beetle, and drove off into the dark with a single police car leading the way.

Back in Ait Bouchent, Akkad abandoned all caution and began filming all the final sequences involving the Kaaba that he possibly could before the Moroccan wrecking crews arrived. He filmed one of the most historically significant scenes of the movie, when Muhammad's disciples conquer Mecca and methodically topple and smash all the pagan idols standing in the Kaaba—announcing the ascendance of the single, unseen Allah. The destruction of the idols marked the establishment of the first Muslim empire, and it initiated a taboo in Islamic civilization against the creation of graven images that would last for more than a millennium. The actors tore down the idols inside the fake Kaaba with raw passion and genuine aggression as Akkad captured it all on film. At night, once the last day of filming had ended, they burned them all in a huge bonfire.

The wrecking crews moved in days later. The Arab League summit was weeks away, and the Moroccans made sure that if King Faisal of Saudi Arabia or any of his representatives decided to pay a visit to Ait Bouchent, they would see no sign of a film set. Two ships from England, meanwhile, docked at the port of Gibraltar to begin the historic move. Akkad was able to salvage most of what he had in around 250 large parcels. Of the hundred trained horses, Akkad chose only sixteen special mounts, eight stars

18.

REVENGE OF ALLAH

Elijah Muhammad died on February 25, 1975. In the centuries-long history of Islam in America that began with the arrival of the earliest slave ships, this was perhaps the single most consequential death. In the four decades that Elijah led the Nation after the disappearance of Master Fard Muhammad, the Nation of Islam had grown into a national organization with hundreds of thousands of adherents. The Nation, and Elijah with it, had also become an economic and political powerhouse with an estimated worth of $80 million. "Muslim Ruler Elijah Muhammad Dies" read the banner front-page headline of the *Chicago Tribune*. The news of his death was front-page news in nearly every major newspaper in the country.

Elijah had been ill for years, battling bronchial asthma, high blood pressure, diabetes, and various other ailments. After hacking and coughing through many public appearances, he had stopped appearing in public altogether, staying mostly at the estate in Phoenix with his wife, Clara. Still, to many of his followers, the news of Elijah's death was a complete shock. They simply could not believe that the messenger had died. Many of them had long believed, as a matter of faith, that Elijah was immortal.

It was far from clear who would succeed him. Though Wallace had rejoined the Nation after Malcolm was gunned down, the relationship between father and son never actually recovered. In the previous decade, Elijah had ejected and then readmitted Wallace to the Nation several more times. Wallace was a Sunni Muslim, and no matter how much he deferred to his father, he never tried to conceal this fact. In this time, several other contenders had emerged. Within the family, one of Elijah's older sons, Nathaniel, who led the temple in Kansas City as minister, was considered by many to be a safer bet than Wallace. Herbert, the boxing promoter who managed Muhammad Ali, was named by *The Washington Post* as a possible heir to the title. Among those outside the family circle, Louis Farrakhan, the minister of Temple No. 7 in Harlem, led the pack. James Shabazz might have been in the running, but he had been murdered a few months after the Hanafi massacre. Instead, Jeremiah Shabazz, the leader of Temple No. 12 in Philadelphia—and one of the most powerful criminals in the higher ranks of the Nation, who might have masterminded the Hanafi massacre—was also reported as a potential challenger.

There was not a lot of time to decide. Elijah had spent his final two weeks in a hospital in Chicago, and during that time, the succession battle was fought feverishly behind closed doors at the Nation's headquarters. There, Wallace made his case by addressing head-on what he knew was the biggest concern about him: his traditional Islamic beliefs and close relationships with Arabs and non-Black Muslims. "Don't think any Arab is coming here to tell you anything," he told the assembly of the inner circle. "If he comes here, he will have to come by me. I don't care if he's been reading the Holy Quran since the day Arabia became sandy. He's not coming here to lead these sheep."

Elijah had died the day before the Nation's annual Saviours' Day celebration, and the organization's top brass decided that the new leader of the Nation of Islam would be announced from the stage at the convention. In front of a roaring crowd of nearly fifty thousand devotees at the International Amphitheatre in Chicago, the also-rans came to the podium one by one to deliver their blessings and praise for their newly chosen leader, Wallace Muhammad. "Allah himself," Muhammad Ali shouted into the microphone, "will visit Wallace Muhammad." The crowd erupted. Dressed in a blue Fruit of Islam uniform, Wallace was hoisted onto the shoulders of the top brass of the Nation onstage as the crowd began chanting, "Long Live Muhammad."

In the weeks that followed, tributes and accolades poured in for the deceased Black Muslim leader. The governor of Illinois, Daniel Walker, declared March 29, 1975, "Honorable Elijah Muhammad Day." The mayors of Hartford and Kansas City delighted the Nation by declaring their own celebrations. Atlanta, Oakland, Compton, Berkeley, Los Angeles, even Khaalis's native Gary, Indiana, all celebrated Muhammad on his death, while Newark dedicated an entire week to him. In Washington,

DC, the Council of the District of Columbia, the city's legislative body, responded to the news by passing a resolution recognizing him as a great Black leader. The praise stood in stark contrast to Elijah's obituary in *The Washington Post*, which referenced the largest mass murder in the District's history; the killings, the *Post* noted, were "in retaliation for letters Khaalis had written criticizing Elijah."

The news of Elijah's death came to Khaalis and the Hanafis after another long, grueling year of courtroom dysfunction and drama. The trial of Ronald Harvey, the Black Mafia kingpin who was being held at Marine Corps Base Quantico for security purposes, began in October of 1974, and it was a brief affair. The prosecution had a solid case. Once again, Amina Khaalis was the key witness. The right side of her face had weakened from the bullet fragments that were still embedded in it, and she had balance problems from ear damage. She was still obviously traumatized, suffering from panic attacks, crippling headaches, and episodes of intense anxiety and depression, and ridden with survivor's guilt from the attack that took her children. She was under enormous pressure as she relived the day of the murder in painstaking detail in front of a new jury and the watchful eye of the press. The defense, aside from a few sloppy alibis, did not present much of a case. On November 21, 1974, the jury found Harvey guilty of fourteen counts of homicide, two for each of the Hanafi victims. As the foreman read the sentence, Harvey, looking the part of a stone-cold murderer, looked on and smiled. As the jury was led out, he yawned and relaxed in his chair.

James Price, the stool pigeon who never cooed, was scheduled to go on trial in early 1975, but he did not make it to the new year. The Nation of Islam had always intended to make an example of him, and he was left exposed to the Nation's wrath in the prison system. As he awaited his Washington trial, Price was serving a sentence for a separate crime in the notorious maximum-security Holmesburg Prison in Philadelphia. On New Year's Eve, 1974, Price was found in his cell, hanging by the neck from a bedsheet. He was reportedly getting ready to appear in front of another grand jury that was looking into ties between Jeremiah Shabazz, the minister of Temple No. 12, and the Black Mafia. The gruesome autopsy report described how he was strangled with shoelaces. His testicles were smashed. His anus had been ripped open with a sharp object that was never found. Next to his body was a note that read, simply, "Revenge of

Allah." There were no witnesses, and the prison guards insisted they saw nothing. "The investigation" into the Nation of Islam's top tier "really died with Price," a federal agent told *The Philadelphia Inquirer*.

Khaalis was always deeply pained by the fact that the District of Columbia had outlawed the death penalty months before his family's massacre. Now, at least one of the assassins had met a gruesome end. More important, though, his death also meant that Amina would not have to take the stand and relive the murder over several days for a third time. Amina had given birth again that year, and Khaalis and Khadija were grandparents once again. To celebrate a new beginning, and to mark an end to a deeply painful chapter in the Hanafis' lives, Kareem Abdul-Jabbar bought a beautiful three-bedroom house five hundred yards from the Hanafi Center for $70,000. *The Washington Star* reported the sale on January 17, 1975, almost two years to the day since the murders. The Hanafis, it appeared, were finally ready to look forward, not backward.

Then, on March 20, less than a month after Elijah's death, Judge Braman wrote an extraordinary memo. John Griffin, one of the Nation's hitmen who had been convicted in the first trial along with three others, was being granted a new trial. The decision followed an apparent misidentification by Amina during the second trial for the ringleader, Ronald Harvey. Braman had previously tried to grant Griffin a new trial immediately following his first conviction, but an appeals court had overruled that decision. This time, Braman cited Amina's misidentification as new evidence. There was no way to stop another trial from taking place. The oppressive darkness that had only just started to dissipate filled the house on Sixteenth Street once again. The gears of American justice, the Hanafis felt, were chewing them up.

19.

PROGRESS REPORT

Wallace wasted no time in overhauling his father's organization. Under Elijah, the Nation of Islam was a political, economic, and social organization above all, aimed at empowering African Americans. The religious myth of the lost tribe of Shabazz was the glue that held the Nation together. As many suspected or feared, under Wallace the Nation was slowly transforming into an organization that put Islam first. Its economic and social functions designed to promote Black empowerment were now auxiliary missions.

In June 1975, four months after his Saviours' Day coronation, Wallace Muhammad held a marathon five-hour public rally in Chicago. It was his first major public appearance as the supreme leader of the Nation of Islam and was attended by an estimated twenty-five thousand people, mostly members of the Nation. Wallace framed his speech as a "progress report," and its aim was to silence the rumors of dissent within the ranks. Wallace began by boasting of the latest numbers: 39,000 new members had entered the fold since Elijah's death, he reported, bringing the estimated total attendance to 750,000 across all the Nation's mosques.

For the first time in the history of the organization, Wallace made a public disclosure of the Nation's financial holdings. He reported a stunning fortune of close to $50 million. The Nation had $6.2 million invested in farmland and another $14.5 million invested in Chicago real estate. A seafood import agreement signed with several foreign countries had cost the Nation $6.3 million but had returned a revenue of $22 million. Halfway through the year, businesses owned by the Nation had already paid out $1.3 million in payroll to one thousand employees, according to Wallace. In the past year, Wallace said, it had paid $1 million in taxes.

During the rest of his address, Wallace hinted at some monumental changes. The most significant, he announced, was the erasure of the so-called color line. The fundamental Black supremacist essence of the Nation of Islam, based on the belief that the white man was the product of a failed eugenics experiment that produced a devilish race, was formally expunged from the Nation's creed. "Although we have caught nothing but hell from the white man for 400 years, we are now evolving," Wallace announced, adding that white people were now welcome to embrace the faith and join the Nation of Islam.

Wallace knew that steering the Nation toward Sunni Islam, no matter how gently or slowly, would alienate many of his father's top aides and maybe even encourage some to defect. Still, to Wallace, that price was worth paying for everything that was to be gained. Foreign Muslim governments, including those of the Arab countries that had demonstrated their awesome power during the oil shock of 1973, were more interested than ever in supporting Muslim groups in America as a means of securing political leverage in the country. Arabs hoped that Muslim organizations in the United States could serve their interests just the way many American Jewish and Zionist groups had come to Israel's aid over the years. For its part, the American government was looking to forge its own alliances with prominent Muslim groups, as it had since the beginning of the Cold War. By shedding its Black supremacist creed, Wallace was making the Nation much more palatable to both America's political leadership and foreign Muslim governments.

Wallace also hoped to mend the awkward schism between the African American and immigrant Muslims in America, whose numbers were growing faster than ever. Finally, by moving the Nation closer to the orthodox Islam that Malcolm X had espoused toward the end of his life, Wallace hoped that some of Malcolm's Sunni Muslim followers might also reenter the fold. Wallace was trying to position his newly inherited organization at the nexus of all these various interests. Losing some support from his core African American base might be worth it if he could achieve his ultimate goal: to be recognized, at home and abroad, as the undisputed caliph for all American Muslims.

Wallace began touring the country, meeting his ministers and others at the dozens of Nation of Islam temples around the country. In line with his orthodox turn, Wallace renamed the temples "mosques" and called the ministers "imams." Speaking more frankly with his imams in private than he did in public speeches, Wallace expressed his desire for African American Muslims to take the reins of American Islam, rather than relinquish them to immigrant Muslims. Sure, they might speak Arabic and other historically Muslim languages, he told the imams, but when it came to speaking English, they were powerless. "No matter how much they know, they're only verbalizing," he said in one of these meetings. "There is no real feeling in what they say because it's not really in their heart and soul."

At the same time, he emphasized to his base how much African Americans had to gain by aligning themselves with Arabs and Muslims abroad. The *ummah*, the imagined global political community of Muslims, had a role to play in American Islam, he said. He put it most bluntly in a meeting with some imams of the Nation in an October 1975 meeting. "The world at large now is very interested in what we are doing," he said. "The same dignitaries and men of high office in business and government" who sought his father were "now seeking me." These foreign leaders, he claimed, "are more anxious now than they were before to get with us, lend us their hand, and help us with their knowledge, resources and their dollars." He dwelled on that last bit: dollars. "We have not millions but billions that we can get if we show the world that we realize what we already have in our hands."

A flurry of changes—organizational, political, and religious—followed in the months after his speech. Wallace abolished the Fruit of Islam altogether. The Nation began following the Islamic calendar in observing the holy month of Ramadan and fasting with the rest of the world's Muslims, rather than fasting at Christmas, as Elijah had prescribed. Similarly, the day of congregational prayer was changed from Sunday to Friday. Such moves were applauded by many mainstream Muslims in America, including Abdul Rauf at the Islamic Center.

Finally, and perhaps most important, Wallace changed the name of the organization from the Nation of Islam to the World Community of al-Islam in the West. While a mouthful, the new name situated Wallace's organization in a strategic geopolitical context and signaled its more global ambitions. Wallace rebranded the nation's newspaper as *Bilalian News*, named for Bilal, the freed Abyssinian slave who had loyally served the Prophet Muhammad—the same Bilal that was one of the central characters of Moustapha Akkad's upcoming film. During the 1976 election cycle, the Nation endorsed candidates for the first time in its history and hosted a formal celebration for the 1976 American Bicentennial.

The moves paid dividends. The ruler of the emirate of Sharjah came for a tour of the organization, for example, and was so pleased with what he saw that he wrote a check for $1 million on the spot. In the fall of 1976, Wallace, accompanied by Muhammad Ali, traveled to the Middle East and Turkey right after Kareem Abdul-Jabbar had traveled through the country himself on a goodwill trip. The following month, in November 1976, Anwar Sadat, the president of Egypt, made a special detour to Chicago during a state visit to meet Wallace Muhammad in person. At the meeting, Sadat announced twelve scholarships for members of Wallace's organization to study at Al-Azhar. It was a landmark gesture from Wallace's perspective. Two decades earlier, Wallace's father, Elijah, had written a letter to the former Egyptian President Nasser, seeking his attention. Now Nasser's successor had sought out Elijah's son.

20.

COMPASS

In the decade that it took Akkad to complete the *Mohammad* project, he took more than 150 flights shuttling among more than a dozen countries across four continents. He had gone toe to toe with some of the most obstinate and powerful religious figures in the world and squeezed petty bureaucrats and towering dictators for cash and resources. On set, he worked with some of the most gifted actors, stage designers, and technical hands in the film business. He had battled sandstorms and was once nearly bitten by a poisonous scorpion in the desert. He had spent years away from his wife and young children, communicating with them mostly through handwritten letters. He now had a full head of gray hair.

He had arrived in America two decades earlier with the dream of becoming a star Hollywood director. Somewhere along the way, though, the film project became something larger than his own ambition. He was convinced that America and the Western world had to be told the glorious story of Islam and its Prophet Muhammad, for whom he was named, to counter the negative stereotypes that had seeped in over the course of a millennium and a half and hardened in recent decades. In the decade following the 1967 war in the Middle East, a messianic spirit had come over him. He now saw himself as being on some kind of divinely ordained mission to spread the message of Islam in America.

Gaddhafi gave Akkad everything that he needed to complete the film—money, apartments to house his cast and crew, even soldiers from the army as extras for the film. Most important, Gaddhafi shielded Akkad from the growing fury of Saudi-backed religious puritans all over the Muslim world. They were outraged to learn that the project had been resurrected in Libya after they had left it for dead in Morocco. Gaddhafi made sure they could do nothing about it. Shooting wrapped up in Libya in 1975, and Akkad then spent a full year in London's fabled Twickenham Studios editing two films simultaneously, one in Arabic and one in English, matching them up almost perfectly frame by frame. A gossip columnist reported that "Akkad has security guards patrolling the Twickenham Studios because he wants no one to see the film until editing is complete." The prints, it was reported, were kept locked in a vault. In the final calculation, Akkad claimed to have blown through $17 million, a price tag that was second in Hollywood history only to the 1963 epic *Cleopatra*.

Akkad premiered his film in London in late July 1976. It was a smaller market, but the country had the largest immigrant population of Muslims of anywhere in Europe. The film received mixed reviews, but the numbers were encouraging, and the film was number one in the box office for the month of August. There were also hints of trouble. Four days before the release, the theater in London where the movie was premiering started receiving threatening phone calls. The Saudi Muslim World League had run an effective global campaign against the film with articles in journals and newspapers around the world denouncing the project as blasphemous and religious leaders issuing statements urging Muslims worldwide to boycott the film. Some in Britain were clearly unhappy, so Akkad decided to change the name of the film for its British release from *Mohammad: Messenger of God* to the more cryptic-sounding *The Message*.

After all this, Akkad might have thought that his troubles were finally behind him, but when he returned to Los Angeles in the fall of 1976, he found no one willing to distribute the film in America. The news of the trouble in London might have scared some off. The fact that he had bypassed Hollywood money may have rubbed people the wrong way. That Akkad was still virtually unknown as a director did not help. Then there was the same old question that many in Hollywood had considered over many years: who wants to watch a movie about the Prophet of Islam, anyway?

Akkad's lawyer introduced him to Irwin Yablans, a stocky and rambunctious small-scale independent distributor in Los Angeles. The son of a Jewish cab driver from Brooklyn, Yablans had himself started as a director of small-budget movies with uninspiring financial returns. Yablans's older brother, Frank, had enjoyed success on the business side of filmmaking, becoming the president of Paramount Studios. Seeing this, Yablans started his own distribution company called Compass International and carved out a niche in films with global appeal. Akkad's lawyer told him that Yablans was thrilled after watching a cut of the film.

When they met in person, Yablans told Akkad that he saw a lot of potential for American audiences. The character of Bilal, the Abyssinian slave, was a masterstroke, Yablans thought. Thanks to the way Akkad had edited the film, Bilal ended up bookending the story. He appeared within the first half hour of the three-hour film, being tortured for disobeying his slave master, and at the end during Muhammad's conquest of Mecca, when he clambers up the Kaaba and makes the first Islamic call to prayer in history—two of the most powerful scenes of the entire film, in Yablans's opinion. The melodic prayer call gave Yablans the chills, and he appeared ready to bet that other Americans would feel the same way. Bilal, he proposed to Akkad, belonged on the poster along with the Academy Award–winning leads, Quinn and Papas.

Yablans, like many others in Hollywood, had heard the legend of Akkad's project in the desert and the seemingly endless pile of cash fueling it. It did not take long for Yablans to piece together that there were, in fact, creditors and investors with petrodollars in the mix. During their earliest meetings, the dapper Syrian, chomping on a pipe, would interrupt their conversations to answer calls from Libya, Kuwait, and Egypt, speaking in rapid-fire Arabic. While America, and Hollywood with it, was still emerging from the economic slump triggered by the 1973 oil shock, the name of the holding company that Akkad created for the purposes of financing the film, Arab International Productions, had a certain heft to it that would have intrigued any sharp businessman. A few weeks later, Akkad and Yablans signed on the dotted line. Yablans would market and distribute the film and get 25 percent of the gains. Akkad would front the money for all costs related to marketing, distribution, and promotion, and keep the rest.

Yablans's plan for a rollout was a limited release in New York and Los Angeles at first. A film like this needed to create buzz in the media capitals before middle America could be expected to pull out its wallet at the box office. Both cities had sizable Muslim populations, both immigrant and

African American. If the film did well, a wide distribution would quickly follow. Yablans told Akkad he knew the perfect theater for the premiere. The Rivoli at 49th Street and Broadway in Manhattan was a grand, historic venue, one of the most storied movie theaters in the city. Its Greek Revival architecture and large, pointed pediment made it appear like more of a monument than a movie house. Inside was a state-of-the-art Dimension 150 curved projection screen, almost 75 feet wide and 30 feet tall. Its acoustics were legendary. It had opened in 1917 and hosted historic movie premieres ever since, including opening nights for *Oklahoma!*, *The Grapes of Wrath*, *Around the World in 80 Days*, and *The Sound of Music*. It was a few blocks north of the Criterion, where *The Ten Commandments* had opened in 1956 during the Suez Crisis.

The Rivoli, the flagship location of the United Artists theater chain, was run by their East Coast head, Salah Hassanein, an immigrant from Egypt—perhaps the only Arab immigrant in the top tiers of the film distribution business at the time. Yablans set up a meeting between Akkad and Hassanein and watched the two Arab men hit it off. The meeting was almost entirely in Arabic, and by the end they had decided on a release date of March 9, 1977.

Yablans began touring cities that might come next after New York and Los Angeles to build buzz. He arrived in Chicago in January 1977 and had a screening for the publisher of *Jet* and *Ebony* magazines. He also arranged a meeting with the Nation of Islam, now known as the World Community of al-Islam in the West. Yablans arrived at the organization's new headquarters in the old Greek Orthodox church whose purchase had been financed, just like Akkad's film, by Gaddhafi. Herbert Muhammad and a few others from Wallace's top brass were there to greet him. The members of the Nation watched the movie in silence and made no comments—the decision to like or dislike, endorse or condemn, was not theirs. Later, Wallace Muhammad had his own private screening and liked the movie so much, he offered to host the Chicago premiere himself on March 24, two weeks after the opening in New York and Los Angeles. Yablans was delighted. There was simply no more influential Muslim in America than Wallace.

At another prescreening in Los Angeles, Akkad and Yablans invited Muhammad Ali to attend. As the film ended, Ali sprang from his seat and reached over a banister to embrace Johnny Sekka, the Senegalese actor who had played the character of Bilal. "Johnny, you have made me so proud," Ali said to Sekka. "I have seen *Superfly*," he said, but "I have never seen a role with such dignity." Sekka was stunned at being embraced so warmly by the champ. He responded by meekly asking Ali for an autograph.

21

ONLY FOUR

In the end, after a lifetime of playing a hand that had been dealt crooked, after getting doors slammed in his face for speaking the truth, after trying to rob banks, after the massacre of his family, after years of watching the gears of the American justice system chew up family members, after years of insomnia and a lifetime of paranoid delusions, it was a movie poster that pushed Khaalis over the edge. He was visiting New York City in February 1977, meeting with members of some like-minded Sunni organizations, when, walking down Broadway in midtown Manhattan, Khaalis passed by the Rivoli Theatre. There, he came face-to-face with what he would understand to be a message from Allah. Between 49th and 50th Streets, a large banner hung across the marquee: "Mohammad: Messenger of God."

Khaalis walked up closer and saw the publicity poster for the film. There was remarkably little human imagery on it. The most prominent image was the unfurled white banner with the name "Mohammad" on it. In the background loomed the Kaaba, and from it emerged a large army of men in robes and turbans, swords and spears raised, mounted on camels and horses, rushing forward. At the top were these words in bold white letters: "In Four Decades Only Four . . . 'The Robe' 'The Ten Commandments' 'Ben Hur' and Now . . . For the First Time . . . The Vast, Spectacular DRAMA THAT CHANGED THE WORLD!" At the bottom, below the image of the horde around the Kaaba, were five stills from the movie. There was a battle scene showing Anthony Quinn landing a sword on the neck of an enemy; the vamp, Irene Papas, staring intensely at an African slave; another panoramic battle scene; and two photographs of the character of Bilal, one of him being tortured, the other of him mounting the Kaaba. At the bottom were the credits, including, in the largest font, "Produced and Directed by MOUSTAPHA AKKAD." The poster announced a premiere date of March 9.

Weeks earlier, the television adaptation of Alex Haley's novelized family saga *Roots* had aired on ABC, watched by more people than any other show in the history of television. It was historic for many reasons, including the fact that it provided the first broad mainstream recognition of the Islamic roots of many of the slaves brought to America. If there was ever a time to capitalize on America's curiosity about the religion, it was now. Khaalis, however, could not see it that way. He could not think of anything other than the filth that surrounded him. Times Square in New York City: was there a seedier, dirtier place than this in all of America for Muhammad's name to appear? Prostitutes on the corners, sex shows and porn palaces, the drugs, the disease, the decay. Khaalis had always hated filth. He did not like a mess. He did not like germs. He did not like it when rules were broken or when the sanctity of Allah's message was violated. His master had given him the name for a reason: the zealot in service of purity.

Khaalis had come face-to-face with the poster at a time of utter hopelessness. Five years after the massacre and exactly two years since Judge Braman had ordered the retrial of one of the Nation's hitmen, the defendant had still not been convicted or acquitted of the crime. The retrial was originally set for March 1976, but the court failed to hold it then. The District and the U.S. government, still suffering from the recession, were essentially broke. There was simply no money for another elaborate, high-security trial. Khaalis, Khadija, Aziz, and Amina herself had pleaded with the government's attorneys to use transcripts of Amina's previous testimony instead of making her appear in front of yet another jury to relive the massacre once again. The government was reluctant to allow it, fearing a jury would not be sufficiently moved without Amina's physical presence there. In the end, with some coaxing from Joe O'Brien, Amina Khaalis agreed to testify. When the trial finally got underway in the fall of 1976, though, it did not take long for her to snap. Faced with an excruciating session of cross-examination by an aggressive defense attorney, Amina walked out of the courtroom during a recess and refused to continue.

Outside, Joe O'Brien tried to convince her to return to the stand, but she and her husband, Aziz, refused and exited the courthouse, returning to the Hanafi Center.

Judge Braman could have let it go and declared another mistrial, but instead, he responded with a bench warrant for Amina. If she did not appear in court and answer the attorney's questions, the judge declared, she could be forced to do so by federal marshals. A week went by, and the Hanafis stopped answering the attorneys' calls. The prosecutors urged the judge to declare a mistrial. The prospect of armed U.S. Marshals arriving at the Hanafi house to arrest Amina Khaalis was horrifying. Would they really seize a woman who had taken five bullets to the head and tear her away from her husband and toddler children in full view of news cameras? What if the Hanafis picked up arms to defend their home? Finally, on October 12, 1976, Braman relented and declared a mistrial. A new trial date was set for June 1977. By this time, Khaalis likely knew he would not make it to another trial.

While all this was unfolding, Khaalis's most important disciple, Kareem, was slowly drifting away from him. Kareem had grown disillusioned with Khaalis, doubting his knowledge and resenting his tight grip on the entire community. Kareem's marriage with Habiba had also unraveled. The two had another child in 1976, but they almost never saw each other anymore, as Kareem rarely visited Washington, DC. While he still sustained the Hanafi enterprise with a stream of cash, Kareem's absence and distance were sapping Khaalis of any hope for the future. It was a loss made even more painful by watching Wallace and Muhammad Ali stick together, travel the world, and continue to grow their organization, whose Sunni religious beliefs were now almost identical to Khaalis's Hanafi group.

Wallace Muhammad was close to cementing his position as the undisputed leader and spokesperson of American Muslims. Even Muhammad Abdul Rauf, the imam of the Islamic Center in Washington, appeared to be signaling his acquiescence to the ascendance of Wallace. In October 1976, while Amina was melting down on the witness stand, Rauf hosted a delegation of Wallace's rebranded group at the Islamic Center in Washington. A few months later, in January 1977, Rauf published a biography of Bilal ibn Rabah, the Black Abyssinian companion of Muhammad. In the preface to the book, Rauf credited "a brother in the Nation of Islam" for inspiring him to write it. There were even rumors that the new president, Jimmy Carter, a deeply religious man himself, would issue Wallace an invitation to visit the White House.

If there were any doubts left about the ascendance of Wallace Muhammad as the supreme leader of Muslims in America, they had been completely erased in late January, when the *Chicago Tribune* reported some big news in a front-page headline: "$28-Million Woodlawn Renewal to include Big Muslim Mosque." The "$14 million to $16 million mosque to be built by the World Community of Islam," the report said, would be "the largest mosque in the Western hemisphere," built on an eleven-acre site in the neighborhood. The proposed domed structure would come with a two-hundred-foot minaret from which the Islamic call to prayer would sound. The announcement was made at Chicago's city hall in a joint press conference by Chicago Mayor Michael Bilandic and Wallace Muhammad. Wallace told reporters that the governments of Saudi Arabia and other Gulf states had pledged to support the project. A reporter asked Wallace if the mosque was being built with oil money. "Not oil money," Wallace corrected him, "holy money."

Outmaneuvered by his nemesis, spurned by American justice, rejected by his star disciple, Khaalis had wandered aimlessly for months in search of a sign. He was confident that a sign would come. He was just as sure that, somehow, someway, he would emerge as the leader of American Islam, the caliph of American Muslims. As Khaalis stared at the poster, dwelled on the images, studied the names, and pondered the date, March 9, 1977, things began to crystalize in his mind. That date was the ten-year anniversary of the death of his beloved teacher, Tasibur Rahman. The thought that Rauf was the one who had performed the funeral made Khaalis's blood boil. Instead of coming to his aid after the massacre of his family, Rauf had kicked Khaalis when he was down, calling his grasp of Islam superficial. That same Rauf now venerated Wallace, the same Wallace who had stood by his own father's side days after Malcolm's murder. Khaalis knew Wallace would have endorsed this film as well.

Khaalis's mind was racing. The general secretary of the Muslim World League had issued yet another statement warning against showing Akkad's film only weeks earlier. Al-Azhar had pulled its support from the film a long time ago. Then why were the Muslims in America allowing this show to go on? Khaalis knew he had found the sign he was looking for. He was being called on by Allah to act. He knew it was time. But how?

The Bureau of Alcohol, Tobacco and Firearms had alerted the FBI and the Justice Department months earlier about alarming and potentially illegal gun purchases leading back to a man named Abdul Aziz, who lived on Sixteenth Street in Washington, DC. One of the ATF agents was a former Washington police officer who had worked the 1973 Black Mafia murder case. He knew the Hanafis well. The ATF feared that weapons were being stockpiled at the address, and the agency wanted to obtain a warrant and raid the house. The FBI and the U.S. attorney's office balked. They had known Khaalis and the Hanafis for years. Khaalis was a strange man, no doubt, but he had never hurt anyone. Raiding the house now would jeopardize whatever chance the Department of Justice might have of convicting the last of the Black Mafia murderers. Khaalis and his family were too valuable as witnesses to lose. The ATF backed off.

Wednesday, March 2, 1977, was the date in the Islamic calendar that marked the Prophet Muhammad's 1,450th birthday. It was an important annual holiday for the Hanafis, and they celebrated as they always did. Khaalis asked Abdul Rahman, a relatively new disciple, to attend the congregational Friday prayer at the Islamic Center that week and make sure Rauf was around. In his sermon, Khaalis emphasized to his Hanafi followers that the day when they would all have to fight to the death to defend Islam would eventually come. Khaalis paid the phone bill for the Hanafi Center early—he did not want the phone line to be disconnected if he was not around. He paid a visit to the U.S. attorney's offices in the old Pension Building downtown but did not meet with anyone. He just wandered around surveying the layout. Someone stopped him and asked if he needed directions or help. "No," he replied, "I got what I want," and he walked out.

PART II

22.

HOLY LAND

The lunch hour began earlier than usual on March 9, 1977, at the headquarters of B'nai B'rith International. Many of the organization's executives were preparing to leave the eight-story structure near Scott Circle in Northwest Washington, DC, for a meeting with Yitzhak Rabin. The Israeli prime minister had been in Washington for a couple of days already on an official state visit to meet the new American president, Jimmy Carter, and was scheduled to join America's most prominent Jewish leaders for lunch at the Shoreham Hotel at noon.

B'nai B'rith was the oldest and most important Jewish organization in America—it was established in October 1843 by a dozen German Jewish immigrants who met informally in New York to discuss ways to organize and bolster the growing Jewish community in the United States. More than a century later, the organization had grown to almost half a million members, touching almost every aspect of American Jewish life. B'nai B'rith had hundreds of lodges scattered around North America, and its student organization, Hillel, had a presence on hundreds of university campuses. The B'nai B'rith Foundation provided financial assistance to hundreds of other institutions in America and abroad. Several Jewish organizations that were core parts of American Jewish life, including the Anti-Defamation League, founded in 1913, were offshoots of B'nai B'rith.

There were few American organizations that were better friends of the state of Israel than B'nai B'rith. It had donated to the Jewish National Fund, which had purchased land in Palestine for the Zionist cause in the nineteenth century. B'nai B'rith established its first lodge in Jerusalem in

1888. Even though it preceded the rise of the Zionist movement in Europe, B'nai B'rith had supported Jewish migration to the Middle East and had been a stalwart supporter of Israel since it appeared on the map. This support became increasingly visible and important during the Middle East wars of 1967 and 1973, when the organization purchased millions of dollars in Israeli bonds, more than any other organization in the world, and mobilized thousands of volunteers, particularly through its Hillel organ, to volunteer and serve in Israel.

The eight-story, L-shaped headquarters of B'nai B'rith, at the intersection of two major thoroughfares, Rhode Island Avenue and Seventeenth Street, was occupied entirely by the nearly two hundred employees of the organization. It was a custom-built structure that followed a fundraising campaign in the 1950s that yielded $1.5 million, around the same time that the Islamic Center was being constructed on Massachusetts Avenue. The building, which had served as the global headquarters of B'nai B'rith since 1957, shared the block with three other large structures. The Gramercy Inn, with its popular Devil's Fork restaurant, was next door. Across the street was the Holiday Inn Downtown. Down the block was the new headquarters of the National Rifle Association, an organization that had only recently decided to become a political lobby after being a hobbyist club for more than a century.

That spring, the building was undergoing its first major renovation at a cost of $2.5 million. A brand-new wing—one of the arms of the L-shape—had practically doubled the office space and allowed the organization to create an entire unit dedicated to serving women. Separate elevator shafts and stairwells were added at the bend of the L, to serve each wing. The first and second floors had a space dedicated to a Jewish museum and a library. Most important, the renovation allowed B'nai B'rith to turn the top floor into a large meeting space, where the organization planned to hold conferences. This conference space on the eighth floor was the only portion of the renovation yet to be completed. The employees in the building—only about half of whom were Jewish—were accustomed to seeing workers ride the elevators or march up and down the stairs and to hearing the banging and clattering from the top floor.

The leadership of B'nai B'rith knew Yitzhak Rabin, the fifty-five-year-old prime minister of Israel, well. Before leading the Jewish state, Rabin had served as the Israeli ambassador in Washington for five important years between the two major wars. He arrived in Washington when the United States was trying to design a Middle East policy that somehow balanced the expectations of Israel and its Arab neighbors. By the time Rabin ended his ambassadorial term in 1973, the United States had essentially abandoned that approach and was instead selling more military equipment to Israel than to any other country in the world. Rabin, in short, had helped make America Israel's closest ally in the world.

President Carter had been in office fewer than fifty days, but it was already clear that the Middle East would be his top foreign-policy priority, perhaps even a centerpiece of his term in office. He was a religious man who had come into office with an interest in the Holy Lands. He had also signaled that he would adopt a more restrained approach to America's heavy support for Israel. On the campaign trail, he had talked about striking a grand peace bargain in the Middle East, and the Israelis were concerned that such a push would come with pressures to concede the territories Israel had occupied and held since the 1967 war.

Still, in his public declarations, Carter had made no indication of backing away from Israel. The previous year, when B'nai B'rith held the largest national convention in its history to coincide with the American Bicentennial, both Carter and Gerald Ford, his Republican opponent in the presidential race, had made campaign stops at events hosted by the organization. The conference came shortly after the spectacular hijacking of an Air France jetliner by Palestinian guerrilla fighters. The aircraft had taken off from Tel Aviv carrying 258 passengers and was forced to land at Entebbe International Airport in Uganda. In an astounding ninety-minute surgical operation on the night of July 4, the crisis at Entebbe had ended when one hundred Israeli soldiers extracted nearly all the hostages safely. Both Carter and Ford had referenced the event in their addresses at the B'nai B'rith convention. "A free people must never capitulate to terrorism," Gerald Ford had said. Carter was a little more oblique: "We should quit being timid, and join Israel and other nations in moving to stamp out international terrorism."

Days after taking office, Carter had dispatched his newly appointed secretary of state, Cyrus Vance, on a whirlwind weeklong tour of the Middle East to gauge the prospects for a peace deal in meetings with leaders in Israel, Egypt, Jordan, Saudi Arabia, and Lebanon. Rabin was the third international leader to be welcomed by the new American president, following visits by the leaders from neighbors Mexico and Canada. Rabin's visit was the first time Carter had the chance to discuss, face-to-face, the prospect of a Middle East peace deal with any of the leaders from the region.

After the harshest winter in the history of Washington, March 9 felt like the first day of spring. The first forsythias had started to bloom, and the city expected to see the first cherry blossoms appear any day. At 9:00 a.m., just as people were arriving for work at B'nai B'rith, and while Rabin was being honored by American University at a ceremony at the Kennedy Center, Carter held a press conference, the third of his presidency, which was carried live on television and radio. In it, he dropped a foreign-policy bombshell. Among other things, he suggested that Israel would eventually have to withdraw to the boundaries that existed before 1967 and give up the land it had acquired from Egypt, Syria, and Jordan in the Six-Day War. He spent nearly the entire press conference answering questions about Rabin's visit and the conflicts in the Middle East.

Toward the end of Carter's press conference, a reporter squeezed in a question about an ongoing hostage situation in Ohio. Even by the standards of the routinely bizarre hostage takings of the 1970s, this one was remarkably absurd. A Black former marine and Vietnam War veteran had taken a couple of hostages, including a local police captain, in the town of Warrensville outside of Cleveland. He was demanding that all white people evacuate the earth, and he wanted a personal apology from the president for all the injustices whites had made Blacks in America endure since 1619. The FBI was negotiating and had relayed the hostage taker's demand to the president.

"Mr. President, I understand that you have agreed to speak on the telephone to the man in Ohio who is holding a police official hostage after he releases him. Are you concerned that this might be regarded as a precedent?"

"Yes, I am," Carter said, adding bluntly, "It is, perhaps, a dangerous precedent to establish."

The Harlem Madcaps play live at Folkets Park, Uppsala, Sweden, on August 21, 1947. Khaalis can be seen on the drums at the rear.
(Upplands Museum, Uppsala, Sweden)

Khaalis performs at Folkets Park in Uppsala on August 21, 1947.
(Still image from the film *Folkets Park och parkens folk*, 1947. Karl-Erik Forslund / Vasternorrlands Museum, Härnösand, Sweden)

The first image of Elijah Muhammad that millions of Americans saw in the 1959 multipart television news program titled *The Hate That Hate Produced*. In this image, he greets Borough of Manhattan president Hulan Jack while Malcolm X stands to his left. On the far right is Hamaas Abdul Khaalis, then known as Minister Ernest X. (*The Hate That Hate Produced* [WNTA], Mike Wallace Papers, Bentley Historical Library, University of Michigan)

Malcolm X, second from left, faces Abdul Rahman Taj, the former grand sheik of Al-Azhar, during his trip to Egypt in the fall of 1964. (Bettmann / Getty Images)

The sprawling set built by Moustapha Akkad's team in the village of Ait Bouchent, fifteen miles from Marrakesh, Morocco, was centered on a replica of the Kaaba in Mecca.

(Leonard de Raemy / Getty Images)

Akkad in Morocco on the set of *Mohammad: Messenger of God*.

(Leonard de Raemy / Getty Images)

Akkad directs Anthony Quinn in preparation for a battle scene in *Mohammad: Messenger of God*. (Trancas International Films, Inc.)

Kareem Abdul-Jabbar and Abdul Aziz lead a group of Hanafis carrying the coffin of one of the slain Hanafis during the mass funeral on January 20, 1973. (DC Public Library, Star Collection, *The Washington Post*)

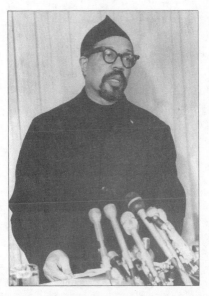

Khaalis holding a press conference a few days after the massacre at the Hanafi Center. (*The Washington Post* / Getty Images)

Muhammad Ali embracing the actor Johnny Sekka after the prescreening of Akkad's film in Los Angeles two weeks before the siege in Washington. (Bettmann / Getty Images)

ABOVE: Wallace Muhammad (third from right) and mayor of Chicago Michael Bilandic (second from left) hold a joint press conference to announce plans for a new $16 million mosque, to be the largest in the Western Hemisphere, in January 1977. (Chicago Sun-Times Media, Inc.)
BELOW: Workmen remove the sign for *Mohammad: Messenger of God* from the marquee of the Rivoli Theatre hours after the premiere screening was halted on the afternoon of March 9, 1977. (Bettmann / Getty Images)

An injured hostage is rushed away from B'nai B'rith on a gurney on March 9, 1977. The U-Haul truck in which the Hanafis drove to the building is parked in the alley behind. (Associated Press)

A group of seven hostages led by Wesley Hymes, clutching his slashed hand, is escorted away from B'nai B'rith by police officers on the afternoon of March 9, 1977. (Associated Press)

ABOVE: Mayor Walter Washington briefs the press inside the pressroom of the Mayor's Command Center late in the evening of March 9, 1977. (Associated Press / Harvey Georges)

RIGHT: City buses and police cars block traffic on Massachusetts Avenue and access to the road from Rock Creek Parkway. (Associated Press / John Duricka)

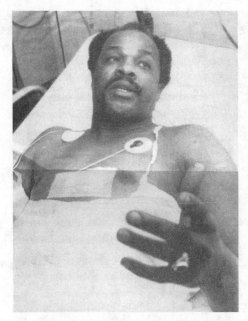

Councilman Marion Barry after surgery to remove shrapnel from the left side of his chest. (*Afro* Newspaper / Gado / Getty Images)

A Washington Police Department sniper aims the barrel of his rifle across Pennsylvania Avenue at the District Building shortly after two Hanafi gunmen took hostages on the fifth floor on March 9, 1977. (Associated Press)

Khaalis is escorted to the entrance of the Hanafi Center by a plainclothes police officer after freeing the hostages early in the morning of March 11. (Bettmann / Getty Images)

Police officers survey the damage on the fifth floor of the District Building after the siege. The blood smeared on the floor was from injured hostages being dragged to safety in the early hours of the attack. (Bettmann / Getty Images)

Hostages are reunited with loved ones at the Foundry Methodist Church in the early-morning hours of March 11, 1977. (Associated Press)

From left to right, ambassadors Ashraf Ghorbal of Egypt, Sahabzada Yaqub Khan of Pakistan, and Ardeshir Zahedi of Iran speak to reporters after the release of the hostages.

(Bettmann / Getty Images)

Muhammad Abdul Rauf at the Islamic Center hours after his release, seated in the chair to which he was tied for nearly the entirety of the siege. (DC Public Library, Star Collection, *The Washington Post*)

Bernard Simon, the director of public relations at B'nai B'rith, with news reporters on the eighth floor of the organization's headquarters, where the hostages spent most of their two days in captivity. (Associated Press / Charles Tasnadi)

Khaalis, pipe in mouth, gestures defiantly at the press gathered outside the Hanafi Center on his way to surrender his passport.
(Associated Press / Charles Bennett)

Khadija Khaalis, flanked by Abdul Aziz (left) and Abdul Qawee outside the Hanafi Center, reads from a prepared statement warning the Jewish Defense League of grave consequences for their planned protest rally a week after the siege. (Bettmann / Getty Images)

Meir Kahane (in the collared shirt), the head of the Jewish Defense League, leading demonstrators outside the Hanafi Center. The Ohev Shalom orthodox synagogue is to the right of the Hanafi Center. (Associated Press / Charles Tasnadi)

Maurice Cullinane, with Sahabzada Yaqub Khan's wife, Begum Yaqub, and Attorney General Griffin Bell (far right), at a party hosted by Ardeshir Zahedi (center) at the Iranian Embassy in Washington, DC, to celebrate the end of the siege.
(DC Public Library, Star Collection, *The Washington Post*)

Captain Joseph O'Brien and Khaalis converse on the grounds of the Hanafi Center with the flags of the United States and Pakistan flying in the background, along with a flag bearing the seven-pointed star of the Hanafi organization. (Associated Press / Charles Bennett)

Captain Joseph O'Brien leads, from left, Abdul Aziz, Khaalis, Amina, and Khadija to the Superior Court of the District of Columbia a few hours before Khaalis was jailed on March 31, 1977. (Associated Press / Barry Thumma)

Captain Joseph O'Brien locks hands with Amina Khaalis at the Hanafi
Center after escorting her and other Hanafis to their home following
Khaalis's arrest on March 31, 1977. (Associated Press / Charles Bennett)

Khaalis, appearing live via satellite connection from the Butner
Federal Prison in North Carolina, during a news program
aired on ABC in January 1983. It was his last national television
appearance. (Still from a video recording of *Viewpoint: Terrorism and the
Media*, originally aired January 18, 1983, preserved at the Vanderbilt Television
News Archive, Vanderbilt University, Nashville, Tennessee)

23.

GUNS OUT

As the president was speaking to reporters that morning at the White House, Abdul Latif, one of Khaalis's most trusted deputies, was in Wheaton, Maryland, picking up a U-Haul truck from a Texaco gas station on Khaalis's instructions. Abdul Latif had been by Khaalis's side when the Hanafis took over the Black Arts Building in Harlem in 1965, and Latif had done years in federal prison for the botched bank robbery in Manhattan more than a decade ago. He was still as loyal as ever to Khaalis. When Khaalis issued instructions, Latif, like all the other Hanafis, knew not to ask questions. He put down a $100 deposit, signed the rental agreement, and drove the twenty-four-foot truck straight to the Hanafi Center on Sixteenth Street, backing it into the driveway at the rear of the house around 10:00 a.m.

As usual, there were a handful of Hanafi men at the center, starting the morning's routine, and Khaalis instructed them to start loading the U-Haul with what was in the garage. The door opened to reveal dozens of firearms piled inside—shotguns, high-powered rifles, revolvers, semi-automatic handguns. In addition to nearly nine thousand rounds of live ammunition, there were also more than forty knives, machetes, and swords, as well as an assortment of other weapons like garrotes, throwing stars, and punji sticks. There were dozens of clubs and hatchets, as well as a crossbow and arrows. There were also gas masks and large canisters of gasoline. Without question, the Hanafis began hauling the arsenal into the U-Haul. As other Hanafi men arrived at the center, they too helped.

A little before eleven o'clock, the U-Haul pulled out of the driveway. Latif was at the wheel, and with him were four others: Abdul Salaam, another veteran Hanafi from New York, and Abdul Adam and Abdul

Shaheed, both in their early twenties and from Cleveland. Finally, there was the youngest, Abdul Hamid, a former cadet at the army prep school whom Khaalis had adopted after finding him in a foster home in 1971. Khaalis had discreetly slipped him a handgun and instructed him to use it if any of the Hanafi men threatened to resist or derail the operation. He was comfortable using firearms thanks to his cadet training—not all the Hanafi men were. Right behind the U-Haul, in a brown 1973 Ford Barwood company cab, Khaalis was being driven by the twenty-three-year-old Abdul Razzaq. Shortly after 11:00 a.m., the vehicles turned onto Rhode Island Avenue. The U-Haul bounced over the curb and pulled into the narrow alley between the eastern side of B'nai B'rith and the Gramercy Inn. The cab jerked to a stop yards away from the building entrance.

Khaalis, wearing a long trench coat, stepped out the passenger door of the car. He marched inside, a few of the Hanafis behind him. They walked purposefully through the entrance at the nook of the L-shaped building. The lobby was manned by a lone uniformed guard with a reputation for being unfriendly and uninterested; employees in the building called him "Stoneface." He did not bother to glance up at the intruders. The Hanafis marched past him and approached the elevators. Khaalis pressed the button pointing up. Just as the doors opened with a ding, he pulled out a long handgun from under his jacket, swung around, and in one swift motion placed it inches away from the guard's nose.

"Get the guns out!" Khaalis commanded his men.

The Hanafis began unloading the U-Haul. They brought in large duffel bags, wooden boxes, and metal containers stuffed with weapons and loaded them onto the elevator that had its doors jammed open. To those on the outside, they would have looked no different from the construction workers who had been frequenting the building for months. Inside was another story. The Hanafis, their guns and knives out, assaulted anyone who had the misfortune of passing through the lobby at that moment. They pistol-whipped the guard until his face bled and dragged him, along with many others, into the museum space in the back. They tied everyone up. Several other B'nai B'rith workers—and even a few people who happened to be walking past the building at the time—received similar treatment.

With the lobby secured, Khaalis moved up a flight of stairs to camp out on the second floor while the rest of the Hanafis split up into two groups. Each group began methodically working its way up the two stairwells serving each of the wings of the building. On the second floor, in the central services room, Wesley Hymes, the supervisor of printing and graphics, had not heard a thing going on outside. The thirty-one-year-old was one of several African Americans who worked in the building and had been a B'nai B'rith employee for twelve years, steadily moving through the ranks. Standing over a light table, with all the printing presses roaring, he did not hear Abdul Adam walk up behind him until the gunman yelled out, "All right, motherfucker, let's move." Adam began shoving Hymes out the door. In the hallway, Hymes hesitated. "Motherfucker, you can't hear too well, can you?" the gunman shouted as he shoved him to the ground and drew from his belt a foot-long knife, raised it high above his head, and slashed it downward. Hymes instinctively raised his arm to block the blade, and the machete slashed his left hand in half.

His thumb dangling from his palm, Hymes made a run for it. He felt the two shots fired from behind land in his arm as he scurried down the hallway and scampered into an open office, wincing in pain. It bought him only a few seconds. Adam, this time accompanied by another Hanafi, entered the room and led Hymes back into the corridor. When Hymes turned the corner to the landing, he was shocked by what he saw: dozens of people were piled on top of each other facedown. He recognized some of his coworkers, who examined his maimed hand and bullet wounds in horror. Hymes was instructed to lie down on top of the pile, and this time he followed the commands. Blood began to pool on the floor. Before too long, he felt the body of a woman climb on top of him. She was whimpering.

Sidney Closter, the fifty-nine-year-old national director of B'nai B'rith, was on the sixth floor getting impatient with the elevator. His conference with a colleague had ended a little after 11:00 a.m., and he was trying to return to his office on the second floor, but the elevator appeared to be stuck. Finally, he gave up and started walking down the stairs. He was on the fifth-floor landing when he was suddenly confronted with the barrel of a gun pointed at his nose. "Freeze," he heard, but his instinct was to flee. He raced down the fifth-floor hallway, desperately looking for an open door. The gunman, in pursuit, fired three shots, but they all missed. Winded, Closter ducked into an empty office and locked the door behind him. He scanned the room for a phone to get word out. Before he could dial a number, he heard a voice on the other side of the door, which he recognized. "Come out, Sid," Albert Elkes, B'nai B'rith's director of membership, said in a deflated voice. "It's no use." Closter knew that Elkes's life depended on his cooperating, so he opened the door and surrendered himself to the gunman.

Alton Kirkland, an African American utility worker, had watched the scene of Closter's surrender from the stairwell on the fifth floor. Minutes earlier, Kirkland had been busy cleaning out a closet on the seventh floor, where the offices for all the top executives were. He noticed some of the secretaries huddled together, speaking in hushed and worried tones about the flurry of calls from the lower floors reporting invaders in the building. Kirkland had volunteered to go see what the commotion was about—he suspected that someone might just be playing games. He was still in the stairwell when he heard three gunshots from below. Then he saw the gunman. Before he could duck back into the stairwell to warn the secretaries, he was spotted. "Hold it," the Hanafi yelled at him. Kirkland bounded up the stairs.

When he returned to the seventh floor, more than a dozen people were already huddled in the office of Yale Goldberg, the director of administration. They were mostly secretaries and assistants, but Kirkland also recognized a few executives. Kirkland locked the door behind him, and they all sat in complete silence listening to their hearts beating. The stillness was occasionally punctured by distant sounds of banging, crashing, and yelling. Then, after almost fifteen minutes, they heard heavy footsteps headed in their direction—it sounded like more than one person was on the floor. The footsteps stopped right outside the door. A moment passed, and a loud thud against the locked door made everyone jump. "Open up in there, we got the building," a man shouted angrily. No one moved a muscle. "Open up or I'm going to kick it down." Another pause. Then the door swung in with a loud crash. Latif stood over the cowering group. "Looks like we found our rabbit!" he said, holding a long rifle in his hand, looking right at Kirkland. "Why didn't you open the door, motherfucker?"

Hands raised in the air, they shuffled out to the hallway and lay facedown on the floor as instructed. Abdul Adam, his bloodstained machete dangling from his belt, approached Kirkland and ordered him to his feet. At gunpoint, Kirkland went from door to door, kicking in each one to look for others who might be hiding. Many of the executives had already left the building for lunch with Rabin, and all the other rooms on the seventh floor turned out to be empty. Adam was frustrated. "You black motherfucker, working for *bwana*," he spat at Kirkland, calling him a slave to his Jewish master.

In a flash, the Hanafi plunged a dagger into Kirkland's left thigh. Kirkland doubled over to clutch it and felt the same dagger pierce the muscles in his back. The blade cut through his spleen, stomach, and liver. The janitor crumpled, wincing and twisting on the ground, as Adam kicked him all over his body. Adam drew out his handgun and pointed it straight at Kirkland's head. It was time to die, he announced. The other captives on the floor, under Latif's watch, screamed and pleaded for Adam to stop. Then Latif lurched at Adam's gun and turned the barrel away. Latif was second only to Khaalis, so Adam knew he was in charge. "Let's take them down," Latif ordered. The hostages arrived at the fifth-floor landing, where they saw a pile of dozens of people lying facedown on top of each other, just like the one on the second floor. The blue carpet soaked up the blood, sweat, and urine.

On the second floor, the pile had grown considerably. Khaalis himself was starting to cut loose on the hostages. When Samuel Fishman, a rabbi and employee of the Hillel organization, was brought down at gunpoint by Razzaq, Khaalis received him by ramming the butt of his gun right into Fishman's face. Fishman's glasses were smashed, and blood ran down his face, obscuring his vision. Then, in the far distance, Khaalis heard the unmistakable sound of approaching sirens. Soon, they heard squad cars screeching to a halt on the street below. Khaalis was confident. He knew the Washington police well. More important, he knew the Hanafis were ready to fight to the death.

24.

GOLDEN VOICE

Robert Rabe, a deputy chief in the Washington Metropolitan Police Department, was at the police headquarters at the Municipal Building on Judiciary Square in downtown Washington, a couple of miles southeast of B'nai B'rith, when he first heard of the trouble. His Motorola Pageboy had buzzed at around 11:20 a.m. with an officer describing a barricade situation in an office building near Scott Circle. The officers on the scene had requested backup and an ambulance. A gunman, they soon reported, was holding hostages inside. Minutes later, when the units on the scene came under fire in the stairwell from the second-floor landing, the requests suddenly became more urgent. They needed the Special Operations Division on the scene right away.

Rabe led the Washington police SOD and was responsible for responding to all kinds of complex situations—crowd control for protests, celebrations, riots—anything that required a large-scale police operation. The forty-nine-year-old had been on the capital's police force for more than twenty-five years. He joined months before his colleague and friend Joe O'Brien did, at the rank of corporal, and had steadily worked his way up to deputy chief. Like O'Brien and many others in the department, Rabe was a military vet. He had served in the navy for a couple of years after the end of the Second World War, and he looked like it. He was stocky, with short-buzzed hair. He spoke in a gravelly voice, with the thick accent of his native New York.

While O'Brien worked in homicide tackling unprecedented levels of murder and violent crime in the capital, Rabe's tenure in the SOD was no less exciting. The capital experienced historic upheaval in those years. The civil rights era demonstrations led to more violent Vietnam War protests in the late 1960s. The riots that followed the assassination of Martin Luther King Jr. were the worst in the history of the capital. More recently, Rabe was the point man for the capital's elaborate Bicentennial celebration in 1976, and for President Carter's inauguration that followed. Despite his gruff demeanor, Rabe's colleagues called him Golden Voice. He had a remarkable talent for calmly negotiating with erratic hostage takers.

Rabe had observed, up close and perhaps better than any single police officer in all of America, the construction of the country's anti-terrorism infrastructure over the previous five years. America's anti-terrorism push began in earnest following the attack by the Palestinian guerrilla group Black September at the 1972 Munich Olympics. The episode exposed weaknesses in the security apparatuses of countries all over Western Europe and in the United States. President Richard Nixon was personally shaken by what he saw and heard. Days after the attack, he asked his national security advisor, Henry Kissinger, "to have contingency plans for hijacking, for kidnapping, for all sorts of things that can happen around here."

The result was the creation of a cabinet-level Committee to Combat Terrorism, the first formal anti-terrorism body in the United States. The committee met for the first and only time weeks after the Munich incident, in October 1972, and created a working group to "devise procedures for reacting swiftly and effectively to acts of terrorism and devise measures to prevent such acts." Rabe was part of that working group. It had met more than one hundred times over five years. They were mostly mid- to high-level bureaucrats and law-enforcement officials from around the country, and they discussed and studied terrorism as a phenomenon, sketching out increasingly complex hypothetical scenarios and drafting responses. At times, Rabe would be the only cop in a room full of diplomats, spies, and military officials.

The 1970s saw a huge spike in political groups using violence to further their goals. During one eighteen-month period in 1971 and 1972, there were around two thousand bombings in America. Most of them were carried out by left-wing groups, Puerto Rican nationalists, and smaller groups like the Symbionese Liberation Army, who wreaked havoc in California. The FBI was the frontline agency for tackling these groups, but the bureau itself came under the microscope after the congressional Church Committee report published in 1975 exposed the grave abuses the bureau had perpetrated under Hoover's leadership.

The previous summer, in May 1976, the working group convinced Kissinger—now serving as secretary of state—to convene a conference of high-ranking officials to discuss "the current, increased danger of major terrorist attacks in the United States requiring urgent preventative and preparatory action." The working group was growing increasingly concerned about something it termed "intermediate terrorism," a scale that was somewhere between events of mass destruction like major bombings and the kidnapping or murder of individual Americans abroad, both of which had been occurring with alarming frequency. There was no federal legislation criminalizing terrorism, and most perpetrators were charged under other federal and local criminal statutes. It was, in other words, a warning of the possibility of a "Munich" occurring in America.

The conventional thinking in Washington at the time was that terrorism was a foreign phenomenon that would enter the United States from the outside. "Counterterrorism," as much as it had developed, was considered the domain of the State Department. It tightened rules around foreign visitors and visa-free transit and entry into the country and made screenings by the FBI, the CIA, as well as the Immigration and Naturalization Service, the norm. "Operation Boulder" tried to screen passengers for their potential connections to foreign terrorists or terrorist sympathizers. The United States also introduced a five-day waiting period for Arab nationals seeking visas. President Ford, who was sworn in after Nixon resigned, increased the CIA's mandate to keep track of foreign militant groups, especially in the Middle East and Latin America.

Meanwhile, the Law Enforcement Assistance Administration, another federal body attached to the Department of Justice, had only a week earlier released a mammoth seven-hundred-page report, "Disorders and Terrorism: Report of the Task Force on Disorders and Terrorism." The largest study of terrorism in America's history had cost upward of $250,000 to produce. The former chief of Washington police, Jerry Wilson, was one of the lead authors. In it, the law-enforcement agencies pressed for more aggressive policing.

As a result of this patchwork of disjointed bureaucratic efforts, the work of fighting terrorism mostly fell on local police departments. Each department had its own way of dealing with events that might or might not be classified as terrorism. The LAPD had a reputation for shooting itself out of situations. The NYPD was known for a more measured approach, mixing the threat of violence with offers to negotiate. Rabe, meanwhile, was a talker, and this was consistent with the Washington police department's general reputation at the time as a progressive department, especially for a force in a large city with a major violent crime and drug problem. Months earlier, for example, Rabe had dealt with a hostage situation in the Georgetown neighborhood, where three men took five hostages at a men's clothing store. Rabe had initially conducted negotiations from the police headquarters, but then moved to a store across the street. Even when one of his SOD officers was shot and rushed to the hospital, Rabe held back and kept talking to the hostage takers until they surrendered.

After sending the SOD to B'nai B'rith, Rabe decided to visit the scene himself. When he arrived in his cruiser around noon, he pulled into the Holiday Inn across the street. One of his sergeants, who could see through the windows, reported seeing fifteen to twenty hostages being led in single file up the stairs. The officer thought he saw one of the gunmen carrying an M1 carbine rifle. "I see a subject," another cop cut in on the radio. "He's got his arm around a female's throat."

Outside, the scene appeared to be a major operation. A police helicopter was already in the air; the cops had set up a perimeter and were diverting traffic on either side. There were several injured people being treated in an ambulance outside, including "Stoneface," whose security-guard uniform was soaked in blood. A fire truck was on standby. A local TV news camera crew was already on the scene, negotiating for space with the police. A K9 unit was idling by the entrance to the building. A lieutenant explained that officers had come under fire from the second-floor landing in the stairwell and that the shooter had appeared particularly bothered by the dogs. Rabe studied the U-Haul parked in the alleyway. The pavement was littered with weapons and ammunition carelessly left behind by the Hanafis. There were also two five-gallon tanks full of gasoline left in the truck. If they had left this much lying around on the sidewalk, how much had they taken in with them?

Rabe stepped inside B'nai B'rith and carefully peered into the stairwell up to the second floor. It was still. He shouted up, introducing himself as a deputy chief in the Washington police. Khaalis hollered a demand in response: if the movie that was showing at the Rivoli Theatre in New York was not pulled before its two o'clock showing, Khaalis would start "cutting some heads off and throw them down the stairs."

What movie?

"Mohammad: Messenger of God."

Who are you?

"Khalifa Hamaas Abdul Khaalis."

Rabe had never met Khaalis, but like so many in the department, he recognized the name instantly. He knew all about the Hanafis and the massacre on Sixteenth Street. They had all seen the family walk in and out of the superior court next door to the police headquarters for four years now. Rabe had a feeling that he would be talking with Khaalis for a while. The first step in a good working relationship, he believed, was a proper introduction. The two men hollered up and down the stairs for a few more minutes. They decided on what titles they would use to address each other: Rabe would call Khaalis "Khalifa." Khaalis would address Rabe as "Chief Rabe."

Khaalis yelled out a phone number and instructed Rabe to call it. It was the phone number for the Hanafi Center on Sixteenth Street. Khaalis explained that he would be calling to check on his family shortly. If there was anything wrong, or if the family had in any way been harmed, he warned, he would begin tossing down severed heads of the Jews he held hostage. Rabe told Khaalis that he would get right to it. He stepped back outside. This no longer felt like a standard SOD job. His "golden voice" would get him only so far. He needed help. A call went out on the police radio shortly after that: "Any unit having knowledge of Captain O'Brien's location? Any unit on the scene if you see Captain O'Brien, they want him inside right away."

25.

ANTI-DEFAMATION

The fifty or so hostages on the second floor were piled up high. The air was getting heavy with the smell of all kinds of bodily excretions, and it was starting to drive Khaalis mad. He hated filth, and he was suddenly engulfed in it. Up on the fifth-floor landing, it was even worse. The carpet was soaking up everything, and the stench was getting unbearable. The Hanafi gunmen on the fifth floor started quizzing the hostages about a larger space in the building. One of the hostages suggested the museum on the first floor. That was a no-go—too exposed, the Hanafis said. One of the women, Besse Ziritsky, an editorial assistant at the *National Jewish Monthly*, suggested the new conference hall under construction on the eighth floor. It was meant for large gatherings, but no one seemed entirely sure what state it was in. One of the Hanafis led Ziritsky up the stairs at gunpoint to see for himself. He returned several minutes later, excited, and passed the message down to Khaalis on the second floor: they had found the spot to hold all the hostages together.

The migration up the stairs began with the fifth floor. The women were led up first, in groups of ten, stalked by one gunman. After the women were transported, the men were taken up in groups of four. Bernard Simon, B'nai B'rith's public relations director, carried Alton Kirkland, the badly injured janitor, up the stairs at the end since Kirkland could no longer walk on his own. All this commotion put the Hanafis on edge, and they turned the humiliation, violence, and terror up a notch. Mimi Feldman, a secretary in her fifties, was spotted by one of the Hanafis as she tried to remove the Star of David pendant from around her neck before marching up. She had not removed the necklace once in eighteen years. "Filthy Jew bitch," the gunman spat out. Betty Neal, another secretary, was kicked in the face by a Hanafi as she stooped to pick up the pair of glasses she had dropped on the floor. David Brody, the local representative of the Anti-Defamation League, was hit on the back of the head with the butt of a rifle. His secretary, Rose Friedman, was shoved onto the floor.

After the fifth-floor landing had been cleared, the hostages on the second floor prepared for their own march. Before they began, though, Khaalis summoned Sidney Clearfield, an executive in the B'nai B'rith Youth Organization. When Clearfield was close enough, Khaalis suddenly punched him in the stomach, and then again as he doubled over. Khaalis told Clearfield he did not like the way that he had been looking at him. Khaalis wondered if he should cut off Clearfield's "prick," stuff it in his mouth, and then toss his severed head down the stairs. After this demonstration, the caravan of hostages began moving in the same way to the top floor, women in groups of ten, men in groups of four.

As the hostages streamed past Khaalis, he picked out a few specific ones, pulling them aside and ordering them to stay back with him on the second floor. In the end, he was left with a group of seven. There were five women, all of whom he confirmed were not Jewish. Then there was the badly wounded print operator Wesley Hymes, who was beginning to drift in and out of consciousness, losing blood from his bullet wounds and his badly mangled left hand. Finally, Brian Golliday, another one of the hostages who had been kicked and badly beaten by the Hanafi gunmen, appeared in need of medical attention.

Four years ago, Khaalis began sermonizing to the petrified group, seven members of his family were executed in their home. He knew that Zionists were behind the plot to wipe out his family. Khaalis was now releasing the group of seven because he had promised Allah he would spare seven innocent lives if Allah would grant him success in his jihad. He went down the line asking each hostage to thank Allah for granting them their freedom. They all thanked Allah. Khaalis then directed them to the open elevator door. He pressed the button for the first floor. As soon as the elevator door closed, he began marching up the stairs himself. It was noon.

The hostages trickled into the eighth-floor conference space, which was known to the employees as the Board of Governors Room. The size of a large hotel swimming pool, it began filling up quickly. As the last group of hostages settled on the floor, Latif took charge. He directed everybody's attention to the firearm that he held, pointed at the ceiling, up near his shoulder. "This is my 357 Magnum," he said. "I don't want to use it so do as you're told." Latif instructed all the hostages to lie down on the cement floor, facedown, and form straight lines by touching the heels of the person in front. It was time for an official head count. The gunmen lined up against the walls all around them and began counting off. Repeatedly, they tried to get an accurate number but lost count along the way. Paul Green, an assistant director in the organization, did not mind the delay. The bones in his face and nose had been smashed to pieces when he was hit in the face with a rifle butt. The cold cement floor offered the first relief for his pain. Finally, after several attempts, the count was completed successfully: 128.

There was a lot of work to be done. The gunmen began assigning specific tasks to groups of men who had escaped pummeling, which included Hank Siegel, a public relations executive in his mid-fifties. A gunman handed him a can of beige-brown paint and told him to start painting over the windows. Another group of younger hostages was told to start moving bookshelves from the offices in the adjacent wing and placing them flush against the windows. Another group began hurling all debris they could find—broken furniture, empty paint cans, folding ladders—down the stairs to completely block access to the floor. When the stairwells were fully barricaded, a couple of Hanafis emptied out the cans of paint thinner and the gasoline they had brought along all over the clutter. They were now a matchstick away from a hellish inferno.

When all the windows had been covered and painted over, the male hostages were told to tie up each other's hands and legs. They used neckties to tie their colleagues' hands behind their backs. Those who did not have neckties were tied up in vinyl-covered electric or phone wire that was pulled from around the room. Alton Kirkland, the janitor with stab wounds, was in no shape to be tied up. His back and leg were both stiff, and he was moaning in pain. Sandi Rosen, one of the executive secretaries who had witnessed the assault on Kirkland on the seventh floor, was cradling his head and mustered the courage to speak up. "He's starting to convulse," she said, pleading for the Hanafis to let him go. Latif considered the situation. He did not want the first hostage to die on his watch. He had a few of the hostages load Kirkland into the elevator and sent him down. "All right now. Just relax. This is going to be your home for a while," Latif said to the others as Kirkland descended.

Shortly after one o'clock, the half dozen gunmen in the room suddenly sprang into action and began yelling at the hostages to sit up. "Get up! Get up and listen!" They started kicking and shaking hostages. Even those suffering bad injuries groaned and grunted into position. The gunmen instructed the hostages to open up a lane stretching down the middle of the conference room. The women huddled to the northern side of the floor and the men to the southern side, leaving, between them, a six-foot-wide aisle. The women with skirts were ordered to cover up their legs and given pieces of vinyl, rugs, jackets, newspapers—whatever was available—for this purpose.

Khaalis walked into the space for the first time. He had bulked up during the years in Washington and now cut an imposing figure at more than two hundred pounds. It was obvious to the hostages that he was the oldest in the group, and it was more than apparent that he was the man in charge. He had changed his clothes. He wore all black now, and instead of a cap, he was wearing a large, imposing turban. He wore dark round spectacles, and a scimitar hung from his belt. He looked like an old Arabian warrior—almost like Anthony Quinn's character, Hamza. Khaalis also had some loose electric wiring visible on his clothes, almost as if he had rigged explosives to his body.

"I am Khalifa Hamaas Abdul Khaalis," he began. "There are no innocent victims in holy war." Over the next twenty minutes or so, as he paced back and forth down the aisle in the middle of the room, he delivered a meandering speech that vacillated between simmering rage and explosive fury. Many of you will die, he explained to the hostages, heads will be smashed, and brains will be blown out. Some heads would be removed from their torsos and tossed out the windows, if necessary. "If you have any sense," he said, "you will pray to your God and be prepared to die."

They were all here because they were "Yehudi," he said, using the Arabic for Jew. "I do not like the Yehudi," he told them. "I do not hate them, either—I do not hate anybody," he said. "Skin color, eye or hair color—none of this matters to me," he corrected himself, "but I do not like the Yehudi." He told the hostages how he had let seven people go free downstairs. They could have been Indian, Italian, Irish, Peruvian, Khaalis said, he did not know. What he did know was that none of them was Jewish.

The Zionists, it was obvious, were the target of Khaalis's operation. They used their "shadow houses" to show Hollywood movies to spread lies, he said. The biggest lie of all, he said, was the Holocaust. Hitler did not kill six Jews, let alone six million. The Zionists ran the CIA to spread chaos all around the world. They conspired with the South African government to kill Black African babies. The *Yehudi* domination of the world, Khaalis informed the hostages, was finally ending. Arabs had all the oil in the world—more precious than gold or diamonds—and they would learn to wield that power soon. Israel, on the other hand, could export only orange juice.

Then, after all that, Khaalis turned to his demands. There was a Hollywood film about Muhammad showing in filth-ridden Times Square, he explained. It was nothing more than a Zionist scheme to defame Islam and insult Muslims and their beloved Prophet. He wanted the film reels removed from the country. The hostages' lives, they would have realized, were in the hands of a couple of film distributors and movie-theater owners. Secondly, Khaalis told them, he needed justice. The men who had murdered his family would have to be delivered to Khaalis here at B'nai B'rith. American justice had failed him. Here in this room, Khaalis would finally carry out Allah's justice. Then, and only then, the hostages would be free to go.

As a final flourish, Khaalis drew a gun from his belt and placed it right against the skull of one of the hostages close to him. Everyone stiffened. "Do you think I am afraid to kill for my faith and die for it?" he shouted. No one answered. A few began weeping. Khaalis replaced the gun in his belt. He was toying with his hostages now. The gun, he explained, was not his preferred choice. "I am fifty-four years old," he said, "but I am strong." He pulled out the scimitar this time and explained that he was capable of cutting off ten heads in succession without trouble. "It will be a clean death," he said. "You won't feel a thing."

His Hanafi accomplices, all six of them, were ready and eager to kill and die for Allah, he explained. Khaalis told all the women to cover their knees and sit modestly. He and all his men were clean family men, he reassured them. They had beautiful Muslim wives at home, as many as they wanted. They were not interested in the women. However, if needed, "we will kill the womenfolk too." The men, on the other hand, should expect no comfort. The sequence of decapitations would begin if his demands were not met. The heads, he explained, would be tossed out the window to show that he was serious.

Finally, he turned to more mundane details that were, however, deeply consequential to the lives of the people who were now his hostages. There were two bathrooms on the floor, he explained. One of them was for the Hanafis only. The 128 hostages would share the other one. The men would have to sit down to urinate because this was the proper and clean way to use the toilet, avoiding splashing. The door to the bathroom would never be closed. The women would be granted privacy for a few moments, but the men would have to conduct their business while being watched by a gunman. The hostages who had already "disgraced" themselves, Khaalis said, would be given some extra pairs of pants or overalls.

One of the older hostages in the group was handed a mop and a bucket. He was the janitor, responsible for cleaning the toilets after every visit. It would have been a strangely comforting task. Anyone with a job, after all, was less likely to be decapitated first. Finally, Khaalis scanned the room for one more volunteer. His eyes settled on a blond woman with blue eyes. She looked to be in her fifties and was wounded from a kick to the face. "What's your name?" he quizzed her. She introduced herself as Betty Neal. Khaalis considered the name for a moment. "You're not a Jew, are you?" Neal told him that she was not. She explained to Khaalis that she had been a secretary at B'nai B'rith for four years. "Then come with me. I don't want these Jew bastards answering my telephone."

Neal rose to her feet and silently followed Khaalis out of the space into the other wing. Together, they retreated into the office of the Anti-Defamation League. There were two phones in the room. Neal told Khaalis she knew exactly how to operate the lines. As soon as she sat down at the table, Khaalis told her to write down two phone numbers. One was for his family at the Hanafi Center, he explained, and the other was for the Islamic Center of Washington on Massachusetts Avenue. He told her to call the Islamic Center first.

26.

EGYPTIAN MISSION

Three Hanafi gunmen timed their arrival at the Islamic Center of Washington, DC, to coincide with the Zuhr prayer, held shortly after noon. Since becoming Muslim a few years earlier, Abdul Rahman, Abdul Rahim, and Abdul Qawee had occasionally attended Friday prayers at the Islamic Center, joining the congregants lined up behind the imam, Muhammad Abdul Rauf. Rahman, the eldest, had attended the Friday prayer at the mosque days earlier. Rahim had also attended classes at the center. Between them, they knew the layout of the complex well. More important, they knew that the five scheduled communal prayers were the only times when the Islamic Center's staff would be separated. The men would mostly retreat into the mosque area, and the women, exempt from praying communally, would staff the office and library near the entrance. Most important, the communal prayers occurred at times of the day when it was almost certain that Rauf would be present.

These three Hanafis were brothers, three of nine children born to parents who lived in the historically Black Anacostia neighborhood of Washington, DC. It was the most depressed, crime-ridden corner of a high-crime city, only five miles away but a world apart from the Islamic Center on glamorous Embassy Row. Rahman was nearing forty, while Qawee, the youngest, was only twenty-two. Rahim, who fell in the middle, was the only one who had left Washington, DC, for any serious amount of time, when he attended Goddard College in Vermont. It was there, while earning his degree in journalism, that he first became acquainted with Islam. When he returned to Washington, he turned two brothers onto the path as well. At first, they began attending prayers at the Islamic Center to learn more about the religion, but they soon found Khaalis at the Hanafi

Center. In 1975, all three brothers took their *shahada* with Khaalis and pledged their allegiance to the khalifa.

Their parents, devout Christians who had raised the children in the AME Church, were perplexed by it all and made no attempt to hide their distaste for Islam and Muslims. Rahman and Rahim were both married with their own families, so there was little the parents felt they could do. Rahman's wife converted to Islam soon after he did, and Rahim married a Muslim woman he met in the Hanafi community. Rahim had a baby, only a few weeks old, who he left at home that morning when he climbed into his brother's cab to take hostages at the Islamic Center.

Rahman parked the Diamond Cab—the rear door had his given name, "C. C. Young," painted on it—at a fire hydrant close to the Islamic Center. The building was shaped like an inverted T with its broad south-facing facade on Massachusetts Avenue. A library occupied the western wing, and the offices were packed into the eastern wing, with windows looking out onto Massachusetts Avenue. Between the office and library wings, at the junction of the T, was the main entrance, which opened to an ornate open-air courtyard with a fountain. This in turn led to the mosque, which occupied the entire long arm of the T that curved fifteen degrees east to point toward the Kaaba in Mecca.

The three Hanafi brothers boldly entered the complex through the front entrance, carrying their firearms, a red canister of gasoline, and a trunk full of ammunition. They knew all the men would be in the mosque, so they made a sharp right turn into the office wing. Walking through the first door, they encountered two women working at their desks. Mushk Ara, a teenage secretary from Bangladesh who had been working at the Islamic Center only a few weeks, and Fauzia Bayoumi, the bookkeeper, were both overpowered quickly and kept quiet as instructed. Next door, Cecile Von Goetz, a South African woman who had been working as the imam Abdul Rauf's secretary for a few months, was alarmed by the sounds of the commotion, but before she could even think of escaping, one of the Hanafi brothers grabbed her from behind and clapped a hand over her mouth, lifting her off her feet. The three women were lined up against a wall in Von Goetz's office. "Keep still!" the men ordered, their weapons drawn, "or we'll blow your heads off."

Around this time, Rauf was concluding the congregational prayer in the mosque. He greeted the congregants afterward and met with a large group of university students from New York, many of them foreign, who were on a field trip to the American capital and visiting its many sites. At around 12:30, Rauf handed the visitors off to his deputy, Abdul Rahman Osman, a heavy-set Egyptian assistant imam, and exited the mosque area. When Rauf reached the office, he did not expect to find the door locked. He used the key he kept with him to unlock it, and the first thing he noticed when he entered was the paper littering the floor. "What happened . . . ?" he began to ask his accountant, who he saw standing against the wall. Before he could complete his question, a gunman had pounced on him from behind and stuck a gun in his back. Dragged by his collar, Rauf was thrown against the wall, where he was lined up with the three women.

Osman was the next to be captured. After assigning the visiting student group to a tour guide, he was walking toward the library wing when he was distracted by the unusual sounds coming from the offices. A visitor, Charles Kraus, a former colonel in the U.S. Army, was at the door waiting to meet with Rauf to return a book on Islam that he had borrowed months earlier. When Kraus had tried to enter, he explained to Osman, a Black man inside had gruffly told him to shut the door and get out. This made no sense to Osman. He dug into his pockets for his own set of keys. As soon as Osman opened the door, he and Kraus were both dragged inside.

Reverend Robert Tesdell, the fifty-eight-year-old gray-haired director of the International Student Center in New York, who was leading the visiting student group, was gawking at the scuffle at the office door from the entrance, entirely unaware of the peril he was in. He had not had a chance to move before the barrel of a gun was pointed at him. Standing next to him was a student from Colombia named Jose Luis Mora. They both froze, and the gunman led them inside the office. A UPS deliveryman, who happened to be delivering the center's mail at that exact moment, watched the entire thing from the sidewalk and ran. He found the nearest uniformed police officer. The cop, who was with Washington's Executive Protection Services, the capital's specialized diplomatic police administered by the White House, instantly radioed the message to the Metropolitan Police Department. At 1:11 p.m., the dispatcher put out the message on the main police frequency: "EPS states subject is holding a hostage at Mass-Ave and Belmont northwest at the mosque. Nothing further, no description, use caution entering the area." Several squad cars peeled away from B'nai B'rith, sirens blaring, and raced west up Massachusetts Avenue.

Inside the offices of the Islamic Center, a heated exchange had erupted between the Hanafis and the assistant director, Osman. They wanted Osman to divulge where the master key for the complex was kept, but he was refusing to tell them. Two of the brothers had their guns pointed at him, and all his colleagues were pleading with him to give up the key, but Osman was taking a stand. "Go ahead and shoot," he kept shouting at the Hanafi men, "I'm not afraid to die." A gunman finally gave him until the count of three to give it up. He got to two when Osman finally gave in.

Meanwhile, more hostages had trickled in. Mustafa Davas, the muezzin responsible for making the call to prayer, was captured along with Muhammad, the janitor, when they wandered in. Finally, Rauf watched with dread as his wife, Buthayna, descended the stairs from the second floor. She had been upstairs in the apartment packing for a trip to New York when one of the Hanafi brothers had caught her unawares and led her down at gunpoint. Finally, when the Hanafis were convinced that no one remained outside, they locked the main door to the office wing with the master key. One of the gunmen went from office to office pulling down the blinds. Soon, they heard sirens nearing.

The phone in Von Goetz's office began ringing. The Hanafis, who were taking stock of their ammunition and inspecting their weapons, froze. Then Rahman, the eldest of the brothers, answered it. "Bismillah ar-Rahman ar-Rahim," he started with the Islamic traditional prayer "In the name of God, the most beneficent, most merciful." He then delivered the standard Muslim greeting "Assalamu alaikum." It was Khaalis from B'nai B'rith. "We have full control of the center," Rahman reported to Khaalis, scanning the faces of the hostages. "We have eleven," he said, "including Rauf."

It had quickly become apparent to all the hostages that the rage of the gunmen was pointed sharply at Rauf. In the short time that they had been holed up in the cluster of offices, he was the one who was pushed, shoved, and threatened like none of the others. Rauf could not tell why. He thought that he recognized the faces of the gunmen, perhaps from when they had attended prayers at the center, but he did not recall ever having had anything to do with them that would have caused offense. The experience would have felt like the holdup in New York City that Rauf endured months after he had arrived in the United States. Back then, however, he instantly understood what the gunmen were after. These young Black men holding the center were inscrutable—until Rauf heard the name of Hamaas Abdul Khaalis.

Rahman summoned Rauf and handed the phone to him. "This is Hamaas," Rauf heard, as he pressed his ear against the receiver. Khaalis was gruff and impatient and unleashed a torrent of abuse at Rauf. Rauf liked playing games, didn't he, Khaalis taunted. Was it all worth it just to be cozy with Elijah Muhammad's "X"s, he asked. Rauf was a traitor, a coward, a sellout. He was the worst thing anyone could possibly be, according to Allah: a hypocrite. Khaalis had known this for a long time, he explained, but there was no better proof of all that than the movie about to play in a New York theater in half an hour. Why had Rauf, from his high perch at the Islamic Center, allowed the holy Prophet Muhammad to be disgraced in this way?

Rauf had not seen the film, but he was familiar with it. As an American imam, he had occasionally followed the drama around the production of the film and had seen the fatwas against it from Al-Azhar and the Muslim World League. He had written an article himself arguing against the need for any film about Muhammad when he had first heard about it almost a decade earlier. How he was possibly connected with the film, however, he was having a difficult time comprehending.

Khaalis was already on to the next subject. He was commenting on Egypt's plans to cozy up with the Zionists in Israel. Carter was looking for a peace deal between the two countries, and Khaalis was sure the Egyptians would sell out the Palestinians. Was that why Rauf was prostituting his Prophet's name, Khaalis wondered? As a favor to the Jews? Rauf could hardly follow Khaalis's thread, but he knew that his life depended on making some sense of it. He listened carefully. He had not seen or heard from Khaalis in a long time, not since they had spoken following the massacre of the family four years ago. Rauf most likely did not realize that exactly a decade ago to the day, the two men had first met upon Tasibur Rahman's death.

Khaalis delivered rapid-fire instructions to Rauf. Khaalis wanted him to call Cyrus Vance, the secretary of state, and tell him what was happening on America's Embassy Row. More important, Rauf would need to start calling all of his diplomat friends and tell them that if the two o'clock show of Moustapha Akkad's film went ahead as scheduled, heads would start dropping out of windows in America's capital. Rauf checked the clock. It was twenty-five minutes to two. There is simply not enough time, he pleaded with Khaalis, but Khaalis had already hung up the phone.

The Hanafi brothers in the office had only one more instruction for Rauf: he would use no language other than English. Rauf's mind was a blank. He simply started at the beginning of the directory: A-Afghanistan. The Afghan ambassador was not in, so Rauf left a message with a counselor and asked them to spread the message to all the Muslim ambassadors in Washington. Realizing how one pointless call had burned valuable minutes, Rauf decided to be more strategic. He called information and asked for the number of the Mission of Egypt to the United Nations in New York City. That was where the movie was playing after all—they could probably act the quickest. Instead, he was connected to the Egyptian consulate in New York responsible for issuing visas and processing passports. Rauf told the person on the line about the film and begged them to spread the word about the need to stop the premiere.

Finally, Rauf managed to get through to the Egyptian embassy in Washington and spoke briefly to Ashraf Ghorbal, the ambassador. Ghorbal appeared to understand; he asked to speak to one of the Hanafis in the office and asked for a phone number where he might reach Khaalis directly. They gave him the number for B'nai B'rith. It was two o'clock. They told Rauf to sit down in his office chair. They tied him down by his arms and legs. After making sure he was securely bound, they placed the canister of gasoline at his feet. If there was going to be a shootout, they would make sure Rauf would burn first. It was not clear if Rauf's phone calls had succeeded in stopping the movie. What they had done was far more important from Khaalis's perspective: the Hanafi attack was now an international diplomatic crisis.

27.

PROJECTION ROOM

The line to get into the Rivoli for the premiere of *Mohammad* went around the corner. Yablans, Akkad's partner and distributor, was pleased at the sight as he circled the block in the hours before showtime. The four hundred–plus seats in the theater would sell out at $4 a seat. Yablans did note that the faces of the patrons were Brown and Black. He knew this would be the case—that was part of the reason they had chosen New York for the premiere. Still, seeing the people lined up on the day of the premiere was a reminder of the long road ahead to mainstream success, which meant breaking into white audiences.

Akkad and Yablans had flown into New York City a few days earlier. The simultaneous openings in New York and Los Angeles were intended to generate buzz in the two media hubs. There was no question that New York was the better place for the director to be. Besides, what city could be better suited for a film about Islam than New York City, the mecca of American Islam? Hundreds of years of American Islamic history had unfolded in these streets. Akkad's wife, Patricia, who had raised three kids almost single-handedly over a decade, had come along. Yablans's wife had also joined them. They had checked into two rooms at the Essex House on Central Park South.

Yablans's plan was to sit in the projection room for the screening. This was his biggest project yet—his ticket to the big time—and he wanted to be there to oversee every technical detail and gauge the audience reactions for himself. They had decided that Akkad should stay behind at the hotel. Akkad had spent plenty of time in projection rooms, beginning in his childhood in Aleppo. It was more important that he be near a phone, so reporters knew where to reach him as soon as the screening ended.

Fifteen minutes before 2:00 p.m., the phone rang in the projection room. Yablans had not even noticed it until it rang. He answered, and it was someone from inside the theater asking whether the movie had already started. Though that was the extent of the conversation, Yablans did not like the sound of it at all. He surveyed the risers. They were almost full, and the audience was buzzing. Yablans kept his eye on the clock. The moment it struck two, he asked the tech crew to start the show.

The lights in the theater dimmed, and the crowd hushed. The reel in the projection room whirred to life. Akkad had worked hard on the opening sequence, and it was one of Yablans's favorites of the three-hour epic. Maurice Jarre, the Academy Award–winning composer, had written an eerie, haunting string score for the prelude on the Byzantine musical scale. Three Arab horsemen appeared on the screen, galloping across the windswept desert at blistering speed. Just as the string orchestra burst into a crescendo, the horsemen peeled off in different directions. Muhammad's message of Islam was beginning to spread. A montage followed that showed the horsemen arriving in the courts of kings and emperors of Egypt, Byzantium, and Persia. The sequence showcased the gargantuan sets that Akkad's team had painstakingly constructed in Libya and Morocco, as well as the elaborate period costumes. In every court, the only Black characters shown were slaves.

At the end of the sequence, the orchestral music flared once again, and the title of the film appeared on the screen in bold red letters: *Mohammad: Messenger of God*. The opening credits ended with "produced and directed by MOUSTAPHA AKKAD." Finally, as a single eerie note hung against a black screen, the following message appeared in white text:

> **THE SCHOLARS AND HISTORIANS OF ISLAM—THE UNIVERSITY OF AL-AZHAR IN CAIRO, THE HIGH ISLAMIC CONGRESS OF THE SHIAT IN LEBANON—HAVE APPROVED THE ACCURACY AND FIDELITY OF THIS FILM.**
>
> **THE MAKERS OF THIS FILM HONOR THE ISLAMIC TRADITION WHICH HOLDS THAT THE IMPERSONATION OF THE PROPHET OFFENDS AGAINST THE SPIRITUALITY OF HIS MESSAGE.**

Then finally, in large letters: "Therefore, the person of Mohammad will not be shown."

The scene opened with a panoramic view of the spectacular set Akkad had created in Morocco, showing a bustling trade hub that was pre-Islamic Mecca on the eve of Muhammad's first revelation from the archangel Gabriel. About twenty-five minutes in, when the movie was just turning to the torture of the Black Abyssinian slave Bilal, the phone in the projection room rang again. Annoyed, Yablans picked it up. He quickly sobered up, however, when the person on the line identified himself as a New York City police officer. He requested that Yablans come down to the lobby immediately.

Like everyone else outside of Washington, Yablans knew nothing about the events unfolding in the capital that morning. The Washington radio station WWRC had first reported the news of the B'nai B'rith takeover at 12:30, and an hour later, the station had broken the news about the Islamic Center. The first news about the hostages in Washington had traveled outside of the District a little before 2:00 p.m., when United Press International sent a story over the newswire about the trouble in the capital. The evening network news broadcasts, the only live national television news at the time, were still hours away. The only way anyone outside the city would have known what was going on in DC was through the phone lines.

When Yablans entered the lobby, the officer was waiting for him. He pulled Yablans aside and summarized, as best he could, the hostage situation unfolding in the capital. Then he pointed to the throng of reporters and camera crews shuffling around outside. They were probably waiting for Yablans to comment, he explained. Yablans felt overwhelmed by all the microphones that were thrust in his face as soon as he stepped out on the sidewalk. The reporters started shouting questions at him all at once and the camera bulbs flashed. Yablans picked a TV camera crew from one of the networks and pulled them inside for an exclusive. It was the only way to control the message that went out. It was a beautiful movie, he said as the cameras rolled; it did not show the Prophet Muhammad. It was a movie about love and the brotherhood of man. The last thing the filmmaker wanted was for anyone to be killed because of it. That's why, he said, he had decided to stop the showing.

Yablans rushed back up to the projection room. He told the tech in the booth to flip the switch on the projector. The houselights came on. The reel whirred, and the audience roared as they snapped out of their spell. Ushers appeared at the exits, directing people to the street. The theater, they announced, was shutting down for the day. As hundreds of patrons emerged into the sunlight, they were attacked by the throng of reporters from all sides, flash bulbs popping and TV cameras trained on their faces. The reporters asked about the movie. "It is a good educational film," one bemused man told a reporter. "They should close down some of the bad films around here," he said, referring to the porn palaces near Times Square.

Yablans rode back to the hotel with a police escort. Inside, NYPD officers already lined the corridors leading to Akkad's hotel room. Akkad was frantically fielding phone calls as Patricia, his wife, looked on, worried. In between calls from journalists, friends and financiers of Akkad's started calling from the Middle East and Los Angeles. Yablans broke the news to Akkad: the screening was canceled. Anthony Quinn, the star of the film, told a reporter who called him that he felt "like a man who has brought a flower to someone only to have it knocked out of his hands and told he was not supposed to bring flowers." Yablans took over answering some of the calls, and Akkad lit his pipe to consider the situation. It was a disaster. At the same time, *Mohammad: Messenger of God* was, once again, making Hollywood history. It was on its way to becoming the biggest story in the country. If things went badly enough, the movie might even become the biggest story in the world.

28.

SPYGLASS

Traffic in downtown Washington, DC, was starting to snarl. Scott Circle, a large intersection fewer than five hundred feet from the entrance of B'nai B'rith and fewer than one thousand yards north of the White House grounds, was now the Metropolitan Police Department's main staging area for the crime scene. The circle served as a crossing for three major arteries: Massachusetts Avenue, Rhode Island Avenue, and Sixteenth Street—and the traffic division was diverting all traffic to three other major traffic circles within five hundred yards, Dupont Circle to the northwest, Thomas Circle to the southeast, and Logan Circle to the northeast. At Logan Circle, Washington police created a zone to process released hostages, treat the injured, and track anyone moving in or out of the crime scene.

The B'nai B'rith headquarters was surrounded by other high-rise commercial and office buildings, many of which now had at least some police presence. The two hotels on the block, the Gramercy Inn and the Holiday Inn, became important nodes in the police operation. The Holiday Inn was receiving non-police visitors to the scene, including friends and families of hostages. Large sections of that hotel were evacuated, and the rooms were offered to loved ones anticipating a long wait. The Gramercy Inn, right next door to B'nai B'rith, was being used for more immediate law-enforcement business. The western side of the hotel, which ran alongside B'nai B'rith's longest wall, was evacuated, and the rooms were made available to the police for surveillance, interviewing witnesses, and temporary evidence storage. Two snipers had also taken up positions at the Gramercy shortly after two o'clock. The Hanafis had successfully obstructed the view onto the eighth floor, and it was nearly impossible to determine what was going on inside. There were, however, still several groups of B'nai B'rith workers trapped in offices on the lower floors, and they were visible through the windows as they were evacuated in brief bursts of police action.

The spectacle had attracted a large crowd of onlookers, especially in Scott Circle, where hundreds gathered over the lunch hour to picnic and gawk. One news report described "several hundred spectators," some of whom had to be removed by police "from every angle they considered to be in possible line of fire." A large group of students at the Charles Sumner School, separated from B'nai B'rith by a narrow alley to the south, had gathered on the roof to catch the action and were evacuated after a police helicopter spotted them and radioed their presence in a panic.

The cat and mouse game with news media was taking up considerable police resources. The TV news crews had descended on B'nai B'rith right around the time that the police had arrived, shortly after 11:30. Most of them were directed by the police to the Holiday Inn, where they tried to take rooms with windows that looked out on B'nai B'rith. The TV crews were hungry for live images. The local NBC, CBS, and ABC network affiliates were using electronic news-gathering vans, or ENGs, which allowed live shots from practically anywhere to be transmitted via satellite signals to the studio or even shown live on air. It was a revolutionary technology that eliminated the need to transport physical film before news broadcasts. The technology, tested at the Munich Olympics five years earlier, made breaking news a visceral experience for audiences, but it also pushed competing stations to take bigger and bigger risks for the most spectacular live images on the ground.

The news channels also tried getting shots from the air. The police had their own helicopter circling B'nai B'rith all morning, but it had spooked Khaalis, and he had demanded that it be taken away. As soon as it was gone, an NBC helicopter swooped in. "Advise them to stay out of the area," the lieutenant in charge of the scene told the news helicopter. "It's interfering with our operation." Air space was an especially sensitive issue at the Islamic Center, where even the police had no access. The center was fewer than one thousand yards away from the Naval Observatory, which was classified as restricted airspace since it housed the vice president's residence. The Metropolitan Police had put in an emergency request to the federal government to send a helicopter to the Islamic Center but was still awaiting an answer from the Secret Service.

On Embassy Row, the police cordons had sliced the city's diplomatic district in half, restricting the movement of embassy staff and cutting off access to the embassies. Massachusetts Avenue was also the main thoroughfare connecting downtown Washington to the Northwest quadrant. Two city buses were used to block the exit to Massachusetts Avenue from Rock Creek Parkway, which carried a heavy load of traffic during working hours. The journalists and gawkers were easier to control at the Islamic Center. It was a high-security diplomatic zone to begin with, crawling with Secret Service, and had much less foot traffic than downtown Washington. In contrast to B'nai B'rith's all-glass facade, the Islamic Center did not offer much of a view to the cameras.

The big question on everyone's mind remained unanswered, and it was articulated over the main police frequency by a lieutenant stationed at B'nai B'rith: "I need to know," he said, "if the situation at Belmont and Mass is getting connected with this one." Rabe had arrived at the Islamic Center around one o'clock with exactly this question in mind. Over the course of the following hour, he had failed to get a definitive answer. The police had tried everything they could think of. One officer outside the center used a bullhorn to shout out a phone number for the gunmen to call but got no response. The police department's communication division followed up with a call to the center, but whoever picked up the phone had quickly hung up. Finally, an officer on the scene dialed into the center from a neighboring residence, and the gunman who answered said the hostage takers would speak only to the chief of police. At that point, Rabe decided it was time to retreat to headquarters. He left one of his lieutenants in charge of the Islamic Center and drove back downtown.

At the headquarters, the chief of the Washington Metropolitan Police, Maurice Cullinane, had been following the unfolding events closely. He was forty-five years old, a few years younger than his friends Rabe and O'Brien, but police work ran deep in his blood. Cullinane was born and raised in Washington. He was the grandson of Irish immigrants who had settled in one of the city's most depressed slums in Southeast Washington, DC, in the mid-nineteenth century. Two of Cullinane's great-uncles had joined the Metropolitan Police Department when it was created in the 1860s on the orders of President Lincoln. Nearly all of Cullinane's own uncles had joined the police force, too. As a child, he would sometimes see them patrolling the neighborhood on horseback. Cullinane's father, the only holdout, eventually became a police officer at Union Station after being forced to shutter his pub during Prohibition.

Cullinane started as a patrol officer in the 1950s and was named chief of police in 1974, soon after the Hanafi massacre trial began in the city. DC was still one of the most crime-ridden cities in America when he took over as chief. The city's heroin epidemic had subsided, but Washington still had a deadly reputation. There were almost three hundred murders in the District during Cullinane's first year. Under his leadership, the situation had started to improve slightly. The year 1976 was the most peaceful the city had enjoyed in a decade, at least when measured by the number of murders, which finally dipped below two hundred for the first time since 1968. Under Cullinane, the police force expanded as well, adding hundreds of new Black recruits, who helped the department gain a reputation as one of the most progressive among those of America's big cities.

Cullinane finally established contact with the brothers at the Islamic Center a little before two o'clock and confirmed what many already suspected: they, like the gunmen at B'nai B'rith, were Hanafis. Word spread over the police frequencies, and the 1973 murders were mentioned as a possible motive. Like Rabe, Cullinane never came to know Khaalis or the Hanafis too well—not like O'Brien, anyway. He did remember meeting Khaalis once a few years earlier. Cullinane was out for lunch with O'Brien in Georgetown when O'Brien asked Cullinane if he would join him for a quick stop at the Aram jewelry store run by Aziz. The family was in limbo between trials, and O'Brien had made a habit of checking in on them whenever he could. Cullinane and O'Brien were close friends, and Cullinane knew how this crime haunted O'Brien, so he'd agreed to tag along. Aziz and Khaalis were both at the store, and Cullinane recalled a cordial meeting.

Khaalis, however, was no longer the cordial man Cullinane remembered when the call came from B'nai B'rith that afternoon.

"Chief Cullinane, I'm going to send your sharpshooters some heads to practice on."

Abdul Latif, using a spyglass in B'nai B'rith, had spotted sharpshooters on the roof of the Holiday Inn across the street, and Khaalis was in a quiet rage.

"You're taking me for a joke?" asked Khaalis.

"We're not taking you for a joke," Cullinane assured him, "we're going to move them."

"I know it hurts. I know it hurts," Khaalis taunted Cullinane. "You're Chief, you're backed up by the Army and Navy and all the American allies, but I have Allah with me and I know it hurts to have to take orders from somebody you don't know nothing about."

"Deputy Chief Rabe has gone outside to make sure the sharpshooters are gone," Cullinane reassured Khaalis.

"My wife said that you were holding up things. Said the police was not releasing information. Now, you better start releasing all of the information."

"What information do you want us to release?" Cullinane asked

"I want the information released that we want that picture stopped, that we have hostages in here," Khaalis said. Then he introduced his second demand. "I want information out that we want those killers that killed my family. That's right. That's right. Justice has not been done," Khaalis said. "Don't tell me nothing about the court system or nothing, I don't care about those revolving doors—they don't mean nothing to me."

Cullinane tried to sidestep this new demand without acknowledging it, but Khaalis delivered Cullinane an ominous threat: "Chief Cullinane," he hissed, "there are men waiting throughout this country. They may not hit you right away but they are watching and they are waiting and they have given their bond and they're very, very serious." Then, Khaalis hung up.

Rabe had returned to his desk after personally ordering the sharpshooters to stand down, when his phone rang.

"This is Sergeant Blake, who am I talking to?"

"You're talking to Chief Rabe."

"Chief, I'm just going to give you an update on the District Building."

"What's at the District Building?"

"Okay, we got one apparently dead in the hallway. His identity is unknown. All right, SOD is cutting loose with gunfire upstairs now."

"SOD is using gunfire on the fifth floor?" Rabe's own unit was in a gun battle in one of the most sensitive buildings in the capital, the building that housed the city's government, and he was hearing the first of it from a sergeant on the scene.

"You see, I'm on the floor underneath them and I hear a lot of shots going on up there."

"On the fifth floor?" Rabe knew that the fifth floor was where the mayor's office was located, along with the entire District Council, Washington's legislative body.

"There's one guard been shot in the head," the sergeant reported.

29

FEDERAL TRIANGLE

On the day that he was shot dead by a Hanafi gunman, Maurice Williams, a twenty-four-year-old reporter for WHUR, Howard University's Radio Ebony, left the studio in the morning to cover a press conference at the District Building on Pennsylvania Avenue, near the White House. Williams had worked at the station for many years, first as a student reporter while earning his undergraduate degree in communications, and later as an intern until he was finally hired as a full-time reporter in 1975. He was the youngest person on staff, and at five-foot-three-inches tall, one of the shortest. The others called him Junior. As he left on that ordinary morning, he passed by the desk of Cathy Liggins, the station manager. "Don't go down there looking like a bum," she joked. Williams was wearing a green pullover sweater and a white jacket on top of it. He smiled, straightened out his clothes, and exited.

He had been on the District Council beat for close to a year. It was exciting work. Until a few years earlier, the District of Columbia had been run by the federal government. A home-rule movement began gathering momentum in Washington in the late 1960s, coinciding with the broader movement for African American civil rights and the city becoming the only majority Black territory in the country. When Williams was attending Coolidge High School in Northwest DC, Black leaders in the city were beginning to demand greater autonomy. President Lyndon Johnson appointed Walter Washington mayor-commissioner in 1967, making him the first African American to lead a major American city. Six years later, Congress passed the Home Rule Act, which allowed the people of Washington to elect representatives to a District Council that was responsible for enacting local laws, albeit with congressional approval.

The inaugural council, elected in 1974, counted some of the most well-known African American politicians in the city among its twelve members. Sterling Tucker, the chair, had considered running against Washington for mayor in the election in 1974, and many of the others—John Wilson, Arrington Dixon, and Nadine Winter—were pioneers of the home-rule movement and veterans of the civil rights movement of the 1960s. None was more famous than the young and ambitious transplant from Mississippi, Marion Barry. A former member of the Student Nonviolent Coordinating Committee, Barry had helped the cause of home rule while working for the Free DC movement and made his political mark with Pride Inc., an organization that provided employment to hundreds of young and old African American ex-offenders. His flamboyant, confrontational style of politics gave him the sort of national name recognition that few others in the DC government had. Rumors were that he was preparing to challenge Sterling Tucker for the council chair in the upcoming election. Few doubted that this would be his stepping-stone to becoming mayor.

The District Building was home base for the council. It was a large American Renaissance–style building situated around 150 yards from the eastern edge of the White House grounds on a historic plot of land known as Federal Triangle. As the name suggests, the plot was occupied by a handful of important federal agencies like the Commerce Department, the IRS, and the Department of Justice. The District Building, on the eastern corner of the triangle, closest to the White House, was one of the few properties on the triangle controlled by the District.

As a young, personable Black reporter, Williams had come to know many of the council members well. He spent many of his working days covering the proceedings of the council, which mostly took place in the chambers on the fifth floor, looking over Pennsylvania Avenue. That is also where the offices of all twelve elected council members were. Sterling Tucker, the chair of the council, had his own office suite, along with the rest of the eleven members of the council, in the western leg of the building, closest to the White House. Walter Washington, who had been elected mayor, and his staff occupied most of the eastern leg, farther away from the White House grounds.

Williams entered the District Building at around 2:30 p.m. to cover the press conference scheduled for Sterling Tucker. He had taken his lunch break with Steven Colter, a young reporter for the *Washington*

Afro American newspaper. The two had ordered burgers at the Blue Mirror restaurant and had talked about their experiences working for Black news organizations. They were young and talented but were unsure if they could succeed in the mainstream, white-dominated press. Focused on city politics, the two reporters were not covering the hostage takings on Embassy Row and at B'nai B'rith.

Just as Williams and Colter were entering the District Building through its eastern entrance, the councilman Marion Barry entered the building through the other side, closer to the White House. He was returning from an engagement with the Northwest Kiwanis Club and was headed to the fifth floor to attend the council's judiciary subcommittee session, which was held every other Wednesday at 2:30 p.m. in the council chambers. Just as the reporters called the western elevator, Barry approached the eastern elevators and was intercepted by Mack Cantrell, a former U.S. Marine and Korean War vet, who had worked as a security guard for the District government since 1971. He was dressed in his uniform—gray shirt and blue slacks—and greeted the councilman politely before giving him the news: "There may be a little trouble on the fifth floor." Cantrell did not know the exact nature of the trouble. He had just heard about it over the radio. He suggested to Barry that it was best if he ride up with him.

As the elevator doors opened on the fifth floor, Cantrell placed his hand on the .38 Smith and Wesson Special revolver in his holster and asked Barry to hang back in the elevator for a moment while he investigated. A police guard, dressed in a blue police uniform, was posted outside the glass doors to the mayor's wing, and Cantrell walked over to confer with him. After a brief conversation, they started down the long, wide marble-floored hallway in the direction of the council members' offices. As they walked past the legislative chambers, already full for the judiciary session, Williams and Colter, the two young Black journalists, exited the western elevator and began walking in the other direction, toward the mayor's office. The reporters and the guards briefly crossed paths. "You going to shoot somebody?" Colter joked, giving the guards a wide-eyed look up and down. Williams snickered, but the guards paid no attention. They had their eyes on the glass doors in front of them. They sensed trouble.

As the guards arrived at the doors leading into the council offices, Cantrell and his fellow guard paused and drew their guns. With his free left hand, Cantrell slowly pried open the large wooden door just a slit and peered inside. A man wearing a long trench coat had his back to the door. Cantrell could see that he was holding a shotgun. Before Cantrell could point his own weapon, in one swift motion the figure turned around, pointed his shotgun at the crack in the door, and pulled the trigger.

Abdul Muzikir, a twenty-four-year-old Hanafi disciple, had grabbed the shotgun as he left his house on Myrtle Street. He had once been an aspiring theater actor, but ever since he'd joined the Hanafis a few years earlier, he had been working as a cab driver, like many of the others in the group. He had once shown a lot of promise. Admitted to Northwestern University's journalism program, he had declined and instead started a job at the Federal Communications Commission in Washington. With him was Abdul Nuh, who was armed only with a long machete. The son of a minister, he was a licensed schoolteacher and former star college football athlete with a bachelor's degree in physical education from Boston University. After teaching elementary school at McCormack Middle School in Boston, Nuh had joined the Hanafis in Washington around the time of the 1973 massacre. Both men lived with their wives and children in the home owned by the basketball star Kareem Abdul-Jabbar on Myrtle Street, where Kareem's wife, Habiba, and their two small children also lived. Nuh had three-year-old and ten-month-old children at home. Muzikir's baby was only a few months old. They had ridden together to the District Building in a 1971 Chrysler Diamond Cab.

Their weapons tucked under their jackets, they had bounded up the western stairwell of the District Building minutes before Williams, Colter, and Barry had entered. Arriving at the fifth floor, Muzikir had immediately taken hostage a police officer standing at a vending machine and dragged him into the western wing, where he and Nuh had ordered everyone inside to lie on the ground facedown. As Muzikir stood guard near the door, his Remington 12-gauge shotgun by his side, Nuh was busy tying up the hands of the captives. Cantrell and his fellow guard were the first officers responding to the reported trouble, and the shot that Muzikir fired was the first one of the District Building takeover.

The burst of #4 buckshot sprayed out of the shotgun shell in a narrow cone. Several of the pellets hit Cantrell's face, one under the left eye. As he fell to the floor, the other guard scuttled around the corner into the stairwell. Twenty feet down the hallway, five pellets hit the side and back of Maurice Williams's body, puncturing his heart and lungs. "I'm shot," he shouted at Colter as he stumbled forward several feet and fell to the floor. Farther down the hallway, another pellet ricocheted off a pillar and lodged itself in the left side of the chest of Marion Barry, who had disregarded Cantrell's instructions and walked into the hallway. He fell to the floor screaming. The remaining pellets pierced the glass door to the mayor's office at the other end of the long hall.

That single shotgun blast had left three bloodied bodies on the ground. Near the entrance to the council members' offices, Cantrell, shot in the face, was slumped over, his fallen hat resting in a pool of blood on the floor. Maurice Williams lay on his back, completely still, his tongue hanging limply from his mouth. Barry sat against a pillar near the council chambers clutching his chest, wincing as he took shallow breaths. He was the only one to move. He scrambled toward the council chambers door, pushed it open, and fell inside. "I've been shot!" he announced. "Call an ambulance." Amid the panicked screaming, someone dialed 911. By this time, Maurice Williams was already dead.

The SOD descended on the building and took control of the scene within minutes. The unit was led by Richard Traylor, the chief of the SOD's civil disturbance unit and the caretaker of the storeroom containing all the arms and ammunition that the police maintained in case of emergency. He was a military vet and a gun nut who, unknown to anyone in the force, was illegally stealing weapons and amassing an arsenal at home. He came armed with a 9mm Uzi automatic machine gun, and he was bristling for action. He ordered the power to the floor cut off and, in the relative darkness, police officers scurried along the length of the corridor taking positions. A few officers quickly dragged Cantrell's limp body into the stairwell, leaving a smear of blood on the floor. Traylor, meanwhile, had dragged a twenty-foot wooden conference table from the council chambers where Barry was being attended to, flipped it over on its side, and used it to barricade the hallway.

In the eerie dimness, the afternoon sunlight filtering through the windows, Traylor spotted a shadow pacing back and forth behind the glass doors of the council members' offices. It was Muzikir's silhouette. He seemed agitated by the darkness. Traylor spotted an ashtray on the ground and hurled it at the shadow. It crashed through the glass next to the door. A startled Muzikir began firing his shotgun into the corridor again. Traylor finally had the pretext to cut loose and emptied the entire magazine of his Uzi, roughly thirty rounds, into Sterling Tucker's office suite. It was a full-blown firefight. The shots echoing off the marble walls and floors made the fifth floor of the District Building sound like a war zone.

Suddenly, the cops who had taken up positions closer to the council offices began shouting at Traylor to hold his fire. They had heard screams coming from inside the council members' offices. Just then, Rabe's voice cut in on the radio. "We have reasonably good information that there may be as many as thirty hostages inside the council office area," he said. He ordered that no more shots be fired until he got there.

Inside, smoke and haze filled the six-hundred-square-foot office suite of council chair Sterling Tucker. The window to the left of the door was partially gone, and the glass to the right of the door had completely shattered. The shots from the Uzi had ripped the plaster off the walls, punctured and shattered glass windows, and left a trail of bullet holes in the metal filing cabinets along the wall. Amazingly, the incoming fire had hit no one. Muzikir, however, had aimed his rifle at one of the hostages lying on the ground during the exchange of fire, and shot him right in his back. Robert Pierce was a fifty-two-year-old retired State Department official. Widely traveled in the Middle East and Europe, he was aiming to start a second career, pursuing a degree in the poverty law program at Antioch School of Law. As part of his law program, he was interning with the city government, and he had been taken hostage when he had wandered into the office. His wrists were tied behind his back as he lay on the floor, and now one of them had been shredded after Muzikir had shot him at close range. He was oozing blood from several puncture wounds from the shotgun pellets.

Muzikir and Nuh checked to see if Pierce was alive. He groaned in pain and complained that he could not feel or move his body below the waist. After some consideration, the Hanafis decided they needed to relinquish control of Pierce before he died. They decided to release their first hostage, a nineteen-year-old intern named Cordelia Wilkins, with instructions to inform the police about the situation inside and tell them that the gunmen were shooting hostages. If the police opened fire again, the gunmen would start aiming for the head, they warned. They also told her to inform the police that they needed the power back on now.

A few minutes after the release of the young woman, police yelled in that they would turn the power on if the injured hostage was released. The Hanafis instructed Carmencita Kinsey, Tucker's secretary, and Helen Keys, another secretary, to drag Pierce out through the shattered glass door and dump him in the hallway. After heaving him over broken glass, the two women were able to get Pierce partially over the threshold of the door into the hallway. The moment they saw the police officers, they both made a run for the stairwell. Pierce was left moaning in pain until a few officers rushed over and dragged him out, leaving yet another long smear of blood on the floor.

The power was turned back on, and a radio in Tucker's office buzzed to life. It was tuned to the WWRC news radio station. The Hanafis and their hostages listened together to the latest reports. The attackers at B'nai B'rith and the Islamic Center were all connected to the Hanafi Muslim group based in the city, the report said. They were making a series of demands, including the cancellation of a film premiere in New York City. A shooting at the District Building close to the White House, the report added at the end, had led to the building's evacuation. Councilman Marion Barry had been transported to the hospital with a bullet wound to the chest. All monuments in the city had been closed for the day.

The news about Barry elated Muzikir and Nuh. "You heard about number one and number two," Muzikir addressed the hostages laid out on the floor in front of him. "Well, this is number three." He began telling the hostages all about Khaalis, about the 1973 murders, and about the injustices the Hanafis had endured at the hands of the Washington, DC, court system. One of the hostages asked a question about the Black Muslims. Another one asked about the trial. Muzikir found himself giving what felt to him like a press conference, answering questions, speaking about the experiences of the Hanafis over the past four years that justified the hostage taking. When the hostages appeared to be satisfied with his answers for the time being, Muzikir turned to Nuh. Maybe they should try to reach Channel 9 on the phone, he suggested.

30.

ONE AND ONLY

Max Robinson was the first journalist to connect the dots. He pulled up in front of the Hanafi Center on Sixteenth Street around 4:00 that afternoon. As the star news anchor for Channel 9 WTOP, the *Washington Post*–owned CBS affiliate, Robinson was probably the most recognizable Black man in all of "Chocolate City." He was born and raised in Richmond, Virginia, and got his start in television in the South after quitting the air force. He left for Washington, DC, in the mid-1960s. Washington had one of the largest African American TV audiences in the country and offered him plenty of opportunities to rise through the ranks.

As a rookie reporter in the capital, he won a prime-time Emmy Award in 1968 for his documentary on DC's old Anacostia neighborhood. He also covered what passed for local news in the city during that time: presidential inaugurations, riots and demonstrations, and the Watergate scandal. In 1971, he became the first African American to anchor the local news in the city, cohosting WTOP's *Eyewitness News* with a white coanchor named Gordon Peterson. His news instincts were sharp, he had a sense of humor, he looked great on camera, and his commanding voice was broadcast perfection. WTOP shot up in the ratings for prime-time evening news thanks to what became known in the city's media circles as the "Max effect."

Robinson also had a history with the Hanafis. He had met Aziz at Aram jewelry store in Georgetown months before the massacre at the center. Robinson was an amateur painter and collected art, so Aziz's store caught his attention soon after it opened. Aram was selling rare and unique pieces from Asia and Africa and even got a brief write-up in *Ebony* magazine. The fact that the shop was Black owned charmed Robinson.

He liked the urbane, sophisticated Aziz. He could tell that the Hanafis were not like Elijah Muhammad's Black Muslims. Aziz told him about the Hanafi Center on Sixteenth Street and how it had been purchased by Khaalis's star disciple, Kareem Abdul-Jabbar. Robinson knew the neighborhood well. He lived not far from there in a high-rise apartment building. Aziz invited Max to join them, but Robinson had never been a religious person, and he told Aziz that he tried to avoid organized religion. Aziz did not push.

Robinson did finally visit the house days after the massacre in 1973. He and another Black reporter from *The New York Times* were the first reporters to enter the premises after the massacre, when Khaalis spotted them standing outside among a throng of reporters and invited them in. The walls were still splattered with blood when Robinson entered; the house had been turned inside out. During the interview, Khaalis explained everything that had happened, switching between rage and mournfulness. "They killed my babies, they killed my babies," he moaned at one point.

Days after the massacre, Khaalis had called up Robinson unexpectedly. Khaalis explained that he wanted to hold a big press conference at the center in which he would accuse Elijah Muhammad of the crime, but he did not know where to begin. He wanted some guidance. Robinson felt terrible for the family. At the same time, he knew that this was a big story, and the trials would become one too. He would need to choose between the story and the Hanafis. He chose the Hanafis, becoming an informal media consultant for Khaalis and the family. He told his producer at WTOP that he could no longer report the story. He did not attend the press conference that he had helped organize, in which Khaalis named Elijah Muhammad and the Nation of Islam as the culprits.

In the months that followed, Robinson became especially close to Aziz. His wife, Khaalis's daughter Amina, was in the hospital. The couple had just lost their child in the most horrific tragedy. After the burials and funerals, there were daily trips to the hospital to care for Amina, and Robinson would sometimes ride with Aziz to keep him company and provide support. One day on the way to the hospital in his car, Aziz looked at Robinson and asked. "Why are you doing this, Max? You know we could be hit at any moment, right?" Robinson did not have a good answer, but he told him that he felt guilty for not engaging with the family earlier, when Aziz had first invited him into the home. Or maybe he just wanted someone to return the favor if something similar ever happened to him. Eventually, though, Khaalis and the rest of the Hanafi community withdrew from the world around them, going deeper and deeper into their dark shell of a home, and Robinson lost touch.

When Robinson heard about the Hanafis again on the morning of March 9, he knew exactly where to go. Everything appeared eerily quiet when Robinson approached the front door. There were some police officers standing at a distance, looking on uncomfortably. They did not dare approach the center. Robinson also noted who was not there yet: other journalists. He knocked on the door.

A series of bolts and locks began clicking open inside. It appeared as if a dozen locks had been added in the years since Robinson had first visited the house. A Hanafi man he did not recognize let him in. He removed his shoes, as he knew he was required to do. As the Hanafi man went to get Aziz, he instructed Robinson to stand and wait near the entrance. Robinson was on alert; he had entered the house expecting a warmer welcome. He scanned the living area and spotted a gun, several machetes, and knives littered around the room. People were going up and down the stairs, paying no attention to him at all.

Suddenly, three men swarmed Robinson, and Abdul Aziz entered the room. Robinson asked Aziz if he might sit down. Aziz reluctantly gestured to his men to allow Robinson to take a seat next to Aziz on a couch. What have you done? Robinson asked Aziz, sounding more like an old friend than a journalist. Aziz was distant and aggressive, sounding to Robinson more like Khaalis than himself. Allah's law required that this be done, Aziz said. There was no other way; justice must be carried out no matter the cost. By that logic, Robinson argued, the Hanafis could as easily take him hostage right there. His was, after all, one of the most recognizable faces in all of DC. He had already considered it, Aziz replied coldly, and decided against it.

They were talking when the phone rang. It was Khaalis from B'nai B'rith. Aziz had a brief exchange with Khaalis and then handed the phone receiver to Robinson. "This is holy war," Khaalis was saying already when Robinson placed the phone to his ear. He was speaking too quickly, his words washing over Robinson, who did not even bother to take notes. He stopped Khaalis in his tracks and proposed a better way to do this. "We need you live on the air," Robinson told him. Khaalis could explain every-thing he wanted to the whole world on live TV. Khaalis liked the idea. The men exchanged numbers, and as soon as he hung up, Robinson headed for the door. He had less than two hours before his six o'clock evening broadcast.

As Aziz and his men watched Robinson fumble with his shoes at the entrance, they all heard a terrifying scream from right outside the door. They rushed out to find one of the large Hanafi guards armed with a ma-chete trying to wrestle a woman to the ground. Robinson recognized her immediately as a reporter from *The Washington Post*. The furious guard looked as if he was ready to end her life right there. Robinson shouted at Aziz, pleading with him to step in and pull his man back. Aziz ordered the armed man away from the stunned woman and delivered loud in-structions to the Hanafi guard: this was jihad, he said, and in holy war, there would be no killing of the innocents. As Robinson climbed into his car, shaken, and began driving back to the WTOP station, he had a real-ization much like the one that Akkad had had a few hours earlier in his hotel room overlooking Central Park. This was the biggest story in Wash-ington, DC, and if things went badly enough, it could become the biggest story in the world. Robinson knew that at that moment he was ahead of every other journalist in the country.

"The One and Only" Channel 9 in Washington, DC, was headquar-tered at Broadcast House in the Tenleytown neighborhood of Northwest DC. It was one of the best spots in the city to grapple with the complex crisis unfolding in the heart of the American capital. All three hostage locations—B'nai B'rith, the Islamic Center, and the District Building—were within a five-mile radius of the station. The station had almost completely converted to an ENG setup for live news, and vehicles were sending in live pictures from each of the scenes. WRC, the NBC affili-ate, had scooped WTOP by breaking the news a full hour before them in the morning. NBC had almost one hundred people working on the story, shuttling in equipment and crews from Chicago, New York, and Burbank, California, to cover the crisis. They also had a helicopter in the air. They were running away with the story. Now, WTOP's star journalist, Max Robinson, had the biggest catch of all: a live exclusive with Khaalis.

Shortly after five o'clock, Robinson and his coanchor were rushed into makeup and then into the studio to start a special news transmission.

By the time WTOP cut live to the news desk shortly after 5:30, Robinson, dressed in a gray suit and maroon tie, a gold watch flashing on his wrist, already had a receiver on his ear and was in conversation with Khaalis. Peterson provided the pithy opening: "We see city council member Marion Barry has been shot, operated on, is in fair condition. Now, my partner Max Robinson is on the phone with the leader of the Hanafi Muslims who are leading this activity. He is talking now. Let's join that conversation."

"What kind of proof are you asking for the film be taken out of the country? How will you know?" Robinson was asking about Khaalis's first demand, which had evolved substantially since the morning. It was no longer enough to simply pull *the movie* from theaters. Khaalis wanted the actual reels of Akkad's film removed from the United States. America was his Islamic jurisdiction, Khaalis suggested, and he wanted that movie out.

"My brothers and sisters and my wife Khadija—"

"So you're saying you'll know when that film is removed."

"Oh yes, it better be, or heads gonna roll, it doesn't matter to me."

"Earlier you told me that something was going to happen in New York."

"I said . . . No, I'm through with that, I'm not going to talk about it."

"You're not going to talk . . ."

"Yeah, no. I'll leave that for the New York people to worry about, all right? Don't you worry about that."

"But once the film is removed from this country. Once . . . you were asking that those responsible for the deaths of—or who killed your children be brought to the B'nai B'rith building . . ."

"And the ones that killed Malcolm," Khaalis cut in.

"And the ones that killed Malcolm."

"That's right, I want them."

"And you're asking for the 750 dollars."

"I've turned down millions of dollars, so it's not the 750," Khaalis's voice began to rise. "But this dog ass Judge Braman, he hold me in contempt of court because I charged the murderers that murder my babies. Now what do you think about that? And you think I'm going to roll over and play dead? What do you think I am? Some kind of jokester? I take my faith serious." His sentences were starting to flow into each other, his pauses syncopated but rhythmical. "You think I raise my children and run all over this country, Max, and raise my boy, twenty-six years old, to be a virgin young man, never touched no man or woman and study and know all of his prayers. And Khadija and I sitting in bus stations and parks. Nothing to eat, no home for our children. Sitting up at night, catching rats, no place to sleep. Sleeping in the car. When I had one—had to sell that. You think I went through all that as a joke, Max? Do you?"

"I understand what you're saying," Robinson replied quietly.

"All right then. I'm very serious about my faith."

Khaalis began yelling commands to his men in the back. "Keep stacking, boys, keep stacking, boys, move it, faster, make 'em move faster, Latif. Work 'em." It was a performance for the live TV audience—a reminder of the action that the cameras could not see. Latif responded by dramatically yelling at the hostages so it was audible in the studio. Robinson glanced up at his producer.

"Hamaas?" he cut in.

"Yes."

"You talked to Police Chief Cullinane a few moments ago."

"Yes."

"What were your demands?"

"Same thing, Max, I'm through, all right. Been talking all day, okay?"

"Thank you, sir."

"All right."

At 6:30, after Peterson and Robinson concluded their live broadcast with more news from the three locations, WTOP switched to the network evening news anchored on CBS by Walter Cronkite. There, too, the Hanafis were at the top of the show. "Good evening. Black Islamic gunmen invaded three buildings in Washington today, apparent revenge for a mass murder four years ago," Cronkite said. A map of DC was displayed behind him with "Islamic Mosque," "District Building," and "B'nai B'rith" labeled. "They took more than one hundred hostages, killed a black radio reporter, and wounded several persons." CBS dedicated almost seven minutes, close to a third of their broadcast, to what Cronkite described as a "bizarre series of events."

Over on ABC, Barbara Walters too began her broadcast with news of what the media were now calling the "Hanafi siege." "A frightening story at the top of the news tonight." Walters described the events at all three locations and played a short audio clip of Khaalis talking about the film to a reporter: "It mocks our Lord Allah, and it mocks our prophet," he yelled.

ABC dedicated more than six minutes to the Hanafi takeover of Washington. Finally, NBC's evening news dedicated its entire first ten-minute segment to the news from Washington and then ended the broadcast with it as well. "The latest from Washington is that there is no latest," John Chancellor, one of the anchors, said at the end. "The situation there is unchanged." He gave the number of hostages as anywhere between fifty and one hundred and fifty. "We don't know what's going to happen tonight."

Nearly fifty million Americans, a quarter of the country's population, got their news from these national evening broadcasts. They all now knew about Hamaas Abdul Khaalis and about the murder carried out by Elijah's men in 1973. They had also learned about the biopic of Muhammad and about Khaalis's jihad against it. Khaalis was finally the most well-known Muslim in America.

31.

JURISDICTION

On a typical day, the Mayor's Command Center on the fifth floor of the Municipal Center in Washington would be staffed by two city bureaucrats who would make sure all the lights were on and the equipment working, and beyond that, not much else. The command center, which was organized under the District's civil defense unit, occupied a part of the fifth floor of the building, where Cullinane and the rest of the top brass of the police had their offices as well. The command center was created on the fly in 1968 when President Johnson declared martial law in the District during the riots that followed the assassination of Martin Luther King Jr. After that, it was quickly formalized and used routinely during massive anti-war and other demonstrations in the early 1970s.

The seven-room honeycomb structure was custom built for the District's Office of Civil Defense. Cullinane had an additional office in there, and there were others for the mayor and his staff and still more reserved for the military. The media had their own space in the command center, with phone lines and amenities like coffee and cigarettes. The command center was a nerve center filled with special telephones with dozens of red, white, gray, blue, and green buttons. Some had direct lines to the military and the White House. The command center had other technology that gave it the ability to pull information from various sources—commercial radio and TV, the police and fire frequencies, National Parks Police, highway and traffic departments, newswire services—creating a centralized databank of information like no other civilian operation in the capital.

At around 2:00 p.m. on March 9, the command center began coming to life. Cullinane and Rabe knew that the only way to keep track of the takeover of Washington was from there. Along with them, in one of the rooms at the center with restricted access, a negotiating team had been slowly assembling all day. O'Brien dropped in periodically, and Earl Silbert, the U.S. attorney who had overseen the prosecutions of the Black Mafia hitmen, was there too. At three o'clock, minutes after the news of the District Building seizure broke, officers from various other DC law-enforcement agencies began pouring in. The Capitol Police, the U.S. Park Police, the Metro Police for the bus and subway systems, and the Executive Protection Services all sent their officers to the command post to operate under the orders of Maurice Cullinane.

The newsroom at the command center, which typically sat empty, was now buzzing with journalists from newspapers, wire services, and local and national TV and radio stations, jostling for space, walking into each other's camera shots. Three large sheets of paper hung from the walls in the pressroom, titled "Mosque," "Dist. Building," and "B'nai B'rith." A running list of numbers of casualties, fatalities, hostages released, etc., was continually updated by the command center staff to keep the press sated.

Shortly after 4:00 p.m., the negotiating team was joined by Special Agent Patrick Mullany of the FBI. The forty-two-year-old had joined the bureau a decade earlier and was one of the first trainers at the FBI's new academy in Quantico, inaugurated months after the death of J. Edgar Hoover in 1972. He had written some of the basic texts of crime-scene forensics and hostage negotiations that the bureau now used to train its agents. He was also the FBI's lead hostage negotiator and one of the founders of the behavioral science unit that specialized in dealing with serial killers, hostage situations, and any other scenarios that required a psychological profile of the criminals involved. For years now, he and a handful of others had been training police departments from all over the country in hostage-negotiating techniques at Quantico. Rabe had trained under Mullany, and the two had worked together at the terrorism working group created after Munich.

Mullany had been in Warrensville, Ohio, that morning negotiating with the Vietnam vet holding the police officer hostage for the second day. Soon after hearing about Carter's decision to speak with that hostage taker, Mullany learned about the situation in Washington and flew there. Mullany had cringed at Carter's decision that morning, and now, in light of what was happening in the capital, it appeared catastrophic. A precedent was set, Mullany feared, and Khaalis would now surely demand access to the president as well.

Mullany had access to thousands of pages of records and files the FBI had compiled on Khaalis and the Hanafis over a period of two and a half decades, but not all. The bureau was forced to destroy many of its records after the Church Committee report of 1975, in which the federal government probed and criticized the bureau's work under J. Edgar Hoover, particularly its COINTELPRO program, which had targeted African American groups ranging from the Nation of Islam to Martin Luther King's SCLC. With what he had, Mullany began sketching out a psychological profile of Khaalis and delivered a sobering assessment. In the bureau's terms, he explained, Khaalis was a "militant fanatic," the most dangerous kind of person to encounter in a hostage situation. He gave Cullinane and Rabe a warning: the longer this went on, the more difficult it would become to get Khaalis, his men, and the hostages out alive.

The FBI had earned a reputation for trying to shoot their way out of hostage situations, especially during the air-piracy era in the 1960s. Cullinane and Rabe had a strong suspicion that because of the precariousness of the situation—shots fired just hundreds of yards from the White House on Federal Triangle—the FBI would be more trigger-happy than usual. The police and the FBI were developing diametrically opposite strategies: the feds were leaning toward a swift conclusion, and the cops wanted to keep Khaalis talking. The rhetoric from the Hanafis was not helping the Washington police's position. Aziz had spoken to a group of reporters at the Hanafi Center, bluntly saying, "A killing room will be set up at B'nai B'rith and heads will be thrown out of windows." Khadija had told a reporter on the phone, meanwhile, that "if it means us fighting to the death also, so be it—babies and all."

Griffin Bell, the attorney general of the United States, had been pondering the question of competing jurisdictions all afternoon. How, if at all, was the affair the business of the federal government? Bell was a newcomer to Washington. He had moved to the city from Atlanta only months earlier and had been the attorney general of the United States for fewer than fifty days. A longtime friend of Jimmy Carter's from Georgia, Bell was one of the earliest confirmed appointments of the Carter administration. His working day had begun at the headquarters of the Central Intelligence Agency in Langley, Virginia, where Carter was swearing in the agency's new chief to replace Ford's pick, George H. W. Bush, who had run the agency for less than a year. By the time Bell returned to his office at the Justice Department building in Federal Triangle, a little after three o'clock, Washington, DC, was under siege and his office block looked like a war zone.

After speaking briefly with Carter on the phone, Bell's next call was to his office of legal counsel. He needed a map for the legal maze. At the time, the United States had no federal statutes directly outlawing such acts as terrorism. Rauf's call to the diplomatic missions and messages to Secretary of State Vance had quickly drawn the State Department into the fray and alerted the federal government's anti-terrorism apparatus. The fact that there were foreign nationals from four different continents held hostage at the Islamic Center would have made the crime the State Department's concern in any case. The District Building on Federal Triangle, meanwhile, muddied the jurisdictional waters even more. The building was still technically District property, but the ensuing panic had forced the federal government to evacuate the U.S. Capitol, where the security had been doubled to almost 440 officers. The federal courts had also suspended business for the day.

One of the most obvious wrinkles was that DC's home rule was still in its infancy, and the line that separated the powers of the local and federal governments was still being worked out. The DC police were accustomed to dealing with the U.S. attorney's office for prosecuting crimes, but when it came to investigations and law enforcement, the FBI and the Secret Service frequently butted heads with the city's cops. It was sometimes unclear what types of crimes were the purview of federal authorities and what should be left to Cullinane's police department or the half dozen other police forces operating in the capital.

There were legal openings for Bell to push for federal jurisdiction if he wanted. The fact that the U-Haul truck the Hanafis had driven to B'nai B'rith had been rented in Maryland and was used to create civil disorder could give the FBI legal standing. The fact that the Hanafis were Muslims and had targeted a Jewish organization also suggested a federal civil rights violation. One obscure law even allowed federal jurisdiction over crimes that involved a mentally ill person coming into possession of firearms from a different state. But Bell was not sure that involving the federal government—and by extension President Carter—was a good idea; would the president want to be directly embroiled in all this?

That afternoon, Bell had met with the two people he thought might help: Charles Duncan, the deputy secretary of defense, and General Lew Allen, the head of the National Security Agency. Bell was looking for firepower from the army and intelligence from the NSA. Bell wondered whether the Pentagon could lend something like stun grenades to the FBI's sniper team—something that could be used to neutralize the Hanafis at all three locations without too many casualties. He wanted the NSA to share surveillance technology that might allow them to discreetly eavesdrop on the three locations without putting anyone in harm's way.

Both men were hesitant. Lew Allen from the NSA had himself testified in the Senate only two years earlier during the Church Committee hearings. In its report, the committee had lambasted Duncan's NSA, along with the FBI, for clear violations of civil liberties of American citizens. The military, on the other hand, was constrained by the Posse Comitatus Act, a Reconstruction-era law specifically prohibiting the military from supplying any material support to the federal government for law-enforcement action on American soil. In the end, Bell's negotiations secured only two army helicopters and some basic equipment for the FBI to use.

After the two left, Bell placed a call to Hamilton Jordan, Carter's chief of staff at the White House, and briefed him on the news. He also received a call from Earl Silbert, the U.S. attorney, who was at the Mayor's Command Center. Cullinane was requesting wiretaps of all three locations as well as the Hanafi Center on Sixteenth Street, and they needed the Justice Department to submit the request.

At 7:30 p.m., Griffin Bell, accompanied by the new director of the FBI, Clarence Kelley, visited the command center. It was time to figure out exactly who was in charge. By the time they arrived, Mayor Walter Washington was also finally in the building. He had been trapped in his office on the fifth floor of the District Building, at the opposite end from where all the action was happening. As the sun set, the police finally took the chance of exposing the mayor to the line of fire and quickly escorted him through the hallway and down the eastern stairwell, out of the building.

The mayor greeted the visitors from the Justice Department, and Bell and Kelley were introduced to the negotiators, who were gathered around a large conference table in the center with phone receivers at all the seats. A large switchboard sat in the middle of the table, and the table was littered with sandwiches, discarded cigarette packs, bottles of aspirin, and piles of scribbled notes from the conversations with Khaalis and others. The men were brought up to speed on the latest developments.

The wiretap surveillance of the telephones on the eighth floor of B'nai B'rith had already started, and police were now monitoring all incoming and outgoing calls. Every word spoken over the B'nai B'rith phone lines was being recorded and would be part of the record. Whenever contact was made with Khaalis from the command center, everyone in the room could listen in on the call, and anyone could join in. Rabe, the lead hostage negotiator, had been doing almost all the talking.

Khaalis and the Hanafis at the other locations had released close to a dozen people, but gunmen at B'nai B'rith still held more than one hundred hostages. Even though some of them had suffered bullet and stab wounds, none of the people released were in danger of losing their lives. The District Building was a different story. There was the death of the young radio reporter Maurice Williams, whose body had remained in the hallway for hours until it was finally removed around 5:00 p.m. The bullet fragments in Marion Barry's chest were found to be less than an inch away from his heart but were safely removed. His doctor had declared him to be in stable condition. Cantrell, the guard shot in the head at close range, was conscious and, amazingly, stable. The news about Robert Pierce, the hostage shot in the back at close range inside Tucker's office, was less positive. His spine had been severed by the shot. Police units on the scene also believed that the two Hanafis at the District Building might also have prepared Molotov cocktails. The Islamic Center was surprisingly quiet and the situation more opaque. No one had left, no one had entered.

There were snipers stationed in various buildings around the city, including the Commerce Building on Federal Triangle, which sat between the White House and the District Building. The FBI's own SWAT team had arrived at around 5:00 p.m. with M16 automatic rifles. Khaalis appeared especially agitated by snipers, so they had been kept out of sight so far. The police had been finally allowed to surveil the restricted airspace over the Islamic Center. The two helicopters on loan to the FBI from the military were also patrolling the sky over the city. Judge Leonard Braman, whom Khaalis had mentioned by name, was under U.S. Marshal protection. There were also a few Black and Jewish members of Congress who had been provided security details. The thousands of people with cars trapped in downtown DC after the District Building takeover had finally been evacuated following an epic rush-hour jam.

Of the demands Khaalis had spelled out on Max Robinson's live broadcast, two had already been met. The movie had been pulled from screens—though the prints of the film were still in Akkad's possession. He had made a bold offer to the Washington police, offering to screen the movie for Khaalis and his men inside B'nai B'rith. After watching it, if they still objected, Akkad vowed that he would burn the film. While this may have been priceless publicity for the film, Cullinane was not sold on the idea and had rejected Akkad's offer and told him to stay away from Washington. Meanwhile, Joe O'Brien, chief of homicide, had delivered an envelope with $750 in it to the Hanafi Center, which he handed to Khaalis's wife Khadija at the door.

Khaalis's final demand—his insistence that the killers of his family as well as the men who murdered Malcolm X be delivered to him—was the most difficult. There was no chance of handing them over to Khaalis for execution. On this question, no one—not the Washington police or mayor, nor the attorney general, or the FBI chief—had any way to deliver. Khaalis had made a demand that appeared to be unfulfillable. Most important, they all suspected that Khaalis knew this was impossible. So why did he insist on it?

After an hour at the Mayor's Command Center, the attorney general and the director of the FBI had seen enough. What had appeared like a deranged act of terrorism hours earlier had become a complex story involving a mentally fragile man intimately familiar with the negotiators in the room. As Bell learned more about Khaalis and his history, the personal, the religious, and the political all seemed to collapse into one. Bell emerged from the command center around 8:30 in the evening. A hoard of journalists was waiting outside and pushed their microphones in his

32

HOG-TIED

Between B'nai B'rith and the Hanafi Center, Khaalis had cobbled together an effective command post of his own. Since first addressing the hostages in the early afternoon, Khaalis had spent most of the day with his new secretary, Betty Neal, in the Anti-Defamation League's offices in the new wing. Khaalis and Neal sat in swivel office chairs occupying two desks set up parallel to each other. Neal sat between the two desks, handling a phone on each. The phones were large switchboard-type beige machines that lit up in various colors as lines went active. Khaalis, alternately, would sit across one of the two tables, puffing on his pipe or a cigarette, taking phone calls that kept coming from all parts of the country and the world.

The phone had been ringing all day without pause. Neal frequently had to juggle calls from reporters, police stationed outside the three buildings or in the command center, family members of hostages, and prank callers. She had been observing how Khaalis reacted to the different callers. Some people or specific subjects set him off in a sudden rage, while others, like the ones from family at the Hanafi Center, appeared to calm him down. Whenever Khaalis left the room, she would take the initiative to filter calls at her will, deflecting some that she knew could pose a danger to her and the hostages. In this way, Neal was the only one in the entire building who encroached on the otherwise complete control Khaalis exercised on the floor.

Khaalis had taken a liking to Neal. The two had chatted between calls all day. They talked about favorite foods as the lunch hour passed without anyone on the floor having eaten anything. She told him about her work at B'nai B'rith, her family and children from a previous marriage, and her boyfriend—she did not tell him that he was a reporter in the Washington bureau of *The New York Times*. Khaalis allowed her to make a phone call to let him know that she was all right. They spoke more than any other two people on the floor did, even more than Khaalis spoke to any of the other Hanafis. The two established what could almost be described as a bond. During one heated conversation between Khaalis and Cullinane, Khaalis made a pledge, seemingly out of nowhere, that even if it all had to end in a shootout and bloodbath, Khaalis would let no harm come to Betty Neal.

To be sure, the Hanafis were prepared for a showdown. A windowless unmarked room on the eighth floor, right in the nook of the L, was the designated armory. All the extra weapons were placed there, nearby in case of a firefight. Hanging above the ammunition was a hand-painted, dark-colored flag with a seven-pointed star (a heptagram) and the number 786 on it—one of the numerological symbols that Khaalis had learned from his master, Rahman, common in Sunni South Asian Muslim practice. The other six Hanafis were decked out for battle. They carried guns, had knives and machetes tucked into their belts and socks, and had ammunition slung around their waists and shoulders. No one in B'nai B'rith doubted their ability and willingness to use any of the weapons.

The gunmen mostly remained confined to the conference room, keeping watch over the hostages. The youngest and gentlest of them, Abdul Hamid, acted as an escort for people visiting the bathroom. Latif and Razzaq, Khaalis's old disciples from New York, would only occasionally visit Khaalis in his office space to check in and keep him updated. Khaalis made occasional visits to the hostages, too. In these brief visits, he made sure to fill his captives with terror. In one visit in the afternoon, he announced the capture of Rauf at the Islamic Center, which got cheers from the Hanafi gunmen standing guard. To celebrate the capture, he handed a periodical to one of his men, Abdul Salam, and directed him to read it aloud to the hostages as a sermon. It was a review of the film *Mohammad: Messenger of God* from a Muslim journal that eviscerated the film for its historical inaccuracies.

In another visit, Khaalis made an example out of one hostage who had been attracting the Hanafis' attention throughout the morning. Charles Edward Mason, a professional handyman, had started his painting job at B'nai B'rith the previous day and was scheduled to complete it on the day he was taken hostage. He was forty-five years old, a former weight-lifter, built sturdy and strong. He had helped paint over the windows at the behest of the hostage takers. When it came time to evacuate Alton Kirkland, the injured janitor, he had volunteered to carry him to the el-evator. The gunmen could sense the gracious and admiring looks he was receiving from the other hostages and reported this to Khaalis.

"Oh, you're a hero? How about I cut your head off?" Khaalis had bel-lowed, towering over Mason in front of all the hostages. When Mason re-sponded defiantly that he was ready to die if it really was his time, Khaalis ordered him to stand up and pistol-whipped him so hard that he fell to the floor and blacked out. By the time he woke up, he was hog-tied, his wrists bound to his ankles behind his back. He lay there, wincing and squirming in the middle of the floor for hours, a reminder to his fellow hostages of the punishment they might endure for crossing the Hanafis. Finally, after several hours, when Khaalis returned to the hostages, he or-dered the painter untied. He then commanded him and one of the female hostages to clean the bathroom.

Such defiance was not the norm. The hostages had mostly been cowed into submission by the evening. They knew that anything could set off Khaalis. One of the female hostages urinated in her pants, for example, and it drove Khaalis mad. The men were all restrained with their hands tied either in front of or behind them. The younger ones had their legs tied, too. The older ones were informed that they would be the first to be beheaded when it came time to start tossing heads out of the eighth-floor window as warnings. No one was allowed to speak, and the few who tried spoke only in brief, clipped whispers and exchanged eye signals. The si-lence hung heavy on all of them.

Khaalis first heard about the District Building takeover from a radio boom box that one of the Hanafis had found on the floor. To Neal, Khaalis appeared confused and perturbed by the news of the District Building, and he quickly ordered the radio be turned off. From his post on the top floor of B'nai B'rith, Khaalis was constantly in communication with jour-nalists and potential interlocutors of all kinds, but there was no actual news media of any kind available on the floor. Other than the phone lines that only Khaalis and Neal could access, the floor was almost hermetically sealed from the outside world. Khaalis wanted to keep his monopoly on information. The job of keeping track of what was happening in the outside world, especially at the other two hostage locations, fell to his family and comrades at the Hanafi Center, specifically his wife Khadija and his son-in-law, Abdul Aziz.

A little before 7:00 p.m., while the attorney general was on his way to the command center, Khaalis spoke to Aziz about the events at the District Building. Like the negotiating team at the command center, Khaalis and the Hanafis seemed unprepared for the violent firefight that had broken out there. Like the team at the command center, he was trying to figure out what to do.

"Who is down there at the District Building?" Khaalis asked Aziz.

"Ah, I don't know," answered Aziz. "I don't know. Ah, they never gave a name."

"All right, you find out from Max, what's—ah, no that's all right. Don't bother about it," Khaalis was clearly holding back. "Just call around and see who's where and who's who and let me know, all right?" He wanted details but was also probably aware that his communications were being monitored. "Just tell me any foolishness, but not on the phone, too much. All right?" Then he hung up. As Khaalis waited for Aziz to call back, he placed a call to the command center, in which he had another coy exchange with the chief negotiator, Robert Rabe.

"Yes, I want communication up at the District Building, whoever is up there," Khaalis demanded.

"Is that the group that has taken over down there?"

"You tell me."

"Well, is that who you want communications with?"

"I want communication with that group."

"Is there any particular person?"

"Get me some communication so I can keep some, ah some sanity to this for a while," Khaalis said to Rabe, who promised to "call right back with the number."

As he waited, Khaalis exchanged a few calls with the Islamic Center. The three brothers there expressed no concern about the news from the District Building. They had fallen into a rhythm with their mostly Muslim hostages. Anyone in need of the toilet, man or woman, received an armed escort and used the bathroom with the door open. Like at B'nai B'rith, the phone was ringing constantly, and Abdul Rahman, the oldest brother and the leader, was answering most of the calls, even ending up on a live radio broadcast once. A radio tuned to the news had sat between the two offices all day long. Like at B'nai B'rith, the Hanafi brothers at the Islamic Center forbade any conversation among hostages, but some of the women managed to speak with one another briefly, often in Arabic. In the evening, one of the Hanafis brought down some food from Rauf's apartment and gave it to the hostages. The Syrian bread and cheese served as dinner for all the hostages, except Rauf, who refused to eat anything. The gunmen, meanwhile, were under strict orders from Khaalis to consume no food.

Rauf remained tied to his chair. Periodically, he would ask to be released in order to say his prayers, and each time, one of the gunmen would call Khaalis to see if he was permitted to do so. Khaalis would have derived a special kind of pleasure from having the power to control if and when Rauf could pray, and he would give his consent or withhold it depending on what mood they caught him in. Once, Rauf was untied to use the toilet. As long as he was in his chair, though, a five-gallon canister of gasoline was kept at his feet, ready to be lit at any moment. The hostage takers and hostages were almost cordial in their interactions, but there was no doubt in anyone's mind that if Khaalis called with an order to execute the hostages, the men would not hesitate for a moment to carry it out.

Khaalis finally connected with Muzikir and Nuh at the District Building a little before eight o'clock, when Neal was able to get a call through to a number provided by Rabe. Nuh picked up the phone and brought Khaalis up to speed. The two men had full control over the situation. From a certain angle in the room, the cops outside in the corridor were in their line of sight and fire. They had placed a rolling office chair with a hostage tied to it right in the doorway to make sure the police would not shoot from this angle. All the other hostages were tied with their hands in front of them. The hostages had been allowed use of Sterling Tucker's private bathroom. There was also a coffee maker that they were able to use, and they could smoke cigarettes. The conversation was short, and Khaalis instructed them to keep focused, keep cool, and keep alert. "Yes Hamaas, yes Hamaas," Nuh repeated, and then he hung up the phone.

As darkness fell, Khaalis instructed Neal to dial the number for the Hanafi Center. As she handed him the phone, Khaalis asked her for the first time that day to leave the room. She was escorted by one of the gunmen to join the other hostages. "Yes, my dear," Khaalis said tenderly as he heard Khadija's voice on the line. She told him how things were at home. They had to administer a Valium to Bibi, Khaalis's paraplegic second wife. Even in her state, she was able to piece together that something terrible was unfolding. Officer O'Brien had come over to deliver the $750 in cash, she reported to Khaalis. He was in tears as he handed over the envelope. "I told Judge Braman he was going to live to regret that," Khaalis responded. Khaalis told her how he had instructed the brothers at the Islamic Center to free the eighteen-year-old Bangladeshi secretary. Her father had called Khaalis pleading for her freedom, and his accent would have reminded Khaalis of that of his spiritual master, Tasibur Rahman.

In a conversation earlier in the afternoon, Khadija had expressed concern that she or the Hanafis had heard nothing from Kareem, concluding, "I guess, it's too early now." Khaalis had downplayed her comment then. "I wouldn't worry about that," he had responded, "I feel good." In the evening Khadija mentioned Kareem once again, and Khaalis cut her short again. "We're not concerned," Khaalis insisted. "He's not in it. Right?" Khadija simply said, "Yes," and reported that "Clay," a reference to Muhammad Ali, the boxer, "is in Los Angeles."

Khadija briefed Khaalis on everything she had seen and heard on TV and radio. She told Khaalis about the official statements made by various Muslim embassies and governments. Khaalis paid close attention to this. His star Muslim hostage, Abdul Rauf, and the prime target of his attack, the Hollywood director Moustapha Akkad, had done their job of making Khaalis's cause internationally known. Khaalis sounded satisfied. Now, as the sun set on the first day, Khaalis decided that it was time to turn the media's attention to his real nemeses.

"You tell all the reporters," he instructed Khadija toward the end of the call, "contact Cassius Clay and Wallace X." The evening news on TV was already dominated by Khaalis, but the morning papers still had hours before they went to print. Khaalis wanted Wallace and Muhammad Ali involved in the story when the morning papers were delivered. Khaalis probably understood that his demand to have the men responsible for the massacre of his family delivered was far-fetched, at best. Wallace, on the other hand, if pushed enough, might just decide that it was in his best interest to submit himself to Khaalis. Khaalis also understood the media well. Framing this hostage crisis as a battle between two sports icons, Muhammad Ali and Kareem Abdul-Jabbar, was ratings gold. "Cassius Clay and Wallace X got to report to me now," Khaalis said.

33.

SPOOKS

Two separate Concorde flights crossed the Atlantic Ocean toward Washington, DC, on the evening of March 9. In one was the British prime minister, James Callaghan, who was on his way to his first formal state visit to the United States at the invitation of Jimmy Carter. In the other was Ardeshir Zahedi, the Iranian ambassador to the United States, who had taken off from Paris. His Concorde had been specially chartered by the French government so that Zahedi could make it to the American capital to prevent a catastrophe. Zahedi served as the chair of the board of directors of the Islamic Center. He had been in Paris, visiting with an ailing friend, when he received news about the hostages in Washington. He landed in Washington and at around midnight arrived at the Mayor's Command Center.

Two other foreign ambassadors, dressed in finely tailored suits and polished shoes, were already in the command center looking entirely out of place among the cops, FBI agents, and city bureaucrats. Ashraf Ghorbal, the Egyptian ambassador to the United States, was one of the first people to find out about the unfolding crisis in Washington when he had received a call directly from Abdul Rauf pleading for help. Ghorbal, Egypt's star diplomat, had arrived in the United States in 1972, just before the massacre at the Hanafi Center at the beginning of Nixon's second term. Ghorbal was the man President Anwar Sadat had assigned to Washington to reestablish the relationship after Nasser had severed diplomatic ties with the country following the 1967 war. The diminutive, bespectacled ambassador had a doctorate from Harvard University in political science and was a deeply religious man. He scheduled his working days around Islamic prayer times and, for a layperson, had an impressive knowledge of Islamic scriptures. As soon as Carter took office, and the new administration's bold plans for a Middle East peace deal between Egypt and Israel became clear, Ghorbal had become one of the most important and sought-after diplomats in the city.

Sahabzada Yaqub Khan of Pakistan, whose urbane sophistication was noticeable in even the most refined scene in the capital, was a master diplomat, most renowned in DC circles as the man who had helped mediate between China and the United States when Nixon sought to reestablish relations with the country. He, too, had arrived in the city months before the massacre at Khaalis's home in 1973. He was born into a royal family, but one that lost its royal status under British colonial rule. He became a soldier for the British, battling in the Second World War in Libya, and remained a prisoner of war in Northern Italy for three years. He spoke Russian and half a dozen other languages. He spoke English in paragraphs with a hybrid British–South Asian accent, and he sometimes demonstrated a stronger command of the language than the American press corps he encountered.

Zahedi of Iran cut a different figure entirely. He represented a country that was not only one of America's closest allies in the Middle East, along with Israel, but also one of the American military industry's biggest clients. Iran placed equipment orders larger than many could fathom. He was also a flamboyant socialite. He was driven around the city in a metallic blue Rolls-Royce and had made the Iranian embassy the talk of the town, with lavish caviar-filled parties that brought a taste of Hollywood to Washington. Zahedi could be trusted to host parties for any occasion and for anyone, from Henry Kissinger to the TV host Maury Povich, for reasons that even Povich, when asked, could not fully explain to reporters.

A *People* magazine profile of Zahedi published less than a year earlier detailed how the "dashing, gregarious" ambassador's very "public smooching" with Elizabeth Taylor was leading to some diplomatic trouble. "The Shah," the article said, "was rumored to be considering calling him home to Tehran." Zahedi, the article noted, had been the shah's son-in-law, before his divorce from the shah's daughter. Zahedi also counted Barbra Streisand, Liza Minelli, Gregory Peck, and Kirk Douglas as friends. Still, his job could be deadly serious as well. Days earlier, an episode of the

CBS show *60 Minutes* had aired a segment about the shah of Iran's secret militia, SAVAK, conducting assassinations of Iranian dissidents in Europe and the United States.

The three ambassadors became involved in the crisis at the formal request of Louis Douglas Heck, the director of the Office for Combating Terrorism, a State Department official with a rank equivalent to an assistant secretary of state. Heck was the only bureaucrat in the entire federal bureaucracy with a portfolio focused on terrorism. Rabe had invited Heck to B'nai B'rith at around 3:30 p.m. to consult. The two men knew each other from the working group of the Cabinet Committee to Combat Terrorism, which Heck had also led in its earliest days. Before this role, Heck had been deputy chief of mission in Tehran from 1970 to 1974 and had come to know Zahedi well. While building the State Department's terrorism portfolio, he coordinated closely with Rudy Giuliani, an assistant attorney general who was leading a similar effort in the Justice Department. Heck's new terrorism group had held only three meetings thus far.

By the time Zahedi arrived, the federal presence in the command center had grown, in spite of the attorney general's statement to the media suggesting that the situation was in the hands of the local police force. Two men with opaque records of work with the government had arrived at the command center shortly after Bell and Kelley left and had mostly observed ever since. They were, in Washington parlance, "spooks." Steve Pieczenik was a specialist hostage negotiator that the State Department would send to any corner of the world. Months earlier, Pieczenik had been involved in the case of TWA Flight 355, which was hijacked by a group of Croatians seeking independence from Yugoslavia. He had also been involved in the creation of the new terrorism bureaucracy under Douglas Heck. The other man, Robert Blum, was more transparently a member of an intelligence outfit and also had a degree in psychology.

Yaqub Khan had already had a conversation with Khaalis before Zahedi arrived. It was brief and it had gone terribly. Khan was not able to get a word in edgewise as Khaalis berated him and his diplomatic colleagues for ignoring the honor of the Islamic Prophet, leaving him to defend it. "You have paved the way to hell, Brother," Khaalis had said to Khan. "I'm on the job and you know it."

With Zahedi there, Khan decided to try his luck again and dialed the number of B'nai B'rith as Rabe and the others watched.

"Assalamu alaikum, how are you feeling, Mr. Khaalis?"

"Alhamdulillah," Khaalis responded, "Allah blessed me with a strong body."

The conversation began pleasantly enough, but Khaalis soon began railing against the diplomats and the Muslim majority states they represented, once again. Khaalis accused them of selling out Muslim interests for strategic relations with the United States and began justifying his own tactics in light of Islamic law, impressing the ambassadors with his knowledge of the Koran and Islamic mysticism. "I know the Book, I know the faith," Khaalis told Khan.

"My dear brother, I know exactly what you're saying," Khan assuaged Khaalis. "It is also worth considering whether this justice should not be left in the hands of the almighty Allah."

"I can't do no more than what Allah lets me do, you know that," Khaalis said. "There's no justice without the sword, you know the Hadeeth as well as I do," he said, using the Arabic term for the recorded tradition of the Islamic Prophet.

Khaalis then turned the conversation to the American Muslims who were in his crosshairs. "This man Akkad," he told the Pakistani ambassador, "should have been wasted long before he made the picture. When he first thought about it. He shouldn't have even been permitted to make it." Abdul Rauf, the imam, "does not make mistakes," Khaalis said. "They are calculated by design, brother, he's been warned too many times." Finally, regarding Wallace Muhammad, Khaalis got right to the point: "Who is giving them the money?" Khaalis demanded. "I want Wallace here in this city. I want to know who's giving them millions when they're playing with the faith. I want to know who these people are."

They spoke for close to half an hour, during which Khaalis did most of the talking. The longer the call went on, though, the wider the chasm between Khan and Khaalis grew. They may have both been Muslims, but Khaalis was an American Muslim descended from slaves, and Khan was a foreign Muslim descended from royalty.

"I've been fighting here. I'm born here. I know the problems in this country," Khaalis lectured Khan toward the end of the call. "Do you think I would go over to your home, your house and try to tell you how to run it, Mr. Khan?"

"My hope and prayer is that Allah may send to you a message of mercy, of kindness, forgiveness, of wisdom," Khan responded. "Whatever, however deep your own sense of injustice might be."

A few hours later, in the dead of the night, after the ambassadors had departed the command center for a badly needed rest, Rabe decided to try his luck with Khaalis. Through years of working on the Committee to Combat Terrorism, he had studied many similar hostage situations, especially during the spate of airline hijackings during the previous decade that ended when the hostage takers were offered safe passage out of the country, a chance to begin a new life elsewhere. The Black Panthers had an entire unit operating out of Algeria made up almost entirely of hijackers, for example. Many hijackers of the time had ended up in Cuba. Would Khaalis take such a deal, Rabe wondered?

"Don't you think we can work this out if we both work it out together?" Rabe asked Khaalis.

"I don't know how," Khaalis replied. "I don't have no suggestions."

"Let me ask you this, Khaalis. Would you be interested in leaving the country?"

"Why?" Khaalis fired back. "Why do you want to get me out of the country? Make it easier so they can bring in pictures like this?"

Rabe tried to backtrack, but Khaalis was incensed. "Who would stand up for the faith? Who? I never traveled out of America in my life except when I was a musician," Khaalis bellowed. "This is my country. My teacher is buried here from Pakistan, my children are buried here, my mother and father are buried here." The mere suggestion had deeply offended him. Khaalis might be a warrior of Islam, sure, but he made it clear to Rabe that he was an American first.

34.

CEASE AND DESIST

President Jimmy Carter woke up at his usual 6:30 a.m. on March 10. From the window of his living quarters in the White House, he could see the District Building fewer than five hundred yards away, where several people, including District Councilman Marion Barry had been shot the previous day. One journalist was dead. Close to a dozen hostages were still being held there. "Holy War of Terror," read the banner headline on the front page of *The Washington Star*. A splash photo of the hostages at B'nai B'rith, silhouettes in the exterior windows, accompanied it.

Jimmy Breslin, the famed columnist from New York, traveled to Washington when the news broke. In his column, also on the front page of *The Washington Star*, he described looking at the White House down Sixteenth Street, "temporal, powerless, a great white ice cream stand, on this night that religious revenge brought Washington to a halt." Next to his column was an "In Focus" sidebar discussing the topic of "Jehad," defined as "an ancient term enshrined in the Koran and preached for centuries by Moslems around the world." No other news made it to the front page of that paper. *The Washington Post*'s front page was similar. It carried two large photos, one of firefighters mounting a ladder to rescue hostages trapped in the District Building, and another of Marion Barry, the bandage on his chest artfully exposed to the cameras, waving from a hospital bed. The only other news that the *Post* squeezed onto page one was buried at the bottom: a federal ban on saccharin, and Carter's proposed Middle East plan that would require an Israeli withdrawal from almost all the Arab land occupied in the 1967 war.

Carter had kept up with the unfolding crisis the previous day after swearing in the new CIA chief. He assigned a few of his close aides to track developments. Hamilton Jordan, his thirty-three-year-old chief of staff, who had worked with Carter ever since he ran his successful gubernatorial campaign seven years earlier, and his deputy, Landon Butler, were on the phone with Attorney General Bell throughout the day. Carter's chief counsel, Robert Lipshutz, had been filtering the updates from many other sources back to the president too. Lipshutz, another Atlanta native and longtime trusted aide of Carter's, took a special interest in the situation. Decades earlier, he had served as the president of The Temple and the Atlanta Lodge of B'nai B'rith. He had deep roots in the American Jewish community, and Carter saw him as a person who might eventually play a key role in selling a grand peace bargain in the Middle East to Zionist organizations in America. In fact, Lipshutz was scheduled to deliver a keynote lecture at the American Zionist Conference's annual event in three days.

The previous afternoon, Jordan, Butler, and Lipshutz had gathered with Carter's national security advisor, Zbigniew Brzezinski, and deputy press secretary, Rex Granum, in the White House to chalk out a strategy after Griffin Bell spoke to Carter. In the cramped space of the West Wing, they sat around a television tuned to the news broadcasts on local channels. Carter's staff had been together in Washington for less than two months, and they were still learning how DC operated. It helped that many of them knew each other from Georgia. After the huddle, Jody Powell, the press secretary, briefed the media. He was tight-lipped but clearly eager to distance the White House from the events unfolding in the District. The FBI was investigating, he told the reporters. "What can be done by the federal government can be done by the Justice Department." Carter had received his final update of the night from Jordan and Lipshutz before going to bed. The two aides had spoken to Griffin Bell after he returned from the command center. They all went to sleep knowing that the Washington police were in charge of the situation. Carter had asked Lipshutz to meet him in the Oval Office first thing in the morning.

For the president, it was the start of another day with a high-profile visit by another important foreign leader. The British prime minister, James Callaghan, had landed in Washington the night before soon after the Israeli prime minister departed. Rabin had skipped the elaborate helicopter-ride farewell planned at the Washington Monument. Instead, he had sped away in a motorcade headed to Andrews Air Force Base after his lunch with the Jewish leaders. Callaghan was scheduled to arrive at the White House with his wife for a welcome ceremony at 10:30 a.m. Carter had only about ten minutes to confer with Lipshutz.

Lipshutz was joined by Hugh Carter, the president's second cousin, who was there in his capacity as a special assistant to the president. Lipshutz had extensive handwritten notes that he had been taking ever since the news broke. The FBI had delivered a twenty-page report to the White House. They had code-named the case DISTAK—District Takeover. The memo was based on the file on Khaalis the bureau had kept on and off since 1955. It discussed his army service, his discharge, his period in the Nation of Islam, his wives and children, and his attempted bank robbery, arrest, and the acquittal on grounds of mental illness. The file also included detailed information on the Hanafi Mussulman Rifle and Pistol Club and the massacre of Khaalis's family, but it included almost no details about the ensuing trials in the DC courts. There were also character sketches of other suspected hostage takers and a list of almost 150 names of the people who were thought to have been taken hostage in all three locations. The report concluded: "No overt action is planned or imminent by law enforcement authorities at this time. All possible strategies are being considered and explored including rescues. Commanding General, U.S. Army Special Forces Fort Bragg, North Carolina, is being consulted."

Lipshutz also carried a memo titled "Stated US Government Position in Dealing with Terrorists" prepared by Douglas Heck's terrorism office in the State Department. The document defined three broad categories of terrorist attacks. "International Terrorist Incidents," "Domestic Incidents," and finally, "Domestic Incidents with International Implications." The strategy for international terrorism was simple: engagement with the "host government" and the in-country embassy but absolutely no concessions and limited dialogue with terrorists. Domestic incidents got the longest treatment, in light of the fact that "different local police do have different policies." The Hanafi takeover fell into the third category, which received the most opaque treatment in the memo. Such incidents, it said, have "been handled by a Cabinet Committee to Combat Terrorism Working Group which is comprised of the FBI, FAA, State, NSC, among others, and which reacts to specific incidents as they occur." There were, in other words, no rules.

Lipshutz had one final document: an executive order that would call in the military to take control in Washington, DC. It cited the powers given to the commander in chief in chapter 15, title 10 of the United States Code, who in turn would hand over powers to the secretary of defense to use the armed forces "as may be necessary" to restore order to the capital. It also authorized him to act on behalf of the commander in chief in making these decisions. "I, Jimmy Carter, president of the United States," the final page read, "do command all persons engaged in such acts of violence to cease and desist." It was essentially a proclamation of martial law in the capital. The last time this had been done was the day after Martin Luther King was assassinated and rioters threatened to overrun the capital. The only other time before that was by President Lincoln, who signed the order during the Civil War.

The clock was ticking, and Prime Minister Callaghan and his wife were scheduled to arrive at any moment. It hardly seemed like the right time to declare martial law. The press secretary was already waiting with the revised version of the remarks that the president would deliver in front of the media with the British prime minister—they had decided to take no questions at this press appearance. For now, Carter decided to stay the course; they would proceed as they had been proceeding for almost a full day now. Any major decisions would have to wait until the prime minister left the White House in the afternoon. They just had to hope nothing catastrophic would happen in the meantime.

A little after 10:30, President and First Lady Carter walked out onto the South Lawn to welcome the British leader. Between the simultaneous crime scenes on Embassy Row and across the street from the White House, the British party had to navigate a meandering route to get there. The grounds were filled with dignitaries from both the United States and the United Kingdom. Mayor Walter Washington, who had been holed up in his office in the District Building for the entire previous afternoon and had spent much of the night at the command center, and Sterling Tucker, the chair of the District Council, whose office held two gunmen and a dozen hostages at that very moment, were also there with their wives.

Lipshutz surveyed the scene on the South Lawn. He could see the corner of the District Building peeking out from behind the Commerce Building in the distance. His eyes then settled on the nineteen soldiers who had arrived from nearby Fort Myer that morning, each standing next to a howitzer cannon, ready to be fired to honor the prime minister with a twenty-one-gun salute after the speeches and national anthems concluded. Without a word, gripped with panic, Lipshutz slipped back into the White House to find a phone and frantically began dialing the command center.

35.

BIG SURPRISE

"Khaalis?"

"Yes, sir."

"Look, the military is having a ceremony downtown on the Ellipse," Rabe began. He hurriedly explained the twenty-one-gun salute and warned that Khaalis and the other hostage takers might hear a series of explosions. "I want you to understand it's not us," Rabe said. "We are not doing anything to you—we are trying to get it stopped," the desperation was obvious in Rabe's voice. "Will you call your other two places and tell them that that is going to happen?"

Khaalis had not slept. He had been on the phone all night, fielding calls from all parts of the world: Australia, Europe, the Middle East. Even in the best of circumstances, what Rabe had blurted out—the military was firing cannons a few hundred yards away from a hostage situation—would have sounded alarming to someone in Khaalis's position. These were not the best of circumstances. Khaalis's voice was hoarse, his body was tired, and his paranoia was unbridled.

"That can be a cover for some foolishness," Khaalis said.

"No, it's not. I—you—you have my word."

"That can be a cover for some foolishness."

"Khaalis, you've got my word. I think I have it stopped. All right, you have my word that we're not coming in there," Rabe pleaded.

"That could be a cover for foolishness," Khaalis's mind appeared stuck in a loop. "I'm not talking about you," he said. "I'm talking about the military."

Rabe was losing Khaalis. "No, no, no. No, that's definitely out, Khaalis. This is a local government, not the military. They're not involved in any way. This is being handled by the Metropolitan Police Department, nobody else."

Rabe had been feeling good about the morning before all this. Soon after sunrise at 6:30, Khaalis had released a handful of hostages from the B'nai B'rith building. A while later, at 7:00 a.m., Khaalis sent another woman with a heart condition down the elevator and with her, some dirty, soiled towels and clothes in order to clean up the space. In exchange, the negotiators had agreed to a few demands: coffee, doughnuts, soap, and Benson and Hedges Menthols for the women—"I won't give them to the men," Khaalis had offered unprompted. Khaalis almost appeared in a good mood. "That's coffee for about 120 people, put it on Mayor Washington," he had quipped. "Don't forget the cups."

The news of the imminent cannon fire had blown away all that goodwill in an instant. Khaalis was becoming more convinced by the second that he was nearing a showdown with the U.S. military. Rabe might not have known this himself, but the military remained on standby, ready with a plan to extract hostages. All they needed was a nod from the commander in chief. After Bell's communications with officials from the Pentagon the previous afternoon, an alert had gone out to select members of the Green Berets assigned to the second and third battalions of the 5th Special Forces Group at Fort Bragg in North Carolina. These select commandos were part of a new special forces unit formed in the mid-1970s, code-named Blue Light, for the exact purpose of responding to the new, amorphous threat of terrorism. Blue Light was following the lead of a few European militaries that had formed such units right after Munich.

On Smoke Bomb Hill at Fort Bragg, a battalion commander had briefed the unit on the hostage crisis in Washington, DC. The president had made no decision yet, he told the unit, and there was no operations order. They were on standby. They began rappelling exercises from helicopters, replicating what a possible landing on the B'nai B'rith and District Buildings might be like. They conducted firing exercises, practicing for a scenario in which they might be required to effectively "neutralize" several hostiles in a shootout. In the end, the military was training to efficiently do what the military was designed to do: smash through the window, kick in the door, and try to kill the Hanafis before they could kill anyone else.

With Rabe still on the line, Khaalis was instructing the Hanafis at his end to make sure the hostages were all tied up. He wanted them to be ready to unleash hell. "You be ready, okay?" he instructed. "Use your machete on them, don't have no mercy." Khaalis directed Latif in the background, making sure Rabe heard. "Latif, alert the brothers to be ready to fight to the death," he instructed. Rabe was desperate to keep Khaalis on the line. "We've been together too long," he pleaded with Khaalis. "I trust you and I want you to trust me." Every minute that passed without cannon fire was one that could be used to walk Khaalis back from the brink, but Khaalis was unmoved by Rabe's pleas. "I trust in my Lord only."

On the South Lawn, Carter and Callaghan were done reviewing the troops and were delivering their prepared remarks from the stage. They now stood next to each other as the band played "God Save the Queen" followed by "The Star Spangled Banner." When the music ended, the two leaders remained frozen in position, waiting for the marines to begin firing the howitzers. They, too, stood frozen in place. For many long, awkward moments, everyone on the South Lawn stood still, unsure what they were all waiting for. Finally, one marine made a decisive move. He marched right up to the base of the stage where the heads of state stood. He delivered an exuberant salute—the nicest possible way to tell the men to get off the stage. The two heads of state glanced around, still confused, and walked off.

Lipshutz had managed to slip the warning to a marine guard stationed at the White House, who in turn had run up to a gunnery officer and briskly explained the situation. The startled officer had passed the message on to the others moments before the cannon fire was supposed to begin. No one was able to tell Carter about it. As the president and the prime minister walked back inside the White House, the staff were waiting at the entrance, blurting out apologies to both men. The British delegation, a White House staffer later reported in a memo, appeared to understand completely.

Rabe had kept Khaalis talking. At a moment like this, Rabe would have liked to pull Yaqub Khan into the conversation. He had an effect on Khaalis that no one else in the party could replicate. "The ambassadors are on the way down here," Rabe told Khaalis, finally letting him get off the phone and hoping that the news might encourage Khaalis. "As soon as they come down, we'll get back to you." Khaalis seemed unappeased. "I've a big surprise, you know," he replied. "I want you to tell Chief Cullinane and all the other forces that I know they can hit in here—SWAT team's going to have a big surprise."

After Mr. and Mrs. Carter bid farewell to the Callaghans, the president returned to the Oval Office, where Lipshutz, Jody Powell, and Hamilton Jordan were waiting for him. It was a narrow escape. Washington was dealing with a subject who was apparently mentally unstable, driven by beliefs and life experiences that none of them could fully understand. Anything could set him off. It was time to revisit the federal government's role in the hostage crisis. Central to this was a simple question: Was this a terror attack on the United States driven by political motivations involving American policies toward Muslims around the world? Or were these the criminal acts of a man deeply disillusioned with the American justice system? Could it be both? Khaalis had so thoroughly blurred the lines separating the personal, the political, the local, the national, the international, the religious, and the psychological that no one could tell for sure.

Carter invited Griffin Bell to join the meeting over the phone. If things ended disastrously, the White House would be caught in the fallout no matter what. On the other hand, leaving things in the hands of the Washington police did create some useful distance between Khaalis and the president, which Carter's team was eager to do ever since he had spoken to the hostage taker in Ohio the previous day. The Hanafis had many more hostages than the lone Ohio gunman. They were much closer. They had a lot more leverage.

For all the frenzied press coverage, the city of Washington was surprisingly functional. With a few exceptions, the city had gone to work as usual on the second morning. The traffic, while knotted and unpredictable, managed to move. The buses were running an hour behind schedule. The functions of government and ordinary life outside downtown continued. Other than the canceled gun salute, the hostage situation had no direct effect on White House activites either. Still, America's capital was one severed head away from becoming a bloody battlefield. If there was any truth to the barely veiled threat that Khaalis had delivered about Sunni Muslim sympathizers around the country ready to rise, the battleground might even extend beyond Washington. Then, there might be no choice but to call in the military.

The decision, ultimately, was the president's. Carter would not have known in that moment that his presidency would eventually come to be defined by a hostage crisis in a place far, far away from Washington. At 12:40 p.m., he placed a call to the command center. Police Chief Maurice Cullinane had never spoken to a sitting president before. He had always thought that if a president ever called, he would speak to a secretary first and get connected through a switchboard, but when Cullinane answered, the man on the line introduced himself as Jimmy Carter. The president started by offering words of encouragement and gratitude. He told Cullinane that he understood that he was dealing with an exceptionally complex situation. Cullinane agreed, "Yes, sir."

The president asked him if he had slept at all.

"No, sir."

The president then told Cullinane that he believed sleep was very important at such a time for clear thinking. He suggested Cullinane find a place to take a quick nap before anything else. Cullinane understood what Carter really meant. This crisis was Cullinane's to handle and his to end. Despite the close call in the morning, the federal government would stand back and follow his lead. At the end of the two-minute call, Carter thanked Cullinane again for all the work he was doing to protect his city and the country and then hung up. The only instruction Cullinane had received from the president, oddly, was to take a nap. Was it a presidential order, he wondered. Cullinane wanted to take no chances, so he retreated to his office, lay down on a couch, and closed his eyes.

His mind was racing too fast to sleep. There was so much that so many people around the world had done and not done to deliver Hamaas Abdul Khaalis to this moment in his life. The military bureaucracy that never placed him in a psychiatric facility, the VA bureaucrats who had stood in the way of extending his GI Bill benefits, the men and women from around the world who had helped make this movie about Muhammad, the judge who had granted retrials one too many times, the dozens of oblivious diplomats in the city who had never as much as thought of making a call to the Hanafi headquarters after a Muslim family was nearly annihilated. Where was Khaalis's own family from Gary, Indiana? So many people had played a part in this. None of those people mattered now. Khaalis towered above the nation, all-powerful, holding the lives of close to 150 people in his hands. Cullinane and his department were the ones responsible for fixing it. As Cullinane lay there, unable to fall asleep, the next crisis of the day was already airing live on TV.

36.

PANORAMA

Over a period of twenty-four hours, Khaalis had handled around one hundred media requests and interviews. He had demonstrated a refined understanding of how the news operated, subtly adapting his message to the different mediums—visual, audio, and print. At times, he also knew specific local and national reporters and their roles in organizations and modulated his tone and message for them. He could even play assigning editor, dangling leads and dispatching reporters to follow them. When he spoke about the news media with his Hanafi associates, he sometimes referred to them dismissively as "designer press."

When Helen Thomas, a star UPI reporter and president of the White House Correspondents' Association, called B'nai B'rith, for example, Khaalis knew exactly who he was talking to. "Why don't you give President Jimmy Carter a nice call? He's a nice ol' country boy," he teased her. "Tell him that it's a very serious situation." To the reporters calling from Detroit and Chicago, he tossed out bloody red meat about Wallace Muhammad and Muhammad Ali and the Nation of Islam. When reporters called from the Middle East or from Los Angeles, he would dwell on Akkad and the film. He anticipated the stories each reporter was writing and then provided them with the pull quotes and headlines they obviously wanted.

He was not letting his secretary, Betty Neal, put everyone through, either. If a reporter or news organization served no apparent purpose at a given moment, he quickly dismissed them. Others, like *The Washington Post*, he purposefully blackballed. This was the paper that had quoted Rauf disparaging Khaalis's knowledge of Islam as "superficial" in the aftermath of the massacre in 1973. He would never forgive Rauf, and he would never forgive the *Post* for that. Some reporters he summarily rejected. When Jim Vance, another Black anchor on local TV, tried to reach out to the Hanafi Center, he told Khadija simply, "I don't like him."

Around 1:00 p.m. on the tenth, a little more than twenty-four hours into the takeover, Khaalis stumbled. It was the lack of food, maybe, or the sleep deprivation, or a combination of many things. Regardless, Khaalis found himself in a situation he should not have been in. An especially daring and dogged producer for a daytime lifestyle talk show, *Panorama*, on the local independent TV station WTTG had repeatedly called B'nai B'rith that morning asking for Khaalis. Neal had tried to deflect her calls, but she'd eventually relented and put her through to Khaalis. She then convinced Khaalis to join the host, Pat Mitchell, live on the air at 1:00 p.m. Mitchell had been hosting the midday talk show for only a few weeks, replacing the previous host, Maury Povich. She had no experience reporting on crime and was unprepared for a live encounter with a sleep-deprived, starving man holding hundreds of people hostage, threatening to decapitate them any instant.

The wheels started coming off within seconds of Khaalis coming live on the air, when Mitchell introduced him to her other guest in the studio, Reverend Steven Abel. "No, just a moment now, just a moment, uh-uh, you didn't tell me you had somebody else there," Khaalis cut her off. "I'm Muslim. You didn't tell me you had someone else there and Reverend Abel and I are not getting into no discussions about my faith and the cross and this and that, no, uh-uh, no, no, no, no." After several painful moments of Khaalis's insults, Mitchell consented to cutting the reverend out of the conversation and was able to turn Khaalis's attention to the hostages and his demands—only to lose him again moments later.

"You sound tired," she noted, as a sensitive daytime talk show host might. "No I'm not tired. That, that, no that's deceptive," Khaalis cut in aggressively. "You come in here, you see how tired I am." Through the previous day, the negotiators had taken care never to put Khaalis on the defensive. Suggesting that Khaalis sounded tired, like the host had, or weak, cornered, or outnumbered, could immediately compel him to a show of force, which the negotiators desperately wanted to avoid. He might just shoot or behead a hostage. "It's my voice," Khaalis continued, "I've been talking. I'm not tired, it's my voice. I've been talking excessively to people calling up here."

The negotiating team was watching Khaalis's slow-motion meltdown live, and they began scrambling to reach the WTTG studio to insist that the talk show let Khaalis get off the phone. Nearly fifteen minutes into the interview, Mitchell and Khaalis were about to discuss the murder at the District Building when, suddenly, Mitchell froze. Her producer was relaying into her earpiece the police's concerns. "I'm afraid that we have to terminate the conversation at this point," she said abruptly. "Thank you for calling in," she told Khaalis, and the line went dead.

The damage was done. Khaalis had not even hung up when he bellowed at Neal to get "the chief" on the line. As Neal dialed, Khaalis decided to get the Islamic Center on the other line and blow off some steam by threatening Rauf. "Tell him he'll be lucky to get out of there without—with his head on his shoulders," Khaalis told one of his Hanafi gunmen to relay. "Tell him I won't kill his wife." Once he was done with the terrorizing, Khaalis stormed out of the office toward the other wing of B'nai B'rith, where the hostages were held. It had been a long, miserable night for the captives. In the middle of the night, around 3:00 a.m., a gunshot had pierced the quiet and awakened those who had managed to fall asleep. They all wondered if a hostage had been executed—they did not know one of the Hanafis had accidentally discharged a bullet. The hostages had perked up in the morning, though, thanks to the coffee and doughnuts Khaalis had requested for them. Some even felt a hint of gratitude toward him. Now, the positive energy evaporated as Khaalis swooped into the room like a dark cloud. If the police were playing games, he yelled, there would be hell to pay. He delivered some news: he had decided that the oldest hostages would be beheaded first. He then stormed back out.

It was not the first time that live broadcasts had threatened to derail the delicate negotiations. WTTG, the same station, had badly blundered the previous evening at around 7:00 p.m. when it aired a forty-second clip of Akkad's film during a news broadcast. The phones at the station instantly started ringing off the hook. People could be slaughtered if Khaalis found out that portions of the film were played on TV in Washington. The same evening, Khaalis heard about one reporter at WTOP who accidentally identified him as a "Black Muslim" on the air. It was a term popularized by Malcolm X and was specifically used to refer to members of the Nation of Islam. Khaalis called the station and demanded an on-air apology, which the reporter was forced to deliver. Another reporter asked Khaalis if he thought he was being dealt with in good faith, leading Khaalis down a dark, paranoid hole. Still another one asked if any deadlines had been set, when the negotiators had carefully avoided any talk of deadlines.

There was another startling broadcast moment on the second morning. At around 9:00 a.m., a WTOP producer was able to connect to Sterling Tucker's office suite in the District Building. The Hanafis allowed Alan Grip, Sterling Tucker's press secretary, to read a statement they had prepared:

"We are Hanafi Muslims to the death," Grip read aloud the message as it aired live. "If the police have any ideas about this room it will put all our lives in immediate danger as well as those of more than 100 hostages at B'nai B'rith, because Hamaas is my father and I will fight and die with my father. And I am prepared to die because they killed our family. This is all for Islam. It is not a personal grudge. It's just that justice should be done."

The reporter followed up with questions.

"I need to know, please, what is the situation in the room that you're being held—how many of you are there and how are you being treated?"

"They want to know what the situation is in here," Grip relayed the question to Muzikir in the background.

"No answer to the number of hostages," Grip replied, "but as far as being treated, we are being treated very well. We've asked for cigarettes, we've gotten them, we asked for fruit for breakfast, they've gotten it, we've asked for a newspaper, we've gotten that. They've allowed us to have our hands tied in front of us, instead of in the back, which is a lot more comfortable. We're allowed to stand or sit or lie down, whichever is more comfortable."

"Coffee," a voice yelled in the background.

"We're allowed to have coffee and tea," Grip added. "We're being treated very well."

Were there any messages that the men might allow to be passed on to those who were concerned about their loved ones taken hostage? the reporter inquired.

"Okay, let me ask," Grip said before relaying the question to the Hanafis.

There was a back-and-forth between the hostage takers and Grip for a brief moment.

Then, suddenly, right before the line went dead, Grip was able to say two panicked words: "No, goodbye." This conversation was the first and only time any hostage's voice was broadcast during the entire episode.

Then, there was Max Robinson. No journalist was as deeply entangled in Khaalis's plot as he was. On the one hand, he was, all of a sudden, a national celebrity. *Time* and *Newsweek* magazines had both sent photographers to take photos of him, and CBS sent out a camera crew to follow him around at work. He got calls from *Newsday, The Wall Street Journal,* the Canadian Broadcasting System, and the media industry magazine *Who's Who,* all looking to profile him. Literary agents were sending out queries about book deals. On the other hand, he was deeply imperiled. In a commercial break during the late-evening news telecast the previous night, Robinson had received a call in the studio from someone threatening revenge for something he had said on the air. "What did I say? What did I say?" he demanded from the caller. "How can I straighten it up if you don't tell me what it was?" he said. As he hung up, he told his colleagues what he thought was happening: "They're going to kidnap me." He called his brother and asked him to take his wife and children to his place. After his broadcast ended, Robinson was escorted from WTOP by two police officers to the Sheraton Park Hotel, where he checked into a room and spent the night under police protection.

Soon after Khaalis's near-disastrous *Panorama* appearance on the second afternoon, Robinson arrived, once again, at the Hanafi Center. This time he was with a camera crew, and they set up on the sidewalk on Sixteenth Street. The center hung over Robinson's left shoulder in the shot, patrolled by a Hanafi man wielding a weapon. Robinson held up a mic, looked into the camera, and began delivering a monologue, telling the story of the man who had been called a terrorist in the morning's papers.

He explained that when you enter the house, you must take off your shoes. "It is holy ground," he said. After recapping Khaalis's demands, Robinson reminded his audience of the massacre at the house four years earlier. Khaalis, he said, had returned home that day to find five of his children and grandchildren hacked to death and drowned. Two adults were shot to death, he said, and his wife and daughter lay unconscious on the floor with bullet holes in their heads. Khaalis and his son-in-law, Abdul Aziz, Robinson said, had witnessed "the kind of horror most of us are spared in our lifetimes." The news media, he reminded the audience, had termed the massacre "the most brutal, the worst crime the nation's capital had ever witnessed." When Robinson had entered the house days after the massacre, he explained, Khaalis "was moaning over and over again inside this house, 'They killed my babies, they killed my babies.'" Robinson told the audience that Khaalis had repeated the phrase the previous day. "But yesterday," Robinson said, "he was not moaning."

Robinson referenced the American flag flying outside the Hanafi compound. "Four years ago," Robinson said, "Khaalis wrote that America should not be a country based on skin power, on gun power. He wrote that no matter what religion you happen to be affiliated with, we are all Americans." Now, Robinson said, Khaalis feels deceived and cheated by the country he loved. He explained how one of the men brought to trial for the massacre had been freed. One died before being tried. Another one was yet to be convicted, four years later. It was clear to him, he said, that Khaalis "is prepared to take innocent lives in his own quest for justice."

Robinson ended his piece before the camera with this: "As for the rest of us, all we can do is wait and pray—pray that the justice of Hamaas Khaalis is not the justice of the sword, but a justice of compassion, compassion for the frightened, innocent hostages he now holds." It was a compassion, he said, "which was too long denied to Hamaas Khaalis and members of his family."

With that, he signed off: "I'm Max Robinson, Eyewitness News."

37.

TRUE PICTURE

Getting Khaalis to eat something, the negotiators believed, was a way to not only calm him down but also to buy some time. Cullinane dispatched Joe O'Brien to the Hanafi Center soon after 1:00 p.m. He was the only one Khaalis would remotely trust to handle something as delicate as food that would enter the Hanafis' bodies. Even then, Khaalis insisted that Abdul Aziz accompany O'Brien and that Aziz never take his eyes off the food. The two, along with Khaalis's brother-in-law, Salim, left the center at 1:25 p.m., carrying hot meals prepared to order at the Hanafi Center for all three locations. There was fried chicken, peanut butter sandwiches, cheese sandwiches, bananas, a candy jar, seven cartons of cigarettes, mouthwash, and, important for Khaalis, throat lozenges.

They arrived at B'nai B'rith first, and then they left for the District Building before finally going to the Islamic Center. There, Rauf was led to the door at gunpoint. As he reached out to grab the brown paper bags from the ground at the doorstep, Aziz stood tall over him, looking down at him. By the time the logistics of the elevators at B'nai B'rith were negotiated and Khaalis sat down to eat, it was almost three o'clock. He had only just started when Neal asked him if he wanted to take a call. It was the National Black Network, the first Black-owned and -operated radio news network in the United States. They were insisting that it was important.

"Yes," said Khaalis.

"Sir, we understand that Wallace Muhammad has arrived in Washington, DC, and we want to know, are you prepared to meet with him?"

"I don't know anything about it," Khaalis replied. "I don't know anything about him having arrived here as yet. Nobody has contacted me."

"Until he personally contacts you, that's when you will believe him?"

"That's right."

"Sir, as far as the meeting with him. Where would you have the meeting?"

"Well, I think that we would wait and see whether or not he's arrived, okay?" Khaalis was uncharacteristically restrained. "I'm going to eat something now, all right?"

"Sir, why do you want to meet with him?"

"I'm going to eat something now, all right?" Khaalis repeated and hung up.

Rumors about Wallace Muhammad arriving in Washington for a showdown with Khaalis had been circulating all day. Khaalis's strategic decision to focus on Wallace and Muhammad Ali in his late-night interview had delivered the desired result. Wallace and Muhammad Ali—Khaalis insisted on calling him Cassius Clay, or sometimes the "so-called Muhammad Ali"—had both been bombarded with interview requests. Some newspapers even ran side-by-side photographs of Muhammad Ali and Kareem Abdul-Jabbar, just as Khaalis might have hoped.

Ali was in a complete media blackout. Wallace, too, stayed away from the cameras, but the number of inquiries did compel him to issue a lengthy press release the previous evening through the World Community of al-Islam's official channels. It came out early enough that it was quoted at length in morning papers. The statement covered, one by one, all the Muslim American men thrust into the spotlight. Akkad's film, Wallace said in the statement, "goes a long way in correcting false ideas about the religion created by earlier movies, which made mockery of Muslim life." Hollywood, he said, had historically "portrayed Muslims as wine drinkers, slave masters and lust-filled harem keepers." If the movie was "discrediting or falsifying the true picture of Islam," Wallace said, "I would be the first to express a desire to see the movie stopped."

Still, Wallace stopped short of endorsing it. The film, he said, "does not satisfy our desires or what we would like to see in a film. We would like to see a better presentation of the early history of Islam." Wallace claimed, however, that "there is general support throughout the Islamic world for this kind of movie." In conclusion, "to stop the violent demonstrations," Wallace said, "the promoters and producers of this movie should stop showing the film."

For Rauf, Wallace had nothing but words of comfort: "We would like to extend our sympathy to those who have been injured or killed thus far and we would like to state our support for the innocent persons being held hostage. We are standing by our brother in the faith, Dr. Muhammad Rauf and his family. Our prayer is that Allah will soon open a way for the speedy and safe release of all hostages and that the mosque be returned to a state of peace."

Finally, Wallace spoke about Khaalis without mentioning his name. "I have no knowledge on the horrifying massacre at the Hanafi center other than what has been given me in the press," he said. It was a dubious claim. The massacre was one of the most notorious crimes committed by the Black Mafia, which operated under the umbrella of the Nation. The murder trial of one of the hitmen from the Philadelphia temple was still pending. Jeremiah Shabazz, the man who had been minister of that temple and had called for the hit on Khaalis's family, was still a high-ranking member of Wallace's organization and most likely drawing a salary from it. Wallace was adamant, though: "I accept no responsibility in this matter."

Instead, Wallace went on the offensive against Khaalis. "The attacks upon innocent persons and threats on human life are, in my opinion, more serious and provoke more concern than the showing of the film," he said. He did, however, leave the door open to possible negotiations. "Any parties that have serious complaints against me as imam, I desire that these complaints be made known to me so that I will have an opportunity to answer them."

Four years after the massacre at the Hanafi Center, the murders were front-page news once again. Wallace had spent two years carefully distancing himself from the troubling and complicated legacy of his father and charting a course for the future, but Khaalis, through his elaborately crafted demands, had tethered him to the Nation's darkest crimes. There were more than one hundred mosques and Islamic centers scattered around the country representing the various religious sects and strains of Islam and ethnic and racial groups of Muslims in the country. In Washington, DC, alone, there were estimated to be thirty thousand Muslims. Khaalis was forcing them all to choose: they were either with Khaalis, who was against the movie about Muhammad, or they were with Wallace, who had endorsed it earlier.

Wallace was no rookie either. He had spent most of his adult life charting his path to the apex of American Islam. He had come out on top in a crowded field, filled with cutthroat and sometimes criminally violent competition. He might have lacked charisma, and he might not have commanded the same adulation as Malcolm X, but he was a crafty operator like his father. As he read the morning papers and saw what Khaalis was doing, he planned his next move.

Wallace called in his legal counsel, Saad El-Amin, for a meeting. El-Amin was a Yale Law graduate who had joined the Nation of Islam in the early 1970s and attended his first Saviours' Day in 1973, weeks after the murders at Khaalis's home. As one of the Nation's two lawyers at that time, he knew all about Khaalis, the murders, and the criminal trials that followed. Even though he never became formally involved in the legal proceedings, he had closely followed the case after Wallace took over the organization in 1975 and made him the top lawyer. El-Amin had helped draft Wallace's statement the previous day, but now, Wallace said, he wanted El-Amin to travel with him to Washington. There, Wallace proposed, he would offer himself up in exchange for the hostages.

Wallace's contacts in the FBI welcomed the proposal. Wallace had worked with them for over a decade, ever since his father first excommunicated him and Wallace had reached out to the bureau to seek protection from the Fruit of Islam. After Elijah's death, the FBI had sensed Wallace's desire to clean up his father's organization and bring it aboveboard. Wallace opened up the books and ledgers for them and began to dismantle the more criminal parts of the sprawling organization. In return, the bureau eased up its surveillance of the organization. Now, the FBI offered to provide him with protection if he came to the capital.

A little before noon, Wallace, his personal secretary, and El-Amin took off from Chicago O'Hare Airport. After the plane landed on the tarmac at Washington National Airport, it stopped short of the jet bridge. The other passengers watched as Wallace Muhammad and his two associates were escorted off the plane and greeted by a group of FBI agents. They all climbed into an official vehicle and drove to a hotel in Arlington, Virginia, on the outskirts of the District of Columbia. An entire floor of the hotel had been cleared for them. The three men were each given a room, but they all gathered in one and sat around a TV set to watch the latest news from the capital.

El-Amin had engineered an exclusive deal with Walter Cronkite's team at *CBS Evening News*. In exchange for taking care of all logistics and setting up a press conference inside the hotel, CBS would get exclusive video camera access to it. They would be the only network to have footage for that evening's news broadcast. At around 4:00 p.m., El-Amin took a seat behind a cluster of microphones in a room set up on the same floor where he and Wallace were staying. Guarded by uniformed police officers, El-Amin made a brief statement.

"There has been a demand for the presence of Wallace Muhammad and he is here," El-Amin told dozens of reporters who had gathered in the brightly lit room. "We had no indication of any enmity that existed between the Hanafi community and the rest of the world of Islam," El-Amin said. Wallace and his organization, he added, were "attempting to get with the officials who have the ultimate responsibility of directing the release of these hostages, so Mr. Muhammad's actions will not be in conflict with theirs." El-Amin stopped short of offering the hostage exchange that Wallace wanted. Instead, he only strongly hinted at it: "no reasonable action will be eliminated, excluded or ignored."

At the end of the prepared statement, the reporters asked several questions. Would Wallace Muhammad appear in public? He would not appear publicly, El-Amin said, until all hostages were safe. Had Wallace reached out to the negotiators? Wallace, El-Amin said, had notified the president, Mayor Walter Washington, and the police chief Maurice Cullinane of his presence in Washington and was prepared to offer his services with ten minutes' notice. None of these people had responded with any request so far. The press conference concluded, the cameras were packed up, and the reporters filed out of the room. Wallace had made his move: at six o'clock that evening, America would find out that Wallace was ready to sacrifice his life for America.

38.

BROTHERS IN ISLAM

The bombshell news dropped at B'nai B'rith a little before five o'clock. Khaalis was engrossed in conversation, once again, with the Pakistani ambassador, Yaqub Khan, when Neal interrupted.

"Mr. Ambassador, hold it right one minute," Khaalis told Khan. "My wife's on the phone, maybe an emergency."

"Yes, dear?"

Khadija wasted no time.

"I just heard on the radio that Wallace has been in town since this morning," she said. "He's within ten minutes of the—of where you are now."

The radio reports said that Wallace was attempting to contact the police and the White House so he could discuss details of how he might present himself to Khaalis, but no one had engaged him so far.

"I knew it," Khaalis hissed. "This is why— That's why there's going to be some nasty things happening around here." He abruptly hung up on Khadija and returned to the line connected to the command center.

"Deputy Chief?"

"Yes," Rabe responded.

"My wife has just heard that Wallace has been in this town since this morning," Khaalis said. "Why haven't you all had him over here and to contact me?"

"I did not know he was in town since this morning," Rabe replied.

Cullinane and Rabe knew that the feds were operating behind the scenes. While President Carter had made clear through his phone call to Cullinane at noon that he wanted the Washington police to remain in charge of the crime scene, federal law enforcement and spy agencies that were part of the negotiating team never truly relented. With every passing hour, they were getting antsier. Mullany, the special agent from the FBI's behavioral science unit, was in constant contact with the bureau's Washington field office and headquarters and did not always bother to brief Cullinane or Rabe on those exchanges. The FBI's tactical team, as well as the helicopters it had on loan from the army, had been in place since the previous evening, ready to engage at a moment's notice. The SWAT team had already drawn up plans to storm the three buildings. The U.S. Army's Blue Light unit was on standby.

Cullinane and Rabe were ill prepared to engage Khaalis on the issue. As far as they were concerned, having Wallace within ten minutes of the scene was an invitation to violence. From the very beginning, the FBI and the police had differed fundamentally in their approaches to tackling the threat, with diverging views on what did and did not constitute progress. As sunset approached on the second day, it became clear to everyone in the room, especially the two police chiefs, that the FBI was eyeing an endgame. They seemed ready to push the situation to the brink instead of allowing the crisis to spill into a third day. To the cops, the introduction of Wallace to the equation felt almost like sabotage.

From Khaalis's perspective, Rabe's plea of ignorance was confirmation of one of two things: it was possible that Rabe was truly unaware of Wallace's whereabouts, or Rabe was lying. Either way, Khaalis might conclude, the police department was losing control of the negotiations.

"I was nice," Khaalis roared, "now I'm gonna be a different man from here on out." He was done with negotiations, he told Rabe. "I'm tired of talking; I'll cut these phone wires."

Khan cut in, urging Khaalis to respond to kindness, as a Muslim should.

"Don't start philosophizing, Brother Ambassador, to me," Khaalis shot back. "I'm not in for it tonight, it's a different night tonight." Khaalis said he was ready for all three locations to be rushed by law enforcement sooner or later. "All they're gonna do is get all these people killed."

Rabe warned Khaalis that "there's a lot of bad information out there," and not to trust everything he heard, hoping to leverage Khaalis's paranoia. "We have talked to the mayor—the mayor is not talking to anybody. None of the ambassadors have been negotiating for you. Nobody can negotiate for you but yourself," Rabe said. Khaalis's faith in Rabe was gone, however. "Connect me with the White House then when I finish with this gentleman," he instructed Neal in the background. "The president might as well know a lot of citizens gonna be slaughtered up here for nothing." A phone call to the White House by an unhinged Khaalis as the sun set on another day of the crisis might be all the prodding the feds needed to end this one way or another. Rabe and Cullinane were getting desperate.

Khan assured Khaalis that "we've communicated to our governments, they are fully apprised of your point of view, your sentiments, your feelings, you can be sure that we are reflecting on your—everything you say here back home."

Then, Khaalis responded with a question that stunned everyone in the room: "When are you coming up here?"

"You want me to?" Khan asked, hesitating.

"Yes, I want you to come here." The negotiators around the conference table exchanged wide-eyed looks. Pieczenik, one of the two spooks in the room, may have been the only one not completely surprised. Ever since he had walked into the command center late on the first night and found the ambassadors looking out of place among the various ranks of American law enforcement, his gut feeling was that they were the key piece of the puzzle. For almost a full night and a full day, he had listened in on the conversations between Khaalis and the negotiators, rarely saying a word. As was his training, he parsed all the conversation with the goal of separating what he called the manifest content—the stated demands of the terrorist—from the latent content: what did Khaalis really want? When Khaalis asked Khan to come to B'nai B'rith, it finally clicked.

By the end of the first day, Khaalis had already received the $750 he had demanded, and while the reel of Akkad's film had not been moved out of the country, Khaalis appeared satisfied with it being pulled off the screens. His only real outstanding demand was the delivery of the Black Mafia hitmen to B'nai B'rith. Everyone, Khaalis included, probably knew that this was an unfulfillable demand. Late at night, that demand had morphed into one for Wallace and Muhammad Ali to surrender themselves. Now, when Wallace's surrender had suddenly become a plausible scenario, Khaalis had pivoted again, this time summoning the ambassador to visit him in the building.

Khaalis simply wanted accountability. He wanted someone he could hold responsible, in the broadest sense, for what had happened to him and his family and for defaming his beloved Prophet. He wanted some-one he could dislike to come face-to-face with him and apologize. Khaalis wanted the enemy to submit to him and ask for forgiveness from all true Muslims. That was not all, however. Khaalis also wanted to be recognized as the most important Muslim in America—the American caliph.

If this was true, then holding court on the eighth floor of B'nai B'rith and exacting revenge on Wallace would achieve little in the way of estab-lishing authority. Even if Khaalis were to execute Wallace right there, it would not grant him Wallace's authority—it might even backfire. The am-bassadors in fine suits, representing three of the most powerful and influ-ential Muslim countries in the world, on the other hand, were the ones with the real power. Foreign governments had enabled Wallace for years, showering him with cash and deferring to him as the leader of America's Muslims. They were always the ones who had the power to anoint leader-ship for Muslim Americans. There would be no better signal to the world of Khaalis's ascendance than a sit-down with these men, when they would grovel and plead for his cooperation and mercy.

"Well, this can be easily arranged," Khan said out of turn, and for the first time stumbling over his words. "We, we can, we can easily set this, this set up I'm not sure of the mechanics, I'd have to ask the . . ." It was up to Rabe to fill in the blanks. With four years of experience under his belt as part of the terrorism working group, Rabe was as prepared as anyone to negotiate, but Khaalis's move had him stumped. He could not begin to fathom the mechanics of sending three foreign ambassadors, from three vital allies of the United States, into the heart of a bloody hostage crisis in Washington. On the surface, it was an absurd proposition. It was also the only path out of the crisis, however narrow, that the negotiators had seen in more than a day. With the feds breathing down their necks, Rabe and Cullinane also thought it might be their last.

"Now you know you gonna have to meet us halfway here now," Rabe said. He countered with an offer that might allow the police to maintain some control. The ambassadors, he said, could meet with Khaalis outside B'nai B'rith on the pavement. "I'm not coming out of the goddamn build-ing," Khaalis said flatly. Rabe reminded Khaalis that his men were hold-ing more than one hundred hostages on the eighth floor. It would be unimaginable for the police to try to harm or arrest Khaalis. Khaalis was not going to take any chances. "I'd be a goddamn fool, you know that."

The men were still grappling with the conditions for a face-to-face when there was a startling thud on the roof of the B'nai B'rith building, over the hostages' heads. It sounded as if something heavy had landed on the roof. The hostages in the open conference space instinctively turned their necks up toward the ceiling. The Hanafi gunmen's eyes shot upward, too, and one of them came running to Khaalis's office to tell him about it.

"You got men on the roof?" Khaalis asked Rabe.

"Huh?"

"You got men up on the roof," this time Khaalis stated it as a fact.

"No, there's nobody up on the roof, Khaalis. I've told you that nobody does anything until the word comes from me or the chief. You have to believe us."

The police no longer knew who controlled the situation, though. For all they knew, the FBI's tactical team or some other agency might already be mounting a rescue operation. Time was running out.

"You should be ashamed of yourself," Khaalis hissed.

For the first time since he had arrived the previous night, the Iranian ambassador, Ardeshir Zahedi, jumped into the conversation. After introducing himself, he made a series of promises to Khaalis in his position as chair of the board of governors at the Islamic Center. He would lobby the secretary of state in the United States, he said, and all the governments all over the world to join Khaalis in denouncing the film. "We'll beg them, and we'll ask them, and we'll command them and we'll demand that they should not show this goddamn film," he tried his best to mimic Khaalis's passion in his thick Persian accent. "They should burn it," he told Khaalis.

The Egyptian ambassador Ghorbal jumped in too. He had heard Khaalis rail against Rauf for almost two days, and he surmised that at least some of that rancor was aimed at Egypt, for their openness to a peace treaty with Israel. "We will be very happy, my dear brother, to come and to see what your grievances are about Imam Rauf," he offered soberly. "If he has done something wrong," the ambassador said, referring to Rauf, "we will correct it." Ghorbal repeated some of Zahedi's promises. "You see, my dear brother, we are all anxious to help in there," he said, adding, "We are all brothers in Islam."

After hearing from all three ambassadors, Khaalis sounded encouraged, but he was still wrestling with the decision. "I don't like it. No, I don't like it. I don't like it. I don't like," he kept muttering to himself. "I don't like nothing where I gotta come down there, no."

"Khaalis," Rabe said, "supposing that I and—myself and Captain O'Brien came over there with the three ambassadors and met you in the lobby? I'll go that far, I'll do that. I'll come in unarmed." The mention of O'Brien seemed to flip Khaalis's mood suddenly. He was finally considering it. "I'm not coming down unarmed myself," Khaalis said. Rabe sidestepped the issue. "You would come down to talk to them and when you finish talking you go right, you go right back upstairs."

"Get Captain O'Brien," Khaalis ordered Rabe, and the deputy chief darted out to find the homicide chief.

"My brother from Pakistan," Khaalis called out to Khan.

"Yes, brother Khaalis?"

"You are my brother, some of my family is over there. I love them very much."

"Indeed. Wonderful."

"Now, I'm going to talk and I'm gonna come down."

The deal was done, and Khaalis needed a handshake.

"We have complete trust in you and we have trust in Allah and we have utterly no fear of any kind," Khan said.

"I don't have fear, brother," Khaalis responded. "I wouldn't care if you had an atomic cannon down there."

39.

CHAIN OF COMMAND

Millions of Americans all around the country sat around their TV sets for a second night to watch the latest from the capital. The previous evening's broadcasts had been filled with numbers of hostages and casualties. On the second night, the news took a deeper dive into the complexities of American Islam and America's uncertain law-enforcement response. Barbara Walters finished her more-than-ten-minute segment on the top story on ABC by telling the audience that she had spoken on the phone with Muhammad Ali, who had ended his media blackout. He had refused to let her record and play the conversation on the air, but Walters read a transcript: "In a subdued voice with no bravado or fight in it, Ali kept repeating he didn't want to be involved," Walters reported. "'If you're concerned about me,' he said, 'don't get me involved.' Finally, he volunteered he would only speak with President Carter. 'Have you tried to reach him?' I asked. 'No.' 'Will you call him?' 'No, but if he calls me, I'll call him back.' 'Are you scared?' I asked. No answer. 'Has anyone asked you to come to Washington?' The final answer: 'No ma'am.'"

An NBC journalist, standing in the bustling newsroom at the command center, meanwhile, reported of a "frightening element" introduced into the situation: "There is a genuine fear," he said, "that these Hanafi Muslims might be engaged in jihad, the Muslim word for holy war." The implication, he said, was that "they might have already decided that they are going to die."

The negotiating team, in the meantime, was working feverishly to make the meeting at B'nai B'rith happen. Attorney General Bell first heard of it in a call from Peter Flaherty, the mayor of Pittsburgh and Bell's designated deputy attorney general, who had stationed himself at the command center since the previous evening. He was a close associate of Carter's and was serving as the president's unofficial eyes and ears. While the proposition might have sounded outrageous, Bell knew of no law that limited the extent to which the ambassadors could get involved in negotiations. Legality aside, the maneuver could badly backfire. In the worst case, the execution of three ambassadors from Egypt, Pakistan, and Iran in the heart of the American capital would turn into its own diplomatic crisis that would surely doom Carter's grand foreign-policy aims in the Middle East. If this was to go through, Bell believed, it would have to be approved by the president himself.

Bell connected with the White House at around 7:00 p.m., where the president was joined by his chief of staff, Hamilton Jordan, and Chief Counsel Lipshutz. The president was hosting a state dinner for the British prime minister at 7:30 and had to be dressed in a tuxedo in the second-floor residence before then. He had only a few minutes to make a decision. Over two days, Carter had carefully kept his distance from the crisis and the decision-making process. If Carter said nothing, he knew the decision would fall right back to the person he had left in charge, the chief of police, Maurice Cullinane. The two men had never met in person. Did Carter want to trust him with this?

After turning over the plan a few times with his aides and the attorney general, the president relayed his stance: he would remain uninvolved in the crisis and in the decision to send ambassadors into the line of fire. Bell understood and immediately called Flaherty with the news: there was no change in the chain of command. Carter was not standing in the way. The authority to make a decision was still with Cullinane.

The three ambassadors were busy seeking clearance from their own respective heads of state. It was getting close to midnight in Cairo when Ashraf Ghorbal connected with Anwar Sadat, the president of Egypt, who indicated his approval. For Zahedi, government was much more of a family affair. He did not consult with his ex-father-in-law, the shah Reza Pahlavi of Iran. Instead, he simply wrote a letter, which he instructed his embassy staff to open in case he never returned. If he did return, he told his staff, and the shah was upset with him, Zahedi would handle the fallout—it could not possibly be more awkward than when he divorced the shah's daughter. In Pakistan, Prime Minister Zulfikar Ali Bhutto had just days earlier won a messy, contested reelection on a socialist platform;

now he was in the crosshairs of what he believed to be a CIA-backed street protest movement led by Islamic political parties in his country. Despite his misgivings about America, he gave Yaqub Khan the green light. If it all turned out well, Bhutto might have calculated, America would reciprocate by stopping its sponsorship of the Islamic political protests against him.

Rabe and Cullinane had worked out an elaborate setup with Khaalis. The three ambassadors would ride with Cullinane in his cruiser from the command center. O'Brien would pick up Khaalis's son-in-law, Aziz, from the Hanafi Center—Khaalis demanded that he be there as well—and they would all rendezvous at B'nai B'rith. Rabe would stay behind at the command center. The negotiations would take place at a table that would be set up in the lobby of B'nai B'rith. When Khaalis had objected that the lobby might be exposed to sharpshooters, Cullinane agreed to pull back the entire police perimeter a full city block and move the table back toward the Jewish museum in the rear of the building. It would be impossible for anyone to see inside. The only outstanding issue was the weapons.

"If we were to go to a peace table, then I don't believe that anyone, anyone there at all should have weapons," Cullinane told Khaalis on the phone. "You would have my word and the ambassadors' word that no one from our side would be armed and we would also like your word as you gave us your word that you not . . ."

"I don't like that," Khaalis snapped back.

If this was to proceed, Cullinane insisted, the two men would have to have faith. "I know that you as the general are going to leave orders with your men, which they will follow," Cullinane said. "And I would like you to understand that as the chief, I'm going to give orders—"

"I'm not a general," Khaalis cut in, "I'm a mujahid. I'm a mujahid"—a soldier of Islam, an executor of Allah's divine will, the one who carries out jihad. "I always carry my knife with me," he said finally.

"Okay, Khaalis," said Cullinane. "If that is your desire."

As he hung up the phone, Khaalis turned to Betty Neal and told her to leave the room for the last time. Her services were no longer needed; she was now just another hostage. She was escorted by a Hanafi gunman to the conference hall and tied up as she took her place on the floor. Not long after, Khaalis walked into the space. He told the hostages that the time for their deaths was near. He recommended that they say their final prayers, and a few of the hostages began sobbing. He said nothing about his upcoming face-to-face negotiations with the ambassadors.

Back in his office, Khaalis dialed the Islamic Center himself this time. He told the brothers there to let Rauf know that he would die very soon. His head, Khaalis said, would likely be removed from his torso. He instructed the three Hanafi brothers at the Islamic Center to ensure all their weapons were loaded and ready to fire. In case the police charged the mosque, they would have just seconds to make sure all the hostages were executed. Khaalis instructed Nuh and Muzikir, at the District Building, to retie the hands and feet of all hostages and, just like the other Hanafis, be prepared with their weapons to execute everyone if the police made a move.

With everyone warned, Khaalis waited. He sat in his chair in the Anti-Defamation League office, closed his eyes, and began to pray. For the first time in almost two days, he was truly alone. As he always would in times of trouble, or whenever he faced an important decision, he beckoned for his master, Tasibur Rahman, to appear to him. When the U.S. Secret Service had met with Khaalis to interview him exactly one decade earlier, a few days after Rahman's death, Khaalis had told them that his master was already communicating with him as an apparition. He was the inheritor of "an inner or mystic line," he had explained to the Secret Service agents, and that gave him extraordinary powers.

Rahman never failed him. He would always come, luminous and wise. Now, on the tenth anniversary of his death, Rahman appeared at B'nai B'rith. Fred, Jerusha, and Gary Richardson, the three stocky white dwarves whom Khaalis had once told army psychiatrists instructed him to hurt others, were no longer there. Rahman was the only one he saw. Without words, they spoke, and Rahman offered his guidance, delivering the truth to Khaalis.

Finally, Khaalis called into the office, one by one, each of his six Hanafi followers who were in the building. They had all joined him in this mission the previous morning without a question and without expressing a shred of doubt. They had come because Khaalis was their khalifa. Now, they were all fighting to the death. Khaalis explained the situation to each of them. He was going down on the elevator to meet with the emissaries of some of the most powerful Muslims on the planet. Each Hanafi listened carefully, quietly. None of them expressed any doubt. It was not their place to do that.

Khaalis designated Abdul Razzaq, one of his oldest disciples, to stay in the office and answer the phones. "Keep that goddamn thing clear," Khaalis instructed Razzaq, pointing to the blinking light on one line. "Keep it clear of any foolishness." If things started going wrong, Khaalis said, he would find a way to send the code word, the fundamental articulation of the Islamic faith in Arabic. "*La ilaha Illallah, Muhammad ar-Rasula Allah.*" There is no God but Allah, and Muhammad is the messenger of Allah. If Razzaq heard that message, the Hanafis at all three locations were to immediately execute all the hostages.

Khaalis had time for one last phone call. He dialed home. Khaalis and Khadija had married in that church in Harlem on a snowy day more than thirty years ago. Together, they had gone to hell and back and suffered endlessly in limbo. "Yes, beautiful," Khaalis said tenderly as she came on the line. They spoke as if Khaalis were not the single most important story in the country at the moment. They talked about the kids and the grand-kids. They joked about neighbors acting strangely. He had already told her what mattered that morning: "I'm prepared to die, dear." She had re-sponded, as he knew she would, "Okay, we're prepared to die too." Khaalis told her that it was time to take the call on the other line. It was Aziz, calling from the B'nai B'rith lobby. They said their goodbye.

"How does it look down there?" Khaalis asked Aziz.

Aziz reported that it looked as expected, but Khaalis was not satisfied. He asked Aziz to perform a closer inspection of the scene. "Let me know what kind of room it is; if it looks safe and windows and all that kind of crap." Aziz placed Khaalis on hold and returned to the line a few minutes later. "Everything is secure back here," he reported. Khaalis asked Aziz to walk to the elevators and wait for him there. O'Brien came on the line and reported that Aziz was "at the elevator now." Finally, at 8:11 p.m., Khaalis walked into an elevator on the eighth floor and pushed the button for the first floor, returning to the lobby that he had entered thirty-four hours earlier.

40.

TABLE SPREAD

Khaalis embraced Aziz as soon as he stepped off the elevator. There were no weapons visible anywhere on his body. He walked right past the police officers—they seemed insignificant—and approached the three ambassadors huddled together. Without missing a beat, Zahedi moved into an embrace with Khaalis. Khan and Ghorbal followed his lead, embracing Khaalis in turn. It was an unexpectedly warm start to the proceedings. It might have injected the negotiators with a rush of confidence, except the ambassadors felt the sharp jab of the heavy metal chain Khaalis wore around his waist. It was not technically a weapon, but Khaalis could easily decide to wield it as one and knock over anyone in the room, perhaps even kill them if he wanted.

Khaalis took a seat at the head of the table. Across from him, at the opposite narrow end, Cullinane and O'Brien sat close together. Zahedi took a seat to Khaalis's immediate right, with Abdul Aziz sitting between him and the two officers. Yaqub Khan took the seat to Khaalis's immediate left, and the Egyptian Ghorbal sat next to Khan, clutching a copy of the Koran. There were seven people at the table.

As soon as they were seated, Khaalis launched into a tirade against the ambassadors. Their weakness was the real reason they had all ended up here. Their sterile stand against the Zionist plot for world domination was what enabled Israel to brutalize Palestinians. Why, with all their oil, wealth, and bombs, were their countries so weak, unable to leverage their power? How did they fail to cancel a movie that ridiculed their dear Prophet Muhammad? Khaalis, in his mind, knew the answer: it was their compromised personal faith that enabled them to "prostitute" Islam for short-term, worldly gain.

Khaalis's harsh words, while disturbing, would have hardly felt new or strange to the diplomats' ears. The rage that Khaalis was expressing was the same rage that these diplomats had seen mounting in hundreds of millions of people around the Muslim world, especially the young, during the Cold War. What would eventually be called "anti-Americanism" was beginning to sweep across the Middle East and Asia, and it often had less to do with America than with the frustrations Muslims around the world had with their own governments. In the case of Zahedi's country, Iran, and Khan's Pakistan, this anti-Americanism was felt in leftist and communist circles too. In Egypt, Nasser's successor, Anwar Sadat, was bracing for blowback from a newly energized Muslim Brotherhood if he did take Carter's lead and pursue a peace deal with Israel. Khaalis's case might have been built around a biopic of Muhammad, but the quivering fury in his voice left no doubt in the ambassadors' minds that Khaalis's grievances were also political.

As the political figurehead of the Islamic Center of Washington, Zahedi apologized, physically lowering himself before Khaalis as he spoke. Zahedi not only apologized for their inability to stop the film from being made and shown, but he also expressed, for the first time, their deep sorrow for what had happened to Khaalis's family four years earlier. All three men had arrived in Washington within a few months of the massacre at Khaalis's home, and none of them had spoken with him about it. The diplomats, Zahedi said, thought it was not their place to involve themselves in a murder investigation, but they were wrong. Hearing the mention of his family instantly made Khaalis break down into tears. It was the first time anyone had seen him weep freely about this. Even his closest family members had not seen him cry. He had shed tears only once, in private while bathing himself. Now, the tears flowed freely.

Over the next three hours, the ambassadors and Khaalis talked, listened, and debated everything from the enigmatic will of Allah to whether the Zionists really did control Hollywood and the media. They discussed the nature of life and death as well as revenge, forgiveness, and, of course, justice. Abdul Aziz and the police looked on quietly. Sometime in the first hour, spotting an opening, Ghorbal carefully stepped into the conversation with his Koran open on the table. The book had a few pages marked.

In the preceding hours, while the police had been negotiating the conditions and details of the face-to-face meeting with Khaalis, the ambassadors had sat down with Pieczenik and Blum, the psychologists, and an Iranian Koranic scholar from Bethesda, Maryland, and role-played the face-to-face meeting. In that mock negotiation, besides picking up important negotiation tactics from Pieczenik, the Muslims had also selected three specific verses from the Islamic holy book, which they decided would be useful in confronting Khaalis in their appeal for peace. A case rooted in Allah's own words as revealed to the Prophet Muhammad was the best option, they believed. Khaalis, it had become more than obvious by now, answered to no less an authority.

The first verse that Ghorbal recited for Khaalis was from the fourth chapter of the Koran, titled "The Woman": "But those who disobey Allah and His Messenger and transgress His limits will be admitted to a Fire, to abide therein: And they shall have a humiliating punishment." In context, the verse was ostensibly about shares of inheritance. This passage included the injunction that daughters and wives, who had historically been treated as property themselves, should become inheritors of wealth. Over centuries, however, some Islamic scholars had read the verse also as a warning about how careful and precise a true believer must be in following Allah's commands. According to one of the most reliable narrators of Muhammad's tradition, Ghorbal would have explained, the Prophet had said that even one small mistake in carrying out the order described in this verse could wipe away seventy years of good deeds. By that same measure, seventy years of sinful deeds could be wiped clean by one good deed that was precisely in line with Allah's will.

Pieczenik and his fellow psychologist Robert Blum would have gleaned from studying Khaalis's FBI file that the need for precision would resonate. During his childhood in Gary, his classmates always knew one thing about Khaalis for sure: nothing upset him more than when things were not done by the book. This precision had led Khaalis to excel as a jazz drummer. It was this same precision that had so impressed the sage Tasibur Rahman that he gave him the name that highlighted his two biggest strengths: zealousness and purity. The ambassadors were urging Khaalis to consider a possibility that they hoped would unsettle him: was it possible that he was misinterpreting Allah's will? They did not dare doubt the righteousness of his anger or even challenge the morality of his acts. How sure was he, though, that his decision to take more than one hundred people hostage was not transgressing the precise meaning of Allah's commandment?

The next verse was from the fifth chapter, "The Table Spread": "O ye who believe! Make not unlawful the good things which Allah hath made lawful for you, but commit no excess: for Allah loveth not those given to excess." These instructions were specifically about the dietary and social restrictions that Muhammad imposed on the Arabs per Allah's revelation. This verse was addressing a specific problem that had arisen among Muhammad's followers. Some of them simply went overboard. Some, being excessively careful, were avoiding foods not mentioned by Muhammad as problematic. Others were practicing celibacy, even though there was no command from Allah to do so. Some went as far as becoming reclusive hermits or even castrating themselves to stay away from sinful sexual thoughts and acts.

In this verse, Allah communicated through Muhammad that it was possible to become overly zealous. Allah is warning Muhammad's followers not to fall into sin in their desire to please Allah. They should not make *haram*, or forbidden, what is actually *halal*, or permissible. The ambassadors wanted Khaalis to consider this question: How sure was he that the film he was protesting was truly a forbidden thing? Was he making *haram* for himself and the Muslims of the world something that was actually *halal*? If so, he was disobeying Allah's command.

Finally, there was another verse from the fourth chapter. "O ye who believe! Stand out firmly for Allah, as witnesses to fair dealing, and let not the hatred of others to you make you swerve to wrong and depart from justice. Be just: that is next to piety: and fear Allah. For Allah is well-acquainted with all that ye do." This verse tackled the crux of the matter: justice. It was also a fitting verse to bring up in the lobby of B'nai B'rith. Islamic historians believed that it had been revealed to Muhammad through the angel Gabriel in response to Muhammad's dealings with a local Jewish tribe.

Muhammad, tradition says, had sent one of his representatives to collect a tax on the fruits and produce of the Jews of Khyber, near the city of Medina, which was under Muslim jurisdiction. When Muhammad's agent arrived there, the Jews offered him a bribe to look the other way, and the tax collector took deep offense. "By Allah! I have come to you from the dearest of the creation," religious texts record the man as saying, in reference to the Islamic Prophet. "You are more hated by me than an equivalent number of apes and swine," he said. In that moment of rage, the man was tempted to avenge what he read as clear disrespect for Muhammad. He considered drawing his sword, but he resisted the urge. "My love for him and hatred for you," he said, "shall not prevent me from being just with you."

Was Khaalis confusing his own desire for revenge with the justice of Allah? "Let not the hatred of others," the verse instructed, "depart from justice." Weeks earlier, standing in front of the movie poster in Times Square, Khaalis had conflated the injustices and violence he had suffered with the insults he perceived against the Islamic Prophet. He held the same people—Zionists and their Muslim agents, Akkad, Rauf, and Wallace—responsible for both. These agents had defamed and humiliated his dear Prophet and had perpetrated or allowed the violation of his home and the massacre of his family. The verse, the ambassadors hoped, would force Khaalis to pull these strands apart and urge him to consider whether his urge to execute the traitorous Jews and their agents was driven by his own urge for revenge. "For Allah," they emphasized to him, "is well-acquainted with all that ye do."

Khaalis fought back, wielding his own knowledge of the Koran and other texts and of Islamic history—it was considerable. Of all the Muslims in the room, after all, the man from Gary, Indiana, was the one who had dedicated the most time in his life to studying the faith and unlocking its secrets. He countered with other verses from the Koran, reciting them in Arabic when he could, and translated them to justify his stance. They went back and forth like this throughout the first hour and into the next. Their central question: what was Allah's true will for Khaalis in this moment? No one in the room knew the answer, of course. No one ever knows the answer.

Zahedi, known more for his fine taste in wine and caviar than for his deep knowledge of the Koran, was mostly quiet during this discussion. When the theological debate appeared to be hitting a wall sometime after 11:00 p.m., he finally turned the direction of the conversation away from faith and toward something as important: family. Zahedi told Khaalis that this moment in Washington reminded him of a story that his grandmother would tell him when he was a young boy. It was a story about her husband, Zahedi's grandfather, whom Zahedi never met. He was a wealthy landowner who one day rode into rival territory on horseback to negotiate a settlement for a conflict over disputed land. The elders of the opposing tribe welcomed him, but as he sat sharing a water pipe with a few of the elders, a group of young zealots from the clan ambushed and stabbed Zahedi's grandfather to death.

The murder sparked a blood feud that would continue for decades. Much later, members of Zahedi's tribe were finally able to capture a few of the men they suspected of murdering his grandfather. They were brought into the village square, and the town was invited to witness their execution. Zahedi's grandmother, as she told it, was invited to confront the men before they were put to death. When she arrived, however, she walked up to the men assembled for execution and surprised everyone by announcing that she had forgiven them. Why did she do it, Zahedi had asked as a child. The fighting, she said, had taken her husband. A continuing blood feud, a cycle of violence, she feared, might also take her children or her grandchildren someday. If she had not forgiven the men, the old woman had said, Zahedi might never have been born.

It was a simple story, but it stirred something in Khaalis. He rose to his feet and approached Zahedi, who rose to meet his eyes. They were of similar height, but Khaalis was much more broadly built. In that moment, Zahedi knew that Khaalis could end his life if he wanted to. Khaalis stared at Zahedi for a moment and then, for a second time that night, held the Iranian in a tight embrace. This time, however, he stayed in the ambassador's arms for a long while and wept like he had never wept for his lost family. The rest of the men sat quietly, trying not to disturb the moment.

As Khaalis settled back into his chair and wiped away his tears, Ghorbal, the Egyptian ambassador, recited another verse of the Koran taken from the fifth chapter: "So pardon them and turn away from them. Surely, Allah loves those who do good." The verse, it is believed, referred to the Christians and Jews who lived alongside Muhammad's Muslim followers in ancient Arabia. Allah had revealed that the Christians and Jews had committed a grave sin by twisting the words that God had revealed to them. The verse, however, instructed Muslims to forgive and turn away. Allah, it is explained a few verses later, will take care of the rest. "He forgives whom He wills, and He punishes whom He wills. And to Allah belongs the dominion of the heavens and the earth and whatever is between them, and to Him is the final destination."

Closing the book, Ghorbal suggested the release of thirty hostages from the eighth floor as a sign of goodwill and forgiveness. It might serve Khaalis greatly not only in his larger life mission but also in the afterlife. Khaalis considered the proposal for a few moments. "Why don't I release all of them?" he finally said. No one spoke. No one knew what to say. Khaalis was serious. He repeated that he was ready to let everyone go. Then, for the first time in almost three hours, Khaalis looked straight ahead at the two cops seated at the opposite end of the long conference table. Khaalis was ready to begin a different kind of negotiation now.

41.

FAIR JUSTICE

The meeting ended around 11:30 p.m. on March 10 with an important understanding: all parties wanted the hostage crisis to end. How, exactly, this would happen remained a puzzle. Khaalis rode the elevator back up to the eighth floor and retreated to his office. When the ambassadors and the police, along with Aziz, exited the building, Earl Silbert, the U.S. attorney, and Peter Flaherty, from the Justice Department, were waiting outside, eager to be briefed on what had transpired. As they conferred on the pavement, news cameras flashed in the distance, capturing the brief huddle.

Everyone knew that the officers and the ambassadors were always going to be the face of the negotiations and nothing more. Any agreement reached in the lobby of B'nai B'rith would have to be taken back up several long chains of command, through the District and federal bureaucracy, probably ending with Mayor Walter Washington and President Jimmy Carter. Khaalis had demanded immunity from prosecution for himself and his eleven men—essentially a clean slate for the Hanafis to start all over again. Cullinane had tried to temper Khaalis's expectations in the lobby. There was a dead reporter awaiting burial, he reminded Khaalis. Councilman Marion Barry was still in the hospital, as were several other injured hostages, one in critical condition. Someone would have to be held accountable for all that. Still, Khaalis did not budge. He had little interest in playing by the rules of the American justice system. One of the accused murderers of his family was still awaiting trial four years later, after all. Plus, Khaalis still held close to 150 hostages. He was still in a position to call the shots.

Flaherty briefed Griffin Bell over the phone a little before midnight.

The attorney general, who had been in touch with Carter's chief counsel throughout the evening, carried the offer up to Hamilton Jordan, Carter's chief of staff. After almost an hour and at least a dozen calls between the U.S. attorney's office, the Justice Department, and the White House, Cullinane received word of the counteroffer the United States was ready to make to Hamaas Abdul Khaalis. It was up to Cullinane to sell it to Khaalis.

In the meantime, Khaalis had spoken with Khadija as soon as he had returned to the eighth floor. News of the face-to-face encounter, she told him, was all over live TV. She also reported two important calls that she had received while Khaalis was meeting with the ambassadors. The first one was from Harry T. Alexander, one of the first Black judges in the DC courts, who had gained notoriety and fame for his bold racial activism from the bench. Khaalis had met Alexander almost a decade earlier when he appeared in front of the judge while facing felony charges after trying to rob a bank single-handedly in 1968. Alexander was no longer a judge and was now a practicing attorney. He had recognized Khaalis from the news, he had told Khadija. If Khaalis made it out alive and was ever to face a trial, Alexander would be interested in representing him. The second call, Khadija said, was from the office of the Saudi-led Muslim World League. They, too, were interested in speaking to Khaalis if he made it out alive. They were eager to help. Khaalis was pleased with all this news. He now had a high-profile defense attorney lined up, and he had the attention of the single most influential Sunni Islamic institution in the world. By the time Cullinane called at quarter to one on March 11, Khaalis was more open than ever to the idea of ending the hostage crisis.

"You gave me a tough job, you know," Cullinane said. "The District Building caused us a lot of trouble, but I think both of us already knew that it was going to cause us some trouble."

Cullinane explained the offer. Khaalis, he explained, would be arrested at B'nai B'rith. "Your arrest will be made by Joe O'Brien," he said. From B'nai B'rith, Khaalis would be taken in O'Brien's cruiser to the police headquarters and then to the DC superior court, the same court in which Khaalis and his family had spent so many days of the past four grueling years. Khaalis would be arraigned and then released immediately on his personal recognizance, Cullinane said. Earl Silbert, who would represent the government at the hearing, would make it clear to the judge that the government had no objection to Khaalis's release. "Joe will then take you directly to your house where you can take your bath and pray, okay?"

"Yes, I'm listening," Khaalis said.

The grand jury would take at least a couple of months, Cullinane explained. Khaalis would have to go to trial for what he had done. For those couple of months, as long as Khaalis kept his nose clean, "you will be home, able to take care of your business, able to take care of your family and the families of the others."

"I'm listening," Khaalis said again.

"Well," Cullinane said, "that's it."

"And then what happens after that?"

"Well—justice—"

"What do you mean by that?"

Cullinane hesitated. He knew better than anyone that selling Khaalis on the idea of American justice was foolish. "I told you when I was up there and I told you that my word was good. Now if you want me to come to court to say that I dealt with you in a very tense situation for a long time, that you always told the truth, that you never lied to me. Any time you ever told me you were going to do something, you did it and I believe you to be an honorable man, I'll be happy to do that."

"That's nothing," Khaalis replied bluntly.

"What do you mean, it's nothing? It's nothing! If you knew what I had to do to come up with a plan like this. What do you mean, nothing?" It was the first time since the start of the crisis that Cullinane had lost his cool. Khaalis sounded almost amused. He asked about his men. Like Khaalis, they would all be arrested, Cullinane explained. Rabe would supervise the arrests at the Islamic Center, and "I'll pick another good man to go to the third place." Like Khaalis, they would appear before a judge. There were no guarantees for bail or bond for anyone other than Khaalis, however. "They'll be treated with dignity," Cullinane guaranteed. "I promise you that there'll be nobody going to beat on them or any way mistreat them and that they're going to receive fair justice as you ask."

Finally, Cullinane reminded Khaalis, as obliquely as he could, of a fact that Khaalis already knew: that American justice favored the powerful. "The publicity that surrounded the last few days," Cullinane told Khaalis, and "the new friends that you have made as a result of this incident" could all help Khaalis. He had two months to build his profile and present his case in the court of public opinion. "That's why I'm having you released just as soon as you leave there and come down to court."

Khaalis pondered what Cullinane appeared to be saying without actually saying it. Over two days Khaalis had gone from a fringe figure in American Islam to the most widely known American Muslim in the country and perhaps even the world. Khaalis had stopped a film reviled by some of the most powerful and influential Muslims and governments in the world. Khaalis had the Muslim World League, and who knew what else, waiting to talk to him.

"We got an agreement?" Cullinane asked.

"All right," Khaalis replied.

A little after one o'clock, Flaherty, Bell's deputy, called the U.S. attorney, Earl Silbert, to inform him of the terms for the Hanafis' surrender. Earl Silbert took careful notes and finally carried the message to the one person who ultimately held all the cards: Harold Greene, the chief judge of the Superior Court of Washington, DC. Green had been chief judge of the court since 1966. He had overseen the entire murder trial involving Khaalis's family and all the retrials that followed. He was the one who had appointed Leonard Braman to the Black Mafia murder case as judge in the first place. He needed no explanation or background about who Khaalis was.

Greene agreed to Khaalis's release, but he had a few requests of his own. He wanted the Hanafi headquarters to be free of weapons, and he wanted to prohibit Khaalis from having any contact with Wallace Muhammad or anyone from that organization. Silbert resisted on both counts. Besides the obvious first and second amendment issues the orders might present, adding more conditions at this stage in the negotiations could derail the precarious agreement, he argued. The mere mention of Wallace Muhammad, he warned, could push the negotiations several steps back. As carefully as he could, Silbert explained to the judge that the limits of compromise had already been reached. Silbert asked if 5:00 a.m. would be too early to convene court, and the judge said he would be there.

Khaalis, meanwhile, gathered his men in B'nai B'rith to inform them that their jihad was over, for now. The police would enter, he explained, and they would all quietly surrender. Khaalis told them to leave all their weapons behind and walk out with dignity. They need not bother about untying or releasing any of the hostages. The police would take care of that.

"There'll be no manhandling, no bullshit like that," he guaranteed the brothers at the Islamic Center.

"Is that all right with you?" Khaalis asked.

"Yes, yes."

"I am your leader," Khaalis said.

"Yes, Hamaas," they said without hesitation.

He called the District Building last. It was the first time Abdul Muzikir, the man who had pulled the trigger killing Maurice Williams, answered the phone.

"Listen to me closely," Khaalis said. "I'm releasing my hostages up here. I want you to do the same."

"Yes, Hamaas."

It was all done in less than five minutes.

Captain Joseph O'Brien called Khaalis from the lobby of B'nai B'rith at around 1:00 a.m.

"What's the status?" he asked.

"I'm coming down," Khaalis replied.

O'Brien said he wanted Khaalis to come down last, probably because he wanted to oversee the arrests of all the others and make sure everything went smoothly. Khaalis, though, insisted that he would be the first to surrender. His men had followed him in on the morning of the ninth. They would follow him out on the eleventh. For the second time that night, Khaalis rode the elevator down to the lobby. Joe O'Brien was waiting there and gently placed handcuffs on Khaalis. As they drove to the police station for processing, the other Hanafis descended one by one, and each was arrested and led out of the building and into the waiting squad cars.

Their guns drawn, a Washington Metropolitan Police tactical team moved in formation into B'nai B'rith a little after 1:30 in the morning. When they burst into the eighth-floor conference space, many of the hostages at B'nai B'rith—only a few would have been fast asleep—believed that the bloody end had finally arrived. The terrorists, they thought, had come "to do it to us," one would later tell a news reporter. The cops yelled at the hostages to get low and stay down on the floor as they spread out and combed the entire eighth floor for booby traps or an ambush from hidden gunmen. After a few tense moments, the tactical team secured the eighth floor. They finally began untying the hostages. Free at last, they hugged, kissed, cheered, and let the tears flow. A few huddled for a quick prayer.

At the Islamic Center, things were quiet in the dark. The hostages were either lying on the floor or sitting in chairs. Several of them had fallen asleep. Buthayna Abdul Rauf was awake, though, and she noticed the two older brothers, Rahman and Rahim, shuffling in the dark. She could tell that they had removed their jackets and their guns before quietly sliding out of the room. She whispered to one of the center employees next to her to put her head down and pretend to sleep. No one dared move. Moments later, the police entered calmly and directed the hostages to the Gramercy Inn lobby for processing. Robert Tisdale, the Christian minister, was asleep. He woke up when the lights were turned on and a police officer was towering over him. "You're free to go."

At the District Building, the hostages watched anxiously as their two captors handled their belongings. The police yelled from the corridor outside, asking the gunmen if they knew what they needed to do. Nuh placed his scimitar on one of the empty chairs. Next, he took off his belt, which had a scabbard attached to it for the machete he had carried in with him. Muzikir picked up his shotgun and pumped it once, staring at the hostages. No one breathed. He then moved his finger over the safety and clicked it on. Immediately, Deputy Police Chief Robert Klotz appeared at the doorway and instructed the men to shed their weapons and come through the doorway with their hands on their heads. They complied. "Is everyone okay?" the deputy chief asked, finally turning his attention to the stunned hostages.

In the basement of the Foundry Methodist Church, two blocks north of the B'nai B'rith headquarters, close to fifty people, family and friends of hostages, had been given food and beds by the Red Cross as they waited. As word spread through the basement that the hostages were being released, they all began rushing for the exit. They left the basement and ran down the empty streets of Washington to greet their loved ones, who were emerging from the building. Before exiting, someone flipped the switch on the panel in the basement that controlled the old Swiss bells hanging over the church.

To the sound of pealing church bells, the hostages and their loved ones poured out onto Rhode Island Avenue at quarter after two in the morning. They fell into embraces. There were more tears, more cheers, and more prayers and flashing news cameras all around. For some of the hostages, the moment marked the beginning of a new life. For many, though, the damage would be irreparable, appearing days, weeks, or even years later. Some would leave their spouses after their release, and some would marry fellow hostages. While some would start new jobs and new lives in faraway places, some would remain stuck in the moment, prisoner of their memories forever. For the time being, though, everyone had to be examined by a doctor and questioned by a police officer. They were corralled and taken to the Gramercy Inn, where they were recorded and processed. Ambulances and three metro buses were lined up outside the hotel to carry all the wounded and injured to the hospital. Jack Carter, one of the president's sons, woke up his father at the White House to deliver the news. Soon after, in the middle of the night, Mayor Walter Washington held a press conference. "The Lord was on our side," he declared euphorically. "I didn't give up anything—what I got was 134 citizens alive."

Khaalis arrived at the DC superior court before 5:00 a.m. escorted by his friend, Captain Joe O'Brien. Fifty reporters along with twenty-one on-duty deputy marshals packed the courtroom. Khaalis was wearing a blue windbreaker, light-colored trousers, brown shoes, and a blue turtleneck sweater. The wood-paneled courtroom number seven was under extraordinarily heavy guard. It was the biggest security presence since the trials of the Nation of Islam murderers had started there three years ago. O'Brien had formally signed the criminal complaint against Khaalis. Chief Judge Greene charged Khaalis with armed kidnapping, explaining that the charge grew out of "a takeover by the defendant of three buildings." The judge placed four restrictions on Khaalis as conditions of his release. He would not travel outside the District, he would give up his passport by March 14, he would not possess any firearms himself, and he must not give any statements to reporters. If he broke any of these conditions or engaged in any more illegal activity, Greene explained, his bond would be revoked and he would be jailed. Finally, Greene instructed Khaalis to reappear at the courthouse at 9:00 a.m. on March 31.

"Do you understand what I have said, sir?" Greene asked at the end.

"Yes, I do," Khaalis responded soberly. Those were the only words he spoke during the proceedings.

At 5:40 a.m., Greene adjourned court. Khaalis walked out of the court-room a free man, for now. As the sun of a new day rose over Washington, DC, Joe O'Brien and Khaalis drove north on Sixteenth Street toward the Hanafi Madh-Hab Center as they had done countless times before. O'Brien stopped the car in front of the Hanafi Center and watched Khaalis as he walked up to the door of his home. "See you later," Khaalis said to a group of reporters gathered outside. Two Hanafis with scimitars stood guarding the front door. Khaalis gestured at them with a salute as he approached. The door opened, and Khaalis disappeared inside, where his family was waiting to greet him. Khaalis had executed a Houdini-like escape that would have made Tasibur Rahman proud. He was asleep in his bed before most of the hostages had even reached home.

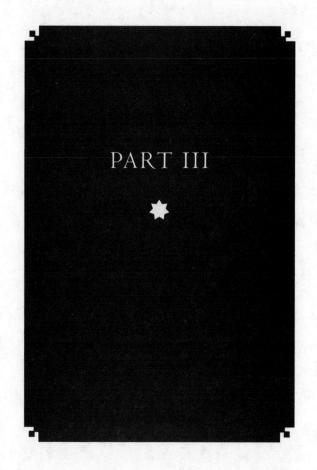

PART III

✶

42.

THINGS GO BOOM

The celebrations in Washington did not last for long. On the morning of the eleventh, the banner headlines told a tale of joy, freedom, and relief. By the time the early edition of *The Washington Star*'s March 12 issue came out, the headlines were grim again: "Release of 4 Gunmen Stirs Outcry." When the other eleven Hanafi gunmen were brought to the courthouse for arraignment, a judge decided to release the three brothers who'd been arrested at the Islamic Center: Abdul Rahman, Abdul Rahim, and Abdul Qawee. There appeared to have been no serious physical violence at that location, the judge observed, and the men's lawyers argued that all had deep, lifelong ties to the District of Columbia and did not pose a flight risk. The judge freed them on bail, pending charges.

"That's outrageous," another judge in the DC court system was anonymously quoted as saying in *The Washington Star* front-page story. "How can he do that? They're terrorists," the judge said. The partisans on Capitol Hill wasted no time in brandishing their tough-on-crime credentials. Senate majority leader Robert Byrd, a Democrat from West Virginia, told reporters that it is "abhorrent in our society that individuals can commit these atrocious crimes and then be out on their own recognizance." Several Republicans saw it as an opportunity to resurrect the Nixon-era law-and-order mantra.

The press frenzy continued. For a third night in a row, the Hanafis dominated the national news. Khaalis would have watched the reports from home this time. "Washington's brush with jihad holy war is over," Cronkite announced at the top of his show. NBC, meanwhile, aired the first public comments President Carter made on the Hanafi takeover of the capital. "The historical nature of terrorist kidnappings," Carter said, sounding more like an analyst than someone who had almost declared martial law in the capital, "is that over a period of time, there evolves a personal relationship between the terrorists and those who they have captured." The negotiations, he said, were "a vivid proof that a slow and careful approach was the effective way."

Journalists and camera crews camped outside the Hanafi Center all day. A few caught glimpses of Khaalis in the doorway several times as he exchanged notes with the police officers guarding the center and welcomed guests who were allowed to visit. He was not allowed to speak to the media, but a *Washington Post* photographer reported to the newsroom that Khaalis appeared calm and not the least bit "antagonistic." Over three evenings, the three major networks had dedicated more than eighty minutes of prime-time coverage to the Hanafis. More than half of NBC's prime-time news had been taken over by the episode. Khaalis was not just the most famous Muslim in America; he was the biggest news story in America.

The Hanafis decided that the boldest statement they could make under such scrutiny was to go on with life as if nothing had happened. Abdul Aziz was back at the Aram jewelry store in Georgetown in the morning, appearing unfazed and almost rejuvenated. He told the reporters swarming the entrance to the store that it was busier than usual. The phone rang frequently. Some people called to express their support, and Aziz encouraged them to stop by and show their support by buying some art or jewelry. Khaalis, Aziz told a reporter, had gone out for a drive that morning. "He wanted to get out for a while," he explained nonchalantly.

That evening, President Carter paid a visit to the traveling King Tut exhibit accompanied by the Egyptian ambassador, Ashraf Ghorbal. Kareem Abdul-Jabbar, now perhaps the second most conspicuous Hanafi in America, flew into the Nassau airport on Long Island, New York, with his Los Angeles Lakers team and was greeted on the tarmac by police officers. Kareem had reported receiving several threatening phone calls, and the FBI had tracked at least one of them to New York. Police officers occupied the entire row behind the Lakers bench at the game that night, and *The Washington Post* reported that one hundred FBI agents were assigned to the game. Asked by a reporter if the events in Washington had affected him, Kareem played it cool as well. "I watched it the same way you did," he replied. "I've got a job to do." He did do the job. The Lakers beat the Nets 84–81. In Washington, the funeral for Maurice Williams, the radio reporter who was shot dead in the District Building, drew eight hundred people, including the mayor and the Iranian ambassador, Ardeshir Zahedi.

On March 14 *Mohammad: Messenger of God* reopened at the Rivoli Theatre in Manhattan and a handful of other theaters in and around New York and Los Angeles. "What happened in Washington is not Islamic at all," Akkad said in an interview after the end of the siege. "That's why I hope the film will be seen so that people may understand the true spirit of love, brotherhood and peace. I am exposed to lots of blackmail, and there is no way some people will change prejudiced opinion, but I want the main Islamic rule to prevail: That you do not prejudge."

The siege had brought the film invaluable publicity. The lukewarm reviews that had preceded the premiere were now meaningless. Millions of people across America had heard about the movie and were curious. For one of the most expensive movies in film history, and one with no wide distribution deal yet, there was no other option. "We have no other plans than to carry on our business in an orderly fashion in a land governed by laws," Akkad said. "We can't allow individuals to impose their will on a majority." One theater manager was more to the point with a reporter, calling the film "an instant hit" and explaining how people had paid cash to buy six hundred to seven hundred copies of the program from his theater as souvenirs.

Mayor Walter Washington was livid about the reopening. He called Irwin Yablans to inform him of his displeasure. Akkad, he said, was putting America in danger. Yablans and Akkad believed that they had already done more than was required of them by pulling the film during the hostage taking. Khaalis may have answered the call of Allah, but Hollywood answered only to the box office. Guaranteeing public safety was the mayor's job, not Hollywood's. At the Rivoli near Times Square, the theater was packed on March 14, just as it had been at the 2:00 p.m. show on the ninth, when it had stopped mid-reel. This time the film played all the way through.

Outside the theater, dozens of people representing an "action committee" of eleven American Muslim organizations, including the American office of the Muslim World League and the Muslim Students Association, stood with placards and banners protesting the re-release. A few of the protesters handed out flyers carrying the official press release by the group, demanding a conclusive ban of Akkad's film. The film, they said in their statement, "contains historical inaccuracies and creates misleading impressions about Prophet Muhammad, peace be unto Him, and his companions." One of the organizers, a Muslim student from India, waved around a document and explained to reporters that it was a detailed letter from the Muslim World League office, a fatwa, describing how even symbolic representations of the Prophet were *haram*, forbidden, blasphemous, a crime. Protests in other cities with large Muslim populations, such as Chicago, followed.

Khaalis would have been heartened to see the movement against the film gaining momentum. Making the cancellation of the film the central demand in the early hours of his operation was always about rallying a broad base of Muslims to a specific cause that resonated broadly. For the first time in his life, Muslims in America, native-born and immigrant, were working together nationally toward a singular cause, following Khaalis's lead. Since Khaalis was not allowed to speak to the press, Khadija became the spokesperson for the Hanafis and kept the focus on the film. "If the picture goes on," she told reporters standing outside the Hanafi Center, a veil pulled over her face, "they know more trouble is coming, worse than before, all over the country." Khaalis, she said, "showed mercy and compassion, so people couldn't call him a terrorist or a killer or a cannibal. If the other parties want to break their agreement, it will be much worse."

From the Hanafis' perspective, the conflict over the film highlighted to Muslim countries around the world, particularly Saudi Arabia, the absence in America of Muslim leadership who could protect religious interests. Wallace Muhammad and his organization were nowhere to be seen, not among the protesters on the streets, and definitely not with the Hanafis. Rauf, meanwhile, was barely beginning to process the trauma of being held hostage and was planning a trip to his homeland, Egypt, to rest and recuperate. With each day that the film controversy stayed in the news, only Khaalis and the Hanafis expressed the conservative Islamic position in the press, solidifying their claim to leadership.

Less than a week after the end of the siege, Khaalis received a cryptic telegram from the Jewish Defense League, a militant Zionist organization based in New York: "Expect immediate apologies for words and actions against Jewish people and God of Israel. We are not B'nai B'rith. Never again." Coming from the JDL, these threats could not be taken lightly. The JDL strongly supported Israel, but unlike B'nai B'rith and other Zionist organizations, it also believed that militancy was essential to protecting Jews and Jewish interests in America and around the world. Meir Kahane, the leader of the JDL and the presumable author of the telegram, was suspected of being involved in various terrorist activities of his own over nearly a decade. The JDL had once bombed the Soviet mission in New York in 1971, for example, to protest the treatment of Jews in the USSR. The Hanafis had long believed, rightly or wrongly, that the JDL had been targeting them. On the first night of the hostage taking at B'nai B'rith, Khaalis had specifically warned Khadija on the phone about the group showing up outside the center.

The JDL had circulated an aggressive flyer on the second day of the siege specifically addressing Jews in America. "The source of such Anti-Semitism is clearly traceable to the Arab States who for years have been inundating America with Anti-Semitic literature and other propaganda," the flyer read. The flyer urged "armed commando action by special police units" as the "way to save hostages." It ended with this message: "JEWS ARM YOURSELVES IN ISRAEL AND IN AMERICA!" After the siege ended, Kahane and his followers were incensed, like many others, about Khaalis's release. Their anger was now directed not only at the Hanafis but also at the authorities in Washington and the "weak" Jewish leadership in the country that was refusing to react.

In a press conference in New York City on March 17, flanked by a handful of tough-looking JDL members dressed in leather jackets, Kahane cranked up the rhetoric, announcing plans for a face-off with the Hanafis in Washington. "We're going to their home to see if their lunatic leader and all other anti-Semites, that are so tough at dealing with women and children, how they deal with us." Kahane said that "black-jacketed, bereted, tough Jews" would gather in front of the Hanafi Center on Sixteenth Street for a demonstration. They would be carrying weapons, he explained. It was time that someone "stood up to demand that Jews, or the authorities, take meaningful action against these anti-Semitic hoodlums." The Hanafis, he said, would "see another kind of Jew, the kind that sent—and sends—the Muslim enemies of Israel reeling in defeat." Asked what he hoped to achieve with such a confrontation, Kahane was blunt: "I would like them to come out so we can beat the crap out of them."

The JDL's announcement was ominous of course, but it was also a dream scenario for Khaalis. The Hanafis were now being equated with Israel's adversaries in the Middle East. Khaalis could not have designed a better excuse for another Hanafi press conference. Once again, Khadija, wearing large square-rimmed reading glasses visible through the thin veil pulled down over her forehead, flanked on each side by a few other veiled Hanafi women and a handful of stern-looking Hanafi men armed with scimitars, read from a prepared statement at the doorstep of the Hanafi Center. "Firstly, we Hanafi Mussulmans are prepared to die defending our faith—Islam," she began. Her husband and his followers, she said "were most merciful and compassionate in releasing people." Drawing a contrast with the JDL's criticism of law enforcement, Khadija spoke admiringly of the Washington police department. "The people in this country are blessed," she said, "to have such a man as Captain Joseph O'Brien," and she also thanked Cullinane by name.

Turning to JDL's threats, she said that the Hanafis knew that the Zionists were behind the "poisonous lessons" that the Nation of Islam spread among African Americans decades ago. The Hanafis, she said, also knew that the Zionists controlled much of the media in America and around the world. As for Meir Kahane and the "Zionist controlled JDL," she said, "they will write their epitaphs in self-destruction and the blood of their people, as we fear only Allah—nothing else." She ended her statement with this: "We, the Hanafi Mussulmans, sincerely warn all Zionist Jews and their allies that we are not alone, and not to be misguided by that they think they see."

Hardly a week had passed since the end of the siege, and Washington was gearing up for another battle in the capital. Mayor Walter Washington, asked about the mounting tensions at a press conference at the District Building, said that "it's very sensitive." He had discussed the situation with Washington police officials, and he was confident "of their ability to handle the entire matter." Cullinane and Rabe's Special Operations Division were in the spotlight again. Khaalis and his men may have lost the arsenal they had carried with them to the three locations, but there was little doubt in anyone's mind that they would be able to defend themselves.

"Have you heard anything with reference to that JDL movement?" O'Brien asked Khaalis on the phone a few days before the Jewish group's planned demonstration.

Khaalis took a long pause. "It's just that it's madness on his part, it's going to be a bloodbath for his people, that's all," Khaalis said matter-of-factly. "He can find that out. He'll know that," he said. "And there'll be no mercy." Kahane, Khaalis told O'Brien, was looking for trouble. "He made trouble in Brooklyn when he didn't want the Puerto Ricans living up there," he said. "He's been a troublemaker over in Palestine too."

"Well, we're in touch with some rabbis now," O'Brien reassured Khaalis, but Khaalis was not impressed.

"There will be no Jewish people that will be spared," Khaalis replied, his rage mounting. "I don't care nothing about the JDL. We're gonna come down hard on all of them if they start any foolishness."

Cullinane, who was there with O'Brien, came on the line. He asked Khaalis about how Khadija and the family were doing, and he tried to calm Khaalis down. "I want you to know that I'm aware as you are about the JDL," Cullinane said. "Joe and I are personally going to take care of the details, Sunday." He reminded Khaalis that the Hanafis were on thin ice. "It's very difficult for one person to fight on two fronts," he warned. Khaalis could not afford any more trouble.

"This man is not going to create no problems for me," Khaalis said. "He's creating problems for himself."

"When you look out your window, you will see me in charge Sunday," Cullinane said at the end of the call.

A team of Washington police officers greeted Kahane at the Washington airport early in the morning on Sunday, March 20. Alan Dershowitz, the Harvard law professor, had played an intermediary role in convincing Kahane to meet with Cullinane face-to-face before his planned rally. The cops escorted him straight to the police headquarters. It was a gloomy, rainy day, but there were busloads of JDL activists headed into the city, Kahane explained to Cullinane and Earl Silbert, the U.S. attorney, who joined in. They tried to convince Kahane to call the whole thing off. The rain would discourage people from coming out, they argued. Cullinane suggested that if they were going to march, it would be best to march a few blocks away from the Hanafi headquarters. Kahane would not budge. The demonstration would be right in front of headquarters, as planned, and the JDL members would be armed with what the law allowed.

When they arrived outside the Hanafi Center, Cullinane and O'Brien saw only two Hanafi guards patrolling the perimeter of the house. They had scimitars slung over their shoulders and machetes dangling from their belts. They were aloof but ready for action. The JDL buses began arriving soon after, each offloading dozens of people, some holding baseball bats and wearing helmets, dressed for a street battle. They unfurled large banners that read "Never again" and "JDL will crush Khaalis" and started chanting slogans. "Who do we want? Khaalis! How do we want him? Dead!" they said. "Be a Jew. Twenty-two," they started chanting, referring to the .22-caliber pistols and rifles their members favored.

The Jewish Community Council of Greater Washington, an umbrella organization in the capital with more than one hundred member Jewish organizations, had cooperated with Cullinane and federal law enforcement in the days leading up to the march by discouraging local Jews from joining. Still, the crowd outside the Hanafi Center kept growing. By the time Kahane arrived, wearing a black jacket and wide-collared dress shirt, the crowd on Sixteenth Street had grown to at least 250 people. The JDL supporters encircled the Hanafi Center, chanting and yelling. Cullinane had come prepared with two hundred police officers dressed in riot gear. They stood in two parallel lines along the perimeter of the Hanafi Center separating the protestors from the two Hanafis standing guard outside. "Meet the real Jew," Kahane hollered at the crowd, speaking atop an upturned trash can. "I want every Jew to have a .22," he said, "and know how to use it." The crowd erupted with cheers. Khaalis is "on our list," Kahane warned. "Never will he walk these streets safely again."

Still, no Hanafis were seen, not even in the windows, other than the two men with scimitars at the fence. Cullinane's appeals to Khaalis to stay indoors appeared to have worked. Eventually Kahane gave up on coaxing Khaalis out. As he concluded his speech, the crowd began marching around the Hanafi Center. "Things go boom in the middle of the night," the JDL chanted as they circled around the block. Finally, around 2:45 p.m., a few hours after he had arrived at the center, Kahane got into a car and was escorted by police cruisers right back to the airport. Other than a brief scuffle between a few JDL members and a bystander holding an anti-Zionist poster, there was no violence at the rally.

Washington had dodged another bullet. Next time—Cullinane was convinced there would be a next time—they might not be so lucky. Two weeks had passed since the siege ended, and not a day had gone by that the Hanafis were not in the news. Khaalis may have been barred from speaking to anyone publicly, but he and the Hanafis had snared the media's attention. As long as Hamaas Abdul Khaalis was a free man, Cullinane feared, the capital would remain a tinderbox.

43

FAITH AND COUNTRY

A few days after the JDL rally, Washington police suddenly took the three brothers from the Islamic Center back into custody. As it became apparent to Khaalis that law enforcement was starting to turn the screws, he decided to dispatch Abdul Aziz on a mission of a lifetime. In the siege and the aftermath, Khaalis had firmly established himself as a central figure in American Islam; the only thing—the big thing—missing was the explicit and strong support of elites in Muslim countries in Asia and Africa—the kind that Malcolm had won after his final mission abroad. On that front, the Hanafis still trailed Wallace and many other groups. Malcolm had traveled to the Middle East toward the end of his life and swiftly unseated Elijah Muhammad as the favored Muslim American in Islam's cultural capitals. Now, Khaalis wondered if Aziz might be able to pull the same maneuver for him against Wallace.

The overtures from foreign Muslims had started to come in over the phone while the Hanafis were still holding hostages. Reports in papers around the world of Khaalis holding court with ambassadors from three of the most powerful Muslim countries in the world had raised his profile and stoked curiosity about him in the Muslim world. Once Khaalis was at home, he started receiving more formal invitations from organizations, but Khaalis had to explain that he had surrendered his passport as a condition of his release. Aziz, however, was in no legal trouble. He had held down the fort at the Hanafi Center for the entire siege, delivered food, spoken to the press, and relayed threats on behalf of Khaalis, but he had never become involved in the mechanics of the hostage taking, and he was careful always to act in coordination with the police. In any case, he was the most seasoned traveler among the Hanafis, as he had taken regular trips to countries in Asia and the Middle East for his jewelry and antiques business. Khaalis, on the other hand, had not left the country in thirty years.

The main conduit for these international contacts was a man named Mustafa Momin, an Egyptian who had built a reputation as a firebrand anti-colonial activist during his time as an architecture student at Cairo University in the 1940s, where he led the student wing of al-Ikhwan, the Egyptian Muslim Brotherhood. He had eventually become a regional spokesperson for the Ikhwan and was present in New York for the 1947 United Nations General Assembly session. It was during that trip that his interest in architecture led him to get involved in the design of the Islamic Center of Washington that was being discussed among some Muslim diplomats. Momin had since split from the Ikhwan but remained an Islamist activist. The revolutionary spirit with which Khaalis and the Hanafis had dominated the U.S. capital had caught his attention and earned his admiration. He contacted Abdul Aziz and offered to connect him with some conservative Muslim clerics in Saudi Arabia and the United Arab Emirates who, Momin suggested, would be eager to endorse the Hanafis. With Momin's encouragement, and without much of an itinerary, Aziz landed in the Middle East as Khaalis's emissary.

Aziz was looking for support generally, but in Saudi Arabia, he was on a very specific mission. In one month's time, the Muslim World League was hosting its first-ever convention of American Muslims in New Jersey. The league, which had recently won recognition from the United Nations as a formal observer body, was sitting atop a new Saudi slush fund of millions of dollars, which was to be distributed to Muslim minority communities around the world. Through its new offices in New York City, it was identifying influential groups and organizations of Muslims in the United States and Canada and inviting them to the conference.

There, they would have the opportunity to meet and network among themselves and, more important, meet Muhammad Ali al-Harakan, the Saudi scholar who now led the Muslim World League, in person. It was a given that any American Muslim who got an invitation to be on stage with Harakan was potentially the recipient of millions of dollars of financing from the Saudis. Wallace was assumed to be on the guest list. Khaalis hoped that Aziz could get him up there instead. The Hanafis' recent encounter with the infamous JDL suddenly became more salient. The Hanafis had already proven their strict adherence to Sunni practice through their spectacular stand against Akkad's film, and their stand against the JDL gave them political heft too.

In Riyadh, the Saudi capital, Aziz had an audience with Sheik Abdul Aziz bin Baz, a high-ranking Islamic cleric who had a seat on the Muslim World League and would one day go on to become the grand mufti of Saudi Arabia. In Sharjah, he met with a man named Sheik Ali Mahmoud, the leader of Islamic affairs in the emirate. The men lavished praise on the Hanafis and even pointed Aziz toward opportunities for lucrative business contracts with friends of the royal family. Still, an invitation to the Muslim conference in America proved elusive. Whenever Aziz brought up the issue, the conversation would always turn to Khaalis's upcoming criminal trial.

As Aziz bounced from one Muslim country to the next, the U.S. State Department kept track of developments. The U.S. embassy in Doha, Qatar, reported that the ruler of Sharjah "is currently mediating among US Muslim sects which were involved in recent terror/hostage operation in Washington." The report said that the sheik, who had only months earlier visited Wallace in Chicago and presented him with a check for $1 million, would be sending a delegation to the United States to achieve a détente between Khaalis and Wallace.

In Washington, Khaalis was getting a similar message from all corners: it was impossible to dethrone Wallace. The Arab states simply would not drop their support for the most influential imam of American Muslims, even if he had supported Akkad's film. The best the Hanafis could hope for was a peace deal with Wallace with some power-sharing agreement. A couple of days before Aziz returned to Washington, Khaalis spoke on the phone with Mustafa Momin, who called from Riyadh. He had no details about Aziz's progress in the Middle East either, but he informed Khaalis that he would travel to the United States himself in the coming days.

"I'm coming to see you next week," Momin told Khaalis. "I'll be in the end of the week in Washington, DC [sic]."

"Alhamdulillah," Khaalis replied, praise be to Allah.

Momin expressed his worry that the Hanafis would target "the brother," Wallace.

"Nobody is going to harm him," Khaalis reassured the Arab. If the Hanafis had wanted, "we could have harmed him a long time ago."

"I will be looking forward to seeing you and see all the brothers and try to plan for a complete peaceful unity between the Muslims," Momin said before hanging up.

Khaalis also connected with Kareem Abdul-Jabbar. The master and disciple had grown estranged, but the crisis pulled Kareem and Khaalis closer together again. Kareem knew that too many people had abandoned and betrayed Khaalis over the years. In his time of trouble, no matter his own mounting doubts and resentments, Kareem did not abandon Khaalis. Indeed, Kareem offered to foot the bill for the Hanafis' legal defense. He sent Khaalis a lump sum and told him to do what he wanted with it.

On Sunday, March 27, four days before his scheduled court appearance, Khaalis finally heard from Aziz in a telegram sent from Jeddah, Saudi Arabia, for the first time since he had left. It was a short note. "Bismillah al-Rahman ar-Rahim," began the telegram with the traditional Islamic prayer. Aziz wrote that he would be back in the country before Khaalis's preliminary court hearing.

Monday morning, Khaalis got another call from O'Brien, who wanted to talk one last time before the court date. O'Brien sounded concerned about Khaalis. He offered Khaalis, Aziz, and Khadija a ride to the courthouse on the morning of the hearing. O'Brien then asked Khaalis about the Hanafis' American flag, which was currently aloft at the center upside down as a sign of distress. O'Brien wondered aloud whether it might be a good idea to turn it right side up once again before he faced a judge. It might send a good message, he suggested. Khaalis was not convinced.

"My first interest is my faith and my country, faith and country, that's what every man has to have," he told O'Brien by way of explanation.

"Well, that's true, and that's the way you felt four years ago," O'Brien observed.

"That's right and I still do."

On March 29, customs officials detained Abdul Aziz when he landed in New York. He was stripped and searched and questioned about his activities and contacts in the Middle East. He said little, and after a while the agents had no option but to let him go. He had enough time during the layover to place a call from an airport pay phone to Khaalis at the Hanafi Center before boarding his flight to Washington.

"When are you going to be here?" Khaalis asked.

"I'm getting ready to catch a flight now. I've got to get an elevator, the Secret Service is waiting for me. Yeah, they just put me to Secret Service."

"Look, I don't give a fuck about the government. Shit. Fuck them. They're not fucking with you. I just want to know when you're gonna be here."

"About an hour and a half."

"What, are they quizzing you?"

"They tried to, I didn't say . . ."

"No, don't say shit to those motherfuckers. I'll kill all two hundred people today. Do you hear that?"

Khaalis was going into a fit of rage.

"What did they do to you?" he asked Aziz.

"Searched me."

"What?"

"Stripped—had me strip down, went through all my things. They were waiting for me."

"You got their number?"

"No, I don't have their number. I just wanted to get away from them, they were getting me really hot."

"O.K., we're gonna, we're gonna get the government for this. All right?"

"All right."

"O.K. Up their asses now. They're playing rough, we're gonna play rough."

Khaalis suddenly ceased his line of inquiry, almost as if he had checked himself. He confirmed the arrival time with Aziz and decided on a place to meet at the airport.

"You got my material?" Khaalis asked before hanging up.

"No, they got it," Abdul Aziz answered.

"Who did?"

"Saudi Arabians."

"Oh good. All right, we'll meet you there at a quarter to three, flight 101."

With the traditional Muslim greeting, they ended the conversation.

A few miles away from the Hanafi Center, at the police headquarters on the fifth floor of the Municipal Center, Maurice Cullinane played back the surveillance tape a few times. His heart was beating fast. He listened carefully, taking notes as he listened to the recording again, and then once again. With less than two days left before Khaalis's scheduled hearing, Cullinane picked up the phone and dialed the number for Earl Silbert, who would represent the U.S. government in the hostage-taking case against the Hanafis. Cullinane explained that he had potential new evidence that he wanted Silbert to hear.

44.

BIG MAN

On the morning of March 31, the day of Khaalis's preliminary hearing, there was news of an extraordinary development in American Islam. Wallace Muhammad and Hamaas Abdul Khaalis, two leaders caught in a years-long bloody feud, had declared a truce. In the days immediately following the end of the siege, Wallace had joined many others in raising the alarm about the agreement to release Khaalis. "Any man capable of seizing the city hall, and the mosque in Washington and the B'nai B'rith temple and that killed a young reporter," he had said, "is capable of killing me." Khaalis had chosen to say nothing to assuage Wallace's fears and instead became intently focused on the re-release of Akkad's film and his battle with the JDL.

As it became apparent to Khaalis, however, that influential Muslims abroad wanted a rapprochement, he began to send out his own signals. A few days earlier, one of Khaalis's allies in Chicago, a young African American imam, had called a press conference at a mosque in the city to announce that the Hanafis "seek to live mercifully among our fellow human beings." Wallace was a "fellow human being and we seek to live mercifully along with him and promote peace along with him."

After Abdul Aziz returned from the Middle East with specific instructions to make peace with Wallace, Khaalis knew he had no choice left. As much as Khaalis wished to deny it, Wallace had steered Elijah's Nation of Islam in the direction of Sunni tradition, boldly staring down his own enemies within the organization in the process. In terms of theology, there was very little separating the Hanafis from Wallace's World Community of al-Islam. The day before his court appearance, he placed a call to Chicago. His best hope now was for a power-sharing arrangement with Wallace. Whether he liked it or not, he needed to be friendly.

The source of the news in the morning's papers was Wallace Muhammad himself, who held a press conference at his Chicago headquarters after the conversation. Wallace told reporters that it was Khaalis who had called him and that he had also spoken to Khadija. Wallace quoted Khaalis as saying: "Look, I want you to know that you have nothing to fear from me. I want peace." In response, Wallace said he had eagerly accepted the peace offering. "Brother Hamaas, that's exactly what I've always wanted," Wallace replied.

Wallace explained to Khaalis that when the Nation of Islam followers had massacred his family in 1973, he was in a period of estrangement from his father, Elijah. He acknowledged that the murderers of the Hanafis might have been a part of the broader organization that his father led, but he doubted that they were true believers and said that he personally had no knowledge of it. Wallace was full of praise for Khaalis. "That was a great move on his part," Wallace said in the press conference, once again, stressing how Khaalis was the one who had called him. "It takes a big man to call another man." The Hanafis, on the other hand, appeared less eager to share the news: "The members of the Washington Hanafi group refused Tuesday to comment," one syndicated story about the truce reported.

Joe O'Brien arrived at the Hanafi headquarters in the afternoon to collect Khaalis. Khadija, Abdul Aziz, and Amina came along to watch the proceedings from the gallery. The hearing was scheduled for 2:00 p.m. Khaalis wore a white turtleneck and snug-fitting military-fatigue-style bush jacket and matching pants. It was the first time that Khaalis had been seen openly in public in more than two weeks. Hundreds of gawkers lined the entrance to the superior court building. Security was tight. Everyone entering the courthouse was searched and their belongings inspected. Special police units with high-powered rifles were positioned at the Old Pension Building across the street. Inside, U.S. Marshals lined the walls of the courtroom, A-211, on all sides. The courtroom itself was packed.

Harry Alexander, the same former judge who had called the Hanafi Center to offer his services while Khaalis was still negotiating with the ambassadors, was representing Khaalis as his attorney. Alexander was one of the first African Americans to graduate from Georgetown Law School and was appointed to the DC superior court bench by President Lyndon Johnson in 1966. He quickly gained a reputation as an activist judge, fighting the civil rights fight hard from the bench, and became a polarizing figure as a result. In 1974, he had even flirted with politics, considering a run for the inaugural DC council, but decided against it. Instead, he had gone into private legal practice, where he sought out high-profile civil rights cases. Thanks to Kareem's generous pledge, Khaalis could afford one of the most high-profile attorneys in the District of Columbia. His presence by Khaalis's side as his counsel sent a clear and strong message: Khaalis and Alexander would wage an aggressive fight and try to put the American justice system on trial as well.

Like Khaalis, Alexander was a showman. The fifty-two-year-old drove a red Cadillac Eldorado and would sometimes wear a necklace that carried a slave identification tag that read, "Sold." On the day of Khaalis's trial, he was wearing a dark suit, a gold tie and matching handkerchief, and a heavy gold chain around his neck. He took his seat next to Khaalis in the courtroom as the assigned judge took his place a few minutes after 2:00 p.m. They did not expect a long hearing. In fact, they had plans for making it an extremely short one.

Alexander's first motion of the day was for a continuance—a delay in the preliminary hearing scheduled for that day. "There was an agreement," Alexander explained, "that Khaalis had fifty days before the preliminary hearing." Khaalis was "expecting some foreign dignitaries with which he wishes to confer," and they are expected around April 15, he told the judge. Khaalis, he said, should be allowed to "confer with these dignitaries prior to the preliminary hearing." He proposed the hearing be scheduled for April 28. Though he did not say this, this date would allow Khaalis to attend the Muslim World League conference in Newark—though he still did not have a formal invitation—and return to DC in time.

The government lawyers protested. The promise of fifty days made to Khaalis by Cullinane was in reference to grand jury proceedings, not a preliminary hearing, they argued. The judge saw no reason to deny Khaalis's request, however, and agreed to have the hearing postponed until April 11. Alexander had bought Khaalis some more time in which he could try to meet with members of the Muslim World League and ingratiate himself with the most influential religious figures in the Muslim world. In the worst case for Khaalis, even if he were to be convicted and imprisoned, there might be a chance that the global Muslim leaders could lobby for a presidential pardon—or, perhaps, Khaalis might even become a pawn in the upcoming Israel-Egypt peace process. After a few more motions, including one requesting permission for Khaalis to speak publicly, the judge asked Earl Silbert if the government had anything to say.

Silbert stood up and introduced a motion that stunned Khaalis, Alexander, and everyone in the courtroom: the government asked the judge to revoke Khaalis's release. Silbert presented the judge with a few pages of a typed transcript of a wire intercept of the conversation between Khaalis and Abdul Aziz, which had taken place "upon his return to this country from Saudi Arabia," Silbert explained. There was also a transcript of another conversation that Khaalis had with a woman, most likely his third wife, Hafsa, right after the one with Aziz. "They were waiting for him," Khaalis was quoted in the transcript as saying to the woman. "All right, they are going to pay in blood for it. I'm gonna kill somebody. And they're gonna die for what they did. It don't matter to me . . . I keep telling people. Now they're gonna pay. Pay in blood. I don't give a fuck. Don't matter to me. They can't do this to the Muslims."

While everyone read the pages, Silbert paused before moving in for the kill. The transcripts, he said, demonstrated that Khaalis had violated the agreement of his release by threatening more violence. The government, he said, wanted Khaalis to be placed in jail immediately with the other Hanafis. Silbert then presented an arrest warrant for Khaalis that was already signed by another judge.

The FBI and the police were both monitoring Khaalis's calls. The judge knew this. Khaalis knew this too. He had said as much in a long conversation with the Iranian ambassador, Ardeshir Zahedi, a few days earlier, when Khaalis invited him to the Hanafi Center for a face-to-face meeting. "I only talk on the phone for what I want them to know," Khaalis had told Zahedi. In the many conversations with Cullinane and O'Brien over the three weeks since the end of the siege, Khaalis had occasionally sounded unhinged and violent. Once, after the JDL rally, O'Brien asked him how he was doing and he answered, "Ready to die," with South Asian Islamic mystical music blaring loudly in the background. "Jews! Jews!" he yelled, before telling O'Brien that his men were "willing to kill one hundred men for each one of his men" and how nobody could stop them. In another call with Cullinane, Khaalis promised "death and destruction like this country never seen before." However, this call with Aziz was different. There was no hint of entrapment. No government official had goaded Khaalis or set him up with a question. Legally speaking, this was the government's best shot.

"I did not anticipate that the Government would, in 1977, utilize this kind of tactic," Alexander rose to object. "I'm shocked," he said. "It is a hot motion." He demanded that the complete wiretap transcript be released immediately and that the government reveal the names of everyone who was bugged in relation to the case, along with transcripts of any other conversations that were obtained. He asked for the government's motion to be quashed on the spot.

The judge allowed Silbert to introduce a witness, Sergeant Robert Sharkey of the Washington police, who worked under O'Brien as a homicide detective. Sharkey had known Khaalis for four years. He was one of the first officers to respond to the Hanafi Center after the family's massacre in 1973. He had also briefly been involved in the hostage negotiations with Khaalis. In a lengthy testimony, he told the court that ever since the murders in 1973, Khaalis had on several occasions talked about taking the law into his own hands. On the second day of the hostage taking, the officer had spoken to Khaalis on the phone, and Khaalis, the officer testified, had alluded to four phases of his attack. "I told you I would get my revenge," he recalled Khaalis saying. "This is only the third of four phases. The fourth phase you can't believe—you can't envision it."

Silbert argued that the early March takeovers at B'nai B'rith, the District Building, and the Islamic Center were the first three phases of an attack on the United States. What Khaalis was caught talking about was a fourth stage that he had planned all along. It was a weak argument—barely coherent—but in the end it was all that the judge needed to reverse what was an unpopular move by the court from the beginning. "The fact of the matter is," the judge concluded, that Khaalis "on previous occasions made threats and on previous occasions, at least on the occasion of the events of March 9 to 11, they were carried out." These latest words, he argued, could not be treated as "idle threats." A little after five o'clock that day, the judge ordered Khaalis detained.

As the marshals approached Khaalis to arrest him, Khadija rushed over from the gallery to hold him, but a few other marshals intercepted her and held her back. After Khaalis was led away, the distraught Hanafis began exiting the courtroom. They were only as far as the courthouse steps when another group of federal marshals swarmed them. They handcuffed Abdul Aziz, arresting him on federal gun charges. At that very moment, federal law enforcement and police teams from DC, Virginia, and Maryland were simultaneously raiding other properties occupied by Hanafis, axing their way through front doors of homes. The men, women, and children inside huddled under gunpoint as tactical teams turned the Hanafi homes inside out. They confiscated dozens of firearms and arrested three more Hanafi men. A few days later, ATF agents along with local police departments in Maryland raided another three homes. In the span of a few days, America struck back against the Hanafis in an attempt to break the back of the organization.

In the evening after Khaalis's arrest, a reporter reached Khadija by phone at the Hanafi Center and asked for her reaction to the extraordinary turn of events. "This country hates Muslims," Khadija said. "They act one way when the brothers come from another country because of the oil," she said; "it puts on another face when they are dealing with us." In the end, she delivered a word of warning: "As soon as the foreign Muslim brothers around the world find out that this country hates Muslims, things will start to roll."

45

INHERITOR OF THE FAITH

On April 4, 1977, four days after Khaalis was locked up, the Egyptian president, Anwar Sadat, landed at Andrews Air Force Base in Virginia to begin an official state visit. As his motorcade exited the airbase, the roads on either side were lined with hundreds of spectators, mostly Arab American immigrants, celebrating the arrival of the most influential leader in the Middle East on a historic trip to America. The press reports in the days leading up to the meeting with Carter had built up expectations, suggesting that the two presidents would discuss the details of what might be a grand, historic peace bargain between Arab countries and Israel.

Two decades after the Suez Crisis, when America began policing the Middle East, the country was more deeply enmeshed in Middle Eastern politics than ever. Now, Carter and Sadat, two religious men seemingly concerned with the fate of the Holy Land, were attempting to write what appeared to be a new chapter for the region. In reality, however, it turned out to be more transactional politics, the kind that Khaalis had berated the ambassadors for in the lobby of B'nai B'rith. While the public statements from Carter and Sadat in the East Room of the White House focused on Palestine, borders, and a potential peace deal, the news reports that followed detailed the military equipment that Sadat was hoping to buy from the United States, including two hundred F5 fighter jets and anti-tank missiles, all adding up to a reported $5 billion. The four-day visit concluded with a press conference in which Sadat said, "for sure, there will be normalization" with Israel.

A few weeks later, a different kind of Arab leader with a different agenda arrived in the country. Muhammad Ali al-Harakan, the former law minister of Saudi Arabia and the secretary general of the Muslim

World League, was going to lead the First Islamic Conference of North America, where, many expected, he would identify the Saudis' preferred candidates for American Muslim leadership. The conference kicked off with the weekly *jummah* prayer on Friday April 22, 1977, at the Holiday Inn in Newark, New Jersey. Several hundred American Muslims, Sunni and Shia, immigrant and African American, representing almost 150 organizations from twenty-nine American states, lined up in neat rows shoulder to shoulder behind Harakan, who led the prayer. Khaalis was in jail as a grand jury trial proceeded. The Hanafis were not represented.

In his sermon, the cleric delivered a message to America's gathered Muslim elite to unite. "Islam is the religion which presents in the totality of its teachings and laws, the oneness of mankind regardless of their color, races, languages," he said in his sermon. "There is no distinction, under the banner of Islam, between the rich and the poor, between the strong and the weak—all form one unit, firm and solid, supporting each other, and not discriminating and disjoining."

The inaugural session of the conference was held that evening at seven o'clock. A panel of speakers took their seats at a long table on the raised stage framed by a large banner in Arabic script that hung on the wall behind it. Harakan took the chair in the middle. Two of the league's American staffers sat to his left. A representative of the Saudi government, another from the United Nations, and one Muslim leader from Canada filled the other seats. In the two seats to Harakan's immediate right sat two men representing the Muslims of the United States: Muhammad Abdul Rauf and Wallace Muhammad. Wallace was listed in the program as Mr. Warisuddin Muhammad—an Arabicized version of his first name, loosely translating to "the inheritor of the faith." The name could almost be loosely translated as "caliph." No one spoke of the spectacular events that had occurred a few hundred miles south in America's capital a little over a month earlier. Still, Khaalis's presence hung heavy over the session. His actions in Washington had laid bare the volatility of American Islam, and there were signs of discord, especially when it came time for the Americans on the panel to speak.

Rauf, arms crossed, was clearly still suffering psychological effects of the traumatic events he had endured. His speech was laced with bitterness and disillusionment over the power plays in American Muslim society. He dwelled on "the ugly rivalry for positions of leadership among those who pose as servants of Islam in America," who "approach influential personalities in Muslim countries, portraying themselves as the only sincere followers of Islam." These people—he was thinking of Khaalis, surely, but also, perhaps, Wallace—"seek to build their own fortunes and aggrandize themselves at the expense of sincere followers of Islam," he said. He attacked what he called the "superficiality of Islamic knowledge on the part of many who pose as leaders of Islam in America." These people, he said, "are fond of making bombastic speeches," but "are quite incapable of distinguishing the wheat from the chaff."

Wallace, the final speaker of the evening, struck a different tone. His remarks sounded almost like an acceptance speech after a political triumph. He began by invoking the memory of his father, "the Honorable Elijah Muhammad, the late leader of the Nation of Islam in America." Wallace boasted of the number of followers he had attracted, which undoubtedly dwarfed the numbers of any other organization in attendance. Since Elijah's death, the membership had grown from fifty thousand to seventy thousand, Wallace reported. "I would say that there are about a million Muslims who identify with our community," he said, and "perhaps another two or three million strong sympathizers who don't yet profess to be Muslims but who say 'I prefer that religion to any other.'"

He thanked the visitor-hosts "from the holy city of Mecca from Arabia, to encourage us, to give us support, to encourage us to unite, to encourage us to move forward in Islam." He noted, bluntly, "they have the knowledge and they have the money." In stark contrast to Rauf, he proclaimed the moment "the best time in the whole history of America for Muslims." He ended his comments with a major announcement. A delegation of "300 Bilalian Americans, 300 Afro-American Muslims," would make the annual hajj pilgrimage to Mecca in Saudi Arabia later that year. The trip would cost a significant amount of money, and while Wallace did not specifically say so, it was assumed that the Saudis would foot a portion of that bill. It was by far the largest group of American Muslims to have ever gone in a group to Mecca. "Pray for us," he said finally, "and pray for our success."

The following day of the conference was reserved for workshops. Hundreds of attendees broke out into subgroups, each one focused on a specific issue and responsible for formulating an agenda that might be carried forward by Muslims in North America. There was a group dedicated to jurisprudence, one dedicated to economic development, one focused on youth, and one specifically on women. Together, the committees agreed on a sixty-two-point roadmap document that would further the Muslim World League's mission in the United States.

The policy proposals and agendas were bland and largely generic, creating task forces, councils, and working groups. The group dedicated to media and representation, however, proposed one highly specific action item, perhaps the only one on the entire roadmap: "The conference expresses its strong objection to the film, *Mohammad, Messenger of God*, as it is unlawful and forbidden in Islam to make any audio-visual figurative representation of Prophet Muhammad, peace be upon him, or of any other prophet of God or of any of their companions. It further urges all Muslim governments to use their good offices to implement this recommendation by stopping the viewing or production of such films."

46.

AMERICAN MUSLIM

A federal grand jury in Washington returned a thirty-two-count indictment in May, with most of the counts applying to all twelve Hanafi hostage takers. The counts added up to almost four hundred discrete charges, and it took almost thirty minutes just to read them in court. The men were charged with armed kidnapping, assault with intent to kill, murder, and several other crimes. All twelve men had acted in concert, the indictment alleged. It was a grand conspiracy. As a result, each one faced charges of murder in the first degree and second degree for the death of Maurice Williams, the radio reporter killed in the District Building. Many of the charges in the indictment carried the possibility of a life sentence.

Khaalis retained Harry Alexander as a lawyer for the trial, while each of the other eleven Hanafi men was given a court-assigned attorney. The Hanafi hostage takers, except for Khaalis, had fallen silent since their arrests. Even with their assigned attorneys, they spoke only when permitted by Khaalis through Alexander. They were still loyal followers, and they would remain so until the end. A few of the attorneys quit before the trial started, completely frustrated by the cult-like power the lead defendant exercised over the rest. They had all agreed to be tried together rather than individually. If Silbert was hoping for any break in the ranks—a stool pigeon like the one he had found among the Nation of Islam's hitmen in 1973—he would be disappointed. All the Hanafis pleaded not guilty to all charges.

The trial began on May 31, 1977, with an all-Black jury of eight women and four men, selected from a pool of 650. None of them were Muslim. The Hanafis arrived at the court together in a prison van escorted by a phalanx of police squad cars. A police helicopter hovered overhead. It was another logistical and security nightmare for the court and the District. Metal detectors were installed not only at the courthouse entrance this time, but also on the second floor, where the courtroom was located. U.S. Marshals lined the corridors of the entire courthouse. The trial was held in Courtroom 11, the same one where the first and largest Black Mafia trial had occurred—where Khaalis had blown up on the witness stand, costing him $750 in lawyer's fees. Inside, the defendants were seated at a long table, with the corresponding defense attorneys sitting behind their clients. A U.S. Marshal stood behind each attorney.

The proceedings began, unsurprisingly, with spectacular theatrics. A good portion of the first day was consumed by heated verbal battles between the judge assigned to the trial, Nicholas "No Nonsense" Nunzio, and Harry Alexander. The point of the argument was a trivial one: Alexander wanted Nunzio to refer to him as "Judge Alexander." Nunzio insisted that he would call him "Mr. Alexander." During a private bench conference, Nunzio threatened Alexander with contempt; he'd accidentally left his microphone on, and everyone, including the media in the room, heard the threat. The trial was hurtling toward chaos before it had truly started.

In any case, the government had its work cut out. Conspiracy charges, which federal prosecutors favored for how broad a net they cast, were not easy to prove. In this case, there had been only one murder, and Abdul Muzikir, the man who had pulled the trigger in the District Building, had been miles away from ten of the other men being charged with that same murder. In order to hold all the men responsible for the criminal acts of one, the government had to prove beyond a reasonable doubt that the men had all planned and closely coordinated their acts under Khaalis's explicit instructions. It was a high bar to clear, but in the absence of any terrorism statutes, this was the best chance they had to convict the men of the most serious crimes committed during the siege.

Rabe was the prosecution's first witness—O'Brien and Cullinane did not testify—and described his dealings with Khaalis over the almost forty hours of the siege. Some of the other officers stationed in the District Building followed as witnesses and helped the prosecution reconstruct, in painstaking detail, what had happened in the hallways of the fifth floor, especially during those early hours when shots were fired and Maurice Williams was killed. The prosecutors presented a large and detailed floor plan for each of the three locations. They rolled out two large glass-paneled displays that showcased the astounding arsenals the Hanafis had brought with them. Repeatedly, the government's lawyers emphasized the vast amount of planning and coordination that must have been required to take over three major buildings in the American capital. In their cross-examination, several of the defense attorneys turned the jury's attention toward Richard Traylor, the trigger-happy SOD officer who fired dozens of rounds from his Uzi during those fateful early hours in the District Building.

The most gripping and compelling testimony came from dozens of hostages from all three locations. They had spent the months since their release coping with what they had endured. Many suffered from some level of post-traumatic stress. B'nai B'rith had sponsored individual counseling sessions and group therapy, which fifty people attended. Many people spoke of not being able to enter an elevator or stairwell without being gripped with terror. Many had trouble concentrating on anything. Some even reported having a fear of taxis, knowing how many of the Hanafis had driven cabs in their city for years. A few reported that they experienced a strange kind of exhausting euphoria: they went out a lot more and found that their emotions—happiness, sadness, fear—seemed to be turned up a notch.

On the stand, Rabbi Fishman of Hillel described how he had been pistol-whipped by Khaalis on the second-floor landing in the first hour of the siege. Paul Green described how he came to suffer multiple facial fractures when hit in the face with a rifle butt. Wesley Hymes, the print operator, explained that the machete and gun attack had left one side of his torso barely functioning. Alton Kirkland, the janitor, spoke about how he feared death while he was being stabbed with a knife and about how he then had a gun pointed at his head by a Hanafi standing over him, ready to pull the trigger. He had had a two-month-old child waiting at home. He had wondered whether he would ever see him again.

Rauf, in his Arabic-accented English and stilted diction, served alternately as a witness to the crime and as an expert on Islamic law and theology, explaining terms like "khalifa" and "Hanafi" to the jury, between testifying to the many occasions when he was threatened with decapitation. Throughout his time on the stand, he referred to Khaalis as "Brother Hamaas." Mushk Ara, the teenage Bangladeshi secretary Khaalis released on the first night, described how the takeover of the Islamic Center unfolded. Robert Tisdale, the minister leading the international student group, described the heated, scary arguments that sometimes erupted between the hostage takers and Buthayna Rauf, the imam's wife, over issues of religious dogma.

Marion Barry, the city council member who was now eyeing a mayoral run, had been suffering from nightmares and replayed the shootout in his head for months. He described what he saw in the moments before he, Mack Cantrell, and Maurice Williams were shot. Days later, Robert Pierce, the man who was shot in the back by Abdul Muzikir inside Councilman Sterling Tucker's office, took the stand. He was in a wheelchair and accompanied by a nurse. He had been paralyzed for life. It was such a pitiful state that the judge ordered the jury out of the room as he entered. The defense attorneys argued for the nurse to be moved away from Pierce—but Nunzio declined.

Two hostages did not live long enough to make it to trial. Charles Kraus, the man who had come to return a book on Islam to Rauf when he was yanked into the office at the Islamic Center, died of a heart attack a few weeks after his release. Mack Cantrell, the security guard shot in the head by the same blast that took out Williams and Barry, was also dead. He had amazingly survived the shot to his head and been discharged from the hospital. Months later, he became well enough to return to work, but on his first day back at the District Building he dropped to the floor soon after entering and never regained consciousness.

Betty Neal, the woman who had acted as Khaalis's secretary, operating the phones from the ADL offices, became a key witness. She was the only hostage who was intimately familiar with many of the conversations that occurred between Khaalis and his men at the other locations, as well as the ones with the Hanafi Center. She was able to provide the prosecutors with damning details about Khaalis's knowledge of the events at the other locations, and she described the nature of the phone calls during the early stages of the siege, before the wiretaps were in place. When the defense cross-examined her, though, she sometimes appeared impressed by how nice and accommodating Khaalis and the Hanafis had been to her and the other captives. She revealed small details about their kindness. Abdul Hamid, the youngest of the hostage takers, for example, had confiscated her cigarette lighter at the start of the siege. As the Hanafis quietly snuck out of the building to surrender to the police, she explained, he slid the lighter back into her pocket.

She was not the only one. Several other hostages spoke about how surprised they sometimes were by how well they were treated. Billy Clamp, a hostage who was gay and cross-dressed, revealed to a reporter that a Hanafi had discovered a lipstick while searching his pocket. A couple of the gunmen called him names and humiliated him, he said, but then later, one of the same Hanafis appeared contrite. "We're only teasing you," Clamp recalled the Hanafi saying, "everyone's born to be different."

More than a month after the start of the trial, after nearly one hundred witnesses had delivered several hundred hours of testimony, the government finally rested its case in early July. When it came time for the defense to present its case, they had only one witness: Hamaas Abdul Khaalis. It was a risky strategy. The Hanafis, however, seemed intent on breaking the back of the notion that there was a conspiracy. Khaalis was the leader, no doubt, but if his testimony could prove that he was not actually in charge, then there might be a chance that most of the Hanafis could not be convicted of the most serious charges.

When Khaalis took the stand on July 11, Alexander asked him to explain the meaning of the word "khalifa." Khaalis explained that the Arabic term meant that he was the leader. He explained that he had been a Muslim "from the day that I picked up the Koran, which is approximately thirty years," dating his conversion back to his entry into the Nation of Islam. Alexander asked him to explain the idea of jihad. "You can have a jihad within yourself," Khaalis responded, which would mean, "if you know that you have some sins within yourself, you pray and ask for the relief of those." Jihad, by that standard, could simply mean the struggle of "getting along with other people." There was another meaning. "Jihad also means to fight against. It means to fight against. That's literally all it means. It means to fight against that which fights you or which tries to oppress you." He was the leader, he admitted, and, yes, he had engaged in jihad.

The jihad, he insisted, however, was against Akkad's biopic of Muhammad. The movie was the "straw that broke the camel's back." This was one pillar of the defense's strategy: the Hanafis did not take hostages as revenge. They were engaged in a holy war. Far from breaking the law, their intent was to uphold the law—it just happened to be the law of Allah. Islam, he insisted, required him to be a patriot. Khaalis described to the jury how he had stood in the middle of Times Square face-to-face with the poster for Akkad's movie. The film "transcended everything," he said. The siege was about the honor of his Prophet, not the personal injuries inflicted upon him by America. "Some of the Muslim World League brothers came to the house just before my being incarcerated," he told the jury. "For seven years they had been contemplating," he said, "trying to stop it." A letter-writing campaign would not stop it, no amount of verbal protest could stop it, not even Saudi Arabia could stop it. Therefore, Khaalis had resorted to the actions under scrutiny in court. "I am dying for the Prophet today, right now, on the stand."

Most important, Khaalis testified, there was no plot. "There was no need to make any plans. There was no need," he insisted. "Allah was the plan." Allah is the plan. Over the tapped phone lines, Khaalis and his followers could be heard saying that phrase, or some variation of it, over and over again. It truly was how they appeared to interpret their own actions in the moment. Perhaps they had purposefully decided to describe the situation as such. While the government had staked everything on the presence of a conspiracy, the Hanafis set out to prove that there was no need to conspire because God was in charge. "Are you not the Khalifa, their leader?" the government prosecutors asked Khaalis during cross-examination. "It was destiny and fate," he responded. The Muslim, he said, "just moves in the name of Allah. They responded to their own conscience," adding, "I don't rule their conscience."

During other parts of his cross-examination, Khaalis frequently launched into anti-Semitic tirades and made no attempts to tone down his hatred of Zionism. If anything, he overplayed it. "We went into B'nai B'rith, because the Zionists are out to not only destroy this country but to destroy the world," he said. He spoke about Palestine and described "the murder of old men and women and children" by Israelis as the most "heinous" crimes ever committed. Still, he said, he had entered B'nai B'rith with no intention to kill anyone. If fact, Khaalis said, if he saw any of his men "was about to kill anyone, I would have killed him."

The day after the defense started, it rested its case.

"A REIGN OF terror landed on Washington," Martin Linsky, one of the U.S. attorneys, said in his closing argument. The jury would "have to determine whether in Washington, DC, in the capital of America, that kind of conduct is acceptable or unacceptable, to be condoned and forgiven, or the men to be brought to the bar of justice." For the closing argument, the government rolled out the racks of weapons and ammunition once again. They quoted from the transcripts of the calls between Khaalis at B'nai B'rith and the other Hanafis at the Islamic Center and the District Building. Allah was not in charge, they argued—it was Khaalis who was running the show. "Can you unleash forces of death and destruction and say, 'Hey don't blame me! I didn't pull the trigger'?" the U.S. attorney asked the jury.

In the two days that followed, each of the twelve defense attorneys delivered their own closing arguments one by one. Together, they painted a picture of the morning of the attack that was like any other morning at the Hanafi Center. Men unquestioningly moving to the rhythm of Khaalis's words. One went out to rent a U-Haul truck; the others began loading it with the weapons. One, who had been tending to the bushes, climbed into the vehicle with Khaalis when the time came to leave for B'nai B'rith. At no point, they said, did Khaalis need to explain what was happening, where they were going, and what they would do. The injustice that the Hanafis had suffered at the hands of America was so deep, so profound, that it lived inside their souls. It was the same place that Allah lived. There was only Allah—and Allah was the plan.

One of the defense attorneys asked the jurors to remember another crisis in Washington, DC, from a decade ago. The riots that followed the assassination of Martin Luther King Jr. were still fresh in their memories. People had risen up all over the country, all at once, to act against injustice in the streets. Were those riots the result of some vast conspiracy, he asked rhetorically. "We are talking about a whole country, thousands of miles apart. Not only were people saying the same slogans, the same identical situations were occurring, the same type of burnings were occurring," the attorney said. "Was that a conspiracy? Did anybody ever say that was a conspiracy? Can anybody ever prove that that was a conspiracy? It can't be done. It can't be done."

How was an insult to a prophet different from the assassination of a civil rights leader? Who can measure the pain caused to a believer by seeing his beloved prophet defamed? The people's response to injustice, he argued, can be organic and sometimes synchronized. The Hanafis had not even bothered taking walkie-talkies in with them, another defense attorney pointed out. Khaalis, another attorney reminded the jury, had to ask Deputy Chief Rabe to help him connect to the District Building. Khaalis had no control over events. There was no conspiracy to harm or kill anyone. The Hanafis had acted instinctively to defend the honor of their prophet and for justice. In the absence of a formal plan, the argument went, only Allah could have guided them.

A defense attorney for one of the Hanafis at B'nai B'rith began his final argument by recognizing how odd it was to have a "religious defense" in a court in the United States. Still, "there are those who think that the Constitution, written as it was so many years ago, and very much alive in this courtroom," he said, "was divinely inspired." The Constitution, he argued, was the byproduct of several illegal actions done for the greater moral good. "Throughout history men have made the mistake of adopting illegal means to gain an ultimate good, an ultimate goal, an ultimate end." In this case, he argued, the morality of defending Muhammad's honor might not be obvious to the jury because there were no Muslims in it. That did not mean, however, that the illegal actions were immoral. The goal was simple: "to have the movie stopped," and nothing more.

The first ballot, cast by the jury before any discussion, was eight to four in favor of acquittal on all counts. For three days and three nights, the jury deliberated. During that time, they sent questions back to the judge on only a couple of occasions. Once, they asked the judge to clarify details of the particular conspiracy law employed by the prosecution. Another time, they asked for one of the transcripts of one of the phone calls, but the judge denied that request. Finally, at 1:35 p.m. on July 23, 1977, after nearly twenty hours of deliberation, the jury informed the judge that they had reached a final verdict. An hour later, in the courtroom, the judge asked Khaalis if he had anything to say to the court before the verdicts were announced. Khaalis rose from his seat and read from a prepared statement.

"Ours is a great country," he began. "My family gave their lives, as many dedicated Americans have, for their faith and country," he said. "We can never and must never forget them nor those who aid the vanguard against the enemies of our country. Always remember our faith, our country. Always remember our faith, our country, America. It is worth standing up for, regardless of what the judgment comes this morning. It is worth going to jail for, which is where I am now, in shackles. It is worth fighting for, which is what I did. It is worth dying for, and I would die a Muslim, an American Muslim man. That is every American's supreme duty."

The jury pronounced three of the Hanafis guilty of second-degree murder: Abdul Muzikir, the triggerman, his partner at the District Building, Abdul Nuh, and Khaalis, the leader of the conspiracy. They faced the stiffest sentences. The Hanafis all listened quietly as the verdicts were read. All told, each one faced up to 125 years behind bars. Khaalis, the leader of the conspiracy, could receive as much as 325 years. After the verdicts had been delivered, some of the jury members broke down and wept. It was strange, imperfect, this cruel thing called American justice. "I can see the troubled looks on your faces," Judge Nunzio told the jury. "Many of you are crying," he observed; "you will leave here crying. But if you weren't crying it would bother me. I would worry about the system."

At the sentencing a couple of months later, Harry Alexander described Khaalis as a patriot. He read out a letter written by Mustafa Momin, the Egyptian intermediary, in his capacity as a representative of the Islamic Center in the United Arab Emirates. "Muslims in the Arab World bear witness," he wrote, "that Khalifa Hamaas Abdul Khaalis is a true Muslim leader who stood for the character and respect of Islam." In his sentencing memo, Alexander wrote this about Khaalis: "His greatest virtue and his greatest fault is his insatiable intolerance for injustice." The judge was unmoved, and Khaalis was given between 41 and 123 years in prison, meaning he would almost certainly spend the rest of his life behind bars.

After his sentence was read, Khaalis turned to salute the Hanafis sitting in the audience. Muzikir, the triggerman, was given the longest sentence, seventy-eight years to life. "The sentence means," Judge Nunzio explained to him, "that you will die in jail." The shortest sentence, between twenty-four and seventy-two years, went to the three brothers at the Islamic Center. The judge ordered the twelve to be scattered in federal prisons all across the country so that they would be prevented from conspiring to commit a similar crime in the future. "There is no question in my mind and in the mind of Your Honor I am sure," said the tearful attorney for Abdul Adam, one of the Hanafis who had acted most violently at B'nai B'rith, "that this is a final chapter in an American tragedy."

As soon as Khaalis was led out of the courtroom, a few deputy U.S. Marshals directed him into a gray sedan. The car was escorted by

U.S. Park Police and took the ramp onto the highway toward Baltimore/Washington International Airport. When Khaalis arrived at the airport, he was escorted onto a private plane. When he asked where he was going, he was told that the plane was headed to Chicago. "I lived in Chicago once," he responded plainly. A few days later, on September 11, 1977, *The Washington Star* ran an editorial on the verdict in the Hanafi case, terming it a success for American justice: "A careful trial preceded the stiff sentences the Hanafi Muslims have received and the sentences themselves serve two sound purposes," the editorial read. "To keep threatening people away from the rest of the community and to make it clear to one and all that we have had enough of terrorism."

47

HOMEFRONT

Mohammad: Messenger of God was a colossal, historic box office bust. The $17 million epic was also a cinematic phenomenon. Its battle sequences, some with thousands of extras, and its byzantine sets and stages were a throwback to the golden age of Hollywood, at a scale rarely seen in Hollywood any longer. With hour upon hour of prime-time network news mentions, and endless column inches of space in newspapers, the film had received massive amounts of publicity. The film even got an Oscar nod a few months later for the musical score by Maurice Jarre. Still, *Mohammad* never secured the kind of wide release that Akkad and Yablans had planned and hoped for.

Though theaters pulled their newspaper ads, the movie was back in theaters on the Saturday following the siege. The Rivoli alone recorded 1,556 people on March 20, the first Sunday. The audience numbers fell after that initial peak and kept falling week after week. When the film grossed $1 million in May, it was playing in nine American cities. A wide release followed in June, but it quickly fizzled. It had a decent run in Japan, then went to a few cities in continental Europe and on to Australia. The Arabic version barely played outside of Libya—the league's influence was strong, and no Muslim government was ready to take a chance. Even though it had become obvious that Muhammad was never seen in the movie, the anger of many Muslims did not abate.

Akkad moved on quickly. That same year, at a festival in London, Yablans introduced him to a young film director by the name of John Carpenter, and Akkad decided to invest $300,000 in a small horror project that Carpenter was working on. The story was about a murderous masked man on the loose in suburban America on Halloween night. Akkad's contribution covered the film's entire budget, and out of this deal, he got a producer title and a substantial cut of potential profits.

It proved to be one of the most lucrative investments in Hollywood history. The film *Halloween* earned close to $50 million in the United States and spawned an era of slasher films and a franchise that would continue for decades. One of the most frightening elements of the film for audiences was the use of an unusual cinematic technique called the subjective camera—for most of the film, a floating camera angle represented the point of view of the murderous protagonist, Michael Myers, the same camera angle that had represented Muhammad in Akkad's debut film.

Akkad's partnership with Muammar Gaddhafi remained strong. In the fall of 1977, Akkad purchased the historic Twickenham Studios in London, where he had edited *Mohammad*, and made it his own property. He wanted to continue bringing Islamic history to the big screen and started planning a biopic of Saladin, the legendary Kurdish Muslim warrior who battled against European Christian armies during the Crusades and won back Jerusalem for Muslims in the twelfth century. He shelved the idea, however, opting instead for one of Gaddhafi's liking—a grand desert epic about the life of Omar Mukhtar, a militant leader and a hero of Libya's anti-colonial fight against Italian rule in the early twentieth century. Months after the release of *Halloween* in October 1978, Akkad was back in the Libyan desert, four hundred miles south of Benghazi, to begin shooting *Lion of the Desert*.

While Akkad was filming in Libya, Iran was being swept by a revolution led by the Shia Muslim cleric Ruhollah Khomeini. The revolutionaries overthrew the staunch American ally, the shah of Iran, Reza Pahlavi, forcing him into exile and bringing an end to the regime that America had helped strengthen in the 1950s. Loyalists and supporters of the shah fled Iran in large numbers as the revolutionaries consolidated power and formed a new Islamic religious government in 1979. Ardeshir Zahedi, the Iranian ambassador to the United States, went into self-imposed exile in Switzerland, where he spent the rest of his life. He would be the last Iranian ambassador to the United States.

Months later, a group of armed revolutionaries launched an attack on the American embassy in Tehran and apprehended fifty-two Americans who worked in the compound, holding them hostage. The Iranian state accused them of being spies and of being enemies of Islam and Iran. It was the second major hostage crisis of Carter's presidency. This one re-mained a fixture on American television news for much longer than the Hanafi episode—for the 444 remaining days of Carter's presidency. The Iranians paraded the hostages in front of news cameras, humiliating them for all of America to see. On ABC, Max Robinson reported on this hostage crisis. He'd been hired the previous year as one of the network's evening news anchors, becoming the first Black network news anchor in American history. The images of the hostages inflicted deep wounds on the Ameri-can national consciousness. Americans had long viewed Islam as an exotic faith that had little relevance to their lives. Suddenly Islam was an evil bent on the destruction of America—an arch nemesis.

Less than two weeks after the embassy takeover, on November 17, 1979, from his prison cell in Chicago, Khaalis sent a letter to the supreme leader of Iran, Ayatollah Khomeini, making a plea for the release of the American hostages.

"My Dear Brother in Islam," Khaalis addressed Khomeini. "I kiss your hand, although I am a thousand miles away in prison." He praised the Iranian ruler for "building a new generation."

Khaalis, too, had once "held hostages also to prevent mockery of our faith (Islam)," he explained. He also explained how his family members had been "martyred" for opposing the Nation of Islam, "who used our faith (Islam) as a joke.

"Hamaas asks you, in the name of Allah," Khaalis then wrote, "to let all the hostages go, American or otherwise." It was, he argued, the way to achieve "your spiritual objectives." He then asked Khomeini to spread the word that "your brother in America" asked "you in the name of Allah, to do this." He signed off with: "Your Brother, Khalifa Hamaas Abdul Khaalis."

Two weeks later, *The Washington Post* ran major portions of Khaalis's letter on its front page under the headline: "Plea from Prison: '77 Hanafi Chief Urges That Ayatollah Relent." The newspaper interviewed Khaalis about the reasons for writing the letter. "We are dealing now with a Mus-lim mind that wants to see that injustices are resolved," he told the re-porter from the *Post*. "From the laws of Islam, I know where he is coming from. But I also know that nothing can be resolved until those hostages are all released." The Muslim Students Association responded by urging the United States government to release Khaalis from prison and dispatch him to Tehran as America's hostage negotiator.

The militant revolutionary Islamic spirit that the Hanafi siege foretold kindled more crises. Days after Khaalis sent the letter to the ayatollah, a handful of armed men charged the large cubical Kaaba mosque in Mecca. The group took control of the compound and held hundreds of pilgrims hostage inside. Their leader was a Saudi man who claimed to be the divinely ordained, true, and rightful leader of Muslims in the world, and his cultish followers demanded that the control of the Islamic holy sites in Saudi Arabia be turned over to him and that the House of Saud be overthrown. In its coverage of the international crisis, *The New York Times* referenced the Hanafi attack on Washington, comparing the situation in Mecca to the one in Washington. Unlike the Hanafi siege, the siege of Mecca went on for nearly two weeks and ended with the killing of many of the militants and hundreds of hostages.

THE HANAFI SIEGE directed the American government's attention to the threat of terrorism much as the Munich massacre had four years earlier, but this time the urgency was felt at all levels. Carter kicked the process off weeks after the end of the Hanafi trial by issuing Presidential Security Memorandum 30, which called for the restructuring of the federal government's anti-terrorism apparatus; it called for "the development of a system appropriate to the special requirements of a domestic crisis situation such as the Hanafi siege." Peter Flaherty, who had spent nearly all the Hanafi siege stationed at the command center, became responsible for coordinating the new bureaucracy. The cabinet commission that Nixon had established in the weeks after Munich was abolished and replaced with a new working group that answered directly to the National Security Council, which had a new executive committee on combating terrorism.

Rhetoric and action on terrorism kicked into high gear in Congress. "Terrorism has long been a problem of international concern," Leo C. Zeferetti, a congressman representing New York City, said on the floor of the House of Representatives on March 16, 1977, but the Hanafi siege, he said, "has shifted the battleground to the homefront." The Act to Combat International Terrorism was introduced in the Senate a few months later, and the following summer the Senate Committee on Foreign Relations held more hearings on "combatting international and domestic terrorism," while the House Committee on the Judiciary released a report called "Federal Capabilities in Crisis Management and Terrorism." In April 1977, the FBI began a program of training hundreds of police officials from departments around the country on hostage negotiations. A long internal review at the FBI followed. The FBI also created a dedicated Hostage Rescue Team that trained alongside the British SAS, the German GSG-9, and the French GIGN units. The FBI's new Special Operations Unit began training alongside the U.S. Army.

In November 1977, the U.S. Army unveiled Delta Force, the first force dedicated specifically to anti-terrorism operations. Delta Force's first major mission was an attempt to extract the fifty-two American hostages at the Tehran embassy. Operation Eagle Claw involved eight helicopters that entered Iranian airspace, but the choppers never made it anywhere near the Iranian capital. The mission failed miserably and ended with the destruction of nearly all the American military equipment and the death of eight U.S. soldiers. The military's anti-terror efforts were off to a catastrophic start. A year and a half earlier, in September 1978, Carter had scored his major Middle Eastern success, helping Egypt and Israel sign a historic peace agreement, known as the Camp David Accords. The leaders of Egypt and Israel won a Nobel Peace Prize for it. Still, the failure of Delta Force's rescue mission and Carter's inability to secure the release of the hostages in Iran likely contributed to his loss in the next presidential election.

As always, the politics of the Middle East reverberated at home. "Moslem Strife Reaches Islamic Center," *The Washington Post* reported in a story in April 1980. Competing factions, the article explained, "urge that strong stands against Zionism and American imperialism be taken by the mosque." African American Muslims, meanwhile, were "agitating for action against what they see as an anti-Black and anti-Islam U.S. society," while immigrant Muslims, "including a number of Iranians and Egyptians," argued "for support of the Iranian revolution and other Middle East Islamic movements." Never one to seek confrontation, Rauf swiftly presented his resignation to the board. Several months later, he received a job offer from a university in the Gulf emirate of Abu Dhabi, and he left America.

After the Hanafi trial, the path was clearer than ever for Wallace Muhammad to act as the presumptive caliph of American Muslims. On July 4, 1977, while the Hanafis were still standing trial in Washington, Wallace made a bold statement at a public event by holding up and waving a large American flag by the pole. "You might not like it, you might not like to hear it from me, you might say it sounds Uncle Tomish," he told the hundreds of adherents gathered there, "but America is the greatest land on the face of the earth." He gave the holiday his own name, the "New World Patriotism Day."

His first major initiative after the Hanafi siege was to launch the Committee to Remove All Racial Images of the Divine. It had a simple aim, as announced in the group's rebranded newspaper, *Bilalian News*: "DESTROY ALL RACIAL IMAGES OF GOD." Wallace began lobbying, for example, for the removal of the image of Muhammad that appeared in a frieze on the U.S. Supreme Court building and began coordinating with Black churches to remove images of Jesus, which were also considered taboo in Islamic tradition. "Nobody since the Prophet Muhammad," Wallace proclaimed, "has ever done anything that is more important in religion than this removing all racial images of worship." The initiative failed to gather momentum.

Wallace's real success after the Hanafi siege was in strengthening ties with foreign Muslims. He formally changed his name to Warith Deen Mohammed and effectively became the agent for all American Muslims in global Muslim power centers. He was made singularly responsible by Saudi Arabia for confirming pilgrimage rights to the country. In May 1979, as the Iranian hostage situation was unfolding, he was the only American invited to attend the tenth annual Islamic Conference of Ministers in Fez, Morocco, where he rubbed shoulders with the most important Muslim leaders in the world. Wallace also had the power to choose which American imams would receive training in Islamic institutes in Saudi Arabia to become scholars. Mosques in his network received cash grants and aid totaling millions of dollars from Arab donors. Wallace was eventually appointed to the World Supreme Council for Mosques, a prestigious committee of the Muslim World League, with only thirty-five members worldwide.

Still, his grip over American Muslim communities was never uncontested. In 1978, the tensions that had simmered between Wallace and Louis Farrakhan blew out into the open. Farrakhan, the longtime follower of Elijah, and the man who was the minister of the Harlem temple when Malcolm was assassinated, broke away from Wallace and reestablished the Nation of Islam in its original form, with its belief in the divinity and superiority of Black people over "white devils." Almost one thousand African Americans who had followed Wallace into Sunni Islam reverted to Farrakhan, who reestablished the headquarters of his organization at the Nation of Islam's original address on Woodlawn Avenue in Chicago.

Khaalis, meanwhile, slowly faded from memory. His name would still pop up periodically on the radar of various groups. Someone claiming to represent the Black September militant guerrilla group, which was responsible for the Munich Olympics massacre, for example, called in a threat to a radio station in Maryland in February 1978, demanding Khaalis's release. Saudi emissaries randomly paid him visits in prison. Even the Secret Service walked into a prison once to inquire about him.

On January 18, 1983, Khaalis unexpectedly got one last opportunity to broadcast his message across the airwaves of America. He was a guest on a live special broadcast of the ABC news show *Viewpoint*, hosted by the journalist Ted Koppel. Khaalis joined the show in front of a live audience at Columbia University by video link from the Butner Federal Prison in North Carolina. His image was projected on several screens, granting him a seemingly omniscient presence in the hall. He wore a blue jumpsuit and the same kind of black hat that he had worn at the press conference he held following the murder of his family. His long goatee was almost all white now, and he had noticeably lost weight since his trial six years earlier.

The topic that evening was media and terrorism, and the other guests on the panel included an officer from the Washington, DC, police's Special Operations Division; Jim Snyder, Max Robinson's producer at WTOP during the siege; another journalist from the *New York Post*; Andrew Young, an SCLC alum who served as U.S. Ambassador to the United Nations under Carter; and a few other law-enforcement and media personalities. Islamic militancy was on the rise worldwide. America's embassies in Libya and Pakistan had been burned down by mobs a few years earlier, and America was paying close attention to Muammar Gaddhafi, who was viewed as the leading supporter of anti-American causes around the world. In 1981, the U.S. had expelled Libya's diplomatic mission in Washington.

Koppel opened the two-hour live event with a ten-minute conversation with Khaalis, introducing him as someone who was "better equipped than most to open our discussion on how terrorists manipulate the media." The show avoided any real biographical details about Khaalis. Koppel did not tell the live audience at Columbia University, for example, that Khaalis was once enrolled in graduate courses there. Koppel did not seem aware of the fact that it was the ten-year anniversary of the massacre at the Hanafi Center either—he made no mention of it, at least. Khaalis, meanwhile, appeared frequently confused. The audio connection was apparently poor, and he pressed on his right earpiece as he spoke. "The media had never entered my mind. I'm not newspaper-happy, Mr. Koppel." Khaalis dismissed the host's suggestion that he had done it all for the publicity.

After his opening interview, the producers cut to Khaalis only when one of the other panelists mentioned him or referred specifically to the Hanafi siege. He was the subject of the conversation, no longer a participant. He sat uncharacteristically quietly and listened. Near the ninety-minute mark of the show, during a question-and-answer session, a law student at Columbia stood up and directed a question to Khaalis. Knowing what he knew now, the student asked, how might he have done things differently? It took Khaalis a few moments to come to grips with the question. "Even as of tonight," he responded, "I have not been able to express the true facts, and you have them right here at hand," he lamented. "The real issue for what went down was the picture, not my family," he said; "it was the picture."

Ted Koppel cut in to remind the audience about Akkad's film, which he said was offensive to many Muslims. "That's correct," Khaalis said, "to a billion Sunni Muslims." Koppel then announced that the connection with North Carolina would soon expire, and they would lose Khaalis. Before he left, Koppel polled the panel: "Should we have had Mr. Khaalis on our show tonight?" he asked the seven people on stage. Six out of the seven guests answered "no." The one panelist who answered in the affirmative was a journalist, who said, "All this theory from people who are not actors should at least be matched from somebody who was an actor saying what was in his head." Some in the audience clapped in support. With that, Koppel broke for another commercial. When the show returned, the screens where Khaalis's image had appeared were blank. It was the last time that Hamaas Abdul Khaalis was ever seen by the public.

EPILOGUE

It was a spectacular terror attack, planned perfectly for the cameras. The first plane struck the North Tower of the World Trade Center in downtown Manhattan at 8:46 a.m. It was another seventeen minutes before the second plane would fly in—more than enough time for camera crews from all the major network and cable television stations, many headquartered within a few miles, to send camera crews to the rooftops of their office buildings to capture the scene. At 9:03 a.m., millions of people around the country and around the world watched the second plane explode into the South Tower in a spectacular ball of fire. Before 10:30 a.m., both skyscrapers had come crumbling down, one after the other, in plumes of smoke and debris, killing thousands of people. The World Trade Center was reduced to dust in front of a global audience.

A third hijacked plane, likely destined for Washington, DC, crashed in a field in Pennsylvania. On the outskirts of Washington, the fourth and final plane crashed into one of the five perimeter walls of the Pentagon, an emblem of America's global military dominance. In its final loop in the sky, the plane passed almost directly over the Lorton Correctional Complex, where Hamaas Abdul Khaalis, nearly eighty years old and legally blind, lived in a prison cell.

The architect of the attacks was the wealthy Saudi turned guerrilla militant Osama bin Laden. He had selected the locations for their symbolic importance and for their role in perpetuating what he said were injustices around the world, especially against Muslims. In a video statement released following the attacks, bin Laden explained the rationale for his jihad. "What the United States tastes today is a very small thing compared to what we have tasted for tens of years," he said. "Our nation"—the

Muslims of the world—"has been tasting this humiliation and contempt for more than eighty years." The time period was a reference to the 1920 Treaty of Sèvres, signed after the First World War between the victorious Allied powers and the defeated Ottomans that led to the eventual downfall of the Islamic Caliphate. In referencing the fall of the caliphate, bin Laden might also have been casually laying claim to the title of caliph for himself—he certainly did become a caliph of sorts for many of the hardcore, violent militant Muslims around the world.

As Khaalis had done a quarter century earlier while speaking to Muslim ambassadors in the lobby of B'nai B'rith, bin Laden assailed global Muslim leaders for shirking their responsibility to protect Islam. "Its sons are being killed, its blood is being shed, its holy places are being attacked, and it is not being ruled according to what God has decreed," he said. "Despite this, nobody cares." He described the violence against Palestinians and Iraqis and lamented how "we heard no denunciation by anyone in the world or a fatwa by the rulers' ulema," referring to religious scholars on state payrolls. In the end, he stated his demands. The American people would never be safe until the people of Palestine were safe, he said. In addition, he demanded that "all the infidel armies leave the land of Mohammed," his homeland of Saudi Arabia.

Three days after he spoke through a bullhorn to first responders amid the rubble on America's Ground Zero, President George W. Bush, dressed in a suit, traveled to the Islamic Center on Massachusetts Avenue. It was still the symbolic headquarters for the faith in America, and the president aimed to demonstrate solidarity with Muslims in America after a week when Muslims of all races and traditions had faced brutal, sometimes deadly assaults around the country. "America counts millions of Muslims amongst our citizens," he said after meeting with a group of Muslim religious and political leaders, faintly echoing what President Eisenhower had said at the center's inauguration four decades earlier. "Muslims make an incredibly valuable contribution to our country." He ended his comments by relaying the feelings of the Muslims he had met with. "They're outraged, they're sad. They love America just as much as I do."

Regardless, the attacks of 9/11 marked a new era for Muslim America, darker than any before. In the years that followed, as America launched new wars in Muslim-majority countries, the country's anti-terror bureaucracy became fixated on the potential threat from Muslims at home. They were surveilled, entrapped, rounded up and thrown into prisons, and deported. Some neighborhoods, especially thriving, bustling hubs of immigrant Muslims, were practically hollowed out.

A quarter century after the Hanafi takeover of Washington, faced with its biggest crisis, Muslim America remained without any strong leadership and as fragmented and fractured as ever. Major Sunni Muslim organizations, like the Council on American Islamic Relations and the Islamic Society of North America, had been formed to fill the void of leadership in the 1980s and '90s. They were frequently led by immigrant Muslims from the Middle East and South Asia and sometimes financed by wealthy Arab governments and individuals. However, no singular leader of the kind that Khaalis, Wallace, Rauf, or even Akkad dreamed of becoming ever emerged from within the ranks. The chasms between African American and Muslim immigrant communities had only widened.

Khaalis missed all of it. During the twenty-five years that he spent swallowed up in the carceral system, he had moved from prison to prison around the country, but he never gave up on winning back his freedom. Every few years, he had friends and acquaintances lobby American presidents for clemency: some had great influence and others none; they came from places as far and remote as Fiji, Sharjah, and Sri Lanka, and as nearby as New York and Massachusetts. Ramsey Clark, the former U.S. attorney general turned gadfly-advocate, had taken on legal representation for Khaalis in the 1980s. When federal appeals failed, Clark asked President Bill Clinton for clemency and pressed for Khaalis's release in 1994 to coincide with the release by Israel of a group of Palestinian militants. "The release of Khalifa Hamaas Abdul Khaalis," Clark wrote to Clinton, "would bring joy throughout the Muslim World and hope to all who believe in justice." Eric Holder, who was a U.S. attorney at the time and would go on to become attorney general of the United States, later advised President Clinton against Khaalis's release. Khaalis himself wrote a letter pleading for clemency directly to Marion Barry, who had become mayor of Washington, DC, two years after the Hanafi siege and was serving his fourth term. That request was declined as well.

Khaalis's health had steadily declined with the passing years. He had heart disease by 1995, and by the late '90s doctors judged him to be legally blind. The royal family of Sharjah picked up some of his medical bills, but Khaalis's condition only got worse. In 2000, at the tail end of the Bill

Clinton presidency, Khadija wrote a personal, handwritten letter to John Podesta, Clinton's chief of staff, once again begging for Khaalis's release. She was suffering from cancer, she explained, and she needed her husband around. "We have undergone much more than the average family," she wrote, "there has been so much in our lives that it would fill a large book."

Even though her request was denied, Khaalis was transferred to the Lorton prison complex on the outskirts of Washington that year so he could be close to Khadija, his children, and his grandchildren, who visited occasionally. Kareem Abdul-Jabbar had visited Khaalis too. The last time the two men saw each other was through a pane of glass during a prison visit. The visits eventually stopped. Khaalis remained fully in control of the Hanafis from inside the prison. He ejected his son-in-law, Abdul Aziz, and his brother-in-law, Salim, from the Hanafi community, for example, for trying to act independently based on their own evolving understandings of Sunni Islam.

By the time the plane flew overhead on September 11, Khaalis was finally scheduled for a geriatric parole hearing, his best chance for freedom in many years. Khaalis had been a model prisoner for a quarter century. He kept clean and organized, and he was an inspirational figure for younger inmates, according to prison records. In 1984, for example, he won the inmate of the month award at Butner Prison in North Carolina for "Outstanding Room/Cubicle Sanitation." He mostly studied religious texts, the same ones that Tasibur Rahman had introduced him to, and when he lost his sight, he still made it a point to slide his prayer beads through his fingers.

The parole hearing was scheduled for November 11, 2001, but in the days after September 11, it was delayed for four months. Like many other Muslim inmates at the time, Khaalis was suddenly transferred to another prison without any explanation or warning. When his geriatric parole hearing finally did occur at his new penitentiary in South Carolina, the date was by coincidence March 11, 2002, the twenty-fifth anniversary of the end of the Hanafi siege. Only one member of the parole board was present, and Khaalis's case was dismissed within five minutes. Far away from family, Khaalis's health began to nosedive. Somewhere along the way, his entire medical file was lost in the maze of prison bureaucracy, and doctors struggled to care for him. He was diagnosed with blood cancer. He grew sicker and was moved to a medical facility in Atlanta. In August 2003, he refused any further medical treatment and was moved back to Butner, North Carolina, where he spent his last days in the prison's medical facility.

There, he wrote his directives for end-of-life care in his own handwriting. He designated Khadija as the person who would make medical decisions for him when he was unable to do so himself. He wrote that he wanted no pork products to be administered to him—a common ingredient in the gelatin used in drugs. He did not want to be euthanized either. Both those things, he explained, are haram, forbidden by Allah. Finally, near the conclusion of the ten-point directive, he wrote this: "Do not remove me from the United States." Khaalis breathed his last at 8:00 a.m. on November 13, 2003. There is no record of a public announcement of his death nor any public obituary. At the age of eighty-one, Hamaas Abdul Khaalis died in complete anonymity. His body was transferred to the Hanafi Center on Sixteenth Street and from there carried to the Lincoln Memorial Cemetery in Maryland. His family and his followers lowered his body into the grave, where he remains buried among the many graves of his children and grandchildren.

OVER THE NEXT several years, the three prominent Muslim Americans Khaalis entangled in his attack on Washington died one after the other. Muhammad Abdul Rauf, the former director and imam of the Islamic Center of Washington, died a year later, in December 2004, of a brain aneurism. After leaving Washington for Kuwait in 1980, he continued to travel around the world, holding various religious leadership positions along the way, but he never worked with Muslim Americans once he returned to the United States. He retired in his house on the outskirts of Washington with his wife. He is buried in Washington National Cemetery in suburban Maryland.

Less than a year later, Moustapha Akkad was lowered into his grave in his birthplace, Aleppo, Syria. It was not planned that way. He had flown from his home in Los Angeles and landed in Amman, Jordan, in early November 2005, en route to Syria to accept a lifetime achievement award from the government led by the hereditary dictator, Bashar al-Assad. With the advent of VHS, and later, DVDs, Akkad's biopic of Muhammad had become one of the most widely watched movies in the Muslim world and a staple in homes of the Muslim diaspora in Europe and the United States. Akkad's message had traveled farther and wider than he could have ever imagined. In this trip to the region, he planned to take a few meetings, in the hope of finally financing his biopic of the medieval Muslim hero Saladin, while he attended a wedding in the Jordanian capital with his daughter, Rima, a mother of two children of her own.

They were in the lobby of the Hyatt Hotel on the evening of November 9 when a suicide bomber detonated himself. It was one of three bombs that went off at three different hotels in Amman that night. Rima died instantly, and Akkad died of his injuries a few days later in a hospital bed. The attack, one of the deadliest in the country's history, was orchestrated by al-Qaeda in Iraq, the insurgent organization that morphed, several years later, into the Islamic State in Iraq and Syria, better known by its acronym, ISIS. Seeking to resurrect the Islamic Caliphate, ISIS seized large swaths of territory and declared its leader, Abu Bakr al-Baghdadi, the new caliph of Muslims.

Wallace was the last of the four men to die. His funeral in Villa Park, Illinois, on the outskirts of Chicago, was held on September 11, 2008. While nowhere near as elaborate or large as his father's, it was attended by hundreds of people. By the end of his life, he had lost the power and influence he had once wielded. Wallace's organization had faced a series of lawsuits from the many descendants of his father, Elijah Muhammad, through several women, laying claim to Elijah's estate, which, they claimed, was indistinguishable from the organization's assets. Wallace declared bankruptcy and disbanded his organization in 1987. Slowly, over time, his stature as an imam also faded. Louis Farrakhan, the man who had resurrected the Nation of Islam under Elijah's old creed of Black supremacy, would emerge as a far more influential political actor.

One of Wallace's last major attempts at relevance came in the nineties, when he began coordinating a group of Black and immigrant Muslim imams and religious scholars. Their goal was to create an entirely new school of Islamic jurisprudence—a purely American one—to add to the handful that had been formulated in a millennium and a half of Islamic history. America's multicultural, multiethnic, multilingual melting-pot Muslim community was truly unique in the history of the global Islamic civilization, he argued; it had earned the right—even the responsibility—to write a new chapter in Islamic jurisprudence. It was a grand task that would have etched Wallace's name in Islamic history alongside figures like Abu Hanifa, the founder of the Hanafi school. This initiative, like many of his others, failed. In 2003, Wallace finally resigned from all his formal religious positions and retreated into obscurity until his death.

The generation born between the First and Second World Wars died, but the struggle to define American Islam did not. It simply passed to the next generation. Less than a year after Wallace's death, a thirty-something real estate developer named Sharif Gamal, born to an Egyptian immigrant father and white mother in America, purchased a large gutted commercial building in lower Manhattan for $4.85 million, two and a half blocks from where the World Trade Center had once stood. The building had been abandoned after the landing gear of one of the hijacked 9/11 planes tore through its roof. Gamal hoped to resurrect the structure with a thriving Muslim community center at an estimated cost exceeding $100 million. The plan was for a thirteen-floor structure that would include a restaurant, a five-hundred-seat performing arts center, a culinary school, a museum, a swimming pool, and a basketball court, among other amenities—an Islamic version of the 92nd Street Y. The top two floors of the building, he proposed, would be a mosque area, and to lead it Gamal tapped Feisal Abdul Rauf, the imam of a small congregation in Manhattan and the son of Muhammad Abdul Rauf.

Feisal was not a trained scholar like his father. He was a student of physics at Columbia University when his father was taken hostage by the Hanafis in 1977. During the siege, Feisal had visited the Mayor's Command Center to consult with the negotiating team, and his name appears on the visitors' logs. After stints teaching high school and in real estate, Feisal turned to the family business—Islam. He began studying religion with his father. After the attacks of 9/11, he felt a calling—or saw an opportunity—to position himself as a Muslim voice of reason who could bridge the growing divide between Islam and America. His book *What's Right with Islam Is What's Right with America* was published in 2004. "Like many immigrants from Muslim lands," he wrote in his book, "I discovered my Islam in America."

By the summer of 2010, Gamal and Feisal's project was one of the country's top news stories. The pair had initially decided to call the space

Cordoba House, after an especially enlightened Islamic caliphate that was rooted in southern Spain at the turn of the millennium, but then changed it to a more New York–sounding Park51. Opponents, many of whom equated all Islam and Muslims with anti-American terrorism, called it by other names: "Ground Zero Mosque" or the "Terror Victory Mosque." In a thirty-second TV spot for his campaign, a Florida gubernatorial candidate called it "Obama's Mosque."

Barack Obama had been sworn in as president the previous year and was celebrated the world over as the first Black president of the United States. He was more than that, though. He was also the son of an immigrant who had been born into a Muslim family in Kenya and had arrived, like Moustapha Akkad, in the United States on a student visa in the 1950s. Like Akkad, Obama's father had married a white American woman. President Obama was born to the couple in 1961. Under the long shadow of 9/11, Obama had carefully crafted the contours of his life story during his presidential campaign, separating his religion and faith from his paternal family's.

The Muslim project in downtown Manhattan became a test for Obama. His first statements on the subject sounded like an endorsement to many. "I believe that Muslims have the same right to practice their religion as everyone else in this country," he said, speaking at the White House, "and that includes the right to build a place of worship and a community center on private property in Lower Manhattan, in accordance with local laws and ordinances." The next day, however, after ruthless backlash from political opponents in an election year, Obama backtracked. "I was not commenting and I will not comment on the wisdom of making the decision to put a mosque there," he told reporters.

A few weeks later, the attention-hungry real estate developer Donald Trump, who was eyeing a presidential run, offered to buy the property from Gamal. In a letter delivered just before the ninth anniversary of the 9/11 attacks, Trump said that he was stepping in because the "inflammatory" and "highly divisive situation" would "only get worse." One of Trump's stated conditions was that any mosque Gamal would build should be at least five blocks farther away from the World Trade Center site. Gamal rejected the offer for what it really was—a clumsy publicity stunt. Trump, however, was right. The situation did get worse for Gamal and Feisal. Through the summer of 2010 and into early 2011, the two

Muslim men were pummeled from all sides. Whatever support the project might have had evaporated in a searing political climate. Even some Muslim Americans began attacking Feisal, accusing him of being a mole who was attempting to wrest the reins of Muslim America at the behest of the American government and the FBI. By the end of 2011, Feisal's attempt to create a new religious power center in a high-rise building in downtown Manhattan had come to an end. Another dream of becoming the American caliph dashed.

Through all this and more, the Hanafi Madh-Hab Center still stands on Sixteenth Street in Washington. What remains is primarily a family compound housing the descendants of Khaalis and his earliest Hanafi followers. Though not a community in any religious sense, they still hold communal prayers, though outsiders are not always welcome. There is no one from the community who has any real religious leadership role. Khaalis's children, grandchildren, and great-grandchildren are musicians and artists; some are lawyers, dentists, and doctors; others are employees in state and federal governments; some still drive cabs. They tend to the khalifa's grave and visit it frequently to pray and ponder. An American flag still hangs on the wall inside the center.

A NOTE ON SOURCES

This is a work of journalism. All the facts in this book derive from sources that I assessed and judged to be reliable. This was easier to do in some cases than in others. In most instances, I was able to confirm facts from multiple sources that gave me great confidence in their accuracy. In other cases, sources provided details that I could not reliably confirm. In those instances, I either left them out or included them based on my best journalistic judgment. In all cases, I strived to be as accurate as possible.

I relied heavily on the journalism of others. Through the 1970s, *The Washington Post*, *The Washington Star*, and *The New York Times*, as well as the Associated Press and United Press International newswire services, ran several hundred articles about Hamaas Abdul Khaalis and the Hanafis as well as about the 1977 attack on the capital and its aftermath. This first draft of history served as a foundation for re-creating the events I describe in this book.

Almost all the dialogue in this book is quoted from wire intercept transcripts or other surveillance records that recorded conversations in real time. In some instances, dialogue is quoted as it was recalled by a person present during a conversation hours, days, weeks, or months after the fact—in police witness statements, depositions, or court testimony, for example. Max Robinson's dialogue with Abdul Aziz inside the Hanafi Center on March 9, 1977, was relayed by Robinson to the journalist Wallace Terry several years after the fact. I have quoted it as it is recorded in the Wallace Terry papers preserved at the Schomburg Center for Research in Black Culture. Khaalis's first conversation with Kareem Abdul-Jabbar is quoted as it appears in Kareem Abdul-Jabbar's 1983 book, *Giant Steps*.

In the course of researching this book, I conducted hundreds of hours of interviews with more than one hundred people. The vast majority of those people were directly involved with the events I write about and spoke from firsthand experiences and knowledge. Many of them also had personal relationships or encounters with Hamaas Abdul Khaalis. They knew him variously as a friend, acquaintance, rival, teacher, mentor, or tormentor, and sometimes as several of the above all at once.

Many Hanafis in Khaalis's immediate circle, including his surviving children, did not cooperate with this project. They either refused to speak with me or declined to speak following requests through intermediaries. (The Hanafis remain private and guarded to this day.) Still, I interviewed several people in Khaalis's extended family, most importantly his brother-in-law, Abdullah Salim, who first met him in 1968, and one of Khaalis's wives, June Roberts, once known as Hafsa, who married Khaalis around the time of the Hanafis' fateful move to Washington, DC, in 1971.

I also interviewed more than a dozen of Khaalis's Hanafi associates. While some remain affiliated with the Hanafi community to this day, others disassociated themselves from the group at various times in the past several decades. Some of them had known Khaalis since the 1960s, but most of those I spoke to joined him in Washington, DC, in the early to mid-1970s. Kareem Adbul-Jabbar declined to speak to me despite several requests. I did interview Kareem's first wife, Habiba, whom he married in 1971, as well as his eldest daughter, also named Habiba, who was born the following year; they were both a part of the Hanafi community in Washington for many years.

Of the eleven men who joined Khaalis in the hostage taking, three have since died. I requested interviews with all remaining eight. Two declined, and Abdul Muzikir, the triggerman in the District Building, never responded to the queries I sent through the federal prison system or his wife. With the remaining five, I conducted nearly a dozen interviews, either in person or on the phone, spanning nearly twenty hours. While they spoke with varying degrees of candor and openness, I judged all of them to be reliable sources.

During the 1970s and '80s, dozens of lawyers were involved in representing or prosecuting the Hanafis over the course of many trials and court cases. I interviewed nearly a dozen attorneys and judges involved in these cases; they provided me with sharp and valuable insight that was not always apparent while studying transcripts and court filings. Most important, I had the opportunity to interview Earl Silbert on several occasions in person and on the phone. He served as the United States attorney for the District of Columbia both during the Black Mafia murders and the Hanafi siege and was involved in all of the relevant trials. Leonard Braman, the judge who presided over all the Black Mafia trials and whose judicial decisions were a key driver of Khaalis's attack on Washington, DC, also spoke to me several times over the phone before his death in 2020 at the age of ninety-five.

Joe O'Brien and Robert Rabe, the police officers who had the most intimate and intense encounters with Khaalis and the Hanafis, both died years ago. Maurice Cullinane, the chief of police, was a close friend of both officers and sat for several interviews with me on the phone and in person. All three foreign ambassadors who negotiated with Khaalis have also died. I did have the opportunity to interview Ardeshir Zahedi of Iran on several occasions on the phone and in person at his home in Montreux, Switzerland, before his death in 2021 at the age of ninety-three.

President Jimmy Carter formally declined to be interviewed for this book, but several members of his White House staff agreed to interviews, including Landon Butler, Carter's deputy chief of staff, and Rex Granum, the deputy press secretary. I also interviewed key individuals from the Department of Justice, including Terry Adamson and Frederick Baron, who both worked closely during the Hanafi siege with Attorney General Griffin Bell, who died in 2009.

The two hostage negotiating specialists from the federal government, Steven Pieczenik and Robert Blum, both spoke with me on several occasions. The lead FBI negotiator, Patrick Mullany, died in 2016 before I could interview him, but Thomas Strentz, a close FBI behavioral science unit colleague who was involved in the hostage negotiations from the FBI Academy in Quantico, spoke with me on several occasions on the phone and in person.

While I did not interview Max Robinson, who died in 1988 at the age of forty-nine, I did interview several journalists who were his friends and colleagues and also covered the Hanafis through the 1970s. Most important was Paul Delaney, the reporter for *The New York Times* who was the first journalist to sit down with Khaalis for a face-to-face interview after the massacre at the Hanafi Center. He spoke with me on several occasions both in person and on the phone and gave me full access to his meticulous and well-preserved notes from the time. Gordon Peterson, Robinson's coanchor at WTOP Channel 9 in Washington, also spoke with me on a few occasions.

Of the nearly 150 people taken hostage by the Hanafis, I interviewed more than a dozen across the three locations. I found that many of the hostages were unable or unwilling to speak about the events, even after several decades had passed, for fear of triggering trauma from the ordeal. Several of the hostages did write about their experiences in the aftermath of the siege, and these accounts were often particularly valuable in capturing the terror and misery suffered at all three locations, especially at B'nai B'rith and the District Building.

Others left behind valuable written recollections as well—and two proved to be especially important. I was able to obtain a copy of an unpublished memoir by Khaalis's son-in-law and right-hand man, Abdul Aziz, titled *Letters to My Children*, in which he describes his activism through the civil rights movement and his time with the Hanafis in tremendous detail. Moustapha Akkad's family shared an unpublished memoir in which Akkad detailed the course of his decade-long film project. I was also able to obtain copies of unpublished memoirs written shortly after the Hanafi siege by two hostages: Alan Grip at the District Building and Charles Kraus at the Islamic Center.

In the process of re-creating events from half a century ago, I knew that written records would be essential to my research.

The FBI turned over more than one thousand pages of records related directly to Hamaas Abdul Khaalis, mostly covering the period between 1954 and 1973. These FBI files provided a thorough chronology of Khaalis's life over that period. Luckily, the FBI records also excerpted large parts of Khaalis's military record, which was destroyed in the disastrous 1973 National Personnel Records Center fire in St. Louis, along with millions of other military files.

The period from the Black Mafia murders of 1973 to the Hanafi siege of 1977 is a thoroughly documented one. The FBI had initiated an investigation of the Hanafis before the massacre, and I was given access to nearly two thousand pages of records related to the Hanafi organization that were compiled by FBI headquarters as well as by field offices in Washington, Cleveland, Baltimore, Chicago, Charlotte, and Tampa. In addition, the Secret Service also maintained records on Khaalis and the Hanafis, some of which were released to me upon request. The Washington police department collected more information on the Hanafis than anyone else during this period, and I was given full access to this material, which is still preserved as evidence at the department's headquarters.

Most important, this period is covered exhaustively in the Department of Justice's records held at the National Archives in College Park, Maryland. The DOJ decided to preserve more than ten thousand pages of material related to the Black Mafia murders and the Hanafi siege as a set of landmark cases prosecuted by the federal government. Many of these records would have otherwise been destroyed as part of routine document-retention policies followed by local and federal courts and agencies in Washington, DC, and elsewhere. The National Archives reviewed and made available to me close to three thousand pages from these holdings as well as audio recordings. Some court records from the first Black Mafia trial were also preserved at the Superior Court of Washington, DC, while the entire transcript of the second Black Mafia trial, involving the ringleader Ronald Harvey, is preserved in its entirety at the Washington police department headquarters.

The Hanafi siege trial, perhaps the first ever "terrorism trial" in American history, was one of many court cases whose transcripts were destroyed by the Superior Court of Washington, DC, more than a decade ago following routine record-retention procedures. I was able to obtain the entire transcript, however, from a former Hanafi member who had held on to the record of more than seven thousand pages, storing it in his garage for almost forty years. The Washington, DC, Court of Appeals, meanwhile, preserved all the court filings from the 1977 Hanafi trial, more than two thousand pages of official records, on microfilm and lent me the reels for a period.

Even without the trial transcript, the forty hours of the Hanafi siege may be as well documented as any two-day period of its era. Several sets of official records provided a moment-by-moment breakdown of those hours, which allowed me to re-create it in granular detail. The District of Columbia Archives holds the entire paper record generated at the Mayor's Command Center—it adds up to nearly one thousand pages and provides a continuous report of the forty-hour period. In addition, all chatter that occurred over police radio frequencies was transcribed in its entirety over several hundred pages and was made available to me by the Washington

police department. This record provided a minute-by-minute account of police activity and of what the police units on the scenes experienced. The
evidence retained by the Washington police also included police incident
reports, depositions, and exit interviews with dozens of hostages from all
three locations. I was also able to obtain the FBI report that contained
separate interviews with nearly one hundred hostages and witnesses conducted by agents in the hours and days after the siege.

Government wiretaps on the three hostage locations as well as the
Hanafi Center recorded dozens of hours of phone conversations. I was
able to listen to portions of these wiretapped conversations on audio tapes.
More important, these conversations were transcribed in their entirety
over nearly two thousand pages and were made available to me by the
Washington police department. These transcripts revealed the visceral
and terrifying human drama unfolding across the capital and conveyed
the urgency of the crisis in a manner that might have been impossible to
fathom otherwise.

In re-creating the events that followed the siege, I relied heavily on
the more than two thousand pages of records on Hamaas Abdul Khaalis
that were delivered to me by the Federal Bureau of Prisons. They offered
insights into Khaalis's years in prison; the detailed medical records particularly allowed me to track his health.

All the information and detail that I gathered would have meant little
had I not had the works of scholars and researchers from many related
fields and disciplines. The work of a few became especially integral to my
project. Patrick Bowen's encyclopedic two-volume *A History of Conversion
to Islam in the United States*, along with *A History of Islam in America:
From the New World to the New World Order* by Kambiz GhaneaBassiri,
allowed me to understand the historical terrain of Islam in America. Karl
Evanzz's deeply researched books on the Nation of Islam, *The Messenger:
The Rise and Fall of Elijah Muhammad*, *The Judas Factor: The Plot to Kill
Malcolm X*, and *Chameleon: The True Story of W. D. Fard* (self-published
under the pseudonym A. K. Arian), together, provided me with an essen-
tial blueprint to understanding the complex workings of the Nation of
Islam. Finally, the character and motivations of Moustapha Akkad might
have remained mysterious without Melanie McCalister's *Epic Encounters:
Culture, Media, and U.S. Interests in the Middle East Since 1945* as well as

some of her other work on the global engagement of African American Muslims.

In the notes that follow, I chiefly cite source material that falls outside the range of sources that I have described here. This includes scholarly papers, news reports, and academic and non-academic books as well as materials published by government sources and, occasionally, unpublished or self-published material. At times, I also use notes to elaborate or complicate specific moments or ideas in the book.

In conclusion: this is a work of narrative journalism, carried out using the tools of the trade. I have attempted to reconstruct the Hanafi siege and the important and historic events leading up to it as completely and accurately as I could, using the most reliable sources that I could find over six years of study, research, and investigation.

NOTES

PROLOGUE

4 *nearly their entire lives*: Abdul Rahman, the eldest, was the only one not born in Washington, DC. The family moved there from Pennsylvania when he was a year old.

5 *most expensive movies*: The 1963 film *Cleopatra*, with a stated budget of more than $30 million, was thought to have been the most expensive movie ever made at the time. Source: Edward Ranzal, "Miss Taylor and Burton Sued for $50 Million on 'Cleopatra,'" *The New York Times* (April 23, 1964): 1.

6 *started monitoring him*: The first entry in the FBI New York field office's file number 105–80–80–1 on subject "Ernest X" is dated May 6, 1954. In it, Khaalis is described as a member of "Holy Temple # 7" and listed as a "Judo instructor" for the Fruit of Islam. While noting his discharge from the military, he is described as "very vicious." The entry includes photos of Khaalis from his Columbia University student ID.

9 *book titled* Look and See: The complete text of Khaalis's self-published book is available online at the website maintained by the Hanafi Madh-Hab Center in Washington, DC: http://al-hanifhanafimdhbctr.com/images/lookandsee.pdf.

9 *short poem*: Hamaas Abdul Khaalis, *Look and See: The Key to Knowing and Understanding—Self-Identity, Self-Culture and Self-Heritage* (Washington, DC: Hanafi Madh-Hab Center, American Mussulmans Headquarters, 1972): 81.

1. PSYCHOLOGICAL WARFARE

13 *Buffalo soldier*: Khaalis's military file was destroyed in the disastrous 1973 fire at the National Personnel Records Center (NPRC) in St. Louis, along with 16 to 18 million other official personnel files. Parts of his military records are, however, preserved in the extensive FBI files on him. His final pay voucher from the army is preserved in the National Archives and has been used to reconstruct some of his military record.

13 *deployed months earlier*: Maggi M. Morehouse, *Fighting in the Jim Crow Army: Black Men and Women Remember World War II* (New York: Rowman and Littlefield, 2006): 136.

13 *"the Casuals"*: John A. Cash, et al., *The Exclusion of Black Soldiers from the Medal of Honor in World War II: The Study Commissioned by the United States Army to Investigate Racial Bias in the Awarding of the Nation's Highest Military Decoration* (London: McFarland Incorporated Publishers, 2008): 97.

14 *born in Alabama*: Lake County Indiana; Index to Marriage Record 1850–1920 Inclusive Vol, W.P.A. Original Record Located: County Clerk's Office; Book B; p. 413.

14 *married in Gary*: County Clerk's Office; Book B; p. 413.

14 *born on August 30, 1922*: Indiana State Board of Health. Birth Certificates, 1907–1940. Microfilm. Indiana Archives and Records Administration, Indianapolis, Indiana. Certificate Number: 40681; Roll Number: 017; Volume Range: 81–85.

14 *largest steel plant in the world*: Ronald D. Cohen, *Children of the Mill: Schooling and Society in Gary, Indiana, 1906–1960* (New York: RoutledgeFalmer, 2002): 4.

15 *earliest Muslims to arrive*: For more on early Bosnian Muslim immigrants, see: Samira Puskar, *Bosnian Americans of Chicagoland* (Charleston, SC: Arcadia Publishing, 2007).

15 *established a "Benevolent Society"*: Puskar, *Bosnian Americans*, 15.

15 *labeled "hazardous"*: Historical redlining map database from the University of Richmond's Digital Scholarship Lab: https://dsl.richmond.edu/panorama/redlining/#loc =11/41.587/-87.464.

15 *not a friendly bunch*: Details of the McGhee family's life, and Khaalis's childhood, are mostly from the archives of the *Post-Tribune* of Gary, Indiana, and the yearbooks of Roosevelt High School, Gary, both preserved in Gary Public Library.

16 *hundred miles away*: "13 Lake Pupils Enter Purdue," *The Hammond Times* (February 8, 1942): 13.

16 *walked into St. Monica's*: Records of Khaalis's baptism at St. Monica's Church in Gary show that Khaalis was baptized on June 23, 1940.

16 *mostly in science and math*: Khaalis's academic transcript from Purdue University shows that he transferred credits from Gary College. He was initially admitted to the School of Agriculture at Purdue but then transferred to the School of Science.

16 *not a welcoming*: Jamar White, Derek Fordjour, and Keith David, *Black Purdue University* (West Lafayette, Indiana, Purdue Black Alumni Organization, 2009). Available online: https://www.youtube.com/watch?v=lMaQyMyQpDc.

16 *dropped five million*: Jeffrey O'Connor Whyte, "Lines of Communication: American Psychological Warfare in the Twentieth Century" (Electronic Theses and Dissertations, University of British Columbia, 2019). https://dx.doi.org/10.14288/1.0378998.

17 *image of President Roosevelt*: Leaflets are on the website of the National WWII Museum, New Orleans: http://www.nww2m.com/2012/11/featured-artifact-operation -torch-propaganda-leaflet/.

17 *Life at the base*: S. Smith, "The African American Soldier at Fort Huachuca, Arizona, 1892–1946" (Columbia: University of South Carolina, South Carolina Institute of Archaeology and Anthropology, 2001).

17 *especially bad reputation*: Smith, "African American," 119.

17 *largest African American hospital*: Smith, "African American," 83.

2. BLACK IS GREEN

19 *playing with big bands*: Some details about Khaalis's early success as a musician in Harlem are derived from a June 2000 letter by Khadija Khaalis to John Podesta, the chief of staff for President Bill Clinton, available at the National Archives.

19 *Black is green*: Todd Bryant Weeks, *Luck's in My Corner: The Life and Music of Hot Lips Page* (New York: Taylor and Francis, 2014).

19 *converted to Catholicism*: Khaalis and Khadija's marriage records are maintained in the original registers at the Church of the Annunciation on W. 131st Street in Manhattan. They indicate that Khadija was born Methodist but was baptized as Catholic at St. Peter's Church in Charleston, South Carolina, on January 29, 1944.

20 *gigs with the scorching Texan*: In interviews with the press, Khaalis claimed to have played among some of the great names of jazz, including Billie Holiday, Max Roach, Bud Powell, Charlie Parker, and J. J. Johnson. Khaalis's claims have been repeated by many over the years. There is, however, no record of Khaalis having played with any of these people. In the promotional material for the Harlem Madcaps' European tour, Khaalis is listed as having played with the trumpeter Oran "Hot Lips" Page. In the complete discography of Hot Lips Page, compiled by Todd Bryant Weeks in his book *Luck's in My Corner: The Life and Music of Hot Lips Page*, Khaalis's name does not appear anywhere. An association with Hot Lips Page would, however, explain how Khaalis was recruited for the European tour because of the trumpeter's association with Don Redman, with whom Hot Lips played at the Apollo. Redman had toured in Europe in 1946, the year before Khaalis's Harlem Madcaps left for their own tour. Regardless, it is clear that Khaalis enjoyed some level of success as a jazz musician during the early bebop era.

20 *landed in London*: A short video recording of the Harlem Madcaps performing at the Norrahammars Folkets Park in Sweden on August 21, 1947, is preserved at the Väster-

norrlands Museum in Härnösand, Sweden. Though the recording has no sound, a few short portions of the video clip show the Harlem Madcaps practicing and playing a live show in front of an audience. One three-second section is a close-up of Khaalis playing the drums while dressed in a suit and tie with sunglasses on.

20 *landing gigs*: "Houston, Bill—basist," OrkesterJournalen, accessed January 1, 2022, https://orkesterjournalen.com/houston-bill-basist/.

21 *courses in history*: Khaalis's academic transcript from CCNY shows him taking some science courses in the first semester, but quickly abandoning them in favor of courses in the social sciences and humanities. He scored mostly Cs, some Bs, and one A, in French.

21 *died suddenly*: Indiana Archives and Records Administration; Indianapolis, Indiana, USA; Death Certificates; Year: 1952; Roll: 09.

21 *courses at the Graduate School*: For the fall semester of 1951, Khaalis was registered for courses at the Graduate School of Arts and Sciences at Columbia University in geography, government, history, philosophy, and public administration.

21 *its unofficial dean*: Reeva S. Simon, *The Middle East and North Africa: Essays in Honor of J. C. Hurewitz* (New York: Middle East Institute, Columbia University, 1990): xv.

22 *In Hurewitz's course*: Academic career file 1951–1978, J. C. Hurewitz papers, Box 105, Folder 22, Hoover Institution Archives.

22 *associated with the religion*: For more on Islamic links to jazz see: Robert Dannin, *Black Pilgrimage to Islam* (Oxford: Oxford University Press, 2005).

22 *article in* Ebony: "Moslem Musicians: Mohammedan Religion Has Great Appeal for Many Talented Progressive Jazz Men," *Ebony* (April 1953): 111.

22 *tens of thousands of Muslims*: Gerhard Bowering, et al. *The Princeton Encyclopedia of Islamic Political Thought* (Princeton, NJ: Princeton University Press, 2012): 398.

3. NO. 7

24 *designated space at the Harlem YMCA*: Patrick Bowen, "The Search for 'Islam': African–American Islamic Groups in NYC, 1904–1954," *Muslim World* 102 (2012): 282.

24 *known variously*: John L. Esposito and Yvonne Yazbeck Haddad, *Muslims on the Americanization Path?* (New York: Oxford University Press, 2000): 242.

24 *earliest recorded appearance*: Erdmann Doane Beynon, "The Voodoo Cult Among Negro Migrants in Detroit," *American Journal of Sociology*, 43, no. 6 (May 1938): 897.

24 *distinct foreign accent*: Michael Muhammad Knight, *Tripping with Allah: Islam, Drugs, and Writing* (New York: Soft Skull Press, 2013), 265.

25 *thousands of Arab immigrants*: Nabeel Abraham, Andrew Shryock, *Arab Detroit: From Margin to Mainstream* (Detroit, MI: Wayne State University Press, 2000): 19.

26 *mentally disturbed Black man*: Patrick D. Bowen, *A History of Conversion to Islam in the United States, Volume 2: The African American Islamic Renaissance, 1920–1975* (Boston: Brill, 2017): 312–313.

26 *disappeared forever*: C. Eric Lincoln, *The Black Muslims in America* (Boston: Beacon Press, 1973): 15.

26 *between four and eight thousand*: Bowen, *A History of Conversion to Islam in the United States, Volume 2*, 286.

26 *vicious succession battle*: Dawn-Marie Gibson, *A History of the Nation of Islam: Race, Islam, and the Quest for Freedom* (Santa Barbara, CA: Praeger, 2012): 28.

26 *mistook him for an Asian*: Karl Evanzz, *The Messenger: The Rise and Fall of Elijah Muhammad* (New York: Vintage Books, 2001): 137, 184.

27 *refusing to register*: Claude Andrew Clegg, *The Life and Times of Elijah Muhammad* (Chapel Hill: University of North Carolina Press, 2014): 84.

27 *some "wise man"*: Bowen, *A History of Conversion to Islam in the United States, Volume 2*, 430.

28 *benefit Black soldiers*: Ira Katznelson, *When Affirmative Action Was White: An Untold History of Racial Inequality in Twentieth-Century America* (New York: W.W. Norton, 2006): 114.

29 *roving minister*: Peniel E. Joseph, *The Sword and the Shield: The Revolutionary Lives of Malcolm X and Martin Luther King Jr.* (New York: Basic Books, 2020): 83.

29   *new, larger space*: David W. Dunlap, *From Abyssinian to Zion: A Guide to Manhattan's Houses of Worship* (New York: Columbia University Press, 2004): 136.

29   *unofficial assignments*: Les Payne and Tamara Payne, *The Dead Are Arising: The Life of Malcolm X* (New York: Liveright, 2020): 377.

4. THE SHEIK

30   *father had presented him*: Luke Ford, *The Producers: Profiles in Frustration* (iUniverse, 2004): 216.

31   *freshly ordained Presbyterian minister*: Jacqueline Larkin, "Maple Plain Educator Cites Key to Unrest in Syria," *Star Tribune* (September 8, 1957): 9.

31   *between 1860 and 1914*: Kambiz GhaneaBassiri, *A History of Islam in America: From the New World to the New World Order* (New York: Cambridge University Press, 2010): 143.

32   *eight-foot-tall Vermont marble statue*: Judith Resnik and Dennis Edward Curtis, *Representing Justice: Invention, Controversy, and Rights in City-States and Democratic Courtrooms* (New Haven, CT: Yale University Press, 2011): 119.

33   *almost always cast as a villain*: Anna Badkhen, "What's Behind Muslim Cartoon Rage," *San Francisco Chronicle* (February 11, 2006): A1.

33   *development of the printing press*: Yvonne Sherwood, *Blasphemy: A Very Short Introduction* (New York: Oxford University Press, 2021): 122.

33   *full-blown ban*: S. Brent Plate, *Blasphemy: Art That Offends* (London: Black Dog, 2006): 90.

33   *two junior diplomats*: Ira Henry Freeman, "Mohammed Quits Pedestal Here on Moslem Plea After 50 Years," *The New York Times* (April 9, 1955): 1.

34   *deeply unsavory bunch*: For more on Arab and Muslim depictions in Hollywood see: Jack G. Shaheen, *Reel Bad Arabs: How Hollywood Vilifies a People* (Northampton, MA: Interlink Publishing, 2009).

35   *prime, thirty-thousand-square-foot*: Muhammad Abdul-Rauf, *History of the Islamic Center: From Dream to Reality* (Washington, DC: The Islamic Center, 1978): 16.

36   *walked a thin line*: Full text of Eisenhower speech: https://www.whitehousehistory.org/press-room-old/u-s-presidents-visits-to-domestic-mosques-fact-sheet.

36   *first tests for the doctrine*: For more on the Syrian crisis see: Reem Abou-El-Fadl, *Foreign Policy as Nation Making: Turkey and Egypt in the Cold War* (Cambridge: Cambridge University Press, 2018): 233–259.

37   *wrote to Harry Cohn*: Kevin Jackson, *Lawrence of Arabia* (London: Bloomsbury Publishing, 2019).

5. HOMEGROWN

38   *sent a cablegram*: Muhammad Fraser-Rahim, *America's Other Muslims: Imam W. D. Mohammed, Islamic Reform, and the Making of American Islam* (London: Lexington Books, 2020): 79.

39   *vast network of business enterprises*: Claude Andrew Clegg, *The Life and Times of Elijah Muhammad* (Chapel Hill: University of North Carolina Press, 2014): 99–100.

39   *first major internal report*: "The Nation of Islam," https://vault.fbi.gov/Nation%20of%20Islam.

42   *sit in on a trial*: The FBI had more than one informant sitting in on the Nation's meetings, and the long-simmering conflict between Khaalis and Sharrieff is described in minute detail in Khaalis's FBI Chicago Field Office's file CG 100–30863.

43   *five-part public television documentary*: "The Hate That Hate Produced," https://archive.org/details/PBSTheHateThatHateProduced.

44   *meeting many important world leaders*: Manning Marable, *Malcolm X: A Life of Reinvention* (New York: Penguin Publishing Group, 2011): 166.

6. SAILOR'S CLUB

45   *slight and small man*: Details about Tasibur Rahman's physical appearance as well as his biographical details are all from Tasibur Rahman's immigration file delivered by the National Archives.

45   *commonly known as Barelvi*: The Arabic name for the Barelvis, pronounced *Ahl-e-Sunnat wa Jama'at*, is also a common reference to Sunni Islam more broadly. There

are several groups in and outside of South Asia that use that Arabic name. For more on Barelvi Islam see: Richa Singh and Anil Maheshwari, *Syncretic Islam: Life and Times of Ahmad Raza Khan Barelvi* (India: Bloomsbury Publishing, 2021).

47 *thousands of child soldiers*: For more on the use of child soldiers by the British in the First World War, see: Shrabani Basu, *For King and Another Country: Indian Soldiers on the Western Front 1914–18* (India: Bloomsbury Publishing, 2016).

47 *thousands of former British Indian soldiers*: Vivek Bald, *Bengali Harlem and the Lost Histories of South Asian America* (Cambridge, MA: Harvard University Press, 2013): 97.

48 *Bengali Harlem*: For more on Bengali Harlem see: Bald, *Bengali Harlem*.

49 *wandering in America*: The claim that Tasibur Rahman was itinerant was relayed by a Hanafi disciple of Khaalis's but it also matches, to some extent, his immigration file, which shows him moving up and down the East Coast.

50 *petty criminal*: The ideas that Fard was a charlatan and that Elijah was a Zionist agent were not uncommon among more traditional Muslim immigrants who were confused by the strange history, doctrine, and practices of the Black Muslims. Khaalis could have easily heard these same claims made by others in the city.

50 *hatched a scheme*: Later in life, Khaalis would claim that he met Rahman upon his arrival in New York City in the mid-1940s and that he joined the Nation of Islam as a double agent with the aim of undermining Elijah Muhammad's movement from the very beginning. There is no evidence of this in the extensive FBI surveillance records of Khaalis. He was almost certainly a true believer in Elijah Muhammad at first.

50 *register a new organization*: The registration for the nonprofit organization was obtained from the New York State Department of State, Division of Corporations.

7. WORLD LEAGUE

52 *doubts about his father's dogma*: "Inheritors of the Faith," Public Broadcasting Service, accessed January 20, 2022, https://www-tc.pbs.org/thisfarbyfaith/transcript/episode_5.pdf.

52 *born in 1933*: No complete book-length biography of Wallace Muhammad has been published. His biographical details have been pieced together from various encyclopedia entries and articles. For more on Wallace's early life, see: Z. I. Ansari, "W.D. Muhammad: The Making of a 'Black Muslim' Leader (1933–1961)," *American Journal of Islam and Society*, 2 (2) (1985): 245–262.

53 *Wallace arranged meetings*: Richard Brent Turner, *Islam in the African-American Experience* (Bloomington: Indiana University Press, 2003): 195.

53 *"If Fard was standing"*: Jeffrey Diamant, *Engagement and Resistance: African Americans, Saudi Arabia and Islamic Transnationalisms, 1975 to 2000* (New York: CUNY Academic Works, 2016): 78. https://academicworks.cuny.edu/gc_etds/1624.

53 *interested in meeting privately*: The most detailed and thorough description and contextualization of this meeting between Malcolm and Wallace was provided by Les Payne and Tamara Payne in their biography of Malcolm, *The Dead Are Arising: The Life of Malcolm X* (New York: Liveright, 2020).

54 *suspending him*: Mattias Gardell, *In the Name of Elijah Muhammad: Louis Farrakhan and the Nation of Islam* (Durham, NC: Duke University Press, 1996): 102.

55 *traveled to Chicago*: This is a claim made by Khaalis during his hostage negotiations from B'nai B'rith.

55 *resurfaced on the front page*: M. S. Handler, "Malcolm X Splits with Muhammad: Suspended Muslim Leader Plans Black Nationalist Political Movement," *The New York Times* (March 9, 1964): 1.

56 *struck a more civil tone*: Peniel E. Joseph, *The Sword and the Shield: The Revolutionary Lives of Malcolm X and Martin Luther King Jr.* (New York: Basic Books, 2020): 290.

56 *multistate international tour*: Edward E. Curtis, "'My Heart Is in Cairo': Malcolm X, the Arab Cold War, and the Making of Islamic Liberation Ethics," *The Journal of American History* 102, no. 3 (2015): 775–798.

57 *Saudi challenge*: Reem Abou-El-Fadl, *Revolutionary Egypt: Connecting Domestic and International Struggles* (New York: Taylor and Francis, 2015): 219.

57 *excerpts from a letter*: M. S. Handler, "Malcolm Rejects Racist Doctrine: Also Denounces Elijah as a Religious 'Faker,'" *The New York Times* (October 4, 1964): 59.

57 *issued a formal letter*: Rodnell P. Collins and A. Peter Bailey, *Seventh Child: A Family Memoir of Malcolm X* (New York: Kensington, 2002): 219.

57 *wife, met with Wallace*: Garrett A. Felber, "Muslim Mosque Incorporated (MMI) FBI File (1964)," *Souls: A Critical Journal of Black Politics, Culture, and Society*, 12, no. 2 (2010): 151–156, DOI: 10.1080/10999941003784961.

57 *brief and blunt telegram*: Taylor Branch, *Pillar of Fire: America in the King Years 1963–65* (New York: Simon and Schuster, 1999): 540.

58 *"a man who has a title"*: Elijah Muhammad, *Blood Bath Teaching: The True Teachings of Malcolm X Seldom Told* (Litchfield Park, AZ: Secretarius MEMPS Publications, 2008): 14.

8. JIHAD PRODUCTIONS

60 *watched from a distance*: Most biographical details of Abdul Aziz's life and his conversion to Islam are taken from his unpublished memoir, *Letters to My Children*, preserved in a private collection. Abdul Aziz published small parts of this memoir online for a civil rights history collective: https://www.crmvet.org/nars/khaalis1.htm.

61 *converted to Sunni Islam*: Amiri Baraka, *The Autobiography of LeRoi Jones* (New York: Freundlich Books, 1984): 207.

62 *nearly fifty police officers*: The FBI kept close track of BARTS, and the FBI records on the organization are available online through the Washington University Digital Gateway: http://omeka.wustl.edu/omeka/exhibits/show/fbeyes/theatreschool.

62 *discovered a shooting range*: Frank Mazza, "Police Stumble on an Arsenal, Come Up with New Racist Sect," New York *Daily News* (March 18, 1966): 2C.

63 *hijacked a taxicab*: Case files for the criminal prosecution that followed the bank robbery were obtained through the New York City Municipal Archives.

63 *helped plan the heist*: In his unpublished memoir, Aziz suggests that Khaalis was in the bank at the time of the robbery but somehow evaded detection.

63 *Tasibur Rahman died*: While no identifiable record of Tasibur Rahman's death could be found in public records, two Secret Service agents interviewed Khaalis at his home on March 20, 1967. In that interview, Khaalis informed the agents that Tasibur Rahman had died on March 11 and that his funeral was on March 14, 1967.

9. DAY OF DOOM

65 *aboard a steamship*: Muhammad Abdul Rauf, *Autobiography of an Azharite American: From the Nile to the Potomac* (Nalai, Malaysia: Universiti Sains Islam Malaysia, 2012): 116.

66 *met with Shawarbi*: Malcolm's involvement with the Riverside mosque is captured among many other places in the short documentary *Malcolm X and the Sudanese*, directed by Sophie Schrago and produced by Hisham Aidi. Available online at: https://vimeo.com/394471323.

67 *held up at the entrance*: It is unlikely that these intruders belonged to the Nation of Islam. The Nation of Islam was eager to build bridges with immigrant Muslim communities during this period, and such an act would not fit that broad mission. It remains unclear, however, what group these men were affiliated with.

68 *in support of the Palestinians*: For more on African American solidarity with the Palestinian cause see: Michael R. Fischbach, *Black Power and Palestine: Transnational Countries of Color* (Stanford, CA: Stanford University Press, 2019).

69 *"evoked commitments"*: Chaim Waxman, *America's Jews in Transition* (Philadelphia: Temple University Press, 1983): 114.

69 *traveled through the Middle East*: Fischbach, *Black Power and Palestine*, 46–47.

69 *pointing to the plight*: It was a dynamic that endured for years to come. In November 1970, a group of African American activists and scholars would take out a full-page ad in *The New York Times* that began: "We the Black American signatories of this advertisement are in complete solidarity with our Palestinian brothers and sisters, who, like us, are struggling for self-determination and an end to racist oppression."

69 *frequent guest on TV*: Abdul Rauf, *Autobiography of an Azharite American*, 122.

10. SPORTS RESCUE

71 *live television interview*: John Matthew Smith, "'It's Not Really My Country': Lew Alcindor and the Revolt of the Black Athlete," *Journal of Sport History* 36, no. 2 (2009): 223–44.

71 *fiery speech in the capital*: "National Report," *Jet* (April 25, 1968): 4.

71 *a no-show*: Johnny Smith, "The reign of Lew Alcindor in the age of revolt," theundefeated.com (March 30, 2018), https://theundefeated.com/features/lew-alcindor-kareem-abdul-jabbar-ucla-boycot-1968-olympics/.

72 *listened to speeches*: Details of Kareem Abdul-Jabbar's early life are compiled from several sources, including profiles in sports and lifestyle magazines over several decades. Abdul-Jabbar himself described some of these events, including his early encounters with Khaalis, in detail in his book *Giant Steps*, published by Bantam Books in 1983.

72 *small pendant*: Kareem Abdul-Jabbar, *Giant Steps* (New York: Random House Publishing Group, 1984): 172.

74 *launched into his pitch*: Abdul-Jabbar, *Giant Steps*, p. 173.

74 *immersed himself*: Abdul-Jabbar, *Giant Steps*, p. 174.

75 *other NBA stars*: Lacy J. Banks, "Kareem Found 'Truth' in Islam," *The Washington Star* (January 19, 1973): A-7.

76 *stay at the Hawkinses'*: Sarafina Wright, "On This MLK Day, Remembering a Charlotte Civil Rights Icon," WFAE Charlotte (January 21, 2019), https://www.wfae.org/local-news/2019-01-21/on-this-mlk-day-remembering-a-charlotte-civil-rights-icon.

77 *scouting properties*: Abdul-Jabbar, *Giant Steps*, 225.

11. SUBJECTIVE CAMERA

79 *summer of 1967*: In his unpublished memoir, Akkad writes that he was troubled by coverage of the war in the Middle East but also of the civil war in Nigeria's Biafra region. In that conflict Muslim and Christian tribes fought viciously and both sides waged targeted public-relations campaigns in the West to mobilize support. Akkad writes that he was disheartened by how Muslims came out looking terrible in the American media during this African conflict.

81 *main beneficiaries of this relationship*: Peter W. Wilson and Douglas F. Graham, *Saudi Arabia: The Coming Storm* (New York: Taylor and Francis, 2016).

12. LOOK AND SEE

85 *purely an Islamic marriage*: Broadly, the Hanafis recognized Hafsa as one of the wives of Khaalis like Khadija and Bibi. Hafsa herself, in retrospect, hesitates to describe her arrangement with Khaalis as a real marriage. Khaalis also had a similar unofficial marriage with another younger woman named Saeeda, which resulted in no children.

86 *idea of a book*: Khaalis first mentioned his plans for publishing a book to FBI agents during a face-to-face meeting in January 1960.

86 *majority of the Muslim population*: Zain Abdullah, "American Muslims in the Contemporary World: 1965 to the Present," *The Cambridge Companion to American Islam*, ed. Juliane Hammer and Omid Safi, Cambridge Companions to Religion (Cambridge: Cambridge University Press, 2013): 65–82.

87 *called themselves the Islamic Party*: For more on Rauf's dispute with the Islamic Party of North America see: Rosemary Corbett, *Making Moderate Islam: Sufism, Service, and the "Ground Zero Mosque" Controversy* (Stanford, CA: Stanford University Press, 2017): 52.

88 *meeting between Rauf and Khaalis*: Rauf described this meeting with Khaalis during court testimony following the 1977 hostage taking in which he was a victim.

88 *funding militants in South Africa*: For more on Gaddhafi's funding of foreign agents see: Joseph Stanik, *El Dorado Canyon: Reagan's Undeclared War with Qaddafi* (Annapolis, MD: Naval Institute Press, 2017).

88 *made national news*: Charles Bartlett, "Libyan Chief Makes Loan for Muslim Base in U.S.," *The Parsons Sun* (May 8, 1972): 6.

91 *old acquaintance of Khaalis's*: Aly Hashim's identity is revealed in police records kept at

Washington police department's headquarters. In these records, Aly Hashim is identified as O'Dell Hayes.

91 *falling out with the minister Malcolm*: For more on Hayes's break with Malcolm see James 7X Najiy's self-published memoir: James 7X Najiy, *The Nation of Islam's Temple #7 Harlem, USA: My Years with Louis Farrakhan and Malcolm X* (United States: James 7X Najiy, 2011).

91 *put Hashim on a salary*: A former member of the Hanafi Madh-Hab Center described Hashim as a language teacher at the Hanafi Center whom Khaalis sometimes called "Odey."

91 *first letter by Khaalis*: Copies of these letters, as well as some of the responses the Hanafis received from various temples around the country, are preserved in Paul Delaney's private papers.

13. SEED OF THE HYPOCRITE

94 *unusually busy at the house*: The massacre at the Hanafi Center is re-created here mostly using court records from the *U.S. v. Christian et al.* trial available at the National Archives: 118.10 Records of U.S. Attorneys, District of Columbia Judicial District. The *United States v. Ronald Harvey*, DC Super. Ct. (Cr. No. 47903–73, Jan. 1, 1975) case is preserved at the Washington police department headquarters.

95 *regional gathering of the Nation*: John W. Griffin, *A Letter to My Father* (United States: Xlibris, 2002): 329.

95 *got their supply*: For a thorough account of the Philadelphia Black Mafia's history and operations, see: Sean P. Griffin, *Philadelphia's Black Mafia: A Social and Political History* (Berlin: Springer, 2006).

95 *merger between the Nation*: James Nicholson, "Philadelphia's Black Mafia," *Today, Philadelphia Inquirer* (August 12, 1973).

96 *"most vicious crime"* John F. Morrison, "Ruthless Killer Robert 'Nudie' Mims Dies in Prison," *The Philadelphia Inquirer* (July 11, 2012), https://www.inquirer.com /philly/obituaries/20120711_Ruthless_killer_Robert__lsquo_Nudie__Mims_dies_in _prison.html.

98 *intense argument*: The only record of this exchange between two Black Mafia members is in the *Washingtonian* magazine article "Hanafi Massacre, Hanafi Siege," published in the February 1980 issue. The account was written by the reporter John Sansing, who had previously been an attorney and was assigned as the defense lawyer to one of the Hanafi hostage takers in the 1977 Hanafi trial. Sansing does not identify the source for his re-creation of this argument between the Black Mafia members, but it is likely that, as an attorney, Sansing gained access to grand jury records, which would have included the written statement by one of the Black Mafia members, James Price. James Price's grand jury testimony was also entered into evidence in a separate trial in Philadelphia but was sealed by the judge.

99 *registered in Hafsa's name*: The police report of Khaalis's traffic accident on the day of the massacre is preserved at the Washington police department as evidence.

14. ASYLUM

102 *invited on the* Today *show*: An audio recording of Khaalis's *Today* show interview is preserved at the National Archives: 118.10 Records of U.S. Attorneys, District of Columbia Judicial District.

102 *the deadly standoff*: The documentary *Hold Your Fire*, directed by Stefan Forbes, which premiered in 2021, is the most detailed account, to date, of the multiday hostage crisis at the Brooklyn sporting goods store.

103 *cartoon strip*: Gerlad 2X, *Muhammad Speaks* (Febuary 9, 1973): S-14.

103 *directly addressed Khaalis*: Melvin 12X, "An American Flag Muslim," *Muhammad Speaks* 12, no. 24 (February 23, 1973): 15. https://jstor.org/stable/community.28592146.

103 *suffered from crippling headaches*: Amina's health condition and challenges are detailed in court filings from *U.S. v. John Griffin* case, DC 178–353, available for view at the District of Columbia Superior Court building.

103 *in a vegetative state*: Bibi Khaalis's brain surgeries were performed by Dr. Jesse Barber

Jr., chief of the Freedman's Hospital neurosurgery division. He was a close friend of Bibi's father, Reverend Reginald Hawkins, and the two had been delegates at the 1968 Democratic National Convention.

104 *series of personal phone calls*: Abdul Rauf confirmed these phone calls from Khaalis during his testimony in the 1977 prosecution of the Hanafis following the hostage taking.

105 *a handful of objects*: A large amount of evidence related to the 1973 massacre at the Hanafi Center is preserved at the Washington police department's headquarters.

106 *to poke around*: For a more detailed account of the Washington police investigation of the murders, see this self-published book by the son of one of the accused Black Mafia members: John W. King, *The Breeding of Contempt: Account of the Largest Mass Murder in Washington, D.C. History* (United States: Xlibris, 2003).

106 *biggest case of his career*: Silbert interview with the Historical Society of the District of Columbia Circuit, conducted in 1992 and available online: https://dcchs.org/sb_pdf/complete-oral-history-silbert/.

108 *another mass murder*: The murder of Major Coxson, a Black drug kingpin, civil rights activist, and politician, is one of the most convoluted and brazen crimes executed by the Black Mafia. Coxson was a close friend of Muhammad Ali who, at the time of Coxson's murder, was the biggest star in the Nation of Islam. Ali and Coxson met in Philadelphia in 1968 and Ali moved to the city shortly thereafter. Ali then moved to New Jersey, again at Coxson's urging, where the two men lived close to one another. Ali even campaigned for Coxson when the latter ran for mayor of Camden, New Jersey, in 1972. Though Ronald Harvey was never charged with Coxson's murder, it is believed that Harvey and Samuel Christian, who both belonged to the group that carried out the massacre at the Hanafi Center, assassinated Coxson because of a major heroin deal gone wrong.

15. TOP RANK

109 *mobilized $2.2 billion*: Patrick J. Sloyan, *When Reagan Sent in the Marines: The Invasion of Lebanon* (New York: St. Martin's Publishing Group, 2019).

16. STOOL PIGEON

113 *six-month-long killing spree*: All four men convicted of the Zebra murders were members of the Nation of Islam, and the organization paid for the legal defense of three of them. It is believed that the murderers were part of a fringe group within the Nation called Death Angels. Many of the members are believed to have joined while being held at San Quentin prison, where, according to some research, Master Fard Muhammad earlier spent years incarcerated.

113 *shootout at a Sunni mosque*: Patrick Doyle, Thomas Raferty, and Harry Stathos, "4 Slain in B'klyn Muslim Gun Battle," New York *Daily News* (February 5, 1974): 3.

113 *its own strong ties*: For more on the the SLA's links with the Nation of Islam see: Jeffrey Toobin, *American Heiress: The Wild Saga of the Kidnapping, Crimes and Trial of Patty Hearst* (New York: Anchor Books, 2017).

113 *Muslim groups in Cleveland*: Earl Caldwell, "Marshal Cinque Is Buried in Ohio," *The New York Times* (May 24, 1974): 38, and "3 Captured and 8 Injured in Cleveland Police Battle: 100 Policemen Called," *The New York Times* (May 31, 1974): 28.

113 *created by an act of Congress*: Following the District of Columbia Court Reform and Criminal Procedure Act of 1970, the DC court system was completely reorganized. While previously felony crimes were tried in U.S. District Court, two new courts were created, the Superior Court of the District of Columbia and the District of Columbia Court of Appeals. While these courts fell under the District of Columbia, the Department of Justice continued to prosecute felony crimes. These changes to the District's court system occurred shortly before home rule in DC was enacted in 1973.

116 *man named David Pasha*: Lawrence Meyer, "Hanafi Prosecutor Criticizes Lawyer," *The Washington Post* (March 29, 1974): B1.

118 *shot in the face*: "Black Muslim Leader in Newark Shot to Death," *The New York Times* (September 5, 1973): 88.

118 *walked into a courthouse*: Chester Goolrick III, "Poindexter Maintains He Doesn't Remember Slaying," New York *Daily News* (May 20, 1976): 1.

18. REVENGE OF ALLAH

125 *battling bronchial asthma*: Claude Andrew Clegg, *The Life and Times of Elijah Muhammad* (Chapel Hill: University of North Carolina Press, 2014): 172.

126 *the biggest concern about him*: Jeffrey Diamant, *Engagement and Resistance: African Americans, Saudi Arabia and Islamic Transnationalisms, 1975 to 2000* (New York: CUNY Academic Works, 2016): 88.

126 *In front of a roaring crowd*: The historic 1975 Saviours' Day ceremony can be viewed online here: https://www.youtube.com/watch?v=qcYb40hKc8w.

127 *found in his cell*: Mike Leary, "Trail of Death Leads to a Hollow Verdict," *The Philadelphia Inquirer* (July 27, 1975): 67.

128 *Braman had previously tried*: At sentencing for the first Black Mafia trial, Judge Braman shocked everyone by granting a new trial to one of the convicted assassins, John Griffin. The judge explained that after reviewing the case, he believed that the impressions of the jury did not ring true. A few weeks later, the U.S. attorney's office filed an extraordinary petition with an appeals court that asserted that Braman had "acted in total disregard to the rules of criminal law," arguing that it amounted to "an abuse of judicial power." The appeals court eventually ruled in favor of the government, reversing Braman's decision.

19. PROGRESS REPORT

129 *five-hour public rally*: Barbara Reynolds, "Muslim Shift from Separatism Told," *Chicago Tribune* (June 16, 1975): 3.

20. COMPASS

134 *gossip columnist reported*: John Austin, "Hollywood Inside: Broken Ankle Delays Film," *The Morning News* (April 15, 1976): 27.

134 *introduced him to Irwin Yablans*: Irwin Yablans, *The Man Who Created Halloween* (United States: CreateSpace Independent Publishing, 2012).

136 *his own private screening*: Gene Siskel, "'Mohammad' Film Plagued by Strife," *Chicago Tribune* (March 10, 1977): 13

21. ONLY FOUR

138 *visiting New York City*: Describing this trip in his court testimony following the hostage taking, Khaalis referred to the moment as "the straw that broke the camel's back."

139 *aired on ABC*: Khaalis discussed the broadcast of *Roots* and his criticisms of it in a wiretapped phone conversation with an unnamed woman following the hostage taking.

139 *an excruciating session*: The cross-examination that eventually broke Amina Khaalis was conducted by Griffin's attorney, Dovey Johnson Roundtree, a renowned Black female civil rights activist.

140 *published a biography*: Muhammad Abdul-Rauf, *Bilal ibn Rabah: A Leading Companion of the Prophet Muhammad* (United States: American Trust Publications, 1991).

142 *potentially illegal gun purchases*: Annual Report of the Bureau of Alcohol, Tobacco and Firearms 1977, (Washington, DC: Bureau of Alcohol, Tobacco and Firearms): 8.

142 *in the old Pension Building*: In the days leading up to the attack, the Hanafis may have scouted several locations. Several of the hostages at B'nai B'rith told police and the jury during the trial that they recalled seeing specific Hanafis in the building in the days prior to the takeover. *The Washington Star* newspaper reported in the March 12 article "Did Khaalis' Son-in-Law 'Case' D.C. Court Building?" that a secretary in the U.S. attorney's office recalled seeing Abdul Aziz in the building two days before the hostage taking.

22. HOLY LAND

145 *most important Jewish organization*: An official timeline of the organization can be found on its website: https://www.bnaibrith.org/history-of-service.html.

146 *fundraising campaign*: Cheryl Kempler, "More Than a Building: B'nai B'rith's Former

Home," *B'nai B'rith Magazine* (September 19, 2016). https://www.bnaibrith.org/past
-magazine-articles/more-than-a-building-bnai-briths-former-home.

146 *first major renovation*: "B'nai B'rith Dedicates New Wing to Its Building in Washington," Jewish Telegraphic Agency (September 14, 1976): https://www.jta.org/archive
/bnai-brith-dedicates-new-wing-to-its-building-in-washington.

147 *selling more military equipment*: William Wunderle and Andre Briere, "U.S. Foreign
Policy and Israel's Qualitative Military Edge: The Need for a Common Vision," The
Washington Institute for Near East Policy, Policy Focus #80, January 2008, 5. https://
www.washingtoninstitute.org/policy-analysis/us-foreign-policy-and-israels-qualitative
-military-edge-need-common-vision.

147 *interest in the Holy Lands*: William B. Quandt, *Camp David: Peacemaking and Politics*
(Washington, DC: Brookings Institution Press, 2015): 33.

147 *Israelis were concerned*: Michael Parks, "Israel Fears Cut in U.S. Arms Sales," *The Baltimore Sun* (February 28, 1977).

147 *largest national convention*: Irving Spiegel, "A Jewish Leader Rebuffs People Who Term
College Economically Unjustified," *The New York Times* (September 13, 1976): 8.

147 *"free people must never capitulate"*: Gerald Ford, "Text of Remarks by the President to
Be Delivered to the Biennial B'nai B'rith Convention, Washington Hilton Hotel, September 9, 1976," Office of the White House Press Secretary, September 8, 1976, https://
www.fordlibrarymuseum.gov/library/document/0248/whpr19760908-014.pdf.

147 *"quit being timid"*: "Carter on Conduct of Foreign Policy," n.d., https://www.ford
librarymuseum.gov/library/document/0205/1672822.pdf.

147 *weeklong tour*: "Cyrus Roberts Vance," Office of the Historian, U.S. Department of State,
https://history.state.gov/departmenthistory/travels/secretary/vance-cyrus-roberts.

148 *third of his presidency*: Jimmy Carter, "The President's News Conference," March 9,
1977, The American Presidency Project, https://www.presidency.ucsb.edu/documents
/the-presidents-news-conference-117.

148 *a couple of hostages*: Reginald Stuart, "Ohio Black Frees White Hostage, Talks to Carter," *The New York Times* (March 10, 1977): 18.

23. GUNS OUT

149 *start loading the U-Haul*: Several Hanafi hostage takers interviewed claimed that they
knew nothing about Khaalis's plan. One of the hostage takers, Abdul Shaheed, said that
even when he was in the back of the U-Haul on the way to B'nai B'rith, he believed they
were on the way to a movie theater to protest the film.

150 *slipped him a handgun*: John Sansing, "No Man Is Told by God What Is the Right Way,"
Washingtonian (March 1981): 73.

153 *plunged a dagger*: The assault on Kirkland is described variously by some of the other
hostages who witnessed it in police reports. Some suggested that Abdul Latif went as
far as to threaten to kill Abdul Adam if he did not stop his assault on Kirkland.

24. GOLDEN VOICE

154 *served in the navy*: J. Y. Smith, "Robert L. Rabe, 62, Dies; D.C. Police Hostage Expert,"
The Washington Post (November 17, 1990): B6.

155 *called him Golden Voice*: J. Y. Smith, "Golden Voice of Police: Chat with Trio Buys
Time, Saves Lives," *The Washington Post* (November 17, 1976): B1.

155 *shaken by what he saw*: One of the first meetings on the Munich issue that Nixon held
was with Jeanne Dixon, a popular celebrity psychic with a nationally syndicated newspaper column who had, some believed, predicted the assassination of John F. Kennedy.
In a fifteen-minute conversation, Dixon relayed to the president her dire and dark
warnings for what was to come to America. Two days later Nixon cited Dixon to his
national security advisor, Henry Kissinger.

155 *first and only time*: The records of the Cabinet Committee to Combat Terrorism are
available through the National Archives, ID 1180969. Additional records related to the
committee are also available in the Armin Meyer papers kept at Georgetown University, ID GTM.061208.

155 *created a working group*: *Public Papers of the Presidents of the United States*, United

States: Federal Register Division, National Archives and Records Service, General Services Administration (1974): 912.

155 *two thousand bombings*: Bryan Burrough, "The Bombings of America That We Forgot," *Time* (September 20, 2016), https://time.com/4501670/bombings-of-america-burrough/.

156 *Church Committee report*: The United States Senate Select Committee to Study Governmental Operations with Respect to Intelligence Activities, widely known as the Church Committee, was spurred by reports of illegal activities by various American law enforcement and spy agencies in domestic and foreign operations. The committee published six volumes, two of which were entirely concerned with domestic surveillance activities. Among other things, the committee exposed the FBI's COINTELPRO operations, which targeted many civil rights organizations, including the Nation of Islam. Because of the report, the FBI was required to destroy large quantities of reports that were found to have been compiled using illegal means. This included some of the records on the Hanafis.

156 *convinced Kissinger*: Tim Naftali, *Blind Spot: The Secret History of American Counterterrorism* (New York: Basic Books, 2009): 92.

156 *seven-hundred-page report*: The seven-hundred-page report by the Justice Department's Law Enforcement Assistance Agency was formally issued the week prior to the Hanafi hostage taking. It may be read, broadly, as a reaction to the Church Committee report that curtailed federal law enforcement agencies' powers of surveillance. By highlighting the emerging threat from terrorism, the LEAA's intention might have been to regain some of those diminished powers. A full hundred pages in the report provided a chronological list of acts of violence and terrorism in the United States. The massacre at the Hanafi Center in 1973 was included in this list. While it mentioned that five people were convicted for the crime, it failed to note that one had been acquitted and one was still awaiting trial. The report is available online: https://www.ojp.gov/ncjrs/virtual-library/abstracts/disorders-and-terrorism-report-task-force-disorders-and-terrorism.

156 *upward of $250,000*: "Davis Warns of 'Pearl Harbor' by Terrorists," *Los Angeles Times* (March 8, 1977): 25.

157 *men's clothing store*: J. Y. Smith, "Golden Voice of Police," *The Washington Post* (November 17, 1976): B1.

25. ANTI-DEFAMATION

160 *kicked in the face*: Betty Neal claimed in police reports and in court testimony that Khaalis kicked her in the face on the fifth floor of B'nai B'rith before the hostages were moved en masse to the top floor. Khaalis strongly challenged this accusation in his own testimony. Prosecutors were not able to prove that Khaalis spent any amount of time on the fifth floor.

161 *did not mind the delay*: For a complete account of Paul Green's hostage experience see: Paul Green, *Forgotten Hostages: A Personal Account of Washington's First Major Terror Attack* (United States: CreateSpace Independent Publishing, 2012).

162 *wore all black*: Diane Cole, "Nobody Promised You Tomorrow," *Baltimore Jewish Times* (February 21, 1992): 42.

162 *loose electric wiring*: Diane Cole, "39 Hours: The Siege Remembered," *The National Jewish Monthly* (May 1977): 6–7.

162 *"innocent victims in holy war"*: "Federal Capabilities in Crisis Management and Terrorism" (Washington, DC: U.S. Government Printing Office, 1978), p. 168

26. EGYPTIAN MISSION

166 *made no attempt to hide*: Joseph D. Whitaker, "Hanafis' Sorrowing Kin: 'We Still Love Them,'" *The Washington Post* (March 13, 1977): A14.

167 *former colonel in the U.S. Army*: Charles Kraus provided the police with a detailed written reflection on his captivity after the incident, which included some context for his presence at the Islamic Center that day. He said his interest in Islam was spurred partly by the negative portrayals of Muslims in Hollywood, specifically naming the 1921 film *The Sheik*, starring Rudolph Valentino. He had visited the Islamic Center months ear-

lier and met with Abdul Rauf, who had personally loaned him a few books that provided a more neutral introduction to Islam and Muslims.

27. PROJECTION ROOM

171 *pleased at the sight*: Irwin Yablans, *The Man Who Created Halloween* (United States: CreateSpace Independent Publishing, 2012): 161

171 *flown into New York City*: Yablans, *The Man Who Created Halloween*, 161.

174 *brought a flower to someone*: Kenneth Turan, "Film Cost $18 Million, Eight Years," *The Washington Post* (March 12, 1977): A18.

28. SPYGLASS

176 *especially sensitive issue*: The P-56B restricted airspace is a circle with a radius of about 1.2 miles surrounding the Naval Observatory on Massachusetts Avenue. It is one of fewer than a dozen designated permanent restricted airspaces in the United States. "DCA Reagan National—Aircraft Procedures," n.d., https://www.flyreagan.com/about -airport/aircraft-noise-information/dca-reagan-national-aircraft-procedures.

178 *created in the 1860s*: "Brief History of the MPDC," https://mpdc.dc.gov/page/brief -history-mpdc.

178 *hundreds of new Black recruits*: Peter Hermann, "Burtell M. Jefferson, Washington's First Black Police Chief, Dies at 96," *The Washington Post* (March 19, 2021).

178 *no longer the cordial man*: This call occurred before the wiretaps were approved at B'nai B'rith, but the transcript is included in the evidence file at the Washington police department. This call was likely recorded by Maurice Cullinane himself in his office, though Cullinane has no memory of recording the call.

29. FEDERAL TRIANGLE

185 *military vet and a gun nut*: Following the Hanafi siege, Richard Traylor began working for the Drug Enforcement Agency. In 1979, there was a huge explosion at his home in the Virginia suburbs of Washington, in which Traylor was badly burned. Investigators found more than one hundred guns in his house, along with "enough gunpowder," one police source told *The Washington Star*, to "level an entire block." Some of the weapons were stolen from the Washington police and others from the DEA. Traylor was tried and sentenced to four months in prison.

186 *smoke and haze filled*: The scenes inside council chair Sterling Tucker's office are described using, among other reports, an unpublished narrative written by one of the hostages, Alan Grip, in the weeks after the end of the siege.

186 *police yelled*: Eventually the hostage takers in the District Building were provided with a bullhorn to ease the communication between them and police.

30. ONE AND ONLY

188 *born and raised in Richmond*: Dhyana Ziegler, "Max Robinson, Jr: Turbulent Life of a Media Prophet," *Journal of Black Studies* 20, no. 1 (September, 1989): 97.

188 *won a prime-time Emmy*: Ziegler, "Max Robinson," 98.

188 *the first African American*: Laura M. Holson, "Max Robinson, a Largely Forgotten Trailblazer: Recalling the ABC Co-Anchor Who Predated Lester Holt," *The New York Times* (June 21, 2015): 8.

188 *met Aziz at Aram*: The Wallace Terry papers held at the Schomburg Center for Research in Black Culture in New York contain transcripts of interviews that Terry conducted with Robinson between 1981 and 1988. In these interviews, Robinson speaks in depth about his relationship with the Hanafis, particularly Abdul Aziz.

188 *amateur painter*: Carla Hall, "The Rise, and Dizzying Fall, of Max Robinson: The Ailing Former ABC Anchor Looks Back on His Troubled Path," *The Washington Post* (May 26, 1988): E1.

189 *another Black reporter*: Khaalis invited two Black journalists into the home for an interview after the massacre. Max Robinson was one of them, and the other was *The New York Times* reporter Paul Delaney, who described the details of the conversation inside the Hanafi Center in an interview with the author.

191   *wrestle a woman*: This scene described by Max Robinson to Wallace Terry was also de-
      scribed by Khadija to Khaalis in a wiretapped phone conversation during the first night
      of the Hanafi siege.
192   *gray suit and maroon tie*: Broadcast available online: https://kaltura.uga.edu/media/t/1
      _tbwrm06p/86446941.
193   *switched to the network*: All evening network news transmissions obtained from the
      Vanderbilt Television News Archive.
194   *Nearly fifty million*: Pew Research Study using figures from Nielsen Media Research:
      https://www.pewresearch.org/journalism/chart/network-tv-evening-news-overall
      -viewership-since-1980/.

31. JURISDICTION

195   *two city bureaucrats*: Frank Van Riper, "The D.C. Command Post—Inside the 'Holy
      War' Room," *Daily News* (March 11, 1977): 4.
195   *part of the fifth floor*: The civil defense unit had its offices on the third floor, but the
      Mayor's Command Center shared the fifth floor with the Washington police depart-
      ment. Cullinane, Rabe, and a few others had offices in both the police department and
      the command center and moved in between locations throughout the siege.
195   *created on the fly*: For more on the history, layout, and capabilities of the command
      center see: *The Mayor's Command Center* (Washington, DC: U.S. Government Printing
      Office, 1971).
196   *agencies began pouring in*: All comings and goings in and out of the command center
      over the period of the siege were recorded in a visitors logbook, which is preserved at
      the District of Columbia Archives in Washington, DC.
196   *joined the bureau in 1966*: Patrick J. Mullany, *Matador of Murder: An FBI Agent's Journey
      in Understanding the Criminal Mind* (United States: CreateSpace Independent Publish-
      ing, 2015): 6.
198   *legal openings*: "Basis for Federal Jurisdiction in Washington, D.C., Hostage Situation,"
      Department of Justice, https://www.justice.gov/olc/opinion/basis-federal-jurisdiction
      -washington-dc-hostage-situation.
199   *met with the two people*: The Griffin B. Bell papers held at Mercer University contain
      Bell's detailed schedules of each day, including all movements and incoming and out-
      going phone calls; they provide a thorough account of his activities over the three days.
199   *looking for firepower*: Griffin B. Bell and Ronald J. Ostrow, *Taking Care of the Law* (Ma-
      con, GA: Mercer University Press, 1986): 155–156.
199   *two army helicopters*: *Attorney General's Annual Report: Federal Law Enforcement and
      Criminal Justice Assistance Activities* (Washington, DC: U.S. Government Printing Of-
      fice, 1977): 38.
200   *monitoring all incoming and outgoing*: The wire intercepts at the four locations came in
      stages. On March 9, at 5:20 p.m., the Department of Justice authorized intercepts of the
      telephones on the eighth floor of B'nai B'rith. The Hanafi Center wiretaps were autho-
      rized on that same day at 10:15 p.m. Five minutes later, the intercepts of the phones at
      the Islamic Center and the District Building were authorized. These authorizations had
      to be approved by a judge, who was able to do so on March 11. The timing and legality of
      these intercepts, and their admissibility in the trial, were challenged by the Hanafis, but,
      ultimately, the judge ruled that the government had met the statutory requirements.
201   *knew this was impossible*: On several occasions throughout the negotiations over the
      phone lines, Rabe told Khaalis that the negotiating team was actively trying to fulfill
      this demand by working with the Federal Bureau of Prisons.

32. HOG-TIED

203   *puffing on his pipe*: Khaalis alternated between smoking a pipe, as was his habit, and
      cigarettes. The Hanafis preferred Camel and Chesterfield brands. During the siege,
      Khaalis also shared his cigarettes with the secretary at B'nai B'rith, Betty Neal.
204   *number 786*: 786 is a numerological expression for the standard Islamic prayer "In the
      name of Allah, the most beneficent, most merciful," used especially in South Asian and
      diaspora communities. The Hanafis most likely absorbed this region-specific conven-
      tion from Tasibur Rahman.

204 *handed a periodical*: In court testimony, hostages variously described the title of this
     journal as the *Citadel* or the *Minaret*. There are several Islamic journals by the name
     of *Minaret* that were published during the 1970s, yet it remains unclear which article
     Khaalis ordered read aloud to the hostages. A long review of Akkad's film that matches
     the description of the one read by the Hanafis did appear in the British Islamic journal
     Impact in 1976.

207 *answering most of the calls*: Other than Khaalis, only Abdul Rahman, the oldest brother
     at the Islamic Center, appeared to take the initiative to speak with reporters at length
     during the siege; he ended up live on air on a couple of occasions. Whether Khaalis was
     unaware of this or was tacitly allowing it is unclear. On the other hand, Khaalis clearly
     instructed Khadija to not let Abdul Aziz, his son-in-law and longtime lieutenant, talk
     to the press, saying, "He's not equipped to do that yet."

207 *Nuh picked up*: Abdul Nuh was the one exclusively answering the phones at the District
     Building while Muzikir was in charge of keeping a close eye on hostages. Because of
     Nuh's clear deference to Muzikir, he was quietly nicknamed "gofer" by the hostages,
     according to court testimony.

33. SPOOKS

210 *chartered by the French government*: No record of any such official charter flight could
     be found; in an interview, Zahedi said he was under the impression that the French
     Ministry of Foreign Affairs arranged the airplane for him.

211 *born into a royal family*: Sahabzada Yaqub Khan, *Strategy, Diplomacy, Humanity: Life
     and Work of Sahabzada Yaqub-Khan* (International Forum Takshila Research Univer-
     sity, 2005).

211 *prisoner of war*: Sam Roberts, "Sahabzada Yaqub Khan, Pakistani Diplomat, Dies at
     95," *The New York Times* (January 31, 2016): A25.

211 *metallic blue Rolls-Royce*: Katharine Q. Seelye, "Ardeshir Zahedi, Who Raised Iran's
     Profile on a Tide of Champagne, Dies at 93," *The New York Times* (November 22, 2021):
     A23.

211 *could not fully explain*: Marlene Cimons, "'Playboy' Envoy Helped to End Siege," *Los
     Angeles Times* (March 12, 1977): 1.

211 People *magazine profile*: Clare Crawford and Parviz Raein, "The Charming Zahedi
     Ponders: Can Liz Taylor Be a Diplomatic Incident?" *People*, vol. 5, no. 23 (June 14,
     1976).

211 *Zahedi also counted*: Telegrams by Hollywood personalities as well as dozens of others
     in government and business are preserved as part of the Ardashīr Zāhidī papers at
     Hoover Institution Library and Archives at Stanford University. Part of Gregory Peck's
     telegram to Zahedi after the siege read as follows: "We are very happy and proud of you.
     Did you promise caviar to the terrorist. All the best."

212 *aired a segment*: "Iran Assassin Teams to U.S., CBS Reports," *Des Moines Register*
     (March 7, 1977): 1.

212 *leading a similar effort*: Giuliani was associate deputy attorney general during the Ford
     administration and in that capacity was handling the Department of Justice's evolving
     approach toward anti-terrorism. Correspondence between Giuliani and Heck and oth-
     ers clearly indicates an emerging turf war over the subject of counterterrorism between
     the DOJ and the State Department.

213 *"how are you feeling"*: In their first-ever conversation, Yaqub Khan failed to say "Assalamu
     alaikum," the standard Muslim greeting, Arabic for "peace be on you." Khaalis used
     that as a pretext to berate Khan for several minutes, and Khan never recovered from that
     misstep in the conversation.

214 *operating out of Algeria*: For more on the Black Panther Party's international section,
     see: Michael L. Clemons and Charles E. Jones, "Global Solidarity: The Black Panther
     Party in the International Arena," *New Political Science*, 21 (1999): 177–203.

34. CEASE AND DESIST

215 *see the District Building*: "Mayor Escaped Bloody Chronology of Raid," *Valley News*
     (March 11, 1977): 39.

216 *Carter's chief counsel*: The Robert J. Lipshutz papers at the Jimmy Carter Library con-

tain an entire section on the Hanafi siege, which includes his handwritten records as well as other documents from the siege.

216   *deliver a keynote*: Lipshutz did end up delivering this lecture at the Zionist conference and landed in some trouble because of it. In his prepared comments, he dwelled on the Hanafi siege and expressed the opinion that the "primary factor" for Khaalis's attack was "a belief that our system has not properly rendered justice." He compared this to the "large percentage of Palestinians" who also "feel that they have been deprived of their rights." Many Zionist and Jewish groups protested Lipshutz's comments as justifying terrorism.

218   *the day after Martin Luther King*: Jonathon Berlin and Kori Rumore, "12 Times the President Called in the Military Domestically," *Chicago Tribune* (June 1, 2020), https://www .chicagotribune.com/news/ct-national-guard-deployments-timeline-htmlstory.html.

35. BIG SURPRISE

220   *had not slept*: The activity over the wiretapped phone lines at B'nai B'rith suggests that there could have been no time when Khaalis could have rested or slept for more than several consecutive minutes.

221   *select members of the Green Berets*: Jack Murphy, "Blue Light: America's First Counter-Terrorism Unit," https://jackmurphywrites.com/wp-content/uploads/2017/05/Blue -Light-Americas-First-Counter-terrorism-Unit2.2.pdf.

36. PANORAMA

226   *the midday talk show*: Pat Mitchell, *Becoming a Dangerous Woman: Embracing Risk to Change the World* (New York: Seal Press, 2019).

229   *looking to profile him*: *Who's Who*, CBS, March 15, 1977, available online: https://www .youtube.com/watch?v=ty54WeAkuKs and https://www.youtube.com/watch?v=LIgK barCoJM.

229   *delivering a monologue*: Available to view online through the University of Georgia's Brown Media Archive: https://kaltura.uga.edu/media/t/1_tbwrm06p/86446941.

37. TRUE PICTURE

233   *I have no knowledge*: Wallace Muhammad was expelled from the Nation of Islam by his father several more times after rejoining in the aftermath of Malcolm X's murder. At the time of the Hanafi massacre, Wallace claimed that he was suffering another expulsion from the organization. Though he may not have had forewarning of the massacre, it is unlikely that he knew only what was in the press. The trials involving the Black Mafia hitmen were ongoing when Wallace gained control of the organization, and Wallace's top lawyer, Saad El-Amin, confirmed in an interview that El-Amin was following the case as it moved through the DC courts.

233   *one hundred mosques*: Patrick D. Bowen, *A History of Conversion to Islam in the United States, Volume 1: White American Muslims Before 1975* (Boston: Brill, 2015): 363.

38. BROTHERS IN ISLAM

237   *already drawn up plans*: Patrick J. Mullany, *Matador of Murder: An FBI Agent's Journey in Understanding the Criminal Mind* (United States: CreateSpace Independent Publishing, 2015): 130.

238   *rarely saying a word*: Neither Steven Pieczenik nor Robert Blum ever spoke over the phone lines, and Khaalis was never made aware of their presence. Still, Khaalis did repeatedly make references throughout the entire episode to "Jewish psychologists in the room." At one point, for example, he said: "No Jewish psychologist or nothing that can talk me out of anything." In another conversation, he appeared to address them directly: "No way in the world some psychologist think he—you gonna debilitate me."

240   *over the hostages' heads*: Several hostages and hostage takers confirmed hearing this sound on the roof on the second evening, but there has never been an explanation for what caused it. It is possible that a federal spy agency was attempting to place additional listening devices on the building. Both the CIA and the NSA refused to confirm the presence of any records related to the Hanafi siege, citing national security exceptions.

39. CHAIN OF COMMAND

243 *unofficial eyes and ears*: Douglas Smith, "Pete Helped Drama End in Success," *The Pittsburgh Press* (March 11, 1977): 1.

244 *only outstanding issue*: All negotiators went into the negotiations unarmed, but Robert Rabe had grave reservations about this arrangement according to Maurice Cullinane.

40. TABLE SPREAD

247 *launched into a tirade*: The three-hour negotiations that took place at B'nai B'rith were not recorded in any manner. These negotiations have been reconstructed from interviews with Maurice Cullinane and Ardeshir Zahedi as well as from press reports that followed.

249 *fourth chapter of the Koran*: The exact translation of the Koran used by the negotiators could not be determined. The translations used in this text are from Abdullah Yusuf Ali's translation, first published in 1934. It is the most widely used English translation of the Islamic holy book today.

41. FAIR JUSTICE

257 *held all the cards*: The Harold H. Greene papers held at the Library of Congress contain the judge's notes that provide a detailed picture of the mechanics of the negotiations and his involvement in them: https://lccn.loc.gov/mm2007085346.

259 *huddled for a quick prayer*: The prayer, led by a rabbi, was the *Shehecheyanu*, a common Hebrew prayer of thanksgiving: "Blessed art Thou, O Lord our God, King of the universe, who has kept us in life, who has preserved us, and enabled us to reach this day."

259 *flipped the switch*: Mike Feinsilber, "Church Bells Ring as 130 Hostages Are Freed," *Bennington Banner* (March 11, 1977): 1.

260 *flashing news cameras*: Charles Fennyvessi, one of the hostages and the editor of *The National Jewish Monthly* magazine, later described hostile feelings among the hostages toward the press upon their release. Many hostages, he wrote, urged him not to write about his experiences. See: Charles Fennyvessi, "Looking into the Muzzle of Terrorists," *The Quill* (July/August, 1977): 16–18.

42. THINGS GO BOOM

265 *partisans on Capitol Hill*: Lloyd Bentsen, the Democratic senator from Texas, said on the Senate floor on March 11 that he was "outraged by the recent events" but "particularly incensed by the release of the leader," before announcing that he had introduced a bill "to suspend all forms of assistance to countries harboring terrorists." After Khaalis's imprisonment, Republican senator Bob Dole issued a press release to "emphasize the urgent need for a law to prohibit the immediate release from custody of terrorists."

266 *welcomed guests*: Khaalis received various guests at the Hanafi Center on the morning of March 11, including the three brothers Rahman, Rahim, and Qawee (who had taken hostages at the Islamic Center) upon their release on bond.

267 *drew eight hundred people*: Alice Bonner and Milton Coleman, "Friends Eulogize Newsman Slain in Hanafi Siege: Newsman Slain in Siege Is Eulogized," *The Washington Post* (March 15, 1977): 1.

267 *representing an "action committee"*: The group included major North American Muslim organizations: Federation of Islamic Association in the United States and Canada; Muslim World League New York office; Islamic Center of New Jersey; Muslim Center of New York; Muslim Students Association of New York; Islamic Service Organization of New Jersey; United Islamic Center of Paterson, New Jersey; Elmhurst Muslim Society; Islamic Center of Corona; International Muslim Society; and the Pakistan Students Association.

269 *various terrorist activities*: Kahane founded the JDL in 1968 as a reaction to simmering tensions between Blacks and Jews in New York City. In its heyday in the 1970s, the JDL turned its focus to Arabs and the Soviet Union for its anti-Semitic policies. One JDL member's plan to assassinate Palestinian Liberation Organization leader Yasser Arafat in 1974 was disrupted by the FBI: Peter Kihss, "J.D.L. Aide Held in Threat To Kill Palestinian Leader," *The New York Times* (November 13, 1974): 1.

269   *specifically warned Khadija*: In addition to Khaalis, Abdul Aziz had also mentioned a potential threat from the JDL in monitored phone calls from the Hanafi Center while the hostage situation was still ongoing.

271   *played an intermediary role*: Alan Dershowitz, "Dialogue and Diversity," *Moment Magazine* (May, 1977): 60.

43. FAITH AND COUNTRY

274   *overtures from foreign Muslims*: The many organizations that reached Khaalis directly over the phone at B'nai B'rith included the National Council of Canadian Muslims, the Nation of Islam, Association of Muslim Scientists and Engineers of North America, Muslim World League's Canadian office, and Blackman's Volunteer Army of Liberation.

274   *most seasoned traveler*: In addition to his business travel, Aziz, along with several Hanafi Muslim women, including Khadija and Amina Khaalis, had also traveled after the 1973 massacre to Saudi Arabia for a minor pilgrimage and then onward to Pakistan.

275   *looking for support*: On March 24, 1977, when Aziz departed for the Middle East, the White House announced that the Egyptian president, Anwar Sadat, would be visiting Washington on an official state visit in the first week of April. It was expected that after hosting Rabin, the Israeli prime minister, Carter would encourage the Egyptian president to engage in a peace process. Peace with Israel was a polarizing issue like no other in the region, and the announcement sent Arab countries into a diplomatic frenzy, which may have helped or harmed Aziz's mission.

275   *recently won recognition*: The Muslim World League gained observer status as a nongovernmental organization at the United Nations in 1974. It opened its formal office to the United Nations in New York City in 1976. The league's American office was led by Ahmad Hussein Sakr, a Lebanese scientist living in America.

276   *Aziz had an audience*: All the meetings listed for Aziz's foreign travels are claimed by Abdul Aziz in his unpublished memoir, *Letters to My Children*. No formal record for these meetings could be found.

276   *Momin told Khaalis*: The wiretaps at the Hanafi Center began once again on March 24, 1977, and went into April.

277   *sent Khaalis a lump sum*: Kareem Abdul-Jabbar, *Giant Steps* (New York: Random House Publishing Group, 1984).

278   *traditional Muslim greeting*: The traditional Muslim greeting, "Assalamu alaikum," used by the Hanafis countless times over the phone, led to serious concern during the trial as the transcribers who had typed up the record of the calls had interpreted the phrase, phonetically, as "Islamic Mayhem." Harry Alexander, Khaalis's lawyer, warned Judge Nunzio that the misspelling might itself become an "international incident." As a result, the jury was never given the transcripts and relied only on the audio recordings.

44. BIG MAN

280   *allies in Chicago*: Keith Ibrahim, who became the conduit for the rapprochement with Wallace, was a young imam at the Umar Farooq Mosque in Chicago. He became one of the leading supporters and spokespeople for the Hanafis during and after the siege. He was interviewed for CBS's evening news telecast and quoted widely in the print media, frequently presenting a defense for the Hanafis' takeover of the buildings.

281   *Wallace quoted Khaalis*: In Washington police department's evidence, a transcript of a conversation from March 26, 1977, exists that may be between Khaalis and Wallace. The caller identifies himself as Khaalis. The receiver is not identified. In it, Khaalis says that an Arab emissary visiting the Hanafi Center recommended that the call be made. The receiver responds positively by saying that "we have to be like a wall." Khaalis then repeatedly offers his help with anything the receiver needs. The two speakers exchange platitudes for several minutes, and at the end Khaalis says that he would call back at 11:00 a.m. the next day. No transcript of any such follow-up call exists in evidence.

281   *one syndicated story*: Bryce Nelson, "Black Muslim-Hanafi Truce Reported," *Los Angeles Times* (March 30, 1977): 8.

283   *transcript of another conversation*: This second call with a female was obtained through a separate FBI wiretap. It is unclear how this conversation was recorded, as it took place

either in person or over a phone line that was not being monitored. The government's attorney claimed that the conversation was heard when someone who was not Khaalis picked up the phone at the Hanafi Center to make a call out and left the receiver off the hook. It also suggests the possibility that the FBI might have had listening devices inside the Hanafi Center but never officially revealed their existence to the court.

45. INHERITOR OF THE FAITH

286 *lined with hundreds of spectators*: "Anwar Sadat Arrives in U.S.," *The State* (April 4, 1977): 1.

286 *two religious men*: Unlike his predecessor, Gamal Abdel Nasser, Sadat had a reputation as a deeply religious and spiritual man. Jimmy Carter, in his 1995 memoir, *Keeping Faith*, wrote that upon first meeting with Sadat, "I noticed immediately a callused spot at the center of his forehead, apparently caused by a lifetime of touching his head to the ground in prayer." See: Jimmy Carter, *Keeping Faith: Memoirs of a President* (Fayette-ville: University of Arkansas Press, 1995): 289.

286 *adding up to*: "Putting Action on Hold to Talk about Peace," *Edmonton Journal* (November 19, 1977).

287 *conference kicked off*: For a full record of the proceedings of the conference see: S. Mazhar Hussain, *Proceedings of the First Islamic Conference of North America, held at Newark, New Jersey, USA, April 22–24, 1977 (Jumada-I, 4–6, 1397)* (New York: Muslim World League, Office to the United Nations and North America, 1977).

288 *cost a significant amount*: Jeffrey Diamant, *Engagement and Resistance: African Americans, Saudi Arabia and Islamic Transnationalisms, 1975 to 2000* (New York: CUNY Academic Works, 2016), https//academicworks.cuny.edu/gc_etds/1624, p. 133.

46. AMERICAN MUSLIM

290 *attorneys quit*: Court records show that in addition to many defendants' refusal to speak to their attorneys without Khaalis's approval, some of the Hanafis, just as the Black Mafia had done years earlier, refused to be represented by Jewish attorneys and petitioned the court for a switch.

291 *refer to him as "Judge Alexander"*: Alexander's theatrics may have done substantial damage to the Hanafi case. When the DC appeals court later upheld the Hanafi conviction, it commented that Alexander "made improper opening remarks to the jury, argued with witnesses, interrupted the court, commented on the testimony and the court's rulings, asked improper questions, and 'baited' the court."

293 *eyeing a mayoral run*: Tom Sherwood and Harry Jaffe, *Dream City: Race, Power, and the Decline of Washington, D.C.* (New York: Simon and Schuster, 1994): 112.

293 *suffering from nightmares*: Jacqueline Trescott, "Marion Barry: Reliving a Nightmare Every Day," *The Washington Post* (April 12, 1977): B1.

293 *dropped to the floor*: Cantrell's cause of death was cardiac arrest, but news reports of his death quoted his wife saying that he suffered from major problems after his release from the hospital. "He complained a lot about his head," she said. He had trouble with his ears and eyes. She also said that he "wouldn't talk to you—he'd just talk to himself." All this suggests that Cantrell did ultimately die because of the injuries he sustained during the District Building takeover and should be counted among the casualties of the Hanafi siege.

293 *became a key witness*: At a conference in Evian, France, in the summer of 1977, a presented paper titled "Dimensions of Victimization in the Context of Terroristic Acts" suggested that several hostages had developed "identification with the aggressor." Betty Neal was particularly singled out: "An important question here is to what extent did the woman who assisted the Hanafi leader lessen the probability of morbidity and aid in the resolution of the conflict?" The report is available through the Department of Justice website: https://www.ojp.gov/pdffiles1/Digitization/60018NCJRS.pdf.

293 *had confiscated her cigarette*: Abdul Hamid was given between 36 and 108 years in prison, the lightest sentence, and Judge Nunzio ordered him free in 1981 to a firestorm of criticism. His release was in limbo for years as the case bounced between the superior court and the appeals court, and Hamid was in and out of prison until 1987, when the appeals court finally approved his release.

294 *risky strategy*: Multiple attorneys and legal experts have suggested to me that an attempt to sever the cases of the Hanafis could have worked in their favor as many would not have ended up serving as much time in prison as they eventually did. Khaalis did not entertain this possibility at the time.

297 *attorney reminded the jury*: Cullinane and several others who were involved with the negotiations and prosecution have expressed the belief that Khaalis truly did not instruct Nuh and Muzikir to take over the District Building and was surprised by the attack and the shootings there.

47. HOMEFRONT

300 *barely played outside of Libya*: R. H. Greene, "40 Years On, a Controversial Film on Islam's Origins Is Now a Classic," *All Things Considered*, National Public Radio (August 7, 2016): https://www.npr.org/sections/parallels/2016/08/07/485234999/40-years-on-a -controversial-film-on-islams-origins-is-now-a-classic.

301 *to begin shooting*: With a reported budget of close to $35 million, *Lion of the Desert*, too, was destined to be a historic flop at the box office. It is estimated to have earned $1.5 million at the American box office.

304 *began training alongside*: The FBI restructuring included the renaming of the anti-terrorism unit to Special Operations and Research Unit. Tom Strentz, an FBI agent who helped found the unit, described it as follows in a 2009 interview with a member of the Society of Former Special Agents of the FBI: "We formed the unit to examine what terrorists did with the intent of developing counter-strategies and investigative techniques."

305 *removal of the image*: In 1997, sixteen Muslim groups petitioned the Supreme Court of the United States to remove the bas-relief of the Prophet Muhammad from the wall of the courtroom where the Supreme Court justices meet. Chief Justice William H. Rehnquist denied the request in a letter, incidentally written on the twentieth anniversary of the end of the Hanafi siege, to the Council on Islamic Relations. The frieze, Rehnquist said, was "intended only to recognize him, among many other lawgivers, as an important figure in the history of law; it is not intended as a form of idol worship." See: Tamara Jones, "Supreme Court Won't Alter Frieze Depicting Muhammad," *The Washington Post* (March 13, 1997): B1.

306 *reestablished the headquarters*: Lorraine Adams, "Mission Mires in 10-Year Heap of Unpaid Bills," *The Washington Post* (September 1, 1996): 1.

306 *live special broadcast*: The two-hour show is available in its entirety at the Vanderbilt Television News Archive.

307 *the last time*: Khaalis's name did resurface in the news one last time in March 1990, when news circulated that Iran was ready to exchange two Americans jailed in the country in exchange for three Black American Muslims jailed in America. The three men included two high-ranking officials of the Black Panther Party, as well as Hamaas Abdul Khaalis, news reports said. The exchange, the Iranians suggested, could deliver the two countries into a "post hostage era." Months earlier, the Iranian supreme leader, Ayatollah Khomeini, had issued a fatwa declaring the South Asian British writer Salman Rushdie worthy of murder for writing the novel *The Satanic Verses*, which fictionalized and was taken by many to ridicule the Islamic Prophet Muhammad. A global diplomatic crisis followed the fatwa, which also led to several deaths around the world. The Iranians, however, made no mention of the blasphemous novel or Akkad's film in their hostage exchange proposal. Instead, the Iranians simply claimed that Khaalis "was fighting injustice."

EPILOGUE

310 *President George W. Bush*: The Bush family's eponymous ancestor George Bush published the first American biography of Muhammad nearly two centuries earlier. Bush was a biblical scholar with degrees from Princeton and Dartmouth. The biography of Muhammad, not surprisingly, was highly critical of the Islamic Prophet and introduced him as an "impostor" in the preface: George Bush, *The Life of Mohammed: Founder of the Religion of Islam, and of the Empire of the Saracens* (New York: J. and J. Harper, 1830).

315 *$4.85 million*: Basharat Peer, "Zero Tolerance and Cordoba House," *Financial Times Magazine* (August 13, 2010).

315 *a thirteen-floor structure*: Peer, "Zero Tolerance."

315 *teaching high school and in real estate*: Jennifer Peltz, "'Peacemaker' or 'Slumlord'?" *The Record* (September 14, 2010): 1.

316 *Florida gubernatorial candidate*: David Gura, "Republican Gubernatorial Candidate Cuts First 'Ground Zero Mosque' Political Ad," National Public Radio (August 17, 2010), https://www.npr.org/sections/thetwo-way/2010/08/17/129252480/republican -gubernatorial-candidate-cuts-first-ground-zero-mosque-political-ad.

ACKNOWLEDGMENTS

This book would have been impossible to complete without the love, support, and encouragement of my family, friends, colleagues, and students. They are too many to name and recognize here individually, but I am greatly indebted to each of them and express my heartfelt gratitude to all of them.

I owe a great debt to the many people who were held hostage by the Hanafis in March of 1977 and decided to share their stories with me. In many cases, these people chose to revisit traumatic moments in their lives and I feel deeply privileged to have earned their trust. I hope this book will prove to be of some value to them all.

I also owe my thanks to the many people who were part of the Hanafi organization and opened up to me with their personal stories. I could not have achieved any real understanding of the organization and of the characters involved without them. I hope that, at the very least, this book will help them make a bit better sense of parts of their own lives.

There are several individuals and institutions who provided valuable material support at various stages of this book project, and I would like to use this space to thank them:

Abdullah Salim and his wife, Umm Salma Salim, were most generous, welcoming me into their home and their lives and providing me with invaluable materials that served as the foundation of this book. Patricia and Malek Akkad shared precious family records with me about Moustapha Akkad's life and works. Tino Zahedi helped me connect with the late Ardeshir Zahedi, who welcomed me into his home in Montreux, Switzerland, and shared from his treasure of documents and memorabilia. Robert L. Rabe shared photographs and documents relating to his grandfather, Washington police deputy chief Robert Rabe.

Paul Delaney lifted my spirits for nearly the entire time that I worked on this book. He generously provided me with full access to his own immaculately preserved reporting materials from the sixties and seventies. Patrick Bowen consistently shared from his treasure trove of primary historical documents and from his encyclopedic knowledge of specific characters and events. Karl Evanzz shared materials related to the Nation of Islam that I would have had an incredibly difficult time finding otherwise.

The staff at Human Rights Campaign, which now occupies the building on Rhode Island Avenue in Washington that was the headquarters of B'nai B'rith, generously granted me access to the building. Joshua Gibson at the Council of the District of Columbia has supported me in various ways ever since I met him on the fortieth anniversary of the Hanafi siege in 2017, including by giving me access to primary materials of great value.

Tom Buckley, a one-man archive of Washington broadcast television history, shared broadcast clips with me related to Max Robinson. Judge John Fisher at the District of Columbia Court of Appeals allowed me access to his own materials and opened doors to many others. Dave Tevelin was one of the few people I encountered in the course of researching this book who had researched the Hanafi siege in detail, and I thank him for sharing various court records with me. Nancy Cohen, who suffered through the Hanafi siege herself, shared important historical documents from B'nai B'rith and materials from the collection of her late husband, Si Cohen, who was held hostage by the Hanafis.

The Washington police department allowed me access to materials related to several investigations and court cases that remain preserved at their headquarters. I want to especially thank Colonel James M. Brown, who helped me navigate the material when I got there. This book may have proven to be an insurmountable task without the help of librarians and archivists at the following institutions who helped me navigate and understand the sprawling materials that related to my book: the Jimmy Carter Presidential Library and Museum; the Gelman Library and the National Security Archives at George Washington University; the Jack Tarver Library at Mercer University; the Hoover Institution Archives; the Brown Media Archives; the Martin Luther King Jr. Memorial Library; the District of Columbia Archives; the Gary Public Library; the Library of Congress; the Public Information Office at the FBI; and the Vanderbilt TV News Archive.

I thank Robert Reed, Laurel Macondray, and Rebecca Calcagno at the

National Archives at College Park, Maryland, for reviewing thousands of pages of archival records. Sam Schuth at the Boatwright Memorial Library helped me find materials from all over the world, in several languages, always with great enthusiasm, knowing well that I would soon come back for more.

I was awarded the J. Anthony Lukas Work-in-Progress Award in 2020 when my book was still in drafts. The award and prize were a lifeline. They allowed me much needed time and space to complete the book and I am deeply grateful for their recognition and support. New York University's Arthur L. Carter Journalism Institute welcomed me as a visiting scholar for two years. The resources at NYU were invaluable, especially at a time when other doors were closing because of COVID. My special thanks to Ted Conover, the director of the institute, as well as to Robert Boynton, who has been a guiding light throughout my journalism career. The seeds of this book are in our conversations about American Islam that started more than a decade ago.

There are many people at the University of Richmond who helped me, particularly my colleagues in the Journalism Department, who afforded me the time and space for reporting and writing and encouraged me to close my office door once in a while. The offices of the provost and the dean of arts and sciences at the university provided me with financial support at various junctures, for which I am deeply grateful.

I owe special thanks to Claire Comey, who worked as my research assistant on this book for nearly the entire four years that she was a student at the university. Without her supreme organizational skills and attention to detail, I might have been lost, especially during the early stages of the project. I owe a great debt to Rollo Romig for all his insightful and valuable feedback that helped me shape the book in important ways.

My thanks to Larry Weissman and Sascha Alper at Brooklyn Literary, who have been championing my work for more than a decade. The specific idea for this book grew from conversations with Alex Star, who first recognized the potential for a story. As my editor at Farrar, Straus and Giroux, he kept me on track with his sharp thinking and thoughtful guidance. I also thank Ian Van Wye and the rest of the team at FSG for all their work on this project.

Finally, I want to acknowledge my wife, Mimi. I am forever grateful for the chance to share this life, and our beautiful children, with her. Without her, this book would never have even been started.

INDEX